OECD Trade Policy Studies

Liberalisation and Universal Access to Basic Services

TELECOMMUNICATIONS, WATER AND SANITATION, FINANCIAL SERVICES, AND ELECTRICITY

OECD

THE WORLD BANK

ORGANISATION FOR ECONOMIC CO-OPERATION AND DEVELOPMENT
THE WORLD BANK

ORGANISATION FOR ECONOMIC CO-OPERATION AND DEVELOPMENT

The OECD is a unique forum where the governments of 30 democracies work together to address the economic, social and environmental challenges of globalisation. The OECD is also at the forefront of efforts to understand and to help governments respond to new developments and concerns, such as corporate governance, the information economy and the challenges of an ageing population. The Organisation provides a setting where governments can compare policy experiences, seek answers to common problems, identify good practice and work to co-ordinate domestic and international policies.

The OECD member countries are: Australia, Austria, Belgium, Canada, the Czech Republic, Denmark, Finland, France, Germany, Greece, Hungary, Iceland, Ireland, Italy, Japan, Korea, Luxembourg, Mexico, the Netherlands, New Zealand, Norway, Poland, Portugal, the Slovak Republic, Spain, Sweden, Switzerland, Turkey, the United Kingdom and the United States. The Commission of the European Communities takes part in the work of the OECD.

OECD Publishing disseminates widely the results of the Organisation's statistics gathering and research on economic, social and environmental issues, as well as the conventions, guidelines and standards agreed by its members.

This work is published on the responsibility of the Secretary-General of the OECD. The opinions expressed and arguments employed herein do not necessarily reflect the official views of the Organisation, the Executive Directors of the International Bank for Reconstruction and Development/The World Bank, or of the governments they represent.

Foreword

The OECD in co-operation with the World Bank held a Services Experts Meeting in Paris on 3-4 February 2005. This meeting was the fifth of its kind in the ongoing OECD work on trade in services and provided an important opportunity for an informal exchange of views on issues of key importance to the current GATS negotiations.

Services liberalisation can contribute to achieving universal service goals. However, complementary policies or regulatory underpinnings may be required. The meeting explored the choices available to governments in terms both of using liberalisation to expand service provision and of regulation and market incentives to ensure greater availability of quality services in liberalised markets. It focused on experience in four sectors: telecommunications, water and sanitation, financial services and electricity. The key questions considered at the meeting include:

- What have countries' experiences been in liberalising services in terms of the impact on ensuring increased and equitable (in terms of income and geography) provision of services? Does the experience of developed and developing countries differ for different services?
- Where liberalisation has been undertaken, what sorts of regulatory mechanisms and market incentives have been used to ensure universal service? Were mechanisms focused on the consumer or the providers? What do we know about targeting assistance to the truly needy and avoiding leakages to other groups?
- To what extent are countries finding that the traditional regulatory measures designed to achieve universal service goals at a particular time are becoming dated or in need of improvement to better reflect today's realities? To what extent are countries looking for new solutions?
- What do we know about the creation of regulatory authorities, with regard to resources required and solutions for countries with limited resources (*e.g.* regional authorities) and necessary assistance and capacity building?

The meeting did not advocate any particular approach; the choice of whether to permit private foreign suppliers is for each country to determine in the context of its own circumstances. Rather, discussions aimed to assist countries' decision-making processes by providing some insights into the experience of countries which have chosen to liberalise to achieve universal service provision and the types of complementary policies and regulatory mechanisms they have used.

This publication therefore focuses on the role of market reform, including trade liberalisation, in obtaining universal access to the services covered at the meeting. It finds that efficiency is a powerful instrument for equity and that the introduction of competition leads to big gains. However, the market alone will not deliver socially desirable levels of access; complementary policies are needed. Command instruments have delivered poor results, while universal access funds have often produced striking improvements.

This publication first contains a summary of the presentations at the meeting and the highlights of the discussions prepared by Hildegunn Kyvik Nordås and Julia Nielson of the Trade Policy Linkages Division of the OECD Trade Directorate and Aaditya Mattoo of the Development Research Group of the World Bank. Next, for each of the four sectors, an overview of the major trade liberalisation issues and the universal access debate is followed by two national case studies (one in the case of electricity) describing national experience in Africa, Asia and Latin America. The volume was prepared with wide participation by the Trade Policy Linkages Division, under the supervision of Dale Andrew. Peer review and editing were co-ordinated by Molly Lesher, Enrico Pinali and Massimo Geloso Grosso. Sébastien Miroudot and Martina Abderrahmane also contributed to the organisation of the Experts Meeting.

Table of Contents

Part IV: Electricity

Executive Summary

Universal Access in Liberalised Services Markets

Aaditya Mattoo
Development Research Group, World Bank

Julia Nielson and Hildegunn Kyvik Nordås
OECD Trade Directorate

Introduction

Access to basic services plays an important role in both individual well-being and a country's economic development. For this reason, general availability of these services to citizens, regardless of income level and geographical location, has generally been viewed as an important public policy goal. However, the precise definition of this goal and the means of attaining it have provoked controversy.

This volume explores whether liberalisation can contribute to achieving universal service goals and, if so, how, and looks at the types of complementary policies that may be required. It focuses on experience in four sectors: telecommunications, financial, water and sanitation, and energy services. For each sector, an overview paper and one or two case studies from developing countries examine the experience of governments in harnessing liberalisation to meet social goals. It is hoped that this cross-sector view will yield general insights which a focus on a single sector may not, and help each sector to generate ideas by drawing upon experience in other sectors. A horizontal assessment can also help us determine how far the services negotiations at the WTO, under the General Agreement on Trade in Services can aid or impede the attainment of universal service goals.

The questions

Defining universal access

There are many definitions of universal service and countries can have different goals. Decisions must be made, first of all, regarding the types of services to which access will be provided. For example, in telecommunications, some countries have focused on basic telephony whereas other (usually richer) countries have also included access to the Internet among their universal service goals. In banking, some have been concerned with basic transactions and savings services, while others have also sought to provide credit services. The second key element of the definition concerns the relative emphasis on availability, price and quality of the service. For example, a focus on setting maximum prices (*e.g.* of energy or water services) has often led to diminished availability and poor quality. Finally, there is the question of the level of access. A distinction is sometimes made between universal service and universal access. For example, in the case of water, universal service aims for a connection in every dwelling; universal access only requires that persons have access to a source of potable water, such as a communal tap. For many developing countries, universal service may be economically less feasible and universal access a more practical objective. So, in each case, the first question is: How are universal access goals defined in different services sectors?

Efficiency vs. equity

There has been much debate in recent years about how universal service or access is best achieved: through government monopoly provision, fully private provision or some combination of public and private funding and provision. Some argue that liberalisation – *i.e.* allowing entry of foreign private suppliers – can contribute to achieving universal service in infrastructural services. Others have argued that liberalisation undermines universal provision, for example, because foreign private providers "cherry pick" richer consumers or the most profitable regions. Issues to consider include:

- What has been the experience of using liberalisation to increase access? How does experience differ between countries and across services sectors?
- Is there a potential conflict between efficiency and equity in specific services sectors? In other words, if a government implements reforms of essential services that are motivated solely by the desire to enhance efficiency – through greater private or foreign ownership or competition or any combination of these – will it worsen access for the poor?

Poor performance by public monopolies in a number of countries has frequently led to the conclusion that pursuit of greater efficiency would not undermine existing levels of equity, and that the market can be relied upon to deliver both greater efficiency and greater access. Where this is true, the pursuit of efficiency-enhancing policies need not be conditional on the implementation of access-improving policies. But the following questions remain:

- Is efficiency a *sufficient* instrument of equity? That is, even if moving to the market improves the *status quo*, can it deliver socially desirable levels of access?
- If not, is it possible to devise mechanisms that improve the market outcome, *i.e.* deliver socially desirable levels of access without sacrificing efficiency, not just in principle, but in practice?

Choice of mechanism

Governments have employed a range of mechanisms to implement universal service policies. These have targeted the service provider (*e.g.* mandatory service obligations, cross-subsidies, direct subsidies from a universal access fund) or disadvantaged consumers (*e.g.* direct subsidies to consumers, vouchers). Several issues arise:

- What sorts of regulatory mechanisms and market incentives have been used to ensure universal service?
- How effective are mechanisms focused on providers in encouraging universal access?

- How effective are mechanisms focused on the consumer? How difficult has it been to target assistance to the truly needy? What are the administrative costs involved?
- Is universal access best assured by government directives or market incentives, or combinations of the two?

Access and market failure

In a number of services sectors, policies to promote access need to take into account policies to remedy other forms of market failure. Informational inadequacies, *e.g.* in financial services, where neither consumers nor financial institutions can fully observe the true nature and behaviour of the other, have prompted prudential regulation. Monopoly power, *e.g.* in water and energy distribution, has prompted fears of under-provision of quality. But high and rigid mandatory quality standards may conflict with wider access.

- How is the design of access policies in specific services sectors influenced by the existence of other forms of market failure?
- If there is a conflict between regulatory standards and wider access, how is the conflict best resolved?

Political economy and institutional context of access

Policies and mechanisms also need to be adapted to institutional and national circumstances and revisited in the light of new developments. In some countries or sectors, interventions have led to significantly improved access, but in others they have undermined efficiency without enhancing the availability of services to the poor. In fact, the mechanisms may even have increased inequality, as the benefits (*e.g.* of subsidised energy and financial services) were captured by the already well-off rather than the poor.

- Why have some countries been much more successful in implementing access policies than others? What role has the institutional and political structure played?
- How is it possible to devise and implement instruments that will not be captured by the politically powerful at the expense of the poor?
- What sorts of cost-effective models exist for creating regulatory authorities in countries with limited resources (*e.g.* regional authorities)? What sorts of capacity building would help?

Access and technological progress

Furthermore, services markets evolve, including as new technologies make service provision easier and cheaper. This can be both an opportunity to extend access to previously underserved populations and a challenge for regulators to ensure that markets function properly and universal service obligations are maintained. Regulatory authorities need to adapt universal service goals and mechanisms to new developments and different circumstances. Issues to consider include:

- What is the role of technological innovation in providing new solutions to universal service challenges?
- Do some types of mechanisms to promote universal service encourage or discourage innovation?

- Are countries finding that the traditional universal service measures are becoming outdated and that new solutions need to be identified?

Findings from the sector studies

The findings from the main papers for each of the four sectors, as well as from the complementary country case studies, are described below.

Telecommunications

The telecommunications sector, driven by technological progress and supported by policy reform, has seen the most remarkable growth over the last decade. Growth, particularly in the mobile segment, has led to striking improvements in access. Traditionally, the existence of network externalities was one rationale for government promotion of wider access in this network industry. The more the subscribers, the more useful the services for all, *i.e.* the gains to society as a whole of additional subscribers are larger than the gains for the individual new subscriber. At the same time, the existence of significant economies of scale meant that telecommunications services were usually provided by a vertically integrated supplier, often a state monopoly. Technological progress in recent years has reduced the significance of economies of scale and made competition viable in ever-increasing market segments. But access to basic infrastructure for service providers and interconnectivity between providers of basic telecommunications remain important regulatory issues in a market-based system. Notwithstanding the remarkable improvement in access, government mechanisms to widen access remain vital in most developing countries, as revealed by the case studies from Uganda and India.

Definition of universal access

While universal service has been achieved in developed countries, universal access is at present a more realistic objective in developing countries. Policies towards this end promote access to telecommunication services on a shared basis through public payphones, public call offices or telecommunication kiosks. What is realistic does, however, change with technology, and universal service is therefore a dynamic concept that needs to be revised as circumstances change. The Indian case study, for instance, discusses whether Internet access should be included in universal access policies. Affordability is also an aspect of universal access in which both technology and regulation have played a role.

Efficiency versus equity

Universal service provision in the integrated monopoly was typically financed through cross-subsidisation of local calls by high prices on international and national long distance calls, on the assumption that the latter services were mainly used by the better-off households. Such cross-subsidisation is evidently unsustainable in a competitive market. Market reforms have therefore involved the rebalancing of tariffs with prices falling for business users and fixed charges and prices increasing for local calls. In Malaysia, for instance, residential line rentals and local call fees increased by 10% and 25% respectively, while long distance and international call fees fell by 20%. Although it can be argued that efficiency has increased at the expense of equity, the impact on equity in the long run may still be positive since price rebalancing provides incentives for extending services to previously unserved areas and market segments.

Access and market

There is clear evidence that market-based provision of telecommunication is an efficient and sustainable way of moving towards universal access. The role of the government is increasingly seen as strengthening market forces through proper regulation. Such regulation typically provides incentives for network development and modernisation, lower prices and greater attention to customer choice. There are nevertheless areas where telecommunications are still not economically viable and government intervention is needed to ensure universal access. Such intervention can however be temporary and reviewed frequently in order to encourage market entry when this becomes a viable option.

Telecommunications liberalisation and the introduction of cellular technology in Uganda have expanded access for the poor and have led to considerable price decreases. Nigeria and a number of other sub-Saharan African countries have also experienced rapid growth in mobile telephone penetration rates and have more mobile than fixed lines. In sub-Saharan Africa 80% of telephones are bought on a pre-paid basis and it is estimated that 70% of households can afford them, while only 30% can afford fixed lines. In India the introduction of competition, coupled with the establishment of a regulator for the sector, have led to significant telecommunications price decreases and improved prospects for universal service. In particular, enhancement of the capability of mobile technology and the potential of combining broadband with telephony is now making it possible to introduce a new model for largely market-driven universal service policies.

Choice of mechanism

Most specific universal service obligations (USOs) are imposed on operators via the licensing process. The regulator may require an operator to install payphones in a given number of localities or to extend services to specific areas. Universal access funds, financed through a levy on operators' income, can be established to subsidise the costs incurred in meeting these obligations. Such levies are typically in the range of 1-5% of revenue; Argentina, Australia, Nepal, South Africa, the United States and many others offer examples of such regulation. Countries such as Chile and Peru have chosen a competitive bidding process, in which the operator that accepts the lowest level of subsidies to carry out the USOs is the winner.

Some mechanisms target the consumer (*e.g.* low-income consumers, disabled people, those in remote areas), for example with specific subsidies. Unlike other sectors, interventions on prices are less common in telecommunications. Most reforms aim at promoting competition in liberalised markets. The issue is therefore how to design universal access mechanisms which are fully compatible with this competitive environment.

Political economy and institutional context

In telecommunications and other network industries, government regulation is necessary to ensure both competitive markets and universal access. In developed countries competitive markets, in combination with targeted subsidies to poor households, delivers universal access. However, this requires a sufficiently independent regulatory body with sufficient capacity. Many countries have established a separate agency with responsibility for administering the universal service programmes, and many, including Uganda, have installed mechanisms for ongoing assessment of the agency's performance.

Access and technological progress

The development and diffusion of mobile technology has reduced the cost of telecommunications substantially and provided access in previously unserved areas and market segments access, including in least developed countries. Further developments in wireless technologies that can be used in conjunction with satellite stations can further improve access for remote areas at commercially viable costs. In Peru, for instance, remote areas are being serviced by VSAT-based telephony provided by a private company after competitive bidding. It is also possible to reduce costs by using the power grid as a communication network, although in poor and remote areas access to electricity is also lacking. Multiple purpose networks could, however, reduce the cost of providing both electricity and telecommunications. A central finding is that USOs should ideally be technologically neutral and focus on outcomes rather on prescribing specific technological choices.

Water and sanitation

One-half of the world's population still lacks access to basic sanitation and one person in five has no access to safe drinking water. Historically, WSS have been provided largely by the public sector. Government provision was seen as necessary to ensure socially equitable access because of WSS's natural monopoly characteristics. Nevertheless, recent years have seen a stronger presence of the private sector in WSS. In developing countries, this has been driven by the need to increase investment and improve infrastructure performance and has often, given the lack of domestic capacity and finance, included foreign participation. But private sector participation in WSS, particularly water services, is controversial. For some, water is not only a public good, but a basic human right, and must be provided by the public sector and shielded from profit motives. Private participation is seen as undermining the ability of governments to regulate the service, a view bolstered by a number of high-profile failures. Others point to private sector success stories and to the failure of many public authorities to provide universal access. This section includes case studies of Argentina, Ghana, Senegal and Nepal.

Definition of access

In WSS, universal access, rather than universal service, is the priority aim. Access goals and definitions for WSS vary greatly between countries, particularly because global improved access goals, as defined by WHO, are extremely modest (although still unmet in many countries). Assessing access is complicated both by the importance of local factors (extreme climates) and the fact that consumers may be unconnected to the network but have access to WSS by other means (*e.g.* water truck, private providers). Affordability is also important and the poor often pay much more than the rich for potable water. In Nairobi, for instance vendors charge ten times more per litre of drinking water than the price for those connected to the network.

Access and markets

WSS remain essentially natural monopolies (competition is possible for sewage treatment, which does not have constraints related to network duplication) so competition has not been *in* the market, but *for* it (through monopoly franchises). Public-private partnerships (PPPs), such as concessions and build-operate-(own)-transfers have emerged as alternatives to privatisation (where ownership is transferred through outright divestiture). Concession contracts grant private companies, typically through competitive bidding, the exclusive right to provide a service for a specified period using existing facilities and/or developing new ones. They thus entail only a temporary transfer of the infrastructure assets, which return to the public authority at the end of the concession period.

However, large-scale contracts of this nature remain a relatively small – and declining – share of the sector. Private investment in WSS now stands at 11%, less than half in volume terms of the 1997 peak. This declining share is perhaps attributable to the mixed record of major contracts, with high rates of renegotiation or financial distress (up to 45% of contracts under some estimates). A recurrent theme in the design of major contracts has been the conflict between keeping prices down (or even reducing them) and extending provision. Such conflicts are rendered more acute if connection charges are maintained for new customers. Currency fluctuations have also exacerbated financial problems.

Arguably, the impact has been greater at the local level via small-scale independent providers (SSIPs). In poorer countries, where water and sewage networks are underdeveloped, SSIPs have developed to serve those left off the network and range from small – and possibly exploitative – vendors to well-run businesses. They increasingly complement existing providers, both public authorities and large concessionaires, which may also use them as subcontractors until the network is expanded. However, small operators may oppose extension of the network for fear of losing their livelihood, or exclusivity clauses can prevent their operation; both are counterproductive in terms of increasing access for the poor.

Choice of mechanism

WSS are capital-intensive services and cost-reflective tariffs have been introduced to generate the investment necessary to maintain, replace, modernise and expand facilities and services. User fees are also seen as crucial to the promotion of conservation principles. But fee increases are one of the most controversial aspects of private sector involvement, as the price fixed under a government monopoly often did not cover the cost of service provision. Given the impact of price rises on availability of services, governments have continued to regulate prices even in liberalised markets. For those who cannot afford even moderate tariffs, governments have various forms of consumer subsidies.

Subsides can be paid in kind (free tranches of water to households or per head, although the former risks discriminating against large households or multi-occupant dwellings) or via cash (*e.g.* operated through the billing system, where a government-funded subsidy is deducted from the consumer's bill, or where social tariffs are cross-subsidised by more expensive ones). But targeting remains difficult in all but the most segregated communities. Targeting by geographical area risks high rates of errors of exclusion and inclusion but means testing can be administratively costly. It has been argued that the most effective form of targeting in many developing countries would be to subsidise connection more than consumption. Not only are consumption subsidies hard to target and handicapped by the need for adequate metering facilities, but they tend to benefit those already connected to the network, not those excluded from it who are likely to the poorest.

At present, the poorest are disadvantaged both in terms of access and cost. The poor often do not have access to water and where they do, they generally pay more because they pay much higher prices to local vendors than wealthier consumers connected to the (public or private) network. Hence it could be argued that for them expanding access is the most critical issue. Yet the emphasis has often been on keeping prices down for existing users, while maintaining connection fees for new users.

A common measure to extend access to service is to include network expansion obligations in contracts with private providers. However, expansion targets may be circumvented or renegotiated if the new customers are loss-makers for the companies so that subsidies are necessary. Transitional tariffs can be useful in supporting expansion, but should be time-limited to avoid regressive effects.

Sub-contracts to, or partnerships with, SSIPs have also been effective in meeting roll-out targets and have also allowed for use of lower-cost technologies. For example, in Manila, concessionaires who operate on a monopoly basis have granted subcontracts to local operators. Water is delivered by the conventional mains to the edge of a defined zone and transported by above-ground pipe connections to meters from which each family makes its connection using low-cost plastic pipes for which they are responsible. This collaboration between a major concessionaire, a local small company and local residents has been viewed as a successful example of increased access. Where exclusivity clauses operate in contracts they can discourage these sorts of innovations.

Standards and quality are also a major issue in the provision of WSS. Both mandatory obligations and market-based instruments have been used, but there can be a tension between expanding access and ensuring that WSS meet basic quality levels, in particular given the important role of SSIPs in expanding access. Many developing countries are introducing flexible regulation to provide incentives for utilities to seek creative approaches to meet service standards, manage costs and ensure that quality is not compromised.

In Argentina private participation through concession proved an unsuccessful experience that left many stakeholders dissatisfied. It represents a case in which the granting of a concession to manage water services was not adequately supported by an independent regulatory framework. An economic crisis together with lack of transparency and discretionary measures adopted in regulating the concession undermined its sustainability.

Experience in Ghana has shown that expanded access does not automatically trigger usage. Nigeria's experience shows that access and customer reach is not always straightforward, and that affordability of service is often questionable even though subsidised schemes are in place. The Nepalese case reveals that in spite of many years of donor investments, some areas did not make progress in water quality and costs were not recovered.

Financial services

Financial services play a key role in economic growth and development. They are mainly provided by the market, but subject to government regulation which focuses on financial risk management rather than universal access. The financial services sector provides a large and increasing number of products, and access to a bank account, credit and basic insurance could be considered basic services subject to universal access policies. The financial services section contains two case studies on India and South Africa.

Defining universal access

Physical access, affordability and product range are three dimensions of universal access. Access also has geographical and socioeconomic dimensions. While bank account coverage is an average of 90% in most OECD countries, it is only about 25% in developing countries. For most developing countries, access to a basic bank account does not exceed 30%, and in the lowest income countries it is less than 10%. However, actual access is hard to measure and lack of use may reflect low demand as well as lack of access. The poor may assume that they will be excluded and may not attempt to gain access. Lack of demand can also be part of broader social exclusion. Many poor consumers do not have enough money to make an account worthwhile. Low literacy also affects the ability to use financial services. Low financial services coverage appears to be more a reflection of poverty rather than a financial sector market failure.

In India only 20% of the population banks, and there is a high degree of reliance on informal providers of savings as well as insurance. In South Africa universal access to basic financial services is part of the government's Black Economic Empowerment policy, but coverage is currently only about 30%.

Efficiency versus equity

Empirical evidence suggests that financial development improves income distribution. Access to financial services, particularly credit and basic insurance, increases economic opportunity and allows poor people to put their skills and other resources to better economic use. Furthermore, broader access and more competitive markets help ensure that credit is allocated on the basis of the merit of the project rather than connections. Hence efficiency is improved as well. However, these outcomes follow developments in the financial sector.

The efficiency versus equity question is somewhat different when the issue is extending financial services to the currently unbanked and uninsured. The administrative costs of opening a bank account, cash withdrawal, payments and loans are about the same, whatever the size of the transaction. For poor customers, these costs can be prohibitive and servicing poor market segments often will not achieve an efficient scale. Policy measures aimed at reducing costs for poor households, whether government provision or services obligations on private sector providers, typically are costly and give rise to inefficiency problems.

Access and market

In developed market economies, financial services are provided by the market, although most countries have special government-provided or government-supported financial services such as student loans, housing loans and rural development funding. In developing countries, physical availability can be limited because it is not economical to establish branches in rural areas. Access is also limited by minimum deposit requirements and collateral requirements for loans. But lack of access is not only due to lack of demand or market failure. Some types of banking regulation can also hinder access. Customer identification requirements, for instance, are obstacles for those without birth certificates or standard addresses. Other examples of regulation that can limit access for the poor are recent anti-money laundering and terrorism financing regulations, while in some African countries women need permission from the male head of household to open a bank account, and minimum capital adequacy requirements create entry barriers for micro-finance institutions.

Increasingly, governments are focusing on encouraging the market to extend access, including by encouraging existing providers to experiment with new products. For example four major South African banks have developed Mzansi accounts, a low-cost banking product. The range of transactions is more limited and there is no credit facility, but fees are lower and the banks pooled infrastructure to maximise the number of ATMs, now numbering more than 12 000 across the country, thereby substantially improving physical access.

In addition to new products, access has been expanded by new types of providers, often operating at the local level where there may be fewer information and enforcement problems. In Mexico close to 50% of credit to the non-banked comes from department stores. In South Africa new legislation will allow retailers and cell phone operators to apply for limited forms of a banking licence and a new legislative framework has been developed for member-based or co-operative financial institutions. Beyond regulation and subsidising low-cost housing and small enterprise lending, the government has intervened little in the market .

Choice of mechanism

A range of approaches have been used to extend access to financial services: direct government provision, subsidies or legislation to require providers to cross-subsidise extension of the service. Experience with government provision and price control has been mixed. While some governments require the national bank, or the postal service, to provide accounts to those refused by commercial banks, others subsidise service provision by commercial providers. However, subsidies do not necessarily result in new consumers, as they can be captured by those who already have access. They may also reduce availability over the longer term.

In another form of intervention, regulators may require providers to advance a certain percentage of their credit to defined sectors (*e.g.* agriculture) or groups (directed credit, priority lending schemes). Regulators can also carve out geographical areas to be served only by designated bank branches which are assigned district credit targets (designated service areas). Two issues arise: whether designated service areas hinder competition and the entrance of non-traditional providers, and the extent to which such directed credit and similar approaches should be mandatory.

In India the regulatory measures include directed credit to priority sectors such as agriculture, small enterprise and micro-credit, among others. It is, however, argued that subsidised services for the poor diminished the number of providers in the market, acted as a strong deterrent to new entrants and did nothing to encourage the development of innovative products. Likewise, interest rate caps had the effect of decreasing the availability of loans by reducing the number of providers.

Some advances in universal access may be more readily achieved via the introduction of foreign competition into the banking sector to bring new technology and know-how. There is also evidence that liberalisation can further enhance access, through both the competition effect on existing providers and direct provision of services by foreign providers moving into those markets. In Mongolia, for instance, the acquisition of a local bank by HS Securities of Japan extended the network of branches and improved access to banking services

Political economy and institutional context

The quality of the legal system, property rights and the presence of mechanisms for obtaining reliable information are found to be important for small firms' access to financial services. Access is also facilitated by general improvements to the infrastructure and the institutional environment, such as the development of national unique identifiers, facilities for credit information sharing and tracking, and improvement of rural infrastructure.

Access and technological progress

Developments in information and communication technology can and already have improved access for poor households in developing countries. Examples are electronic payment over mobile telephones and electronic financial services kiosks in post offices and supermarkets. In addition, information technology can help reduce the administrative costs of financial transactions through better management of information such as credit records. Brazil, India and South Africa, among others, have explored using the postal services network for extending access to financial services.

Electricity

The electrical power sector consists of a vertical supply chain from primary energy carriers to power generation, transmission, distribution and finally trading. In most countries, the tasks from generation to distribution have until recently been performed by a vertically integrated monopoly. However experience in an increasing number of countries has made it clear that private sector participation and competitive markets are possible, but require adequate regulation. Reforms typically involve unbundling of the vertically integrated incumbent monopoly and opening up generation and trading to competition while regulating transmission and distribution, which remain monopolies.

It is, however, fair to say that experience with reforms has been mixed. Internally inconsistent regulatory measures have resulted in financial distress in a number of cases. In some countries capacity utilisation is very high and prices have therefore been volatile. Investment in new capacity is needed to stabilise prices, but although a well-regulated liberalised market can generate sufficient incentives for investment in new capacity, it has been argued that such incentives have been lacking. According to the International Energy Agency (IEA) the necessary investment to enable service provision to keep pace with demand over the next 30 years is USD 4 trillion in OECD countries and USD 5.7 trillion in non-OECD countries

Defining universal services

Universal services and universal access cannot easily be distinguished since electricity is not a service suitable for sharing from a common facility. Therefore, the relevant aspects of universal access are physical access and affordability. Physical access has by and large been achieved in the OECD countries, including in remote areas. By contrast, in many developing countries both physical access and affordability remain major challenges. While Latin America and East Asia had achieved connection rates of nearly 90% and 87%, respectively, in 2000, in South Asia over 800 million people remain without access to electricity (India's connection rate is 43%) and in Africa, particularly sub-Saharan Africa, the vast majority of the population has no access.

Efficiency versus equity

The consumption of electricity requires complementary electrical appliances which a large proportion of the population in least developed countries cannot afford. In least developed countries, therefore, subsidised electricity may well mainly benefit the relatively well-off. In least developed countries there may also be a trade-off between physical access and affordability. If a sufficiently large share of households cannot afford to pay a price that covers the cost of production, universal access could become a serious financial burden for the government. It should however be noted that electricity can improve welfare substantially for poor households even if their demand is limited to, say, lighting and a radio. Electric lights would for instance allow school children to do their homework even if they have to help out on the family farm during the day.

The efficiency versus equity trade-off is less problematic in middle-income and high-income countries. If a relatively small share of customers cannot afford a price that covers costs, government transfers to households combined with subsidies for rolling out the necessary infrastructure can ensure both efficiency and equity, provided there are proper regulation and well-targeted transfers. Subsidies are typically funded through a levy on sales. Another measure that has been used to ensure affordability is a price discount for poor households. In a market-based system cross-subsidisation is not an option and the electricity provider must to be compensated for such programmes.

The two case studies, Brazil and the Philippines, are both middle-income countries. In the Philippines universal physical access has largely been achieved in urban areas, while rural electrification programmes aim at obtaining access to electricity in all villages by 2008, up from 91% in 2004. In Brazil generation capacity is concentrated in the south of the country where most households have physical access, while in the north about 20%of households do not. The country aims at providing universal access at the village level by 2008.

Access and market

The question of access and market is a difficult one in the electricity sector. The fact that essential parts of the industry are close to natural monopolies means that markets alone cannot provide efficient solutions. Capacity and incentive problems related to government provision usually imply that it cannot provide efficient solutions either. Striking the right balance between the market and government regulation is thus a challenge, even for advanced OECD countries. Nevertheless there is evidence that private ownership and unbundling in the sector improves capacity utilisation and productivity, but that improvements only materialise when accompanied by competition and independent regulation. In least developed countries, governments often lack resources for the large-scale investments required to extend physical access, and, unless there are trade opportunities in electricity or related energy-intensive industries, private investors may also be reluctant. Therefore donors have a role to play both for financial and technical assistance, the latter in terms of building capacity for regulation.

The Philippines has implemented extensive but gradual reforms towards a regulated market-based sector. A wholesale spot market has been established, the National Power Corporation has been privatised and an independent regulatory body established. Brazil has also introduced competition at the wholesale level.

Choice of mechanism

The policy measure for ensuring affordability that are the most in keeping with a properly regulated market-based electricity sector is public transfers to poor households. These are considered better targeted and less distorting than price differentiation or discounts for the poor and are used for instance in Germany. Price regulation is nonetheless common in the electricity sector. The Philippines has mandated tariff reductions and lifeline rates for a minimum level of consumption for low-income households. In Brazil households with no more than 50kW installed capacity do not pay for connection.

Mechanisms that mainly aim at keeping prices down through the use of market mechanisms require regulation. In particular access to the monopoly transmission and distribution networks need to be regulated in order to ensure that there is competition in generation and trading. If the incumbent is a vertically integrated electricity provider, it can easily abuse its monopoly in transmission and distribution by giving its own generating and trading arms access to the network at better terms than new entrants. Ideally regulation should keep prices close to long-run average costs. However, regulators need to make sure that there are sufficient incentives for cost efficiency, innovation and investment. These are not always easy to reconcile. Price caps can be too tight, discouraging innovation and investment, or they can be too lax, discouraging cost effectiveness.

Policy measures aiming at physical access include government provision and subsidised private sector provision. Electrification of rural areas is often not commercially viable and special rural electrification schemes are common. Both the Philippines and Brazil have such schemes. In the Philippines, universal access is mandated in each franchise area serviced by a private distributor, while in economically unviable areas a government corporation provides services, funded by a levy on sales. Brazil has a special programme for electrification of rural areas. Universal service obligations are compensated for through subsidies to the supplier. In addition incentives to develop alternative sources of energy have been introduced. Chile has privatised and re-regulated its power sector. Resources for rural electrification come from the government, but are allocated to projects through an annual bidding system.

Political economy and institutional context

The transition period to a market-based and financially sound power sector can be politically difficult, and the degree of difficulty largely depends on the state of the power sector prior to reform. Reforming a sector in financial distress with poorly maintained infrastructure often implies tariff increases. A credible commitment to reform in the face of pressure from interest groups has proven difficult and the reform process has often taken place in spurts interrupted by reversals and setbacks.

The evidence unanimously shows that successful power sector reforms require an independent regulatory body with adequate resources. Both the Philippines and Brazil have established an independent regulatory body.

Access and technological progress

In the electricity sector off-grid power supply solutions such as solar power, wind, biomass and fuel cells, among others, have been promising alternatives to expensive grid extensions to remote areas or poor communities with low electricity demand. Unfortunately, alternative small-scale (or micro) electricity generation has remained promising for decades and reliable low-cost technical solutions have not as of yet become available on the market.

Summing up and research priorities

The contributions in this volume reveal that despite polarised positions and vigorous debate, there is a reasonable consensus on a number of propositions. First of all, the *status quo* is unacceptable. In most developing countries, current levels of access are hopelessly inadequate in the sectors considered here. Given the levels of poverty in many poor countries, even a perfect sector policy environment is unlikely to deliver universal access to telecommunications, (formal sector) financial services, electricity and clean water. Differences in income are a key factor in explaining why some countries are more successful than others in implementing access policies and why subsidised services benefit only the relatively well-off in some countries. Likewise, when financial and regulatory capacity is limited, it is necessary to set priorities. For instance where access to safe drinking water is lacking, universal access to telecommunications may have to wait.

Most people care about both efficiency and equity. Those for whom the priority is poverty reduction and the attainment of social goals would like to see these goals met efficiently, *i.e.* without a waste of resources. And those who seek to ensure greater efficiency in service provision are also sensitive to the need for more equitable access, both because it is desirable in itself and because it is a condition for sustainable reform.

Perhaps more significantly, in each of these sectors, efficiency is a powerful instrument of equity. More efficient production and allocation delivered improved access, and conversely inefficiency penalised the poor. Moreover, clear lessons have been learned about efficiency-enhancing policies. The big gains come, not from a transfer of ownership – from public to private, or national to foreign hands – but from the introduction of competition. Given the acuteness of market failure in many services, effective regulation is essential to realising efficiency gains. So regardless of equity concerns, on purely efficiency grounds greater competition and effective regulation are desirable. It is also evident that neglect of efficiency would impose a cost in terms of equity, *e.g.* if a monopolist exploited consumers by providing expensive or poor quality services.

The issue of whether the poor have slightly better or slightly worse access under private rather than public provision is a divisive distraction. The emphasis on this question merely reflects a desire to buy freedom to focus on efficiency. However, even in the most efficiently run sectors, reliance on the market would not deliver socially desirable levels of access. It is, therefore, vital to devise efficient instruments to widen access, a task in which surprisingly few countries have so far been successful.

In general, command instruments (*e.g.* directed lending in financial services and roll-out obligations in telecommunications) and price controls (*e.g.* artificially low prices for water, electricity and lending) delivered poor results, hurting both efficiency and equity. In contrast, certain fiscal instruments (notably universal access funds that were competitively allocated in a technologically-neutral manner) produced striking improvements in access. Yet the former were frequently observed, and recourse to the latter is rare. The issue of how the choice of instruments is influenced by the political context, the state of technology and the level of institutional development, and how these factors should influence policy prescriptions, must remain a research priority.

A key finding was the tension between regulatory standards and access (*e.g.* stronger prudential standards may inhibit the emergence of micro-finance institutions and create an unwillingness to lend to individuals without conventional collateral). Hence, policies to promote access and policies to remedy other forms of market failure cannot be formulated independently. The tension is particularly acute in countries like India with a growing stake in international trade in services (which creates pressure to adopt international standards), while much of the population has inadequate access to essential services (which creates a need to develop locally appropriate standards). More research is also needed on the costs and benefits of multiple standards.

Trade and foreign investment policy were seen as less important for access than policies affecting overall market structure, private participation and the regulatory framework. Foreign presence was often of peripheral significance, sometimes helpful but never an impediment to wider access.

In principle, multilateral negotiations can foster reform in services, as in goods, by eliminating or reducing protective barriers through mutual agreement and by lending credibility to the results achieved through legally binding commitments. The expectation is that more open markets and greater predictability of policy will lead to more efficient provision of services. That is the rationale for the GATS. But the GATS has so far had little impact on actual policy even in sectors like basic telecommunications and financial services which were heavily negotiated, let alone those like water and energy that have so far received only limited attention.

The most serious charge against the GATS is not its meagre harvest of liberalisation – after all the process has only recently begun – but that it deprives governments of the freedom to pursue pro-poor policies. It is argued that its rules threaten public education, health and environmental services, outlaw universal service obligations and subsidised supply, and undermine effective domestic regulation. If one looks at the GATS in its current form, these charges do not seem well-founded, for three reasons. First, services supplied in the exercise of governmental authority are excluded from the scope of the GATS, although the definition – services that are not supplied on a commercial basis or competitively – offers scope for clarification. Second, even in sectors that have been opened to full competition, the Agreement does not prevent the pursuit of domestic policy objectives, including through subsidies or the imposition of universal service obligations, as long as these do not discriminate against foreign suppliers. Finally, the Agreement recognises the right of members, particularly developing countries, to regulate to meet national policy objectives, and its current rules on domestic regulations are hardly intrusive.

However, the concerns usually expressed are not so much about what the GATS is but what it may become after the current (and any future) round of negotiations, which will aim for more liberalising commitments and new rules in areas such as domestic regulation. Informed debate would undoubtedly help ensure that future GATS rules and commitments reflect broader development concerns and not just the dictates of domestic political economy or external negotiating pressure.

At this stage, however, the main issue is not so much what the GATS forces countries to do or what it prevents them from doing, but that it does not – indeed cannot – ensure the complementary action that is needed to deliver pro-poor liberalisation. This raises a legitimate concern: in a complex area like services, trade negotiations alone could lead to partial or inappropriately sequenced reform. One possibility, already visible in some cases, is that less emphasis will be placed on introducing competition than on allowing a transfer of ownership of monopolies from national to foreign hands or protecting the position of foreign incumbents. Another is that market opening will be induced in countries that have not developed regulatory frameworks and mechanisms to achieve basic social policy objectives. These flaws could conceivably make the poor worse off. The problem is accentuated by the difficulty of reversing inappropriate policy choices that have been translated into legally binding external commitments.

The danger of adverse outcomes would be substantially reduced if two types of activities receive greater international support. The first is increased policy research and advice within developing countries and elsewhere to identify the elements of successful reform and to separate the areas for which there is little reason to defer market opening from those for which there is significant uncertainty and a need for tempered negotiating demands. An even greater need is for enhanced technical and financial assistance to improve the regulatory environment and pro-poor policies in developing countries. The development community is already providing such support, but a stronger link could be established between any market opening negotiated internationally and assistance for the complementary reform needed to ensure successful liberalisation.

Part I

Telecommunications

Chapter 1

Universal Access to Telecommunications in a Competitive Environment

Patrick Xavier
Faculty of Business, Swinburne University of Technology, Melbourne

This chapter provides an overview of the major issues relating to universal access and universal service provision. It explores whether and, if so, how liberalisation can contribute to achieving universal service goals and the types of complementary policies or regulatory underpinnings that may be required. It discusses the choices available to and used by governments in various countries to ensure greater availability of quality basic telecommunications services in liberalised markets.

Introduction

The provision of telecommunications services plays an important role in both individual well-being and a country's economic development. For this reason, general availability of telecommunications services – to all consumers regardless of income level and geographic location within the country – has generally been viewed as an important policy goal. There has been much debate about how the goal of universal service is best achieved: through government monopoly provision, fully private provision or some combination of public and private funding and provision. Some have argued that liberalisation (*i.e.* allowing entry of competitive suppliers, including foreign private suppliers) of telecommunications services can contribute to achieving universal service. However, others have feared that it may undermine universal provision if, for example, foreign private providers "cherry pick" the consumers with the greatest capacity to pay or the most profitable regions, leaving less profitable customers or regions underserved.

This chapter provides an overview of the major issues relating to universal access and universal service provision. It explores whether and, if so, how liberalisation can contribute to achieving universal service goals and the types of complementary policies, or regulatory underpinnings that may be required. It discusses the choices available to and used by governments in various countries to ensure greater availability of quality basic telecommunications services in liberalised markets. Drawing together the broad conceptual issues and the main conclusions emerging from available empirical evidence, cross-country as well as case studies, it addresses a number of key issues:

- How are universal access goals defined in the telecommunications sector?
- Is there a potential conflict between efficiency and equity goals?
- How has liberalisation – particularly in terms of eliminating barriers for foreign providers – affected access to telecommunications services for the poor?
- Where liberalisation has been undertaken, what sorts of regulatory mechanisms and market incentives have been used to ensure universal service?
- Did policies aimed at ensuring universal service use mechanisms directed at the consumer (*e.g.* subsidies, vouchers)?
- What sorts of mechanisms have been used to encourage service providers to increase provision of services to previously unserved or underserved regions or consumers? How effective have such mechanisms been? Did the mechanisms or policies used encourage providers to develop new or innovative solutions to universal service problems or did they focus on the use of existing technologies and solutions?
- What is the role of technological innovation in providing new solutions to universal service challenges?
- What sorts of regulatory bodies exist to regulate the service in question? What sorts of approaches, if any, were used to attain cost-effective administration of these bodies? What technical or capacity-building assistance was provided?

The chapter first discusses how universal service goals are defined. It then examines the impact of market liberalisation, especially the evidence of success in terms of achieving the promised benefits of liberalisation, and finds considerable evidence of success in terms of increased penetration of telecommunications service, especially in wireless services and significant price declines. However, for some parts of the market, such as service provision to inhabitants of rural and remote areas, support from government has been required. Therefore, the support mechanisms used to encourage service providers to increase provision in previously unserved and underserved areas are evaluated before turning to support mechanisms aimed at assisting consumers more directly. Efforts to improve the cost-effectiveness of universal service administration are next discussed, and a brief conclusion follows.

How are universal access/service objectives defined?

Although the terms "universal service" and "universal access" are closely related and are sometimes used interchangeably, they have different meanings. Universal service refers to the provision of telecommunications services to all households within a country, including those in rural and remote (high-cost) locations. Universal service policies also focus on ensuring that the cost of telephone services remains affordable to individual users.

While universal service may be a realistic policy objective in developed countries, universal access is a more feasible practical goal in many developing countries. Universal access policies seek to increase access to telecommunications services on a shared basis, such as a community or village-wide level. Universal access programmes typically promote the installation of public payphones or public call offices in rural and remote villages or low-income urban areas in order to provide a basic and initial connection to the telecommunications network (see Box 1.1).

The major dimensions of universal service and universal access goals are:

- *Availability*: The level of service (including quality of service) is the same wherever a person lives or works, so that residing in a high-cost rural or remote area does not affect the person's ability to access communications services.
- *Affordability:* The level of services is affordable for everyone.
- *Accessibility:* A person with a disability can use the service; the level of physical and mental ability does not disadvantage that person in terms of access to communications services.

No standard universal service definition

Universal access and universal service are not fixed concepts, and there is no single standard definition of what should be included within the scope of such obligations.

The statement on universal service provision in the Reference Paper attached to the 1997 WTO Agreement on Basic Telecommunications (Section 3) is very general. It acknowledges "the right" of each member country "to define the kind of universal service obligation it wishes to maintain", and it states that such obligations will not be regarded as anti-competitive *per se*. However, it qualifies this right with the proviso that universal service obligations should be "administered in a transparent, non-discriminatory and competitively neutral manner and [should not be] more burdensome than necessary for the kind of universal service defined by the Member".[1]

1. According to Roseman (2003), this provision balanced the concerns of Canada and the United States which had achieved virtually universal service largely by means of private operators, with the scepticism

Box 1.1. Universal access policy in China

In July 2002, the Ministry for Information Industry (MII) unveiled a blueprint for the so-called "village to village project" under which unconnected rural areas across the country were grouped into regions and assigned to one of the major telecommunications operators (China Telecom, China Netcom, China Mobile, China Unicom, China Railcom and China Satcom) in accordance with the company's size and financial capacity.

China Mobile was made responsible for providing universal access to over 6 112 villages in Sichuan Province. China Telecom's responsibility included 3 457 villages in Inner Mongolia, and China Unicom was given responsibility for providing universal access in 1 680 villages in Guangxi. China Railcom and China Satcom, two of the smallest operators, were assigned 193 villages in Henan and 132 in Sichuan, respectively. The main objective of China's universal access policy is provision of voice telephone service to all villages.

- The short-term goal is for at least 95% of villages to be provided with telephone services by the end of 2005.
- The medium-term goal is for all villages, hospitals and other organisations to be connected to the public telecommunications network by 2010.
- The long-term goal is for all organisations and families to be connected to the public telecommunications network by 2020.

There have been complaints that the plan is burdensome and unfair. For instance, China Railcom complained that the cost of building networks in Henan province was much higher than for its competitors because many of the province's counties, unlike those of other provinces, were not pre-laid with fibre-optic cables. While other operators need to lay only 5 kilometres of cable from the nearest county seat to the village, China Railcom claimed it may need to install 50 to 100 kilometres. There have also been complaints that assigning specific operators to provide universal access to specific provinces impedes flexible solutions to the universal access challenge and does not facilitate use of the most appropriate technology for villages/provinces. For instance, a wireless operator may be able to supply service in mountainous regions more cost-effectively than a fixed line operator.

Support for the establishment of a universal access fund with the flexibility to compensate operators for the differing costs involved in providing universal access to replace the "village to village project" has been increasing. The Ministry of Finance would be responsible for managing the fund, while the MII would draft the plans for the various universal access projects.

Source: China Ministry for Information Industry.

Universal service requirements can vary considerably depending on the level of development of a country's telecommunications infrastructure. For instance, in developing countries a universal access programme may aim to achieve the installation of one payphone to cover a remote area, while in developed countries it may aim to provide not only voice but also data services (see Box 1.2). In fact, there is now debate about whether the scope of universal service should be expanded to include advanced services, such as the Internet and broadband services.[2] Indeed, governments in an increasing number of countries are already installing programmes to improve access to the Internet. However, such government assistance programmes are distinct from the mandated delivery of universal service obligations, irrespective of income and location, which is the focus of this study.

---

of the Europeans and others regarding the ability to achieve universal service objectives without direct governmental interventions.

2. For a discussion of the issues relating to this debate see Xavier (2003).

To know whether universal access is achieved, it is important to know precisely what type of access is desired; specific goals for individual service and community or shared access should be made clear. It is also important to make clear what types of services are targeted: voice only, voice and data, fixed line and mobile, Internet, broadband, etc. Moreover, as universal service is a dynamic concept, its definition and coverage will need to be revised as conditions in a country change. Decisions relating to the scope and extent of universal service requirements are generally made by the responsible ministry and the legislature. This is because decisions relating to the scope of universal service should take into account social, political and development considerations which are appropriately made through a country's legislative and political processes. Regulators and policy makers have a critical role to play in determining measurable targets for universal access/service and monitoring achievement of these targets.

EU universal service directive

The approach to universal service in the European Union provides an example of a recent redefinition of the nature and scope of universal service to be applied across a number of relatively developed countries. The EU regulatory framework adopted by the European Union in February 2002 sets out the three main elements of universal service: provision of access at a fixed location, provision of directory enquiry services and directories, and provision of public pay telephones. EU member states are free to impose other obligations on telecommunications companies, but if they do so, other market players cannot be required to contribute to the resulting costs.

Provision of access at a fixed location. A fundamental requirement of universal service in the EU is that all "reasonable" requests for connection to the public telephone network at a fixed location and for access to publicly available telephone services at a fixed location are to be met by at least one operator. The connection, as well as being able to support local, national, international and facsimile calls, must also be capable of supporting data communications at bit rates that are sufficient to permit "functional" Internet access, taking into account the prevailing technologies used by the majority of subscribers and technological feasibility.

Directory enquiry services and directories. The universal service obligation in regard to directory information includes: the provision of a comprehensive printed directory of subscribers to all end users free of charge at least once a year; the provision of a comprehensive national and international telephone directory enquiry service to all end users, including users of public pay telephones; the obligation to keep a record of all subscribers of publicly available telephone services in the state, including those with fixed, personal and mobile numbers.

Public pay telephones. The regulator can impose obligations regarding the provision of public payphones to meet the reasonable needs of end users in terms of geographical coverage, number of telephones, accessibility of such telephones to disabled users and quality of services.

With the dramatic take-up of prepaid and post-paid mobile telephony, payphone revenues have steadily declined. As a consequence, further reductions in the number of payphones in both urban and rural areas may be unavoidable. However, payphones continue to provide a key service to some, including disadvantaged consumers, and remain important for universal access in many developing countries.

In the United Kingdom, universal service providers have to publish plans to remove the last remaining public payphone from a particular local call area, and then consult on those plans for 42 days (during which time local public bodies can veto the proposed removal) (Box 1.2). In its consultation document on universal service (Ofcom, 2005), Ofcom proposes retaining this local veto system, with an extended 90-day consultation period and an appeals process to help resolve disputes. Ofcom is also consulting on the need for new guidelines regarding the obligation to provide payphones to make the system clear and consistent. These guidelines would take account of: the number of households in the area; the distance from nearest alternative public call box; the number of calls made from a call box and its profitability; and the status of mobile phone coverage in the area.

Box 1.2. Universal service obligations in a developed economy (the United Kingdom)

Under the UK Communications Act 2003, Ofcom requires BT and Kingston Communications to provide a range of universal services:

- Public payphones.
- Low cost schemes to help those on low incomes.
- Telephone lines capable of delivering dial-up Internet access.
- Special services for people with disabilities.

Source: Ofcom Web site at www.ofcom.org.uk.

Table 1.1 provides an indication of the nature of universal access and universal service programmes in various APEC economies. The cross-country comparison of economies in the APEC region is interesting because it includes developed as well as developing countries.

Impact of telecommunications market liberalisation

Why primary reliance on market forces is critical

Figure 1.1 indicates two separate gaps that need to be addressed with quite different mechanisms in the quest for universal service.

The market efficiency gap is the difference between what markets are actually achieving under current conditions and what can be achieved through further market liberalisation and vigorous pro-competition regulation. The market efficiency gap should be perceived in terms not only of present technology but also technological prospects on the horizon (discussed below).

The access gap refers to the people (*e.g.* those living in rural and remote areas) who would remain beyond the limits of the market unless additional service delivery is stimulated through subsidies to encourage service provision.

Table 1.1. Universal service in various APEC economies

	Scope	Provider	Funding
Australia	Telephony, payphones and 64k/s access	Incumbent	Operator levy administered by the Australian Communications Authority
Brunei Darussalam	Payphones, fax and internet	Incumbent	Indirect government subsidy
Canada	Telephony and dial-up internet	Incumbent	National fund financed by operator levy
Chile	Payphones and telecentres	Contestable by minimum subsidy auction	Interconnection and government fund (FDT) administered by SUBTEL
China	Install payphones in each administrative village	Six telecom operators assigned to specific provinces	Universal service fund expected to be set up with financing through operator levy
Hong Kong, China	Telephony	Incumbent	Universal Service Contribution paid by external service providers in proportion to their external traffic volume
Indonesia	Install payphones in over 40 000 villages within 3-5 years	Incumbent or other operator selected by the regulator	From 2004, a 0.75% operator levy on revenue (after bad debts and interconnection fees)
Japan	Telephony	Incumbent	
Korea	Telephony, broadband and internet	Designated by a committee	
Malaysia	Telephony and 128 Kbit/s Internet access in selected areas	Designated providers	USP fund with operators contributing 6% of revenue
Mexico	Telephony and from 1995 mobiles	Incumbent.	Interconnect fees
New Zealand	Telephony	Incumbent for local residential service	Operator levy
Papua New Guinea	Emergency services	Incumbent	Government
Peru	Payphones and telecentres with internet access	Contestable by minimum subsidy auction	Interconnection charges and operator levy of 1% on revenues.
Philippines	Telephony	All operators	The licensing regime requires mobile and international operators to build fixed lines
Russia Federation	Telephony	Contestable	Operator levy
Singapore			
Chinese Taipei	Telephony	Contestable	Operator levy
Thailand			
United States	Telephony	Various	Operator levy
Vietnam	Telephony		Interconnection and a fund financed from contributions from telecommunications companies and other government sources.

Source: de Ridder, J. and P. Xavier (2004), "Stocktake of Progress Towards Achieving the Vision of a Fully Liberalised Telecommunications Market in APEC Economies", Australian APEC Study Centre, June.

Why rely primarily on the market?

Those who support primary reliance on market forces argue that the greater the market supply, the fewer the areas or people needing subsidy assistance (and the greater the capacity to assist them). In this view, the most effective way of addressing universal access and universal service objectives in a *sustainable* way is to encourage market-based, commercially attractive businesses to address the task.

Primary reliance on the market is preferred because government-funded or philanthropic programmes are vulnerable to modifications or reversal for political or budgetary reasons, for example when a government of a different political ideology comes into power. Besides, a government-driven programme may be accompanied by red tape and bureaucratic inflexibility.

This is not to say that government should not be involved, but rather that government action can be more effective if it helps maximise the role of the private sector so that government can focus on areas the market is unable to serve. This approach also minimises the subsidies required.

It is important to recognise that subsidisation programmes can in fact limit or distort competition in rural and remote areas, because potential market entrants may be discouraged if they have to compete against a subsidised provider that offers service at prices significantly below costs. The advantages of such programmes are likely only to be short-term if they result in adverse long-run outcomes that distort the nature, extent and speed of technological innovation and investment

Figure 1.1. The market efficiency gap and the access gap

Dimensions applied to the network

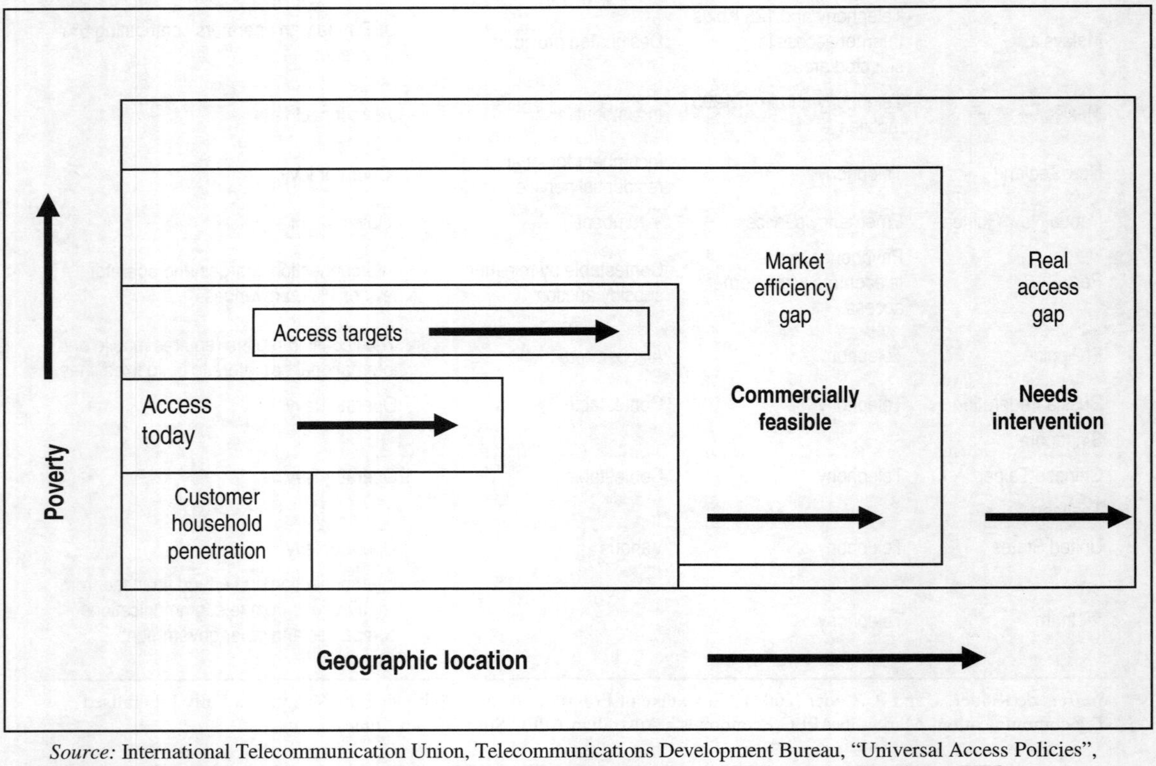

Source: International Telecommunication Union, Telecommunications Development Bureau, "Universal Access Policies", Paper presented by Susan Schorr at the ITU – WTO Workshop on Telecom & ICT Regulation Relating to WTO Obligations and Commitments, WTO, Geneva, 1-7 December 2004; and Intelecon Research 2001.

There are also concerns that subsidy programmes, especially if unnecessary or premature, may assume that the market will fail; may involve guessing what the market and services will be; may deny some market operators the opportunity to offer commercial services because of subsidies paid to other operators; may provide or subsidise services which many users may be able to pay for on a normal commercial basis; may deter market entry owing to the costs that universal access policies impose on market participants; and may impose a considerable cost on consumers (since operators may pass the universal access costs on to them).

Moreover, arguments on behalf of uneconomic telecommunications subscribers should keep in mind that other (economic) subscribers should not bear an unreasonable cost burden.

There is a broad perception that where pressure to be commercially successful is absent, operators have fewer incentives to ensure good service, especially in areas with less competition and lower profits. This may result in unreliable lines (and less disposition to improve the technology used), poor line location, poor customer service, fewer incentives for efficiency, poor access to phone cards, etc.

The role of policy and regulatory frameworks would be to strengthen market forces since this will result in network development and modernisation, lower prices, greater attention to customer choice, and the flexibility to facilitate accelerated market diffusion of services, even to niche areas once considered uneconomical.

Market forces and technological development

As significant changes in rural universal access are increasingly likely, there is a legitimate concern that universal service programmes should not impede or distort the entry of new technology. Such changes will stem from the new suite of wireless technologies such as Wi-Fi and WiMax (which promise telecommunications coverage over a radius of about 50 km) which could provide inexpensive Internet access and voice service to rural and underserved communities. Such developments can help make rural and low-income markets profitable, affordable and sustainable, but they require an environment in which market forces can facilitate innovation and creative business initiatives.

Mobile communications offer an example of technology extending the limits of market forces to reach those unserved by the fixed network, often at lower cost.[3] Mobile operators have translated this lower cost base into affordable prepaid packages that give low-income users a basic network connection. Prepayment allows operators to lower operational costs and reduce credit risk, but because it also gives users more control over expenditure than traditional postpaid solutions, it increases accessibility for low-income users. Mobile services are increasingly available to rural users as well. Indeed, wireless expansion can mean that some operators that specialise in provision of rural service can provide service even in the most remote areas.

---

3. Much of the cost advantage of mobile telephony networks stems from the fact that the access network is shared among subscribers. Once the access network is in place, the marginal cost of adding another subscriber is very low, mainly the cost of a handset. This contrasts with traditional fixed wireline networks where the incremental cost of adding additional subscribers is significant as each subscriber has dedicated access network infrastructure. Hence the cost of adding a mobile subscriber is much lower than that of adding a fixed wireline subscriber. The role of mobile communications in universal access is covered in greater depth in Oestmann (2003).

Competition has resulted in lower prices and lower prices have meant greater affordability and thus better access. Mobile has brought other innovations as well, such as public mobile payphones and SMS. Indeed, as SMS is cheaper than voice, mobile users can engage in a kind of email. Some argue in fact that mobile has virtually eliminated the universal access problem for many of the urban poor and for many rural users as well.

Technological neutrality for cost-effective delivery of universal access in rural areas

Wireless communication technologies, such as fixed wireless access and very small aperture terminals (VSATs), can be effective means of establishing telecommunication networks in rural areas because they are cheaper and easier to install than wired telecommunications (see Box 1.3). For example, in sparsely populated rural areas, wireless communication technologies can be used in conjunction with satellite stations to achieve coverage of isolated settlements over long distances.

Box 1.3. An example of VSAT-based provision of rural telephony

In 1998, Peru's telecommunications regulator (FITEL) invited tenders for a 20-year, subsidised concession to provide rural payphones in the remote regions of Tumbes, Piura, Cajoramarca and Amazonas. Participants submitted bids indicating the lowest government subsidy they would be willing to accept to build the network.

The solution selected by FITEL was based on VSAT technology. The cost-reducing principles behind the winning solution, submitted by GVT del Peru, included the following:

- VSAT-based thin route telephony with up to three voice channels per VSAT.
- Low power consumption (approximately 40 watts per VSAT), as 90% of sites lacked commercial electricity supply.
- Star network topology using a 7.6 metre Hub station in the capital city and a 1.2 metre or 1.8 metre remote VSAT station in each town.
- Use of simple, rugged payphones with a prepaid system instead of coins, to reduce the number of field trips to payphone installations.
- Centralised network management system at the Hub.

Based on this configuration, GVT del Peru proposed to cover the costs of building, installing and operating the network with a government subsidy of USD 4 9 million over five years. The remaining costs would be borne by the operator and recovered from service revenues. According to FITEL, the public subsidy amounted to USD 11 per inhabitant.

Source: OSIPTEL (2003).

With spectrum becoming an increasingly important resource, spectrum allocation and management policy need to be reviewed with a view to allowing more flexible use of spectrum, including spectrum trading and liberalisation. This will enable: the market to play a bigger role in deciding how much spectrum should be allocated to different uses; faster, flexible access to spectrum, including unused and underused spectrum; the development of new, spectrum-efficient technologies; and innovation in the use of the spectrum and spectrum-based products and services (Xavier and Ypsilanti 2006).

Satellite systems have also been developing technologically improved ways to serve rural areas. Prices for VSATs have fallen rapidly, allowing manufacturers to expand sales of VSAT systems into low-end applications such as rural telephony.

Power line. Use of the power grid as a communications network – known as "broadband over power lines" (BPL) in the United States, and "power-line communications" (PLC) in Europe – appears finally to be receiving official acceptance. In October 2004, the FCC approved the use of power-line technology in the United States. Advocates of the technology argue that it promises several advantages, offering not only voice but broadband, with connection speed not dependent on distance from the telephone exchange (as with DSL) or on the number of customers (as with cable). Also, unlike its rivals, power-line offers uploads at the same speed as downloads and promises to offer far more capacity than today's cable networks. Moreover, the technology will reportedly[4] allow utilities to monitor what is happening on their power grids in real time, down to local substations; read power and water meters without entering customers' premises; and manage peak loads by, for example, turning down a residential air conditioner remotely while a customer is at the office, in return for a lower tariff.

"Stratellite" technology. Floating in the stratosphere at an altitude of about 20 kilometres (13 miles), a "stratellite" would behave just like a geostationary satellite, hovering over a particular spot and relaying radio signals to and from the ground. Like satellites, these airships would be able to provide wide-area mobile telephone coverage, paging and other communications services. It is claimed that such airships will be much cheaper to launch and maintain than satellites and can do things that satellites cannot.

There is considerable excitement over the prospect that stratellites would be able to provide wireless broadband coverage, akin to Wi-Fi, over large areas. Advocates claim that a single airship could potentially provide coverage over an area of about 800 000 square kilometres. It should thus be possible to create "hotzones" of coverage encapsulating entire cities and the surrounding countryside, rather than the smaller Wi-Fi "hotspots" found in airports and coffee shops. Moreover, stratellites are expected to cost much less than satellites (about USD 20 million each) and can be reused. After hovering for 18 months they can be recovered for servicing and relaunched.

This is not to say that the technologies mentioned above will live up to their promises, or that one should be preferred to another. It is simply to say that the market must be kept open and that universal service programmes should maintain technological neutrality so as to allow the most cost-effective technologies available now and in the future to be introduced to address the challenge of universal access/service (and the opportunity of "leap-frogging" developing countries to the technological frontier).

Evidence of the success of market liberalisation

Experience around the world has shown that the entry of private telecommunications operators into the market improves teledensity and increases the profitability of telecommunications operators by providing incentives for efficient operation, greater levels of investment and network rollout.

Further scope to enhance market forces. There is still considerable scope to enhance the role of competitive forces in delivering universal service. For instance, in the APEC

4. For a discussion of promising new telecommunications technologies, see for instance, *The Economist*, "Technology Quarterly", 4 December 2004.

region, while only two economies (Brunei Darussalam and Papua New Guinea) have a monopoly in the fixed network, in most economies the incumbent operator controls more than 90% of local access lines. This means that there is still very limited competition in the supply of customer access lines and this influences the ability of market forces to help achieve universal service. In markets that are now focusing on broadband, the lack of effective choice in the fixed local loop has become an important policy issue.

Impact of market liberalisation. The impact of market liberalisation on universal service can be assessed in particular through: increased levels of teledensity and lower prices (which improve affordability). More general analyses of the impact of market liberalisation, including impacts on productivity, investment, quality of service, etc., are available in the various editions of the OECD's *Communications Outlook* (which is updated every two years). These present a wealth of data and analysis showing that market liberalisation has been fundamental to the growth of the telecommunications sector in OECD countries. As the 2005 edition concludes: "the opening of markets promoted competition, and in turn, brought a tremendous expansion of access and increasing innovation in services" (OECD, 2005).

Increased teledensity. Total teledensity (*i.e.* both fixed line and mobile) has increased in all countries. Owing to the popularity of mobile service (and ADSL which makes a second line for Internet use unnecessary), some economies have seen declines in fixed teledensity. Indeed, mobile teledensity now exceeds fixed line in most APEC economies. Moreover, the coverage of mobile service now averages 99% across OECD countries. Prepaid customers have been a major driver of mobile usage and in 2003 represented an average of over 40% of all customers (OECD, 2005). These trends have significantly affected availability and affordability of telecommunications and are very relevant to universal service.

Lower prices. Lower prices help to address universal service by improving affordability. Since 1998 domestic long distance revenue per minute in relatively developed economies has fallen by 25% in Australia to 50% in New Zealand and Chinese Taipei. Chile and Russia are the only two developing economies where domestic long distance prices are higher than they were in 1998. In the Philippines, Peru and Mexico, prices are 40% below 1998 levels and in Malaysia and China they are between 50% and 60% lower.

In the developed APEC economies (except Korea and Singapore), international prices have fallen more than domestic long distance prices because that is where profit margins are highest and competition is fiercest when competition begins. There is additional pressure on international prices from call-back operators, simple international resale (where this is permitted), and now VoIP or Internet-based voice services. International prices have fallen by between 45% (United States) and 69% (Hong Kong, China). Among developing economies, international prices have hardly changed since 1998 in Chile, Vietnam, Indonesia and Russia, although they have fallen between 40% in Mexico and 70% in China and the Philippines.

Mobile service is still a premium service in terms of call prices, but it has the attraction of low up-front connection fees (*i.e.* handset plus SIM card), instant access (*i.e.* no waiting list) and control of budget; over 60% of mobile services in developing economies is prepaid.

The other distinctive feature of price changes resulting from market liberalisation has been increases in line rentals. Australia has had the biggest increase in line rentals for residential customers since 1998 (47%) with no change before 2000. Among the other developed economies in the APEC region, Hong Kong (China) and Chinese Taipei have seen large increases since 1998. The implications of price rebalancing are discussed below.

Developing countries

The World Bank has observed that when competition, privatisation and pro-competitive regulation were introduced into telecommunications markets in Latin America, basic line rollout grew approximately three times faster than in countries with a state monopoly provider and twice as fast than in those with private monopolies. Similarly in Africa, countries with liberalised telecommunications networks had costs of Internet access eight times lower than those with closed markets.

Many studies (*e.g.* Ramamurti, 1996; Ros, 1999; Bortolotti *et al.*, 2001; Li and Xu, 2001) confirm[5] that provision of service by private operators in the telecommunications sector improves teledensity and profitability.[6] In the Asian region, most countries that have liberalised their fixed, mobile and data markets have levels of teledensity and Internet use which are higher than countries that have relied on the provision of services through an incumbent monopolist.

Part of the reason for the success of mobile telephony in reaching more people in both urban and rural areas has been the innovative pricing structures which have been developed as competitors battled to win market share from rival operators. As Hodge (2002) observes, approximately 80% of all mobile phones in southern Africa are bought on a prepaid basis. This means that the subscriber pays no monthly connection charges after purchasing the phone. Contrasting this with the high access fees for fixed line telephony, Hodge estimates mobile phone use is affordable for 70% of households, while fixed line connections are affordable for only 30%.

A similar conclusion emerges from an examination of information relating to the status of competition and privatisation in fixed and mobile markets in Africa and the levels of teledensity and universal access in the region (see Box 1.4). In the countries surveyed, fixed line facilities were almost non-existent in 1997 and privatisation of the incumbent operator was at an early stage. By contrast, most countries had introduced competitors in their mobile market segments by 2002 and had more liberal provisions regarding foreign ownership of mobile operators. As a consequence, teledensity of mobile is higher than that of fixed services in most countries. By 2002, in all but one of the countries surveyed, mobile subscribers had grown from an insignificant base to the point where they outnumbered fixed line subscribers. By contrast, fixed line growth has been

---

5. For a discussion of many of the recent econometric studies which have examined the links between liberalisation and network rollout and operator performance, see Fink *et al.*, 2002; Parker and Kirkpatrick, 2003; and Kessides, 2004.

6. However, the level of competition largely depends on the effectiveness of the regulatory agency in creating a level playing field for all operators, and requires the regulatory environment of the telecommunications industry to be conducive to a well-functioning competitive market. This can be achieved through legal and regulatory mechanisms that promote, among other things: fair and non-discriminatory interconnection between telecommunications operators; cost-oriented tariffs and the elimination of internal cross-subsidies; as well as recourse to a strong and truly independent regulatory agency, capable of enforcing rules. Regulators also have the challenge of creating market-oriented incentives that make service provision to poor and rural areas commercially viable.

flat and in some cases negative with only negligible improvements in fixed-line teledensity.

Box 1.4. Nigeria's GSM umbrella people

Nigeria is Africa's most populated nation with some 124 million inhabitants in 2002. Until August 2001, Nigeria had one of the lowest teledensity rates in the world. In February 2001 the government awarded three 15-year mobile cellular GSM licences for USD 285 million. The rise in the number of mobile subscribers has been dramatic, reaching 2 million by March 2003. Mobile coverage was initially limited to Lagos, the largest city, but has now spread to 219 out of 550 local government areas. Although handsets and prepaid cards are expensive, service is being extended to those who cannot afford a mobile handset and prepaid card through so-called "umbrella people".

Many Nigerian streets are now decorated with umbrellas marking the stands operated by makeshift GSM resellers, whence the nickname of these entrepreneurs (most of them young women). All they need is an umbrella, a plastic table and some chairs, a Subscriber Identification Module (SIM) card and a handset and they are ready for business. An interesting development is the procurement of handsets and subscriptions to each of Nigeria's three mobile service providers, followed by the hiring of "subcontractors" (often young boys or girls) to operate each handset, tripling the potential returns. Critics of GSM services in Nigeria have disparaged the high tariffs and substandard services rendered by operators. But GSM has indisputably played a role in helping to provide universal access in Nigeria, while also appearing to give low-income Nigerians an avenue for gainful entrepreneurship.

Source: ITU (for background on the Nigerian market) and an editorial in the *Daily Trust*, Abuja, Nigeria, 29 April, 2003.

The conflict between efficiency and equity

In many countries, the extension of universal service has been promoted by the cross-subsidisation of line rentals and local call charges by high prices in international and national long distance call revenues. As competition drives prices towards costs, cross-subsidies cannot be sustained. New entrants are largely attracted to providing services for which prices are well above costs (international and long distance) but avoid local markets where prices are often below cost. To defend market share, incumbent operators are forced to reduce long distance prices, thereby reducing the gap between price and cost that makes them vulnerable to competitive entry. To offset the fall in revenue from long distance calls, incumbents have increased line rentals and frequently also local call charges. This is commonly referred to as "price rebalancing".

Table 1.2 shows the price rebalancing that has occurred in OECD countries as a whole. There have been significant rises in fixed charges. But usage prices have declined significantly for both residential and business users, especially since 1997, although this has been offset to some extent by significant rises in fixed charges. The overall fall in prices has been greater for business users (especially large corporate users) than for residential users. These price decreases do not take into account the price falls made available through the price discount schemes that have been accessible to a growing number of both business and residential consumers.

According to OECD (2005), "While the direct impact of rebalancing has been to shift the relative weight of charges, the decline in usage charges is directly attributable to increasing competition. For business users the gains have been particularly noticeable with increased liberalisation. Most of the gains have been made since 1998, coinciding with widespread liberalisation in that year. The rise in prices in 2004 may reflect less price competition as some firms exited the telecommunications market following the end of the financial bubble in the sector."

Table 1.2. OECD time series for telephone charges

	1990	1997	2001	2003	2004
Residential					
Fixed	100	112.97	129.13	132.21	145.23
Usage	100	81.29	55.83	53.50	55.75
Total	100	93.97	85.15	84.98	91.54
Business					
Fixed	100	113.07	126.90	126.52	137.73
Usage	100	86.46	55.54	54.65	56.56
Total	100	91.78	69.82	69.02	72.80

Source: OECD, *Communications Outlook 2005*, OECD, Paris.

Similar trends in price rebalancing are observable in developing countries. For instance, in March 2002, the Malaysian government implemented major tariff rebalancing, reducing long distance and international call fees by more than 20%, while increasing maximum residential line rentals by 10% and local call fees by 25%. Although rural line rentals did not increase, it is claimed that the changes will "provide incentives to industry players to invest in infrastructure roll-out particularly to the rural areas" (OECD, 2005).

Price rebalancing is accepted by regulators since it is recognised that higher line rentals and local call charges that better reflect costs are economically efficient and necessary to make local markets more attractive to new entrants and increase competition/contestability. However, such price increases are also politically unpopular and may be considered unfair as subscribers in these local markets are vulnerable because they cannot migrate to a competitive supplier (since none exists). Also, the largest beneficiaries of price rebalancing are those who make significant international and long distance calls, often large corporate users and the relatively wealthy, while the costs are borne by low users.

There is also concern that sharp increases in monthly rental charges can reduce affordability and thereby threaten the quest for universal service on the fixed network. Some may argue that this is not undesirable if mobile telephony is a cheaper technology to deploy and tariff rebalancing for fixed service makes the cheaper technology relatively more attractive. However, Internet connection, especially high-speed connection, still depends largely on access to fixed-line service. In light of all this, an increasing number of countries apply price cap regulation based on "equity" considerations as a means of controlling the nature, extent, speed and direction of price rebalancing. For instance, a price cap regime can limit the increase in monthly charges (*e.g.* to no more than CPI + 2%) as in the United Kingdom and Australia.

Mechanisms aimed at the service provider

How have regulators sought to implement national access targets and affordability goals, once these have been defined? Generally, governments have imposed two types of universal service obligations (USOs) on operators. The first is a general obligation to provide service to all customers willing to pay for service at the regulated price. This obligation may be limited to certain geographic or population groups, such as a requirement to serve rural areas with population above a certain level. In addition, policy makers and regulators have imposed obligations to extend certain types of designated services to a specified number of subscribers or localities. These network build-out obligations are often incorporated into operators' licences (see Box 1.5).

Box 1.5. Examples of universal service provider designation

In Finland, the obligation to provide access at a fixed location is designated to the SMP operator (or secondarily to the operator with the biggest market share) in that particular area.

In the Netherlands, the USO is awarded to the operator with the lowest net cost.

In Austria, an auction is to be used, and if there is no tender, the USO will be designated.

In Greece, the designation mechanism has been changed. Whereas the incumbent has traditionally been the USO provider, since the liberalisation of the telecommunications market, a competitive tender mechanism may be used.

In China, the six telecommunications operators were each assigned responsibility for providing universal access in the form of two public payphones to each village in a number of designated provinces.

In the United Kingdom, BT is the designated USO provider.

In Ireland, the regulator re-designated the incumbent operator as the USO provider following a detailed consultation process. A request for expressions of interest from alternative operators to become a USO provider was also made, but no expressions were received.

In Norway, the USO provider is designated by the ministry based on criteria described in the regulatory framework.

In Denmark, the USO provider is designated on the basis of market share (combined with other criteria described in the telecommunications directives), but the legislation also allows a public tender.

In Germany, in situations where a universal service is not being adequately provided or there is reason to believe that such provision will not be ensured a USO will be imposed. First, a voluntary solution, *i.e.* provision of universal service without compensation, would be sought. Should there be no voluntary solution, the legislation gives two options: the USO may be imposed on the provider with a dominant position, or the USO provider may be selected by an auction process.

In Mexico, the incumbent operator (Telmex) was required, as part of its privatisation, to install payphones in 20 000 rural areas over a five-year period to meet the policy goal of ensuring some telephone access in all villages with at least 500 residents.

Universal access/service fund

Costing a universal access programme has proven a complicated and contentious task. In principle, costs should be based on the "forward-looking" long-run incremental cost of efficient provision. However, many elements of judgment are involved in estimating this cost. This may cause problems because an operator providing USO will have strong incentives to exaggerate the cost of provision to increase the subsidy received. For example, in Australia, the government's estimate of universal service cost was several times lower than Telstra's. This led to the provision that to claim a subsidy from the universal service fund, Telstra had to disclose its calculations of "loss" to operators "paying" for universal access. If Optus was dissatisfied with the cost estimate, it could challenge the estimate and could also ask the regulator to designate Optus as the universal service provider. This approach maintained the pressures of a contestable market.

An advantage of this approach is that it made the costing process transparent and placed responsibility for cost verification on the parties with relevant information and strong incentives to be vigilant about exaggerated costs (since they had to pay for the costs). Such an approach is consistent with sensible regulatory practice which makes operators resolve issues themselves as far as possible to reduce regulators' information requirements and workload. To some extent this helped to contain the disposition to exaggerate the difficulties and cost of universal service delivery.

Use of a universal access fund would allow more flexibility than mandating a particular operator using a specific prescribed technology. Also a universal access fund is more transparent, the cost can be much lower, and it can be designed to be competitively neutral (*e.g.* by requiring a broad range of operators to contribute to a universal service fund) and technologically neutral (see Box 1.6).

Box 1.6. Features of a good universal access fund

- Independent administration, not related to telecommunications operators.
- Transparent financing.
- Market and technology neutral: does not favour incumbent operators or new entrants or specific technologies.
- Funding targeted to specific beneficiaries (*e.g.* high-cost regions, unserved rural areas, low-income populations, education and health sectors).
- Subsidies should be relatively small and should only subsidise the uneconomic portion of service; operators should finance the rest.
- Competitive bidding process for universal access projects: *i.e.* lowest bidder should be awarded subsidy and right to build and operate networks to expand service.

Source: World Bank (2002), "Telecommunications Regulation – A Handbook", November.

In developing countries, universal access funds have emphasised ensuring basic public access (*i.e.* voice-grade fixed access to the public telecommunications network). With the growing importance of the Internet to national economies, some funds are also supporting public access to value-added services, including Internet access. In Chile, the government has redefined its universal access fund, which has been successful in extending basic telecommunications to rural and low-income areas, to support telecentre projects. In India too, telecentres are eligible for subsidies from the universal service fund.

Contributions from operators

What percentage of revenue should be payable by operators? This will largely depend of course on the amount of subsidy funding required. In countries that have installed a universal access fund, the levy has ranged from 1% (Argentina, Brazil), to 5% (India) or 6% (Malaysia). Table 1.3 gives some examples of contributions required from operators in a range of countries.

Table 1.3. Examples of universal access/universal service funds

Country	Source of revenue	Administering agency	Method of allocating funds
Argentina	1% of all operators' gross revenues	Operators (virtual fund)	Government to determine based on its goal to increase fixed teledensity and mobile teledensity.
Australia	Levy on operators depending on market share by revenue	Australian Communications Authority (ACA)	USO provider (currently incumbent Telstra) submits claim based on evidence of "net costs". Until 2003, claim was assessed by ACA using large scale USO model but this approach is currently under review.
Brazil	1% of service providers gross operational revenues earned from the provision of telecom services	Anatel, regulatory agency	
Chile	Government's budget	Subtel, regulatory agency	Subsidies distributed through competitive bidding (lowest bid wins)
Colombia	5% of national and long distance operators' revenues plus funds from licence fees	Ministry of Communications	Subsidies distributed through competitive bidding (lowest bid wins)
India	5% levy on the revenue of telecommunications operators	TRAI (the telecom regulator)	Subsidies distributed through competitive bidding (with lowest bid winning)
Malaysia	Fixed and mobile network operators contribute 6% of their weighted revenue from designated services to the Fund	Malaysian Communication and Multimedia Commission (CMC), regulatory agency	During an interim period (1999-2002), Telekom Malaysia was the only operator with access to funds. Starting in 2002, other operators were invited to submit proposals for USP and be compensated from the fund through a competitive process
Nepal	2% levy on the revenues of the incumbent operator, ISPs and mobile operators.	NTA (Nepal Telecom Authority)	Subsidies distributed through competitive bidding
Peru	1% of all operators' and CATVs' gross revenues	OSIPTEL, regulatory agency	Subsidy goes to lowest bidder
South Africa	0.16% of all operators' revenues	Universal Service Agency, specially created unit to manage fund	Subsidies mainly awarded to telecentre projects and areas of greatest need
Uganda	1% levy on all sector participants including telecom operators, the postal service, couriers, ISPs	Uganda Communication Commission, the regulatory agency	Subsidies distributed through competitive bidding (lowest bid wins)
United States	6.6% levy on operators' interstate end-user revenue (which is passed on to customers as a "Universal Service Fund fee on monthly phone bills)	Universal Service Administrative Company (a private not-for-profit-corporation)	A number of programmes, including: high-cost support mechanism; low-income support mechanism; rural health-care support mechanism; schools and libraries support mechanism (E-rate)

Source: Intelecon Research 2001, and other sources.

In deciding upon the contribution to be obtained from operator revenue, consideration should be given to the extent to which this revenue base might shrink because of the development of technologies that can bypass the traditional telephone network, such as VoIP, and because of the increasing inability to distinguish between local and long distance revenues[7] owing to the emergence of service packages that bundle local, long distance and international services.

7. In the United States, for example, all telecommunications companies that provide service between states, including long distance companies, local telephone companies, wireless companies, paging companies and payphone providers, are required to contribute to the Federal Universal Service Fund. Carriers

Not all countries have been enthusiastic about establishing a universal service fund (USF). In the European Union, for example, a universal service fund may be established by a member state if it concludes that the incumbent would be significantly competitively disadvantaged if designated as the universal service provider. It is notable that (so far) only France and Italy have decided to establish a universal service fund.

Contribution from government taxation revenue. Clearly the government can make a contribution to a USF from general taxation revenue as Chile has done.

Contribution from spectrum auctions (3G), spectrum pricing and privatisation. Some of the proceeds from telecommunications licence fees, including spectrum-pricing fees, can be contributed to a USF. Also, part of the proceeds of spectrum auctions might be allocated to USO purposes. For example, there is a strong case for auctioning 3G licences and/or charging operators allocated a spectrum licence fees based on the "opportunity cost" of the spectrum allocated. In addition, a proportion of the proceeds of privatisation of telecommunications operators could be allocated to support universal access and universal service programmes and, indeed, programmes to bridge the digital divide. For instance, in Australia, 5% of the proceeds from privatising the second tranche of Telstra's shares were allocated to improving conditions in rural areas on the rationale that this constitutes an equitable sharing.

Contribution from local government and other government departments. Telecommunications can help to deliver improved service to education, health, agriculture, e-government and telecentres in rural and remote regions. Thus a number of government agencies might contribute to a USF to support telecommunications access. Allocating responsibility for delivering programme outcomes to key spending ministries can have other benefits, such as a shared sense of ownership across participating ministries and local government. In addition, telecommunications operators can form partnerships with local government agencies to help ensure that the initiative contributes to local economic development. Small business support could also be enlisted. Any telecentres established are likely to be in a central location which is probably suitable for business activities. During the day a telecentre could be used for training for Internet use, etc., while at night it could be used for business activities. For example, it could be a suitable location for telecommunications operators to market their products, sell their prepaid cards, etc., along lines of one-stop shopping.

Asymmetric interconnection charges. Asymmetric interconnection fees could be used to increase revenue from rural service. Higher interconnection charges could be charged for termination in rural and remote areas to reflect the higher costs of providing termination service in these areas. Such an approach is used in Chile and Peru, for example. Asymmetric interconnection regimes can be particularly important to rural operators. Since rural operators' income may be largely based on incoming calls, asymmetric interconnection rates affect whether they will be financially viable. Such asymmetric interconnection charges can reduce dependence on government subsidies.

Competitive tendering for providing universal access in Latin America

In 1994, the Chilean government set up a fund financed by the national budget to improve access to public telephones in rural areas. The goal was to award subsidies

---

providing international service must also contribute. The contribution is calculated as a specific percentage of interstate and international end-user revenue.

through competitive bidding (see Box 1.7). The fund's budget in 1995 was aimed at covering 1 285 localities and permitting access to basic telecommunications services for the third of the population without access at that time. From 1995 to 1999, the Chilean government paid subsidies of USD 21 million to support 183 projects providing public access telephones in 5 915 localities serving a population of about 2.2 million. The bidding process was successful beyond expectation and the fund had to commit only 48% of its budget to achieve 90% of its plan (Wellenius *et al.*, 2004). In fact, bids requiring zero subsidy were made for 51% of the localities. Furthermore, the programme led to private telecommunications investments several times the amount provided by the fund. The ITU estimates that each USD 1 of subsidy generated private investment of USD 1.4 in public access telephones and USD 5 in individual lines and other services (ITU, 2003). Within five years of its establishment the fund had succeeded in extending access to basic voice telephony service to the majority of Chileans living in rural areas.

Box 1.7. Steps in using a competitive tendering approach

A competitive tendering approach comprises the following main steps:

- The government defines the broad objectives, target population and levels of funding for the subsidy programme. It also establishes key service conditions such as types of service to be provided, quality standards, maximum retail prices and duration of service commitments.
- Specific service needs and choices are primarily identified by prospective beneficiaries and communities. Economic and technical analysis is used to select and prioritise projects likely to be desirable from the perspective of the economy at large but not commercially viable on their own, and to determine the maximum subsidy justified for each project.
- Private firms submit competitive bids for these projects. Subject to meeting service conditions, bidders are free to develop their business strategies, including choice of technology.
- Subsidies are awarded to bidders requiring the lowest one-time subsidies. Alternatively, bids are invited for fixed subsidies and awarded against other quantifiable service measures, such as the lowest price to end users or the fastest roll-out of service.
- Subsidies are paid in full or in instalments linked to implementation of investments and start of service.
- Service providers own the facilities and bear all construction and commercial risks.
- No additional subsidies are available downstream for the same services.
- The government monitors and enforces service quality and pricing standards, protects users against arbitrary changes of service, and provides investors with stable regulatory rules.

Peru too uses a competitive tendering scheme to place public access telephones in selected rural localities. It differs from the Chilean scheme in that it also requires Internet access cabins to be provided in district capitals and in that it is funded by operator levies rather than government (see also Box 1.8).

As Table 1.4 shows, the amount of subsidy actually bid for and granted can be less than half the maximum offered by the funds. However, the averages hide a wide range of experience, from zero subsidy in some of the early Chilean tenders to 100% of the offered amount in later rounds.

Table 1.4. Examples of funding universal access in Latin America

Country	Source of finance	Period	Localities served	Max subsidy given (USD millions)	Subsidy given (USD millions)	Subsidy per locality (USD)
Chile	Government budget	1995-97	4 504	24.2	10.2	2 256
		1998-99	1 412	14.4	9.8	6 919
		2000	143	1.9	1.8	12 727
Peru	1% operator levy	1998	213	4.0	1.7	18 800
		1999	1 937	50.0	11.0	5 700
		2000(a)	2 290	59.5	27.8	12 100
Colombia	Operator levy & government contribution	1999	6 865	70.6	31.8	4 600
Guatemala	Spectrum auctions	1998	202	N/A	1.5	7 587
		1999(b)	1 051	N/A	4.5	4 282
Dom. Republic	2% operator levy	2001	500	3.8	3.4	6 800

(a) Implementation delay due to disqualification of the subsidy winner and subsidies awarded to second bidders.

(b) Actual fund disbursements, excluding subsidies won but network not implemented owing to operator failure.

Source: Björn Wellenius (2002), "Closing the Gap in Access to Rural Communication: Chile 1995-2002", November.

Competitive tendering has a number of advantages, including:

- The speed with which tenders can be conducted and thus quick implementation of universal service arrangements.
- The ability to reveal information about each bidder's true valuation of the cost of providing universal service obligations.
- The increased incentives for bidders to decrease costs in order to win the tender to provide service in particular areas.

Table 1.5 summarises some success factors in the use of competitive tendering.

Demand side initiatives

Demand side initiatives are also important. For instance, a government's significant purchasing power can help to increase a country's telecommunications infrastructure in rural and remote areas, particularly when used to initiate demand aggregation. The "core" of aggregation possibilities includes schools and health institutions, agencies interested in promoting telemedicine, public safety, community networks, community learning centres, tourism-related products, teleworking, etc. Demand aggregation has been successful in attracting telecommunications supply, including broadband, to rural and remote areas in a number of countries (Xavier, 2002).

Box 1.8. Universal service and competitive tendering in India

The approach to universal access in India provides an interesting example of the way in which a country with a very large population and number of rural villages addresses this issue.

Through the Universal Service Obligation Fund, a bidding process was used to provide rural community phones in 48 310 villages with a population in excess of 2 000 in which no other public telephone facility was available. The process reportedly resulted in lowering the cost of the project by about 17% from the reserve price.

The USO Fund administration is proceeding with plans to cover all 570 000 villages with public phones. It has already signed agreements for disbursal of subsidies to support the more than 520 000 village public telephones already installed. Bids for the remaining 57 000 villages have also been invited. Agreements have also been signed for replacing more than 180 000 village public telephones on multi-access radio relay (MARR) technology.

In addition, the Department of Telecommunications will invite bids to set up Tele-Information Centres to provide access for both voice and data in villages with a population of more than 2 000. So far, over USD 100 million in subsidies have been disbursed to the universal service providers.

Support through the USO fund is also being provided to subsidise the capital and operating cost of Direct Exchange Lines (DELs) installed in rural areas after the beginning of 2002. About 3.1 million rural DELs had been installed as of the end of March 2004. Bids have also been invited for providing telecommunications facilities to new rural subscribers.

Source: Telecommunications Regulation Authority of India (TRAI).

Table 1.5. Competitive tendering for subsidies: some critical success factors

Demand factors	Supply factors	Enabling environment
Limited or no capital contributions are required from users	Several firms are qualified to bid for subsidies	Elements of market-oriented legal and regulatory framework are in place
Subsidies can be easily targeted to poorest users	Business opportunities are aligned with operators' strategies	Government has access to stable and reliable sources of subsidy finance
Service features are tailored to user needs and preferences	Project components are cost-effectively packaged	Private investors have access to long term financing
Services have considerable growth potential		Donors and different tiers of government are able to coordinate financing policies
		National infrastructure networks are already relatively developed
		Institutional capacity is in place to implement and manage a competitive subsidy mechanism

Source: Wellenius, B., V. Foster and C. Malmberg-Calvo (2004), "Private Provision of Rural Infrastructure Services: Competing for Subsidies," World Bank Policy Research Working Paper 3365, August.

Mechanisms aimed at assisting the consumer

Market forces, even where efficient, are less able to serve low-income, disadvantaged or disabled consumers in both urban and rural areas. A number of schemes involving subsidies and other assistance programmes exist in various countries to help ensure that disadvantaged customers have access to basic telephony services. Most offer a concession on certain charges for basic telecommunications services to eligible old-age, disadvantaged, disabled or low-income consumers. Discounts are usually offered on connection charges, monthly access charges and usage charges so that the rate of growth of a "lower quartile bill" is constrained. In the United Kingdom, the universal service provider is required to offer special services to customers with disabilities, including text relay (which translates voice into text) for those who are deaf or hard of hearing, special format telephone bills for those who are blind or have only partial sight and a priority fault repair service.

In Australia, the incumbent carrier, Telstra, is obliged under its Carrier Licence Conditions, to offer products and services to address the needs of low-income customers. Telstra's "Access for Everyone" scheme has programmes that target low-income Australians in the following segments: age pensioners; people with a disability; transient and homeless people; job seekers; people from non-English speaking backgrounds; indigenous Australians; low-income families. Similar schemes exist in a number of other countries such as the United States, the United Kingdom and Ireland (Table 1.6).

Table 1.6. Addressing the needs of the disadvantaged in the United States, the United Kingdom and Ireland

Country	Scheme details
Ireland	Vulnerable user scheme.[1] Customer gets line rental and EUR 5 worth of calls for EUR 23.65 per month. Once the EUR 5 worth of calls is used, user pays double the usual rates for the next EUR 6 worth of calls. Caller will therefore not be more than EUR 1 a month worse off under the scheme.
	The aim is to limit increases in the size of vulnerable users' telephone bills if they have relatively low levels of usage. The median bill of customers who use the scheme will not increase by more than CPI-0%, the cap on the current lower quartile bill.
United Kingdom	Light user scheme.[2] Eligible consumers get a rebate on line rental as long as they spend less than GBP 15.07 a quarter on calls. The amount of the rebate increases as the call bill gets smaller.
United States	Lifeline.[3] A federally funded scheme which reimburses carriers for providing discounts on monthly phone bills. The scheme allows low-income consumers to save at least USD 5.25 a month and up to USD 10.00 a month off their monthly phone bills.
	Some states (*e.g.* Nebraska[4], New Jersey[5], Tennessee[6]) provide additional support of up to USD 3.50.
	People living in indigenous tribal lands can also receive further benefits.
	The scheme is open to low-income consumers participating in other low-income assistance programmes such as food stamps or energy assistance programmes.
United States	Linkup.[7] Provides savings of up to 50% of the installation fees of a new line, up to USD 30.

1. Details available at www.comreg.ie/_fileupload/publications/ComReg0348.pdf.
2. Details available at www.bt.com/Pricing/index.jsp and then click on Residential, Other Call Schemes, Light User Scheme.
3. Details available at www.lifelinesupport.org/li/components/lifeline.asp.
4. www.psc.state.ne.us/home/NPSC/usf/ntap_usf/ntap_usf.html.
5. www.bpu.state.nj.us/home/TelephoneAssistance.shtml.
6. www.state.tn.us/tra/teleassist.htm.
7. Details available at www.lifelinesupport.org/li/components/linkup.asp.

In addition to specific subsidies targeted at disadvantaged and low income groups, various other approaches are sometimes used to ensure that consumers are able to access affordable telecommunications services. These usually take the form of price controls and price capping requirements on the dominant operator to ensure that prices for basic telecommunications services do not increase by more than a specified amount. In Australia, for example, the price for untimed local calls was capped at 22 cents for calls made from a residential or business phone, and 40 cents for calls made from a public phone; line rentals charged at residential rates were not to be increased without prior consultation with the regulator; Telstra had to notify the minister in advance if it intended to alter charges for directory assistance services, and the minister could disallow the proposed changes if they were considered against the public interest; and Telstra was to offer a line rental service to schools at a price at or below the standard line rental offered to residential customers.

Price caps in Australia (and in other countries applying price cap regulation) are designed both to provide assistance to low-income consumers so that they have access to affordable local call services and to ensure that metropolitan and non-metropolitan call prices remain at broadly similar levels and safeguard rural consumers from high local call prices.

The phoneless

Even where well-designed universal access/universal service policies have succeeded in increasing teledensity and telephone penetration to international best practice levels, a percentage of the population is likely to remain without access to a telephone service in many countries. This is true even in countries like the United States and Canada where over 90% of the population has access to a telephone. Studies in the United States (FCC, 1996, 2000, 2003) and Canada (Human Resources Development Canada, 2002) indicate that there are many contributing factors, only some of which might be tackled through universal service policies. They include:

- *Poverty and unemployment*. A study by the FCC concluded that low income and unemployment had a significant negative impact on telephone ownership in the United States. It found that approximately 30% of welfare and public assistance recipients did not have telephone service. In addition, more than two-thirds of the households without service had annual incomes of USD 15 000 or less. Approximately 50% of households headed by females with children living at or below the poverty line did not have a telephone (FCC, 1996). In Canada, approximately 88% of those without a telephone had incomes below the Statistics Canada Low Income Cut Off (Human Resources Development Canada, 2002).
- *Mobility*. The FCC study found that tenants were six times more likely than owners to be without a telephone. In Californian regions with telephone subscriber levels below 90%, more than 50% of phoneless people had lived at their current address for less than one year (FCC, 1996).
- *Minority groups*. Telephone penetration rates for minority groups in the United States have been estimated to be 8 to 10 percentage points lower than for the general population (Schement and Forbes, 1998). Similar results have been found for Canada. For example, in the Manitoba region, where average penetration in 1997 was 97.8%, the average penetration rate for First Nation communities was 73.2% (Human Resources Development Canada, 2002).

Many of these issues clearly go beyond the scope of universal service programmes and may be overcome only through appropriately designed social, employment and incomes policies. Nevertheless, there is scope for well-targeted assistance provided as part of a universal service programme to alleviate some of the barriers to phone ownership. Practical options with the potential to assist in reducing phonelessness include:

- Reviewing disconnection procedures to help customers unable to pay for long distance service to stay connected to local service. Information collected in the United States and Canada indicates that many of the phoneless were disconnected because of difficulties in managing their use of and payment for long distance services.
- Providing low-cost or free blocking services for long distance or expensive information-related services.
- Providing "quick dial" or "warm line" service so that customers who have been disconnected continue to have access to emergency services.
- Requiring telephone operators to offer customers the option of an instalment payment plan or a bad debt repayment plan, thus allowing customers to maintain local call service while making repayments.
- Providing more substantial discounts on monthly access fees for basic telephony service for those meeting eligibility requirements. One of the main reasons given by non-subscribers for their inability to have a telephone service is that existing subsidy schemes do little to offset the high cost of monthly access charges levied by telecommunications operators.[8]
- Ensuring greater awareness of assistance programmes through public announcements and targeted advertising. In the United States, some states have set up "marketing boards" to market and publicise Lifeline, Link-Up and other assistance programmes available to existing and prospective telephone customers.

Towards more cost-effective universal service administration

Towards systematic development of a universal service strategy

With the rapid development of telecommunications, countries should already be thinking or rethinking longer-term policies. In the context of universal access/service policy, this means bearing in mind how shorter-term programmes support longer-term universal service and digital divide policy objectives in an increasingly competitive, technologically dynamic telecommunications environment.

Experience suggests that a country should develop a systematic universal service strategy in order to identify the sources of any identified problems and address them with tailored cost-effective measures. Any redefinition of the scope of universal service and universal access should also be based on a transparent, systematic review of a country's universal access objectives and targets. In Australia, Hungary, the United Kingdom and India, for example, the strategy development procedure commenced with a public consultation document that sought the views of various stakeholders. This approach to defining universal access and universal service obligations would be consistent with the transparency required by the WTO Reference Paper provision relating to universal service.

A systematic review of universal service programmes should be based (at least) on the considerations set out in Box 1.9.

8. In Canada, for example, almost 70% of those unable to afford a telephone service cited high monthly access charges as the primary reason. See Human Resources Development Canada, "Eliminating Phonelessness in Canada: Possible Approaches", March 2002.

Box 1.9. A systematic review of universal service programmes

1) Clear and specific articulation of the objectives and coverage of universal service

It is crucial to specify the intended beneficiaries clearly. It would therefore be helpful to break down the broad objective of universal access into a range of distinct, realisable and measurable targets for its subcomponents.

2) Identification of barriers to universal service

Such information is necessary to guide the development of effective universal service policies.

3) Identify schemes that could cost-effectively address the identified barriers to universal service

To maintain the benefits of a competitive or "contestable" market in the delivery of universal service, the option for replacing a universal service provider by a more cost-effective supplier should be preserved.

4) Estimate the cost of programmes for universal service

The costing principles, process and outcomes should be transparent and subject to audit; they should be subject to regular disclosure.

5) Consider the relative merits of alternative mechanisms for funding universal service

6) Establish a mechanism for funding universal service in a sustainable way

7) Ensure regular monitoring and evaluation of performance in the delivery of universal service against a pre-set delivery schedule and targets

8) Ensure regular public reporting of progress in achieving universal service

Criteria for sustainable USO support

Experience also suggests that the choice of implementation mechanisms for universal access delivery should be guided by a range of criteria, including:

- *Sufficiency:* Does the mechanism ensure comparability of service and prices between urban and rural customers in a sustainable manner?
- *Affordability:* Does the mechanism enable providers to offer the supported services in an affordable manner?
- *Competition:* Does the mechanism minimise distortions to competition? Does it encourage and facilitate competition by precisely targeting support to high-cost disadvantaged customers?
- *Flexibility:* Is the mechanism able to evolve as new technologies are introduced, as competition develops and as the definition of USO changes over time?
- *Protection and advancement:* Does the mechanism prevent degradation of the existing infrastructure and the current level of service? Does the mechanism produce an investment incentive to upgrade facilities used to provide universal service?
- *Portability:* Can the mechanism provide all eligible operators with an appropriate amount of support in a competitively neutral manner?
- *Predictability:* Does the mechanism enable an operator to determine in advance the amount of support it will receive on behalf of a customer?

- *Practicality:* Is the mechanism economically and administratively viable?
- *Transparency:* Is the mechanism transparent and open to monitoring and review?
- *Cost-effectiveness:* Does the mechanism enable objectives to be achieved at least cost?

The administration of USO programmes

Cost-effective administration of universal service programmes is also important. For instance, while some universal service funds (*e.g.* in Colombia) are administered by government ministries, others are administered by the regulator (*e.g.* Australia, Peru, Chile). Countries such as the United States and South Africa have set up a specific agency to deal exclusively with the administration of the universal service programmes.

Some studies have concluded that a separate and independent regulatory agency achieves the best results in regard to universal service in both developed and developing countries (Garcia-Murillo and Kuerbis, 2003). However, whether an industry regulator or an agency specifically set up to provide universal service is responsible for administering the universal service framework, the principles of economical, effective and efficient administration should be followed. This means that the universal service framework must be transparent, accountable, targeted, proportional and consistent in its decisions.[9]

Countries have used various mechanisms to ensure transparency and cost-effectiveness in the administration of universal service funds. These have included regular reporting mechanisms to the public and to the government; regular and independent auditing of the financial and procedural administration of the funds; and the creation of procedures for regulatory impact assessment of the rules and regulations created by the regulatory agencies for the implementation of universal service policies.

Performance measurement, efficiency review and auditing

The United States, Australia, the United Kingdom, Hong Kong (China) and Uganda have installed mechanisms for ongoing assessment of the performance of the agency responsible for the universal service framework and the auditing of programmes used to deliver universal service. The assessment can take the form of financial auditing of the cost and revenue information upon which the universal service cost is calculated and allocated among operators,[10] performance auditing of the practices and procedures

9. *Transparency* refers to the regulatory process being open to public scrutiny. This may involve the requirement to circulate draft decisions for comment, consult with the public generally and with interested or affected parties prior to making decisions and publish decisions once they are made. A transparent regulatory regime allows the public to appreciate the grounds for regulatory decisions. *Accountability* involves the regulator being answerable to the public, the minister or parliament. A targeted regulatory framework is one which ensures that regulatory decisions are meant to resolve the specific issue at hand and do not unintentionally affect other markets or industry participants. *Proportionality* is concerned with ensuring that the breadth, depth and severity of regulation is proportional to the problem it is designed to resolve. That is, the scope and intensity of regulation should reflect the seriousness of the problem it is attempting to resolve. Finally, *consistency in regulatory decisions* involves the regulator's actions being predictable over time and across similar issues. This provides certainty to public and private sector participants and provides incentives for investment and private initiative by reducing regulatory risk.

10. These audit reports are sometimes published and open to public scrutiny. See, for example, the approach adopted by the Uganda Communications Commission, www.ucc.co.ug/draftreg/universalService.doc).

employed by the agency in administering the universal service framework, and auditing of the recipients of universal service funds.

For example, in Australia, the National Audit Office undertakes performance audits of the Australian Communications Authority (ACA) to assess the effectiveness of its financial management and the adequacy of its administrative practices as they relate to the administration of the universal service framework. The audit evaluates the ACA's universal service levy collection practices, levy assessment systems, arrangements for banking of receipts, recordkeeping systems, levy collection risk management policies, internal accounting systems, and reporting and corporate governance arrangements.[11] Similarly, in 2001 the United Kingdom undertook an efficiency audit of several industry regulators, including the then telecommunications regulator, Oftel, to assess whether the operations of these agencies provide cost-effective and responsive regulatory processes and outcomes.[12] In the United States, formal audits of E-rate beneficiaries (both service providers and applicants) are conducted to assess overall programme compliance and to identify instances of overpayment of universal service grants.[13]

Regulatory impact assessment

A number of countries require regulatory agencies to undertake a regulatory impact assessment as part of the decision-making framework. Regulatory impact assessment requires assessing the costs and benefits of each option considered by the regulatory agency, followed by a recommendation supporting the most effective and efficient option.[14]

Assistance towards cost-effective administration of universal service programmes

Understanding the principles of best practice is necessary but not sufficient. The skills to implement these practices, which are often in short supply, especially in developing countries, are also needed. Various programmes now provides technical and capacity-building assistance to developing countries, including programmes to enhance regulatory effectiveness. International bodies providing assistance are: the World Bank, the International Telecommunication Union (ITU), the Commonwealth Telecommunications Organisation (CTO), the World Trade Organization (WTO), and the OECD. In regard to universal service, the ITU, for instance, has conducted capacity-building workshops and supported visits by experts to advise on the design, development and implementation of

---

11. See, for example, The Auditor-General, Audit Report No. 32, *1999–2000 Performance Audit Management of Commonwealth Non-primary Industry Levies*, Canberra, 2001.

12. WS Atkins Management Consultants, "External Efficiency Review of the Utility Regulators", February 2001.

13. www.fundsforlearning.com/cgi-bin/NewsList.cgi?world=§ion=&rec=392&cat=E-rate.

14. Regulatory impact assessment involves consideration of seven key elements: a clear description of the problem or issues which give rise to the need for action; an assessment of the desired objectives the regulator wishes to achieve; the options (regulatory and/or non-regulatory) that may constitute viable means for achieving the desired objectives; an assessment of the impact (costs and benefits) on consumers, business, government and the community of each option; identification of the key affected parties and assessment of the level of consultation undertaken with affected parties; identification of a preferred option; and a strategy to implement and review the preferred option. See UK Office of Regulatory Review, 2001; Oftel, 2002; OECD, 2000.

programmes. The WTO and World Bank have also participated in such action. The OECD's various programmes, such as the regulatory reform programme, have contributed to capacity building. But far more is needed.

Conclusion

This study concludes that market liberalisation in the telecommunications sector has resulted in improved telecommunications penetration and lower prices in overall terms and, accordingly, affordability. The penetration of mobile telecommunications has increased spectacularly, largely because of competition and technological developments such as prepaid service. As a result, the number of households without telephone service has declined significantly.

Valuable experience has been gained regarding the ingredients for a successful policy approach.

With the dramatic changes in telecommunications technology now occurring (and those on the horizon), it seems especially important that governments harness the full support of market forces to address universal access and universal service. This includes adopting a technology-neutral policy and facilitating market entry of new entrants, including those with new technologies, into telecommunications markets to allow quickly introducing benefits of technological developments leading to convergence and next generation networks (NGN) (Xavier 2006).

Policy measures, such as market liberalisation supported by effective pro-competitive regulation, are probably as important as declining technology costs. But there are areas that seem beyond the reach of market forces alone. Here, mechanisms used to support service providers appear to have been successful in providing incentives/subsidies to encourage provision in areas not previously supplied. In some cases, mechanisms directed at low-income, disadvantaged consumers may be more effective in helping to ensure that such customers can obtain affordable service, choose tariff packages, control their expenditure and pay their bills in ways that are more tailored to their needs.

Systematic monitoring and evaluation based on good up-to-date data is critically important to ensure that universal service targets are being achieved on schedule. Also important are regular audits of the economy, efficiency, and effectiveness of the administration of a universal service programme.

References

Bortolotti, B, D. Siniscalco and M. Fantini (2000), "Privatization and Institutions: A Cross-country Analysis", Working Paper 375, CESifo.

Federal Communications Commission (FCC) (1996), Common Carrier Bureau, *A Review of Current Interstate Support Mechanisms*, February 1996.

FCC (2000), Telecommunications Industries Analysis Project, *Closing the Gap: Universal Service for Low Income Households*, August, Washington, DC.

FCC (2003), Industry Analysis and Technology Division, Wireline Competition Bureau, *Telephone Penetration by Income by State*, May.

Fink, C., A. Mattoo and R. Rathindran (2002), "An Assessment of Telecommunications Reform in Developing Countries", World Bank Policy Research Working Paper 2909, October.

Garcia-Murillo, M. and B. Kuerbis (2003), "The Effect of Institutional Constraints on the Success of Universal Service Policies", World Bank, Washington, DC.

Hodge, J. (2002), "Infrastructure Service Liberalisation in Southern Africa – 'Managed Liberalisation' and Emerging Lessons from Telecoms", October.

Human Resources Development Canada (2002), *Eliminating Phonelessness in Canada: Possible Approaches*, March.

International Telecommunication Union (ITU) (2004), Telecommunications Development Bureau, "Universal Access Policies", presented by Susan Schorr at the ITU-WTO Workshop on Telecom & ICT Regulation relating to WTO Obligations and Commitments, WTO, Geneva, 1-7 December.

ITU (2003), "Trends in Telecommunication Reform 2003: Promoting Universal Access to ICTs: Practical Tools for Regulators", www.itu.int/publications/docs/trends2003.html.

Kessides, I. N. (2004), *Reforming Infrastructure: Privatization, Regulation, and Competition,* World Bank and Oxford University Press, Washington, DC and New York.

Li, W. and L. Xu (2001), *Liberalization and Performance in the Telecommunications Sector around the World*, World Bank, Washington, DC.

OECD (1995), *"Universal Service Obligations for Telecommunications in an Increasingly Competitive Environment*", OECD, Paris.

OECD (2000), *Reducing the Risk of Policy Failure: Challenges For Regulatory Compliance*, OECD, Paris.

OECD (2005), *Communications Outlook 2005*, OECD, Paris.

Oestmann, S. (2003), "Mobile Operators: Their Contribution to Universal Service and Public Access", Intelecon Research & Consultancy Ltd, January.

Ofcom (2005), "Review of the Universal Service Obligation," 10 January, www.ofcom.gov.org.uk.Oftel (2002), *Regulatory Option Appraisal Guidelines: Assessing the Impact of Policy Proposals,* London, June.

OSIPTEL (2003),"Telecommunications Sector in Peru, presentation to APEC TEL28" by Liliana Ruiz de Alonso, www.apectelwg.org/apec/atwg/previous.html#16.

Parker, D. and C. Kirkpatrick (2003), "Privatization In Developing Countries: A Review of the Evidence and the Policy Lessons", Aston University Centre on Regulation and Competition, July.

Ramamurti, R. (1996), "The New Frontier of Privatization", in R. Ramamurti (ed.), *Privatizing Monopolies: Lessons from the Telecommunications and Transport Sectors in Latin America*, The Johns Hopkins University Press, Baltimore, Maryland.

de Ridder, J. and P. Xavier (2004), "Stocktake of Progress Towards Achieving the Vision of a Fully Liberalised Telecommunications Market in APEC Economies", Australian APEC Study Centre, Melbourne, www.apec.org.au/docs/stocktake.pdf.

Ros, A. (1999), "Does Ownership or Competition Matter? The Effects of Telecommunications Reform on Network Expansion and Efficiency", *Journal of Regulatory Economics* 15 (1).

Roseman, D. (2003), "Domestic Regulation and Trade in Telecommunications Services: Experience and Prospects under the GATS", in *Domestic Regulation and Service Trade Regulation*, Aaditya Mattoo and Pierre Sauve (eds.), World Bank and Oxford University Press, Washington, DC and New York.

Schement, J.R. and S.C. Forbes (1998), "The Persistent Gap in Telecommunications: Toward Hypotheses and Answers", August, Washington, DC.

UK Office of Regulatory Review (1998), *A Guide to Regulation* (Second Edition), London, December.

Wellenius, B., V. Foster and C. Malmberg-Calvo (2004), "Private Provision of Rural Infrastructure Services: Competing for Subsidies", World Bank Policy Research Working Paper 3365, August.

Wellenius, B. (2002), "Chile: Closing the Gap in Access to Rural Communications: Chile 1995-2002", November, World Bank, Washington, DC.

World Bank (2002), "Telecommunications Regulation—A Handbook", Washington, DC.

Xavier, P. (2002), "Bridging the Digital Divide—Refocusing on a Market Based Approach", Australian APEC Study Centre, Melbourne. www.apec.org.au/docs/Bdd.pdf.

Xavier, P. (2003), "Universal Service Obligations and Broadband," *Info,* May.

Xavier, P (2006), "What rules for universal service in an IP-enabled NGN environment", paper presented to an ITU Workshop on Next Generation Networks, 23-24 March, www.itu.int/osg/spu/ngn/documents/Papers/Xavier-060323-Fin-v1.pdf.

Xavier, P. and D. Ypsilanti (2006), "Policy Issues in Spectrum Trading", *Info*, April.

Chapter 2

Uganda's Approach to Universal Access to Telecommunications[1]

F.F. Tusubira
Makerere University

This chapter presents Uganda's approach to universal telecommunications services and universal access and evaluates both the government's strategy and its impact.

1. Based in part on F.F. Tusubira (2004).

Introduction

Developing countries, especially least developed countries (LDCs), face many challenges when they try to ensure that all citizens have access to telecommunication services, which are recognised as an aid to efficient social and economic transactions and as a means of obtaining economically useful information. The international economic environment and the failure of government-owned telecommunication companies to perform efficiently has meant that provision of access, especially in LDCs, must be achieved through the private sector, and Uganda is no exception (Shirley *et al.*, 2002). Because the private sector is largely driven by the need for profit, appropriate policy and regulatory interventions are needed to avoid permanent marginalisation of the poorer sections of society which, in Uganda, constitute most of the population.

The target population and the circumstances

Uganda is a landlocked country located in East Africa. Its population was 24.7 million in 2002, according to the 2002 Census, and is estimated at 26 million for 2004. It covers 236 040 square kilometres, of which 15% is water.

Between 1991 and 2002, Uganda's overall population grew at an average of 3.4%, with an urban population growth rate of 6%, due in part to rural-urban migration. The high growth rate is attributable to an increase in the fertility rate[2] coupled with a decline in child mortality[3]. The human development index improved from 0.338 in 1996 to 0.507 in 1999, but declined to 0.449 by 2001, before recovering its positive trend and increasing to 0.493 in 2002 (UNDP, 2003). If the current growth rate persists, the population will reach about 32 million with a density of 162 (up from the current 126) persons per square km within ten years. At present, 50% of the population is less than 15 years old, and the female-to-male ratio is 100:96. Most of the population is rural (21.8 million rural to 3.7 million urban in 2003).

The current macroeconomic strategy centres on a government-enabled, market-driven approach to economic development, supplemented by appropriate pro-poor policies[4] to encourage socioeconomic development. Figure 2.1 shows GDP growth and per capita trends over the last seven years. Per capita income declined from USD 315 in 1997/98 to USD 200 in 2003/04, the lowest in East Africa, owing to population growth and depreciation of the shilling. Absolute poverty declined somewhat in the late 1990s but increased from 33% in 2000 to over 39% in 2003/04.[5] To date, average revenue per user (ARPU) for the main telecommunications companies is estimated at USD 20, and with a per capita income of USD 200, very few people are able to afford telecommunication services without compromising other necessities. This captures one of the key challenges to universal access in Uganda: affordability.

2. The fertility rate in Uganda from 1995 to 2000/01 was estimated at 6.8 children per woman, owing, among other things, to the early age at which women begin childbearing.

3. The infant mortality rate per 1 000 live births was 100 in 1990 and dropped to 79 by 2001.

4. Vision 2025; Poverty Eradication Action Programme; Plan for the Modernization of Agriculture; Universal Primary Education; etc.

5. Uganda Poverty Participation Assessment Project report 2003.

Figure 2.1. Real GDP and per capita growth, 1997/98-2003/04

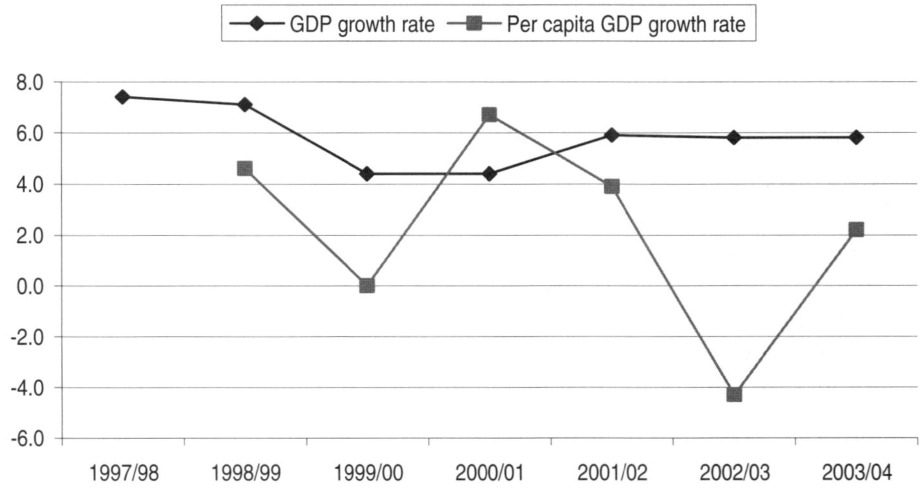

Telecommunications sector prior to reform, motivation for reform, and the voice market structure

Telecommunication and postal services throughout the East African Community (Kenya, Tanzania, Uganda) were historically run by the East African Posts and Telecommunications Corporation (EAP&TC) and the East African External Telecommunications Company. The split of the Community in the late 1970s led to the establishment of the Uganda Posts and Telecommunications Corporation (UPTC), which operated by decree from 1977 and under the UPTC Act from 1983. Up to 1993, UPTC was the monopoly provider of both telecommunications and postal services in Uganda, and was at the same time the sole regulator, under the direction of the government.

The initial period of the monopoly (1977-86) was also the period of the worst governance in Uganda's history. Telecommunications actually dwindled owing to lack of maintenance and expansion programmes to the point where obtaining a new line required high-level political connections, outright bribery or waiting periods in excess of two years. There were no social targets (including rural communications development) whatsoever for the sector. Indeed, ownership of a telephone was a basis for political suspicion about involvement in subversive activities. The number of lines in service by 1986 is estimated to have been fewer than 40 000 throughout the country, all of them effectively in the capital city and three other major towns. The public call box infrastructure had totally broken down.

In 1987, Uganda's Economic Recovery Programme was started, initially relying on parastatal companies with new management and later, after this failed to work, led by the private sector. One of the outcomes was the establishment in 1993 of the Inter-ministerial Committee on Investment in Telecommunications. This Committee formulated recommendations that were the precursor to subsequent sector reforms. Although the initial motivation for this effort was to address the consistently poor performance of UPTC and the desire to reduce government subsidy to the sector, the review process included broader considerations and objectives that were captured along the process of reform.

Owing to increasing demand for services, especially by investors (it was quickly realised that investors found poor telecommunications to be a very strong disincentive), the government took action to license operators even before the law was in place. The first mobile service provider, Celtel, was licensed in September 1993 to provide nationwide mobile services. Another operator, Starlight Communications, was licensed at the same time to provide trunked mobile radio communications services but failed to obtain sufficient customers and eventually closed. Celtel's business strategy targeted only the elite, pitching prices at a level that was out of reach of even Uganda's middle class. From 1993 to 1998, Celtel signed up fewer than 5 000 customers.

MTN, licensed in 1998 after the law was in place, came from South Africa with market experience and a business model based on setting low entry costs for consumers and a prepaid model. They expected to get 10 000 customers in the first year, but got 7 000 on the first day, and the network collapsed due to overload. This was the start of the access revolution which, for the first time, brought communications services, albeit on an occasional basis owing to cost, within the reach of all citizens.

The entry of Uganda Telecommunications Ltd (UTL) as the privatised successor company to UPTC in 2000 created true competition and presented a real challenge to MTN. Subsequently, Celtel adopted and refined the MTN market approach and, while it still has the smallest number of customers of the three operators, it is now seen as an innovation leader in services and tariff packages.

There is therefore effective competition in the voice market, with three providers covering the entire country, two of which (MTN and UTL) are allowed to provide fixed-line services. Owing to the principle of technology neutrality, fixed lines may be wireless if they provide toll quality service and use home zone billing (cheaper than mobile tariffs). All the mobile service providers are owned by foreign investors, even though the government still holds 49% of the equity in UTL which it plans to make available to the public through an issue of shares. The boundary between fixed and mobile is blurred from both the market and regulatory aspects. From the regulatory point of view, the only demands are toll quality and home zone billing. From the consumers' point of view, convenience and ease of entry are the overriding factors.

Even before the Rural Communications Development Fund (RCDP) was implemented, the market had gone a long way towards making available access based on cellular technology, now the basic access platform. Figure 2.2 shows the rapid growth in subscribers. Uganda is a relatively small country, and as service providers have moved to cover highways and small urban centres, they have provided signal coverage in many rural areas. High uptake of mobile technology and the opportunities it opens up for small businesses have used this platform to provide telephone access to rural areas far beyond the level anticipated in 1996. More importantly, many service providers have become commercially viable because of Uganda's demographic patterns (especially the tendency to have both urban and rural homes). The Uganda Communication Commission (UCC) has encouraged small operators of telephone kiosks as well as Internet cafes of all sizes by waiving all licensing requirements for such operators. The resulting free competition has ensured that users get the lowest prices consistent with commercial operation.

Competitive pressure has also driven tariffs down to a level where even the poorer sections of society can afford to make a call (compared to the more expensive alternative of making a journey to achieve the same purpose) (Figure 2.3). The overall conclusion is that liberalisation and entry of foreign investment capital have benefited the poorer sections of society in Uganda.

Figure 2.2. Growth in fixed and mobile subscribers in Uganda, 1996-2004

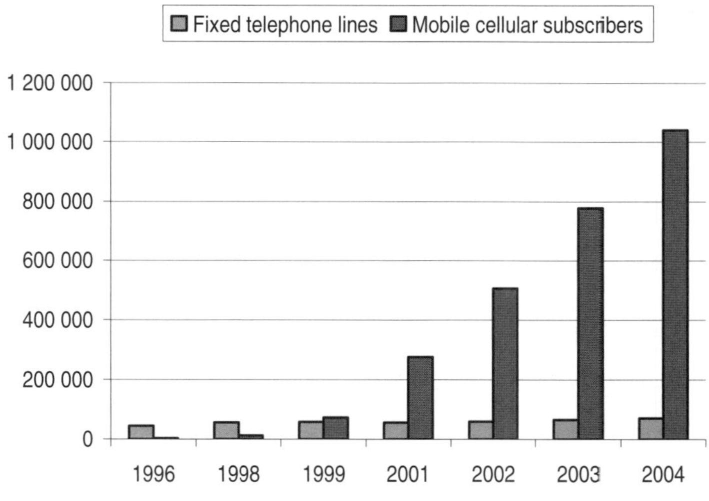

Source: Uganda Communication Commission.

Universal access: policy, regulation, and goals

When telecommunications sector reform started in Uganda, it was explicitly recognised from the start that the kind of liberalised market envisaged by the government policy framework would lead to marginalisation of the poorer sections of society. The policy and regulatory mechanisms aimed at addressing this marginalisation were:

- Like other African countries, pragmatically adopting universal access rather than universal service as the first frontier.
- Incorporating rollout obligations in the two national operator licences to ensure, to the extent possible and without compromising the business plans of operators, access for areas that would be seen as non-viable in the short to medium term, with some specificity of focus on local government access.
- Providing protection (through a period of limited competition under a duopoly) to the first major investors. This was partly to attract investment and partly to compensate for the universal access rollout obligations.
- Tariff regulation for what were at that time called basic telephony services – basically traditional wireline voice – seen as the main service needed by the poorer sections of society. There was no provision at the time to regulate the cost of mobile access which was viewed as a value-added service. Paradoxically, this has become the basic access platform in Uganda.
- The requirement in the Uganda Communication Act, 1997 (Laws of Uganda, Cap. 106) to establish a Rural Communications Development Fund (RCDF).
- Provision in the law for a funding mechanism: the law permits a levy of up to 2.5% to be imposed by the UCC to support rural access. This in essence provides funding for public-private sector partnerships that address rural access.

Figure 2.3. Evolution of fixed and mobile tariffs, 1995-2003

Connection and monthly fees, 1993-2003
UGX

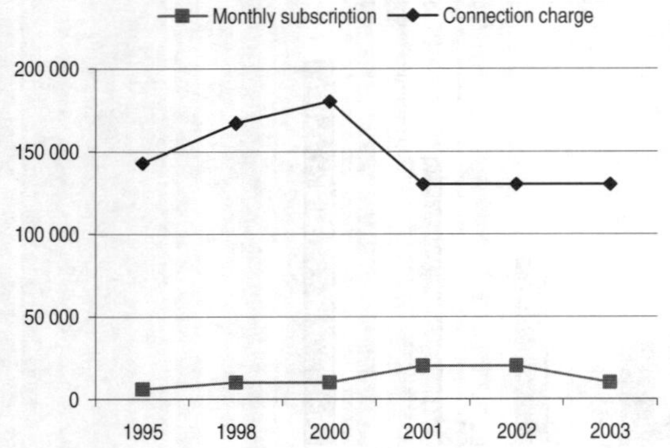

Tariffs for classic landlines, 1995-2003

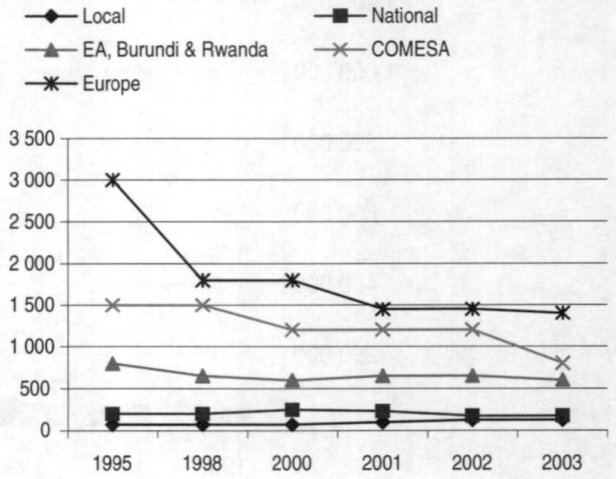

Movement of mobile connection and subscription rates, prepaid, 1995-2003

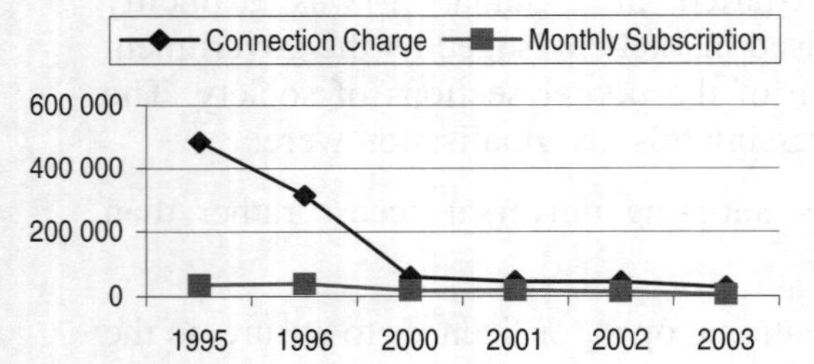

Movement of local mobile rates (on network, off network and M2F), prepaid, 1995-2003

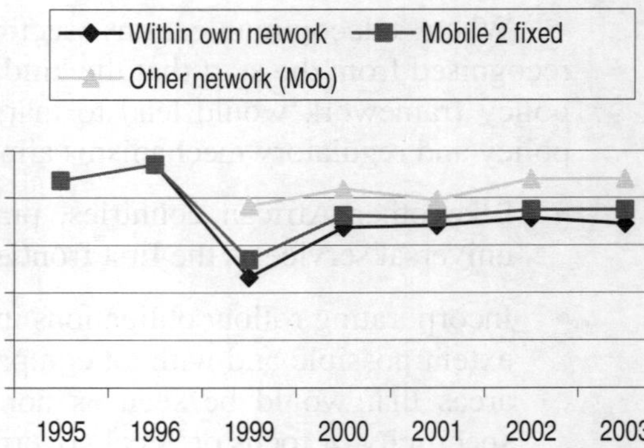

Source: Uganda Communications Commission Telecomm Sector Policy Review.

The initial universal access goals in Uganda were very modest and were only spelled out, in terms of rollout obligations, in the licences issued to the two national operators. The target was to have at least one public telephone in each county.[6] The UCC subsequently moved to establish a more systematic framework for defining and achieving universal access, the Rural Communications Policy and Strategy (UCC, 2001).

In developed economies, "rural" often means sparsely populated and rich and sometimes sparsely populated and poor. In LDCs, it almost always means poor, whether densely or sparsely populated. Clearly, the nature of intervention and the sustainability

6. Uganda has a system of decentralised government, with the district a semi-autonomous political (with a directly elected political head) and administrative unit. It currently has 56 districts. Each district has three to four counties, and each county has three to four sub-counties.

challenges change according to context. The aim of government policy was to address access for those citizens whose income levels (or location) keep them out of the telecommunication environment. By making "rural" synonymous with "poor", UCC targets the communication needs of the rural poor, as well as the peri-urban and urban poor, under the RCDF.

The starting point for Uganda's Rural Communications Development Policy (RCDP), was not a detailed statement of policy with specific policy objectives: It was a broad statement of intent: "to increase the geographical distribution and coverage of services throughout the country".

Rural communications development: the intervention concept

RCD is aimed at creating equity of opportunity leading to improved human development. It is therefore important for the RCDP to capture human development concerns and targets. This means that policy makers and regulators need to understand human development and its challenges in order to translate general policy statements into a good RCDP whose performance can be objectively evaluated.

The first challenge is therefore the identification of entry points for intervention. It is wrong to assume that rural communities in LDCs, which are often illiterate or semi-literate, do not know what they want. Technocrats tend to use a desk identification of what they see as the challenges and prescribe solutions (much as multilateral agencies sometimes prescribe solutions for LDCs).

Rural communities only need to learn about the opportunities technology offers to enhance their activities. They are then quite able to put the technology to use. Apart from leading to solutions that are more likely to succeed, engagement of rural communities also promotes ownership and sustainability.

The level of information needed varies from community to community, ranging from information to address health problems to information leading to better production and marketing for the area's economic activities. In identifying the underlying challenges, it is important to capture the key economic activities in the country's rural areas, including details of income and expenditure patterns.

RCD can address the underlying challenges, but requires full awareness of information needs. The real value of an RCD intervention will not be felt unless the information needs are addressed, not by the RCDF, but by the sector ministries (*e.g.* health, agriculture, education). This underscores the importance of a multi-sectoral approaches to rural development.

Uganda recognised that the varying definition of "rural" across the world meant that imported solutions were unlikely to succeed. An example was the then popular approach of implementing multi-purpose community telecentres, as was indeed done by various development agencies in Uganda. The Nakaseke multi-purpose telecentre, for example, has taught Uganda and others valuable lessons. Grants used in setting it up and keeping it running are estimated to be in excess of USD 200 000. It has had some impact, but far from what should have been expected from that level of investment. The format was also clearly not sustainable. The RCDP was therefore based on field research in Uganda (including pilot trials to test if small start-ups could be sustained with the income of poor rural communities), expert input and public consultations. The policy and strategy adopted consequently departed from the common infrastructure interventions that only address access and to some extent affordability in order to address specific needs. The

Uganda Communications Commission's RCDP identified the challenges of utility (in light of ICT literacy and awareness of opportunities), access and affordability. These dictated the strategy and the interventions:

- *Utility*: Awareness and literacy are addressed by supporting training centres in each district, reinforced by demonstrating utility through support of district information Web sites whose management is devolved to local governments.
- *Access* is addressed through the establishment of communication centres (telephone, postal outlet) in each sub-county, and also support of commercial Internet cafes.
- *Affordability* presents a major challenge, especially since the sustainability of any initiative is a major concern. It was decided to address affordability through capital support for private sector operators and also to promote competition in order to minimise usage costs. The policy also permits the use of asymmetrical interconnection rates in favour of rural operators, but the impact has not yet been evaluated. Direct intervention via consumers (vouchers, etc.) was ruled out as not sustainable.

Based on overall cost estimates for achieving targets in each category, percentage ceilings based on total funding available are set each year for content development, small start-ups, training, tele-kiosks, and network rollout, including provision of public payphones (over and above the rollout obligations).

Based on these planned interventions, basic access goals were set as follows[7]:

- Ensure that all sub-counties with at least 5 000 inhabitants have access to basic communications services (one payphone and one postal outlet) by the end of 2005, with an additional phone for each additional group of 5 000 people or part thereof. This typically establishes a public payphone within 5 kilometres (1 hour by foot or 10 minutes by bicycle) of every person in the country.
- Support the establishment of an Internet point of presence (PoP) in every district of Uganda by 2004.
- Introduction of ICT use in at least one "vanguard" training institution in each district by 2005.
- Promote provision of communications services as a profitable business (general) with interventions that also help reduce cost.

Managing and funding the interventions

Management

The role of the Uganda Communications Commission is regulation and it therefore does not have the capacity to oversee the RCD. Moreover, the stakeholders in RCD are different from normal regulation stakeholders. Government departments that focus on rural development and marginalised groups also need to be involved. The UCC therefore set up a separate board by statutory instrument, with representation from the UCC, the Consumers Associations, the Ministry responsible for Communications, the private

7. Contracts for the rollout of the major programmes were executed during 2005, with sufficient funding to meet all targets by the middle of 2006. An evaluation has not yet been conducted.

sector, the financial services sector, and the Uganda Institution of Professional Engineers. Apart from policy guidance and monitoring oversight from UCC, the board operates independently.

Two staff members are engaged to run the desk of the Rural Communications Board, and there is a staff time allocation from the regulatory and support functions of UCC. To date, the administrative cost of managing the fund, including staff time from other UCC staff, is less than 10%, and consultancy costs are not expected to exceed 5% of disbursements. The RCDF is obviously well-managed. This is partly the result of letting the private sector craft technology solutions for service provision, rather than doing them in house, which would call for more staff time.

To date, capacity building for the RCD staff has focused on project management, procurement and rural communications development. More broadly, capacity building in interpretation of and approaches to universal access is a priority for all staff in UCC because universal access is recognised as a key challenge. The UCC is a member of the NetTel@Africa[8] Capacity-building Network for ICT Policy Makers and Regulators, and is gaining more expertise through peering, short workshops and formal training via the network. UCC is becoming a recognised example of good approaches to RCD.

Sources of funds

All interventions have to date been supported by the RCDF for which a levy on the gross income of all licensed service providers is the principal source. This was initially set at 1%, rather than the 2.5% permitted by law, as an incentive for service providers to increase investment in the sector. Development partners have also given additional support, including:

- IDRC support for policy and strategy research (CAD 200 000).
- A World Bank grant of USD 5 million under the Energy for Rural Transformation Project towards implementation. Consideration is being given to an additional grant of USD 6 million.

Table 2.1 shows revenue and expenditure projections under the RCDF.

Funding strategy

The basic funding strategy is the smart subsidy: "The RCDF shall be used to establish basic communication access, through smart subsidies, to develop rural communications. That is, the RCDF shall be used to encourage commercial suppliers to enter the market but not to create unending dependency on subsidy."

Apart from small start-ups for which a one-off grant is given to subsidise the capital investment, minimum subsidy open bidding is used to provide defined infrastructure and/or services in a given locality. The maximum subsidy available is stipulated in the bid documents and is simply a financial incentive to bridge the gap between commercially viable and non-viable (in the short term) operations. The rollout stipulated in the bidding

8. This network was mooted and started by the Regulatory Association of Southern Africa, TRASA, with support from USAID and the National Association of Regulatory Commissioners (NARUC). The network has expanded to East and West Africa with the support of USAID, the UK Department for International Development (DfID) and Sweden's Sida. See www.nettelafrica.org/. DfID and Sida support is through the Catalysing Access to ICTs in Africa (CATIA) initiative. See www.catia.ws/.

documents must be achieved, the subsidy is a direct grant, and there is no explicit or implicit exclusivity granted either for the service or for the geographical area of operation.

Table 2.1. RCDF revenue and expenditure projections, 2002-05[1]

Expenditure	Total planned (USD '000)	Actual to 2004 (USD '000)	Remarks
Public telephony Infrastructure for 154 sub-counties	6 000	150	Major implementation through World Bank funding. No disbursement yet due to long World Bank procurement procedures
User rural packages	250	(?)	
Internet PoPs	1 000	90	Major implementation through World Bank funding
Internet exchange point	100	100	Fully implemented 2003
Vanguard ICT projects	1 650	360	
Rural postal franchise	500	14	Major implementation through World Bank funding
ICT training capacity investment	250	150	
ICT awareness and content creation	250	171	
Administrative costs		114	8.5% of disbursement to date
Consultancy costs		299	This includes consultancy for the World Bank funded components that are rolling out in 2005, for about 3-5 % of overall expenditure after the major components are in place.
Total	10 000	1 448	
Income			
Levy	11 000	6 000	Does not include 2005; Possible eventual shortfall of USD 2.5 million
Grants	5 000	5 000	Grant committed. Additional USD 6 million grant under consideration
Total	16 000	11 000	Private sector input expected to make up the shortfall

1. All figures rounded.

Progress on implementation

Up to 2004, it was estimated that USD 1.5 million from the RCDF had leveraged a further investment of about USD 1 million from the private sector. The leverage ratio was initially low because many of the initial disbursements were outright grants to small start-ups. More recent data from 2005, with the major projects starting, show that for each USD 1 from the RCDF the private sector is contributing USD 2.5. Procurement procedures under the World Bank unfortunately delayed implementation of the key components of the RCD programme for more than two years. When these are fully implemented, it is expected that the private sector will have invested USD 3 for each USD 1 from the RCDF. The invitations to offer and bid documents have also been deliberately technology-neutral, permitting bidders to deploy the most cost-effective technology solutions to meet service rollout and quality requirements. The UCC takes the view that since it is the service providers who lay their money on the line, they are the best qualified to choose the best technology.

Through subsidies from the RCDF to various companies, the following projects have so far been implemented: 20 Internet PoPs were established in various districts (there are 56 in all); establishment of 26 district websites (www.dip.co.ug); establishment of four Internet cafes; establishment of three ICT training centres; and provision of 66 public payphones.

In addition to the major interventions supported by the World Bank listed in Table 2.1, the following projects funded by UCC and the private sector were completed during early 2005: establishment of 30 district websites, provision of Internet cafes in 11 districts, establishment of ICT training centres in 45 districts and provision of 200 public access points.

Impact

Evaluation of the impact on development is difficult, especially since no evaluation methodology was established as part of the programme. Infrastructure rollout therefore becomes the main indicator for evaluation. The discussion therefore necessarily includes subjective qualitative statements on impact.

Unfortunately, the impact on human development can only be qualitatively assessed. This was not a key consideration at the policy formulation stage and was therefore not integrated into monitoring and evaluation. The following comments, while subjective, are nevertheless demonstrable:

- The spread of mobile phones has created synergy, with the spread of private FM radio stations. Today 68 stations are operational in Uganda and provide near total national coverage in local languages. Where radio used to be a passive tool for disseminating development information, it is now a public interactive tool and discussion forum through the very popular phone-in programmes. Daily programmes range from political debates and other topical issues to health issues (AIDS, malaria, ante-natal and post-natal care, immunisation), agriculture, education, gender issues and the environment.
- Internet cafes and ICT training centres have opened new business opportunities for many small operators, creating literacy and awareness and opening their horizons to bigger markets and opportunities.
- The infrastructure achievements are discussed above.

Internet access

Considering the liberal regulatory environment, growth of the Internet and data market has remained far below expectations. Total incoming and outgoing Internet bandwidth is only about 100 Mbps, and there are fewer than 200 000 computers in Uganda[9] and almost no Internet hosts (low bandwidth means that there is a preference to host outside Uganda, though implementation of local peering is beginning to attract local hosting for local markets). A halving of prices (from about USD 8 000 per Mbps per month down to about USD 4 000) towards the end of 2004, the deregulation of the ISM band for wireless Internet access, and the waiver of licensing requirements for ISPs that do not own IDGs, are expected to spur growth.

9. See Uganda E-Usage Survey Report at www.researchictafrica.net.

Figure 2.4 shows trends in international incoming and outgoing bandwidth. Uganda accesses the Internet only via satellite, making it inherently expensive, but this alone does not justify the high cost. Like all of East Africa, Uganda has no access to the international optical fibre backbone.

Local loop access costs remain high for dial-up customers (tariffs are still time-based), and this is compounded by the continuing slow speeds (typically less than 5 Kbit/s for dial-up). It currently costs at least USD 3 (telephone tariff only) to download a 1 megabyte file via a dial-up connection. Leased lines for larger clients are available but still expensive owing to limited competition.

Figure 2.4. International incoming and outgoing Internet bandwidth, 1999-January 2005

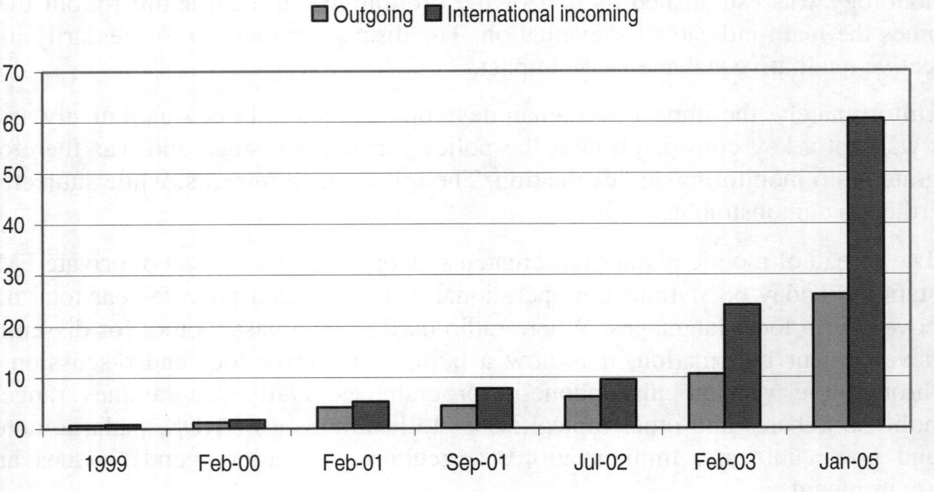

New directions

An evaluation of sector performance to date (Tusubira *et al.*, 2003) identified shortcomings, weaknesses and gaps in the sector policy which, combined with the impending end of the duopoly regime, have necessitated the formulation of a new sector policy.[10] With specific reference to RCD, the following weaknesses in the current policy were noted:

- Human development objectives did not play their rightful role in policy formulation. While related challenges were captured in the current policy, rollout had no linkage to the development objectives set by the different arms of government (health, education, agriculture, governance).
- The absence of higher-level enabling policies, like a national ICT policy, meant an *ad hoc* approach that did not take into account the interface with other ICT sectors (broadcasting, electronic and print media).

10. This new definition is captured in the new Telecommunication Sector Policy 2005 which is now undergoing a public consultation process.

- With the exception of the Energy for Rural Transformation Project (for which a grant was obtained from the World Bank), there was no co-ordination or creation of synergy with other initiatives targeting rural development. In Uganda, these include the Plan for the Modernisation of Agriculture, universal primary education, health sector initiatives and decentralisation of government.

The formulation of the new telecommunications sector policy has been holistic, based on the need to support achievement of human development goals (in response to the millennium development goals) through Uganda's Poverty Eradication Action Programme. With this approach, universal access addresses the question: "What minimum infrastructure and services must be in place (where and when) in order to enable the human development plans and objectives of the different sectors?" This has led to a revision of the universal access targets to include accessibility, by the year 2010, to a minimum of one voice and data network point specified as follows:

- Institutional data[11] access points of speeds of not less than 128 Kbit/s for all universal primary education schools and post-primary institutions; all educational institutions; government health units at LC111; population centres exceeding 1 000 people; agricultural extension units and other public institutions as may be subsequently determined by UCC in consultation with the service delivery arms of government.
- Public data access points of speeds not less than 128Kbit/s within each sub-county (LC111) of the administrative districts of Uganda (2004).
- Public voice access points within each local council second-level (LC11)/parish of the administrative districts of Uganda (2004). This means that there will be a payphone typically within at most 10 minutes by foot by 2010.
- Interconnection of all higher local government capitals by Gigabit optical fibre as part of the national data backbone.
- Pricing relying on competitive pressure, regulatory and fiscal incentives, and a high level of productivity among service providers to ensure affordability in marginalised sectors of society.
- There will be technology neutrality in both policy and regulation.

It should be noted that the universal access targets are over and above the universal service targets set for the year 2010:

- A universal service target of 20% of the projected population, up from the current 4.2%.
- Internet connection at speeds greater than 128 Kbit/s to at least 10% of households, up from the current figure of less than 1%.

The new approach emphasises the use of private-public partnerships (PPPs) to ensure rollout of sufficient infrastructure to all areas and is expected to provide a better platform for creating equity of access without compromising efficiency. While RCDF has been operating as a PPP funding mechanism, the proposed PPPs would call upon local and central governments to play a role in sector funding beyond the levy, for example by

---

11. The entry level in the new policy is based on a national data backbone that will carry all services.

incorporating optical fibre capacity along with the road and power transmission infrastructure.

Conclusion

Uganda is still on a learning curve for successful implementation of universal access. Key components have not been implemented, and a full evaluation is not yet possible. The policy iteration before the conclusion of the first phase is however noteworthy, in essence providing an online feedback mechanism that permits current implementation to be modified as necessary. This is indeed being done. Thus, while it is too early to claim success, there are clearly indications of success.

References

Shirley, M., F.F. Tusubira, F. Gebreab and L. Haggarty (2002), "Telecommunications Reform in Uganda", World Bank Development Research Group, Policy Working Paper 2864, June. www.researchictafrica.net/.

Tusubira, F.F. (2004), "Rural Comunications Development – A Tutorial Paper Based on the Uganda Case" International Seminar on ICT Policy Reform and Rural Communications Infrastructure, 23 August-1 September, organised by the European Bank for Reconstruction and Development and the Japan International Cooperation Agency (JICA), Fujisawa and Tokyo, Japan.

Tusubira, F.F., I. Kaggwa and F. Mukholi (2003), "The Uganda Telecommunications Sector Performance Review, 2003", www.researchictafrica.net/.

Uganda Communications Commission (2001), "Rural Communications Development Policy for Uganda", July 2001, www.ucc.co.ug/rcdf/about.html, and *Uganda's Approach to Universal Access and Communications Development and Funding: A Guide Book for Policy Makers and Regulators*, published by the Uganda Communications Commission and the International Development Research Centre (IDRC).

UNDP (2004), *Human Development Report*, United Nations

Chapter 3

India's Experience with Universal Service Obligations in Telecommunications

Harsha Vardhana Singh
Telecom Regulatory Authority of India

This chapter describes India's success in its efforts to ensure universal access and universal service, particularly to poor rural areas.

Introduction

The focus of universal service obligation (USO) programmes has generally been on access to telecommunications service. For countries with relatively high teledensity, providing access under USO meets the social objective of providing the general public with telecommunications services. For countries with low teledensity, such as India (Tables 3.1-3.3), meeting this objective requires a focus both on access and on provision of individual phone connections. When teledensity and coverage for access are limited, provision of individual connections significantly helps to improve effective access.

Table 3.1. Waiting list for rural direct exchange lines, 2000-01 to 2003-04 (March to April)

Million direct exchange lines (DELs)

1999-2000	2000-01	2001-02	2002-03	2003-04
1.65	2.48	1.28	1.31	1.37

Table 3.2. Number of telephones (fixed and mobile) and telephone density

Year ended 31 March	Fixed lines (DELs)	Mobile telephones	Number of telephones (fixed + mobile) per 100 population
	Millions		
1948	0.08	--	0.02
1951	0.10	--	0.03
1961	0.33	--	0.08
1971	0.98	--	0.18
1981	2.15	--	0.31
1991	5.07	--	0.60
1992	5.81	--	0.67
1993	6.80	--	0.77
1994	8.03	--	0.89
1995	9.80	--	1.07
1996	11.98	--	1.28
1997	14.54	0.34	1.56
1998	17.80	0.88	1.94
1999	21.59	1.20	2.33
2000	26.51	1.88	2.86
2001	32.44	3.58	3.53
2002	37.94	6.43	4.29
2003	40.62	12.69	5.11
2004	42.84	33.69	7.17
31 Dec 2004	44.76	48.00	8.62

Table 3.3. Village public telephones (VPTs), public call office (PCO), and teledensity, 1999-2000 to 2004-05

Financial year (April to March)	VPTs	PCOs	Urban teledensity	Rural teledensity	National teledensity
	Thousands		Per 100 persons		
1999-2000	375	658	8.23	0.68	2.86
2000-2001	410	885	10.37	0.93	3.53
2001-2002	469	1 078	12.20	1.21	4.29
2002-2003	513	1 493	14.32	1.49	5.11
2003-2004	522	1 924	20.79	1.55	7.17
April-Sept. 2004	524	2 278	n.a.	n.a.	8.10

Note: The total number of villages is 607 491.

With technological development and diverse services available on the same platform, *e.g.* Internet or broadband, universal service obligations must broaden to provide access to these services as well. Thus, the scope of USO keeps evolving, and, in countries with low teledensity, must include both access and individual phone connection. Meeting this objective requires the development of suitable mechanisms and a range of policies that must be co-ordinated so as to enhance their combined effect. Ultimately, the aim should be to make the system as self-sustaining as possible, so that universal service obligations are largely met through growth and commercially viable activities.

The story of universal service/access in India is one of the evolution of both its scope and the requisite mechanisms. In India today, owing to a sharp reduction in costs, a major increase in competition and consequently a sharp decline in tariffs, a largely market-driven process is now possible (Table 3.4). Emerging technologies are now enhancing the capability of mobile technology, and by combining broadband with telephony a new, primarily market-driven, USO model can ensure access and services to villages. This can result in linkages between access, which is a conventional USO type of activity, and phone on demand provided through individual connections, which can be achieved through normal commercial investment without financial support.

Table 3.4. Present and proposed coverage of mobile networks

	By area	Population coverage
Present coverage of mobile networks (population coverage 20%)		
Towns	1 700 out of 5 200	About 200 million
Rural areas	Negligible	Negligible
Proposed network coverage of mobile networks by 2006 (population coverage 75%)		
Towns	4 900 out of 5 200	About 300 million
Rural areas	About 350 000 out of 607 000 villages	About 450 million

Background

Until about the end of the 1990s, the Indian telecommunications sector was marked by supply constraints, persistent waiting lists and poor availability of public phones; low teledensity seemed likely to persist for a long time. Achieving universal service/access objectives seemed difficult, and there was little basis for expecting the situation to improve markedly. The few basic service providers were struggling to establish themselves, cellular mobile service was considered too expensive to be of interest to the "common man", effective competition was not in place in most of the country. The need was felt for reliable media in order to provide adequate telephony services nationally, and the government sought high up-front licence fees from new entrants, which basic and cellular mobile service providers found difficult to pay. The outlook was therefore uncertain, or even, according to some, dismal.

Box 3.1. Main regulatory bodies for universal service

Two key government departments play a lead role in USO policies, the Department of Telecommunications (DOT) and the Department of Information Technology (DIT), both in the same ministry. The DOT has the main responsibility for government policy for communications, which includes *inter alia* licensing and spectrum policy. Certain policy functions have been transferred to the telecom regulator, the Telecom Regulatory Authority of India (TRAI). Section 11 of the TRAI Act (www.trai.gov.in) specifies the regulator's functions. TRAI is an independent statutory body, and it functions include, *inter alia*, recommending USO policy as well as ensuring effective USO policy implementation.

The Universal Service Fund (USF) is administered by the USF administrator's office in the Department of Communications, and it functions independently with respect to its policy mandate. The USF administrator's office is headed by the administrator and has two divisions, one dealing with technical matters (with four persons) and another with finance (five persons). The organisations' budget expenditure for April 2003-March 2004 was about USD 200 000. The USF has its office on the premises of DOT and therefore saves on this expenditure.

The USF administrator's office was established with experts from the Department of Telecommunications. The office has interacted with international experts to obtain insights on how USO policy is implemented in other countries and to seek answers to queries regarding their own work, including estimation of relevant costs, etc. They have conducted a major costing exercise together with a large national research institute, the National Council for Applied Economic Research (NCAER). In general, however, they have functioned by addressing matters on the basis of their own capacities. A handbook with relevant information, like the handbook prepared earlier for telecommunications regulators, would be helpful.

Today the situation is very different, and the outlook is optimistic. In fact, operators in India are now in a position to provide rural telephony in several areas on a commercial basis, *i.e.* without financial support. Moreover, the rural telephony targets now include provision of broadband. Indeed, India is well placed today to achieve an objective that would have been unthinkable a few years ago. The beginnings of the change can be traced to three important events of the late 1990s:

- The establishment in 1997 of the Telecom Regulatory Authority of India (TRAI), which provided an alternative institution for managing or recommending relevant policies (see Box 3.1). The TRAI, together with the government, has played a major role in promoting and sustaining competition, and in developing a market environment that has completely changed the parameters of performance and expectations in the Indian telecommunications sector.

- The announcement in November 1998 of the Licence Policy for Internet Service. This policy revealed a change in the government's perspective, as it focused on a low entry charge and open entry, both of which facilitated competition. This reorientation has increasingly been apparent in the case of other licences as well. For example, TRAI's recent recommendations on a unified licence emphasise a decrease in the licence fee, facilitating entry and flexible operations. A similar perspective can be seen in TRAI's ongoing consideration of spectrum policy (www.trai.gov.in).

- The most important event was the announcement of the New Telecom Policy of 1999 (NTP 1999), which brought a number of far-reaching policy changes to the scope of universal service and the manner of achieving it. Section 6 of NTP 1999 emphasised both access and provision of telephone lines on demand to subscribers and extended the scope of universal access to include data services (see Box 3.2). In addition, NTP 1999 instituted a fund to provide financial support for universal service/access. In line with this policy, the Universal Service Fund (USF) has started operating in India under a USF administrator.

A point which cannot be overemphasised is that once universal service is no longer limited to universal access, it is necessary to consider an overall policy package, which has to be developed in a consistent manner. The need for co-ordination is also apparent in the fact that certain social or universal service objectives and targets are contained in Section 2 of NTP 1999, *i.e.* they are separate from the section dealing with the USO (see Box 3.2).

Thus, a broad set of policies must be put in place to achieve growth of affordable telephony covering large portions of the country and to meet the evolving objectives of USO policy. Today, India is well placed to move towards achieving USO objectives that encompass conventional telephony, access to broadband, and provision of more than one public telephone in larger villages. This dramatic change is due to certain key factors:

- Experience in the mobile sector since 2002, where exceptional growth has been linked with a sharp decrease in prices. This shows that at reasonably low prices, there is likely to be an unexpectedly large demand for the service (Figure 3.1).
- A major focus by the regulator on further stimulating growth through competitive price declines by reducing the burden of policy-related costs, facilitating infrastructure sharing and encouraging the provision and efficient use of scarce resources such as spectrum.
- The presence of an extensive fibre network for about 90% of the telephone exchanges that cover virtually the whole nation.
- Rapid progress in changing the terms and conditions of licences to provide greater flexibility of operation and reduce possible conflicts arising from different service-specific licences (*i.e.* the move towards unified licensing).
- Decline in costs and enhanced scope of mobile technology due to technical changes (both recent and likely in the near future).
- The emphasis at the highest levels on removing constraints inhibiting growth in the infrastructure sector, with special emphasis at present on telecommunications services in rural areas.
- An initiative to consider comprehensively a number of initiatives in the non-governmental sector which focus on spreading access to, and use of, the Internet and broadband.

Box 3.2. Sections 2 and 6 of New Telecom Policy 1999 (NTP 1999)

Section 2. Objectives and targets of the New Telecom Policy 1999

The objectives of NTP 1999 are:

- Ensure access to telecommunications, which is of utmost importance for achieving the country's social and economic goals. Availability of affordable and effective communications for citizens is at the core of the vision and goal of the telecommunications policy.
- Strive to provide a balance between the provision of universal service to all unserved areas, including rural areas, and the provision of high-level services capable of meeting the needs of the country's economy.
- Encourage development of telecommunication facilities in remote, hilly and tribal areas.
- Create a modern and efficient telecommunications infrastructure taking into account the convergence of IT, media, telecommunications and consumer electronics and thereby propel India into becoming an IT superpower.
- Convert PCOs, [public call offices] wherever justified, into public teleinformation centres with multimedia capability such as ISDN services, remote database access, government and community information systems, etc.
- Transform in a timely manner, the telecommunications sector into a more competitive environment in both urban and rural areas in order to provide equal opportunities and level playing field for all players.
- Strengthen research and development efforts and provide an impetus to build world-class manufacturing capabilities.
- Achieve efficiency and transparency in spectrum management.
- Protect the country's defence and security interests.
- Enable Indian telecommunications companies to become truly global players.

In line with the above objectives, the specific targets that NTP 1999 set were:

- Make available telephone on demand by the year 2002 and sustain it thereafter so as to achieve a teledensity of 7 per 100 by the year 2005 and 15 by the year 2010.
- Encourage development of telecommunications in rural areas by making it more affordable through a suitable tariff structure and making rural communication mandatory for all fixed service providers.
- Increase rural teledensity from the current level of 0.4 per 100 to 4 per 100 by 2010 and provide reliable transmission media in all rural areas.
- Achieve telecommunications coverage of all villages in the country and provide reliable media to all exchanges by 2002.
- Provide Internet access to all district headquarters by 2000.
- Provide high-speed data and multimedia capability using technologies including ISDN to all towns with a population greater than 200 000 by 2002.

Section 6. Universal service obligation

The government is committed to provide access to all people for basic telecommunications services at affordable and reasonable prices. It seeks to achieve the following universal service objectives:

- Provide voice and low-speed data service to the 290 000 unserved villages by 2002.
- Achieve Internet access to all district headquarters by 2000.
- Achieve telephone on demand in urban and rural areas by 2002.

The resources for meeting the USO would be raised through a "universal access levy", *i.e.* a percentage of the revenue earned by all the operators under various licences. The government, in consultation with TRAI, would determine the percentage of revenue assigned to universal access. The implementation of the USO for rural/remote areas would be undertaken by all fixed service providers which would be reimbursed from the funds from the universal access levy. Other service providers would also be encouraged to participate in USO provision subject to technical feasibility and be reimbursed from the funds from the universal access levy.

Figure 3.1 Cellular mobile growth and effective charge per minute for 400 minutes of use/month (both incoming and outgoing minutes)

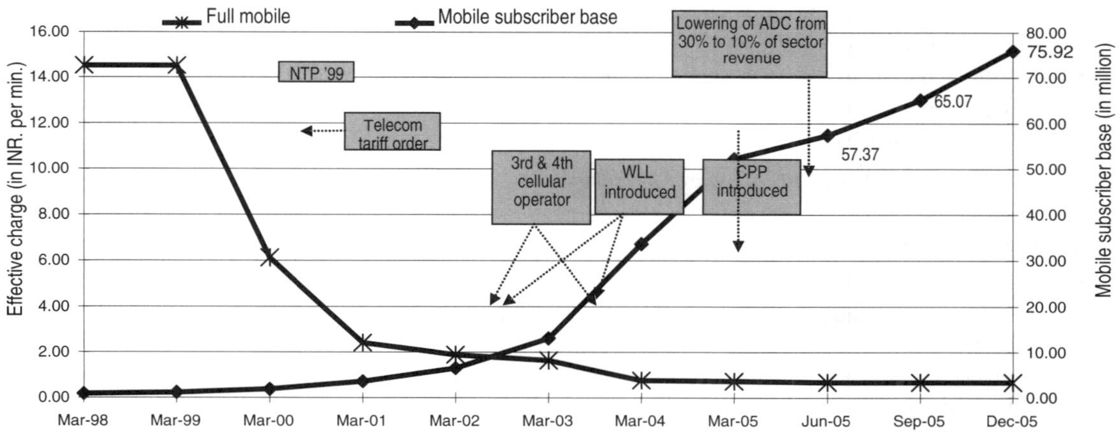

Goals of universal access/universal service in the Indian telecommunications sector

Initially, the USO policy framework only addressed universal access to telephony in both rural and urban areas. India's USO policy initially focused on access to public telephones in the target areas. It began with provision of universal access in a specified area (*e.g.* one public phone per hexagon of 5 kilometres, the entire country having been divided into hexagons), then one to each Gram Panchayat, and later, as specified in NTP 1994, one village public telephone (VPT) per village and in urban areas one public call office (PCO) per 500 persons.

While the initial USO policy focused on universal access, the wider objectives of affordability and spread of telephony, which are a part of overall social objectives, were also emphasised in various ways, including through relatively cheap monthly access tariff for subscribers, free call allowance and low usage charge for a specified number of call units. Tariffs in rural areas were kept below those in urban areas.

Over time, the scope of universal access broadened to include Internet and data services. While NTP 1999 continued to emphasise VPT, it also included provision of access to low-speed data services to villages and Internet access to all district headquarters (about 8 000 locations). Under NTP 1999, universal service was extended beyond access and also included extending the subscriber base to cover both access and provision of individual phone connections in urban and rural areas on demand.

The goals of universal service have continued to evolve to encompass the Internet and universal access to broadband owing to TRAI's recent recommendation on broadband and the government's broadband policy. Achievement of some of the additional objectives of NTP 1999, especially those pertaining to provision of reliable media to all exchanges, has put India in a very strong position to achieve the more recent USO objectives, including broadband.

Box 3.3. Factors affecting supply and demand for rural telecommunications

Supply of access and communication services

Policy specifying the requirement (with cross-subsidy or possibly some financial support):

- Directs the incumbent to fulfil targets for access (especially VPTs): initial phase of providing public access to villages.
- Specifies targets in licence terms and conditions: initial licence regime.
- Provides (through incumbent) reliable media (fibre) links to exchanges or specified parts of the country: an objective under NTP 1999.
- *Policy incentives or relaxing of policy constraints*
- Provision of finance through the USF collected from a levy on the revenues of the sector: established under NTP 1999.
- Use of mobile phones for public telephony by using mobile phones as community phones.
- TRAI recommendation for allowing niche operators with no entry fee for service areas much smaller than for normal licences.
- A scheme allowing the postman to carry a mobile phone when delivering letters to villages: government policy initiative.

Other policy initiatives

- Government E-Governance Programme also involving state level initiatives. To provide a basis for carrying supplementary services, and also for public-private partnerships.
- Increase competition by allowing open entry for all services (mobile being subject to spectrum availability) and create a framework for enhanced competition.
- Reduce policy-imposed costs on operators (*e.g.* licence fee, spectrum charge, levies, etc.) so that operating costs decrease and the increased margins are passed on through competition as lower prices.
- Promote infrastructure sharing among operators through a systematic policy to address this matter.
- Seek/develop new technologies, or improved ways of addressing specific problems that may be adversely affecting implementation of USO, *e.g.* Bharat Sanchar Nigam Limited (BSNL) plans to use solar-powered batteries together with wireless in local loop phones in rural areas with power supply problems.

Market/private initiatives

- Tailor different tariff packages, especially prepaid, for different clienteles.
- Beginnings of infrastructure-sharing agreements among operators.
- Systems in rural areas to extend the coverage of mobile phones, *e.g.* the phone provider is informed of the address and time at which a phone call is to be made, takes the phone to the specified place at the specified time, and after the call the receiving party pays a charge for the service.
- Seek/develop new technologies and uses to enhance market coverage.
- Non-governmental and commercial organisations provide Internet kiosks which are used for multiple purposes, including training, education, health and of course, communication.

Demand for access and communication services affected by:

- Increase in income and population.
- Tariff policy, especially tariff ceilings and specified free call allowances keeping in mind affordability and social objectives of increasing teledensity
- Telecommunications service made available as technology developments make it possible to supply services in areas at prices which were earlier not possible.
- Price declines through competition-reducing margins.
- Cost decrease due to initiatives to reduce the burden of policy-induced costs/levies/fees, etc., which in a competitive environment translate into lower prices.
- Decline in the price of customer equipment owing to market or policy-induced reasons, so that market entry costs decline.

The extension of the scope of USO policy and the additional objectives linked to USO imply a need to rely on a broader mix of policies under the USO policy framework itself and through complementary policies.

Mechanisms to encourage service providers to increase provision of services to previously unserved or underserved regions or consumers

India has adopted a mix of policies over time. Its initial efforts can broadly be defined as improved coverage and affordability. More recent efforts include specific steps to promote growth by addressing supply constraints, reducing policy-imposed costs, and providing reliable links for voice and data (Box 3.3).

Initially, public sector monopoly operator addressed the USO objective by gradually establishing village public phones. Quite a large number of villages remained unconnected at the end of the 1990s (see Table 3.3).

Subsequently, other methods were also used to achieve USO (or social) objectives. Holders of a fixed service licence (called "basic service licence") were required to provide VPTs in the area in which they operated. In addition, obligations to extend the network to various parts of the licence area were specified for both basic service and cellular mobile service licences; the roll-out obligations were more stringent for basic service (see Annex 3.A1). When wireless in the local loop with limited mobility service was allowed, the licence contained a specific requirement that the service provider should cover the urban, semi-urban and rural short distance charging areas (SDCAs) equally.

Greater affordability was achieved by setting tariffs for fixed line service lower in rural than in urban areas. Now, even though the operator is free to set tariffs, rural tariffs for basic services have been kept relatively low. Similarly, charges for public calls have been specified at levels below the peak call charge for fixed line, and the call charge is lower for rural than for urban public call offices. Likewise, for the Internet, the government had earlier specified that if an Internet service provider was not available for dial-up within a local call area, a long distance dial-up connection would be charged at the local rate. More recently, both the regulator and the government have emphasised cheaper dial-up charges for the Internet, and the tariffs have been sharply reduced.

The earlier strategy for meeting USO or social objectives through mandatory requirements under the licence was not successful because the new private basic service licensees covered only six of the country's 23 circles (often corresponding to states), with one in each circle in the initial phase of market opening (Table 3.5). Even for the six areas, operations were delayed for various reasons. The basic service licensees did not fulfil the requirement to install VPTs and instead paid the penalties specified in their licences for failing to do so. The public sector operator – formerly the Department of Telecom Service Operator and now Bharat Sanchar Nigam Limited – has continued to be main provider of VPTs. Out of a total of about 607 000 villages, VPTs have been installed in about 520 000. Of these, BSNL has provided about 511 000, and the six private operators have provided 9 171.

Table 3.5. Basic service licensees that entered the market in the initial phase licence area (service provider)

Rajasthan (Shyam Telelink)	Gujarat (Reliance Telecom)	Maharashtra (Hughes)
Punjab (HFCL)	Andhra Pradesh (Tata Tele)	Madhya Pradesh (Bharti Telenet)

The mechanism for promoting USO has changed over time. NTP 1999 altered not only the scope of USO but also the means of meeting the policy objective. It was changed from mandatory requirements to financial incentives in view of the introduction of competition and recognition of the lack of success of the mandatory requirements (Box 3.4).

Given the limited finances available, USO policy has prioritised the USO items covered in NTP 1999. While NTP 1999 does not prioritise USO objectives, USO policy implemented through the USF has given greater priority to telecommunications access in rural areas, with lower priority to Internet access, and still lower to extension of the subscriber base or to provision of telephone on demand (see the USO Guidelines at www.dotindia.com). A bidding process among existing operators is used to decide the extent of support from the USF. An exception is the support for meeting operational costs for phones in rural areas established prior to 1 April 2002 (see below), which has the same priority as access: the 8.6 million direct exchange lines involve support of about USD 265 million.

Financial constraints also meant that initial support for telephone on demand was limited to the areas with the "most pressing" requirements. Out of the 2 647 SDCAs, the smallest units for network configuration for call delivery of basic service, within which all calls are local, only 486 were classified as rural and eligible for support from the USF (see the USO Guidelines www.dotindia.com). As defined in the census, "rural" is much broader than the SDCA coverage that initially qualified for USO funding.

The scope of USF policy has evolved even within the short time of its existence. An important change brought about by the Indian Telegraph (Amendment) Rules, notified on 26 March 2004 (see "Indian Telegraph Rules" at www.dotindia.com) is that support for phone on demand has been extended beyond the 486 SDCAs; funding is now provided for rural DELs in all net-cost-positive SDCAs. Preliminary estimates suggest that this would cover new rural DELs in about 1 580 SDCAs. Further, these rules also take account of complementary policies that provide additional funding to operators.

Box 3.4. Selected features of the Universal Service Fund

- The Universal Service Support Policy came into effect on 1 April 2002.
- The universal service levy is 5% of adjusted gross revenue (AGR) and is contributed by all operators except value-added service providers like Internet service providers, voice mail or e-mail.
- The USF was given statutory status under the Indian Telegraph (Amendment) Act, 2003. It is a non-lapsable fund. The Act provides that credits to the fund include not only amounts received towards the universal service obligation, but also any grants and loans made by the central government. The fund is to be used exclusively for meeting USO goals.
- Contributions from telecommunications service providers over the financial years 2002-03 and 2003-04 reached INR 16.53 billion and INR 21.43 billion, respectively. In addition, a sum of INR 6 billion was allotted over the two years and was fully disbursed.
- The requirement for the current financial year is INR 27 billion. An allotment of INR 12 billion has been made and has been fully disbursed. Anticipated collections during the current financial year are estimated at about INR 40 billion.

The USO policy now being implemented has extended the scope of the USO beyond that of NTP 1999. It includes, for example, a second public telephone in villages with population exceeding 2 000, the upgrading of VPTs to public telecommunications and info centres (PTICs) and the replacement of VPTs installed prior to 1 April 2002 working on Multiple Access Remote Radio (MARR) systems, which were ineffective for various reasons, including power supply problems in rural areas and unsatisfactory performance of the equipment, especially owing to lack of spare parts. Likewise, keeping in mind the need for higher speeds for data service, there is a provision for both low-speed (below 128 Kbps) and high-speed (128 Kbps and above) PTICs (see the USO Guidelines at www.dot.gov.in).

Extending the use of USO funds for additional activities is under consideration by the USF administrator and the government. The Department of Telecommunications, the regulator and the Planning Commission are considering how USO policy support should evolve through funding from the USF and other initiatives. These include consideration of additional initiatives for financial support for mobile telephony towers and fibre to nearest point to boost teledensity in rural areas. Another important policy focus is better co-ordination among diverse initiatives so as to maximise the combined effect.

On the basis of experience, the USF administrator has adjusted the components of USO support to improve its effectiveness. Initially, the practice was to obtain a bid for a seven-year period, with a mid-term review to assess whether any change was required in the estimated funding, and payment of the capital and operational cost subsidy as an annual stream during the relevant period. While the initial phase of the USF programme was implemented within this framework, there was a lack of response to the request for bids for the second public phone in villages with a population of more than 2 000. The reasons for the lack of interest were examined, and meetings were held with service providers to improve the policy's effectiveness. The period of seven years was then reduced to five years, the mid-term review was dropped, and most of the capital cost (depreciation, return to equity and cost of debt, or about 90% of the capital expenditure as a whole) was paid up front to increase certainty for investors. Since the five-year period begins a couple of years after the programmes initiated under the seven-year scheme, both cover the period up to the financial year 2009-10.

Other adjustments include a change in the mechanism for settling claims, so as to improve the effectiveness of the USO scheme. Until 30 June, 2003 all claims were settled in Delhi by the USF administrator. Settlement was then decentralised and the regional offices of the Controller of Communication Accounts of the Department of Telecommunications settles payments in the region where the USO investment takes place.

It is expected that the financial viability of currently assisted activities will improve over time, reducing their need for USO support. For instance, there will later be a review to consider whether support is required in the next phase of the USF programme for public phones, because provision of long distance call service within a few years should make such phones financially viable. Likewise, with multiple services possible on high-speed Internet or broadband, revenue will increase and average costs will decrease.

The USF administrator has tried to improve the transparency of actions taken by service providers to meet USO objectives. For example, it has asked service providers giving public access service to indicate on their website the names of villages that they serve.

Policy makers have continued to seek new ways of promoting universal service. Additional USO initiatives could be considered to increase flexibility of the policy regime and to involve public-private partnerships. An example of increased flexibility is the creation of a special category termed "niche operators" under TRAI's recent Unified Licence Recommendations. If the regulator's recommendations are accepted and converted into policy, these operators would be allowed to operate without an entry fee in the local call area (SDCA), provided that the SDCA has a rural fixed teledensity of less than 1%. Likewise, the Unified Licence Recommendations propose allowing Internet telephony. With the spread of Internet kiosks to rural areas, this would allow the provision of voice services together with data services if government policy allows Internet telephony.

Examples of public-private partnership include towers erected by certain state governments to be used by private sector service providers for Internet service in rural areas, or the establishment by state governments of a network for e-governance which can be made available to private parties for a fee to give additional services (see the Kerala state project in Annex 3.A2).

Most telephony access in villages and towns is provided by BSNL. The technologies used by BSNL for most VPTs include MARR (81 847 VPTs, to be replaced by wireless in local loop), fixed phone by landline (238 694), satellite (299), and wireless in local loop (190 351). BSNL's legacy network, particularly for the rural area, is being upgraded. Steps taken include upgrading of present rural automatic exchanges, and conversion of single base modules to remote switching units. Satellite-based public phone technologies are being used to cover remote and isolated areas.

Wireless in local loop technology is increasingly being used for rural access and provision of phone connections, even by private operators. Efforts have also been made to combine mobile technologies with procedures that enhance telephone access. For example, the government (together with BSNL) has put in place a scheme for postmen in rural areas to carry a wireless in local loop phone to be used for telephone access in the villages they cover. At present, 2 592 postmen cover 11 013 villages under this scheme. Independent entrepreneurs are also providing such service on demand, with two different types of schemes. In one, the phone is taken to a person who makes a phone call (and pays for the call); in the other, the phone is taken to a person who receives a call at a specified time and this person pays for the service.

Efforts to provide Internet service to rural areas also involve both government and non-government efforts, with private companies or non-governmental organisations sometimes taking the initiative. The development of radio-based technologies is resulting in much greater flexibility than earlier envisaged, at costs substantially below those for fixed line. Annex 3.A2 gives two examples of the technology used, the main features and the products covered (for information on other initiatives, see www.trai.gov.in). Given the diverse activities focused on common or related objectives, steps have been taken to co-ordinate these efforts and to make them more effective and sustainable.

A major component of the government's policy to improve teledensity and provision of telecommunications service has been the opening of markets and steps to increase competition and enhance flexibility. Access services were opened up in the mid-1990s, with a duopoly in both fixed line and mobile services markets, and licences were awarded for telecom circles (mostly the equivalent of provinces/states) (Tables 3.6 and 3.7). In 1999, the licence fee regime was altered and linked to revenue rather than bids. This facilitated operations and sustained industry growth. By 2001, the government had opened up national and international long distance services, and open entry, subject to specified conditions, was allowed for all licences except cellular mobile for which only four operators per licence area were allowed owing to spectrum constraints.

Table 3.6. Number of private cellular service providers (CMSPs)

Service area	CMSPs initially licensed	New CMSP licensed since 2001
Rajasthan	2	1
UP (East)	1	1
Gujarat	2	1
Maharashtra	2	1
North East	2	-
Karnataka	2	1
Punjab	2	1
AP	2	1
Haryana	2	1
Kerala	2	1
UP(West)	1	1
West Bengal	1	-
MP	2	1
Assam	1	-
Bihar	1	-
Himachal	2	1
Orissa	1	-
Tamil Nadu	2	1
Delhi	2	1
Mumbai	2	1
Chennai	2	1
Kolkata	2	1

A unified access service licence was introduced in 2003, which offered the possibility of providing fixed or mobile services under a single licence. The revenue share licence fee was also reduced at that time. More recently, the TRAI recommended a unified licence regime that makes it possible to offer any telecommunications service under a single licence, subject to allocation of spectrum. It also recommended still lower licence fees, allowing Internet telephony, and providing for a special category of small operators to be allowed easy entry in smaller areas (local call areas) with less than 1% fixed line teledensity, as noted above. The easier entry and licence fee conditions have led to intense competition, as can be seen by the number of operators in each licence area (Table 3.7). Today, India has three operators with licences for access service in all areas (the two public sector incumbents are treated as one operator), one operator with licences for all areas except three hilly areas, and ten others that are present in one or more licence areas. The combined effect of intense competition, cost reduction due to technological developments and the policy decision to keep termination charges for fixed as well as mobile calls low have led to India having among the world's cheapest mobile tariffs. This has expanded the market base in an unanticipated manner (see Figure 3.1), and markedly changed prospects for rapid progress in meeting teledensity targets.

Table 3.7. Mobile operators with unified access service licence (UASL) or cellular mobile licence

S. no.	Service area	UASL*	Remaining cellular mobile licensees
1	Delhi	3	3
2	Mumbai	3	3
3	Chennai	3	3
4	Kolkata	3	3
5	MH	3	3
6	GUJ	3	3
7	AP	3	3
8	KTK	3	3
9	TN	3	3
10	Kerala	3	3
11	Punjab	5	2
12	Haryana	3	3
13	UP-W	4	2
14	UP-E	3	3
15	Raj	3	4
16	MP	4	3
17	WB&A&N	5	2
18	HP	4	3
19	Bihar	4	2
20	Orissa	4	2
21	Assam	2	2
22	NE	1	3
23	J&K	3	1

Source: UASL List as per DOT information 15 May 2004.

A major new factor is that with the decline in costs, USO objectives may be achieved through normal commercial investment, *i.e.* without financial support. As Table 3.4 shows, the country's population, including rural, covered by mobile network is likely to increase from the present 20% to about 75% in two years through commercial investment.

Effectiveness of the mechanisms used

Initially, USO policy focused on low tariffs for low users, particularly in rural areas, and a mandated programme to establish VPTs. Subsidies to consumers were provided only through low prices for access and calls. The high cost of service provision and relatively low tariffs and usage in rural areas meant that the service provider required subsidies to meet USO objectives. The system did not succeed in meeting either the USO objective of access or government's teledensity target. NTP 1994 already recognised the need for additional funding, and the telecommunications sector was opened up. With competition, the cross-subsidy to low access and usage tariffs provided by the tariff structure could not be sustained, and an alternative mechanism had to be found for the requisite financial support. The mandatory conditions set in the licence agreement did not succeed in meeting the USO objective, and the USF was established (see Box 3.2).

The USF provides the required financial support through a competitive bidding process. India now has at least two highly competitive operators which have won different bids for USF support. In analysing efficiency in meeting USO objectives, both access and individual connections should be examined in order to understand the specific issues pertaining to each as well as the links between them.

Access

The present programme for access under USF should be effectively implemented within a couple of years. It has been in place for a short period of time and sets greater priority on access, both for VPTs (including replacement of MARR VPTs and additional VPTs in villages with more than 2 000 inhabitants), and for public tele-info centres, or Internet kiosks. By March 2007, the MARR VPTs should have been replaced and the public phone programme (including the high-speed public tele-info centres programme) fully implemented. It is likely that by that time, USO may also include broadband.

In assessing the effectiveness of meeting the access requirement, one needs to consider not only the establishment of the link but also its continued functioning. Repairs and maintenance of access becomes crucial with intensity of use. The effect of an increase in phone connections on sustainability and effectiveness of access is likely to be positive.

As Box 3.3 shows, promoting access requires specific initiatives, possibly including laying fibre or building the network by the public sector or with its support. In addition to general policies, additional or supplementary policies are required to bridge the gaps. Moreover, the policy framework must also include incentives for non-governmental or private-sector investments that help achieve the social objectives of USO.

For affordable access, any policy specifying a low price must be supplemented by a policy to reduce policy-imposed costs; otherwise, the policy will result in a greater burden and the need for more financial support. Reducing policy-imposed costs is an alternative for enhancing financial viability, with wider and better ramifications. It makes the investment more attractive, provides the possibility of a price decrease through market response rather than decree, and has an impact that spreads to both access and provision of individual lines.

Like reduction of policy-induced costs, investment in access is more attractive if revenue-earning opportunities increase. In telephony this would imply enabling calls earning higher revenue (*e.g.* STD calls). Access to the Internet and broadband offers better and more flexible potential for earning additional revenue. The USO programme for access should thus quickly move to incorporate broadband.

Individual connection

The rural waiting list for fixed line and the low rural coverage of mobile show that the constraint is supply rather than demand. To increase supply, all factors that reduce costs, increase revenue-generating activities and allow the market to expand either through price reductions or the flexibility provided by technology (mobility and scope of products) should be a key focus. If the cost of some activity is high, *e.g.* provision of communications facilities in rural areas, a price reduction without a cost reduction will only result in a greater burden. It is therefore important to implement policies that will lead to cost reduction, including sharing of infrastructure, increasing flexibility of operations and reducing other policy-induced costs.

Changes in telecommunications technology are enabling operators to give multiple services using the same equipment, the cost of carriage of data has come down immensely, and radio-based technologies are opening up great opportunities especially in rural areas. Policy makers must create a facilitating environment which allows the benefits of these developments to reach as widely as possible. India's experience is that once telecommunications tariffs fall below certain threshold levels, there is a quantum jump in the market available (see Figure 3.1). The objective should be to reduce tariffs to such levels through competition rather than decree. With competition, the market will choose the most suitable products and technologies, and lower prices in a competitive environment are a better stimulus for market growth. Since fixed costs are a large share of total costs in telecommunications, market growth will mean an even greater capacity to reduce prices and increase market size. This would prepare the ground on both the demand and supply side for the service to penetrate rural markets: the demand side owing to the lower price for the service, and the supply side because of economies of scale and scope and ongoing cost reductions due to technological change and competition. This would also have the various beneficial linkages mentioned in the context of access, including reducing pressure on access and providing supplementary forms of access.

The USF process for inviting bids for individual telephone connections in net-cost areas has begun. At the same time, the government has taken a number of initiatives to increase competition and flexibility. Another point that emerges strongly from the Indian experience is that the policy maker must have a short-term focus for achieving major gains, because large changes can be achieved within a relatively short period. For example, As Table 3.2 shows, in the last ten years, teledensity has increased about ten times. To achieve a similar result in the previous period, it took more than 30 years. The table also shows that each year's absolute increase in teledensity is now greater than the total teledensity achieved in India in the half century following its independence in 1947.

Annex 3.A1

Licence obligations regarding VPT and/or rollout obligation of old basic service operator (Madhya Pradesh service area)

Target	Cumulative no. of DELs to be commissioned	Cumulative no. of village telephones to be commissioned*
Within 12 months from effective date	10 000	5 500
Within 24 months from effective date	100 000	11 000**
Within 36 months from effective date	150 000	16 500**

* Subject to compliance with the percentage indicated at "D" for all other purposes, such as monitoring performance at the end of every quarter in respect of VPT coverage until all villages have VPTs.

** At present villages to be covered number 52 387. However, if it is necessary to cover more villages, this is to be taken care of in compliance with "D" below.

D. VPTs to be commissioned in each quarter: (a minimum of 11% of total DELs commissioned during the quarter).

Rollout obligation of cellular mobile licence

36.1 The Licensees shall endeavour to cover the entire Service Area at an early date and notify on quarterly basis the areas not covered by the licensee's system. In Metros, 90% of the service area shall be covered within one year of the effective date. In Telecommunications Circles, at least 10% of the District Headquarters (DHQs) will be covered in the first year and 50% of the District Headquarters will be covered within three years of effective date of licence. The licensee shall also be permitted to cover any other town in a District in lieu of the District Headquarters. Coverage of a DHQ/town would mean that at least 90% of the area bounded by the Municipal limits should get the required street as well as in-building coverage. The District Headquarters shall be taken as on the effective date of licence. The choice of District Headquarters/towns to be covered and further expansion beyond 50% District Headquarters/towns shall lie with the Licensee depending on their business decision. There is no requirement of mandatory coverage of rural areas.

Rollout obligation of BSO licence in 2001

9.3 (a) The LICENSEE undertakes to fulfil the following minimum network rollout obligations:

Phase	Time period for completion from effective date of licence agreement	Cumulative % of coverage in terms of point of presence to be achieved at SDCA level at the end of each phase	% of performance guarantee that can be released on fulfilment of obligations under col. 3
I	2 years	15%	--
II	3 years	40%	20%
III	5 years	80%	30%
IV	7 years	100%	50%

9.3 (b) However, coverage beyond 80% SDCAs in a service area may be done jointly with another licensee (excluding BSNL/MTNL).

9.3 (c) The rollout obligations specify the list of SDCAs category-wise in terms of (a) rural; (b) semi-urban; and (c) urban. Licensee has to fully ensure that each of the named categories is covered in equal proportion during each phase of the rollout obligations.

Annex 3.A2

Two Examples of Technologies Used for Rural Connectivity

CorDECT technology

The corDECT technology was jointly developed by TeNeT (Telecommunications and Computer Networks Group of IIT Madras) and Midas Communication Technologies Pvt Ltd. TeNeT has over the past few years incubated several companies which have developed various technologies suitable for rural areas in developing countries (see below). The focus has been on building a scalable and successful business in rural areas, using:

- Technology that is cost-effective, affordable, robust, scalable and capable of delivering the relevant applications.
- A clear business model, which addresses all market, stakeholder and operational needs.
- An organisation exclusively focused on the rural market.

An exchange and a base station are installed at the *taluka* or county where fibre is located. This exchange functions at a temperature of 55 °C and does not require air conditioning. The total power requirement is 1 kW. This capability solves the problem of lack of power in small towns in India. Also, when power in unavailable, a one kW generator can be easily obtained and used as backup. CorDECT is capable of offering simultaneous voice and Internet access and can deliver a 35/70 Kbps connectivity to villages within a radius of 25 kms from the fibre-connected taluka.

The next-generation corDECT technology aims to deliver a 80/150 Kbps-sustained rate on each Internet connection. The TeNeT group is also working on a solution that combines satellite and terrestrial wireless to provide low-cost connectivity to rural areas covered by mountainous regions and forests.

Within the above framework, an organisation/company called N-Logue uses this technology as a rural service provider whose sole focus is providing commercial telephone and Internet connection to every village in rural India. The company is prohibited from operating in urban areas by virtue of its charter. N-Logue follows a three-tier operational model based on demand aggregation at the village level, servicing the kiosks in terms of local linkages and technical assistance at the district/taluka (or county) level, and connectivity and content servicing handled by N-Logue on a national level.

N-Logue aggregates demand in small villages by creating an Internet kiosk with a computer, an Internet connection, a printer and accessories such as a web/digital camera in each village. The kiosk is the hub of rural connectivity, providing communication services (e-mail, chat, browsing), as well as other needed applications like education and training, health care, agriculture consultancy and e-governance. The kiosk operators need regular support in terms of maintenance, connectivity and handling of other local issues. It was therefore decided that a middle tier of local service providers (LSPs) would be formed to service the needs of the kiosk operators in every county or taluka. The LSP is located in a town not more than 15-20 km from each village. This enables the LSP to reach a kiosk in about 60-90 minutes in case of an emergency.

N-Logue provides the connectivity backbone for the operations, co-ordinates with multiple technology providers for relevant applications and content, trains LSPs and kiosk operators, sources critical supplies for kiosks including the hardware and software, co-ordinates with regulators and policy makers to ensure service availability, and markets the services to the community with the help of the LSPs and kiosk operators.

The existing language software was found to be quite expensive to install at the village kiosk. This led to development of CKShakti, an office suite package in the local language, a relatively cheap package that offers most features normally found in other software in English. It also has a dual language option, which facilitates switching between the local language and English. CKShakti is available in three dual language packages as well as in English.

A video conferencing software (iSEE) which can function at very low bandwidth, was also created to facilitate communications and applications such as telemedicine, education, agri-consultancy. Likewise, a low-cost remote diagnostic kit has been launched at the incubation stage. It is placed in kiosks and enables a doctor to measure a person's temperature, blood pressure, pulse count and ECG remotely. A low-cost (USD 1 000) ATM has also been developed specifically for rural applications, to offer non-cash transactions, micro-deposits, credit and other services catering to the rural area.

Kerala's state-wide data network initiative with a pilot project at Malappuram for Akshaya, using MMDS technology

The State of Kerala has decided to roll out a state-wide data connectivity project. In November 2002, a pilot project was launched under "Akshaya", as part of the Kerala State IT Mission, with the aim that at least one member of every family in every village in a backward district, Mallappuram (3 600 km^2 of densely forested mountainous terrain), should be computer-literate and should have access to the Internet and to the state Intranet. Today Malappuram has over 500 computer centres, each with five PCs interconnected to the state data centre and the outside world over wireless. It is the largest wireless IP network of its kind in the world. The Akshaya centre in one village has even started medical transcription. Another is planning to start distributed business processing outsourcing (BPO) operations.

Akshaya uses MMDS, an IP-based, low-cost, multi-point wireless technology which is circuit-switched and delivers a shared bandwidth of 4 Mbps (*i.e.* extremely high speeds) capable of interactive voice, data, video and entertainment services on one platform. Emphasis was placed on developing a system which offered practical, reliable and economically viable options, which could be scaled up and replicated. The programme is run, in conjunction with the Kerala state government, by Tulip IT Services Ltd. The model used by Tulip involves:

- Setting up the main gateway along with the network operating centre and data centre at Mallapuram.

- Extending the functionalities of this gateway, to about 20 points of presence using point-to-point radio links (the backbone network).
- Thereafter, installing WipLL base stations (the access network).
- As the centres sign up for service, installing WipLL customer premises equipment at the training centres and they are up and running.

The network has high bandwidth scalability, starting as low as 16 Kb and scaling up to 4 Mb, is voice-enabled from day one and voice services in the closed user group can be made available immediately, supports streaming video so that e-learning and telemedicine programmes can start from day one, and provides bandwidth on demand from the beginning.

The model is entrepreneur-driven, with adequate room for provision of value-added services and services to non-governmental organisations and businesses in the district to make it economically viable and self-sustaining.

At the same time, to leverage the advantages of this infrastructure, the government of Kerala has started implementing the next phase of the initiative of connecting the Gram Panchayats, other government organisations and bodies that are part of an effective e-governance model. All would ride on the same network rather than having each department try to create its own infrastructure. The system would set up a "data umbrella" over the entire district to provide voice, data, video and entertainment.

Part II

Water and Sanitation

Chapter 4

Universal Access in the Water and Sanitation Sector

Robin Simpson
Senior Policy Adviser
Consumers International

This chapter presents an overview of the question of access in the water and sanitation sector. It draws attention to problems of definition, discusses sectoral reforms and their impact and mechanisms for developing a framework of universal service. It looks at contract stipulations, pricing devices and consumer subsidies and evaluates their effectiveness in terms of increasing provision for the poor. Possibilities for alternative technologies are considered. The chapter also discusses the role of regulatory bodies and the sustainability of reforms involving the public and private sectors.

Introduction

The importance of water and sanitation services is so evident as to hardly need spelling out. Just a few figures indicate their importance for economic development, public health and social welfare, not to mention environmental conservation and cultural and even aesthetic considerations. To take some of the most vital statistics, according to the United Nations Development Programme (UNDP), "in the 1990s the number of children killed by diarrhoea – the result of unsafe water and sanitation – exceeded the number of people killed in armed conflicts since the Second World War" (UNDP, 2003). Further, according to the United Nations World Water Development Report (2002), improved water supply and basic sanitation extended to the present day "unserved" would reduce the burden of infectious diarrhoea by 17%, while a fully developed piped water service and full sanitation service would reduce this burden by a massive 70%. There are a host of other such indicators, but to list them would be to belabour the essential point: there are rich prizes to be won in human terms from well-directed investment in this sector.

When liberalisation of water and sanitation services[1] is understood to mean entry of foreign private suppliers into a given market, there has been huge controversy for a range of reasons. The controversy is intensified by the "life and death" nature of the product, the inherently monopolistic nature of much of the service, and the market concentration of the major international water and sanitation services providers. This makes the issue an intensely political one. This chapter tries, as dispassionately as possible, to explore whether "liberalisation" can contribute to improving access to water and sanitation services, and if so, under what conditions. It addresses various key questions:

- How are universal access goals defined in the water and sanitation services sector?
- How has liberalisation, particularly in terms of eliminating barriers for foreign providers, affected access to services for the poor?
- What sorts of mechanisms, if any, have been used to encourage service providers to increase provision of services to previously unserved or under-served regions or consumers?
- Have policies promoting universal service used mechanisms aimed at the consumer (*e.g.* subsidies, vouchers)? If so, how were these mechanisms targeted at the truly needy and was "leakage" of resources to other groups avoided, if at all? What were the administrative costs of any such assistance schemes?
- How effective have the above mechanisms been in extending access?
- Have the mechanisms or policies used encouraged providers to develop new or innovative solutions to universal service problems or have they focused on the use of existing technologies and solutions?
- What sort of regulatory bodies have been established to regulate the service?
- How sustainable is the reform process in the long term?

1. In this study, sanitation is taken to refer not to street cleaning and public refuse disposal, but rather to sewerage and other forms of disposal of human waste.

The chapter is structured as follows. The following pages first discuss the definition of access before examining the impact of sectoral reforms and the mechanisms used to move to a framework of universal service,[2] considering them under contract stipulations, pricing devices and consumer subsidies, evaluating their effectiveness with a view to increasing provision for the poor. Next, adaptability to alternative technologies is considered. The discussion then turns to the role of regulatory bodies and the sustainability of reforms involving the public and private sectors. The chapter ends with a summary and distilled conclusions.

What is liberalisation?

There is a tendency to assume that privatisation or private-sector participation (PSP) is the same as liberalisation, and indeed "reform". This is a dangerous assumption, even when national boundaries are open to foreign participation. Liberalisation can bring benefits in the form of technical expertise and business experience as well as "leveraged" capital. But restricted competition among foreign oligopolists for unpublished long-term contracts running fixed infrastructures under weak regulatory regimes cannot accurately be described as liberalisation. Consumers International, one of the less PSP-hostile NGOs in the field, described much of the development of private-sector participation in this field during the 1990s as "false liberalisation" (CI, 2001).[3]

One of the paradoxes of this sector is that liberalisation involving Northern companies is not actually practised very much in the North. The United Kingdom's water industry is certainly open to foreign ownership, but it is not competitive in any meaningful sense at the retail level or even at the licensing level as licences are, in effect, permanent. In contrast, the French system is competitive in terms of tendering for contracts, but in practice very few companies are present in the French market (Mohajeri *et al.*, 2003).

This is not surprising. Complete reticulated systems – that is, physically connected networks – such as those that exist in most OECD countries, are the ultimate example of a natural monopoly. In such countries, attempts to introduce competition "in the market" are essentially marginal and have been noted, if at all, by those working for domestic consumers as essentially irrelevant if not detrimental. An example is the responses by UK consumer organisations to the UK government's attempts to explore the possibilities of retail competition in water (www.ncc.org.uk). Competition "for the market" (such as bids for concession contracts) is a different matter, but the extent to which this can be described as liberalisation depends on the conditions under which the competition takes place.

It is not the intention here to enter into a precise terminological debate. Nevertheless, it is important to put the different forms of private-sector participation into perspective. There is a wide spectrum of PSP, ranging from divestiture of assets, which is actually very rare, to "outsourcing" from within traditional public utilities. Intermediate points, starting from the "public" end of the spectrum, include management contracts, leases and concessions, including build-operate-transfer (BOT) systems. Table 4.1 gives a schematic

2. As the object of this paper is to discuss universal service, *i.e.* to the general public, the industrial/commercial market is not considered, although there are links, for example cross-subsidies between commercial and domestic consumers.

3. The case study on Argentina presented in Chapter 6 illustrates this point.

presentation, including allocation of responsibilities and risks between the private operator and the public body with commissioning responsibility.

Table 4.1. The PSP spectrum[1]

Option	Asset owners	Investment	Revenue collection	Operation	Length	Risk
Management contract[2]	Public	Public	Public	Private	3-5 yrs	Public
Lease or *affermage*[3]	Public	Shared	Private	Private	8-15	Shared
Concession	Public	Private	Private	Private	25-30	Private
BOT[4]	Shared	Private	Private	Private	20-30	Private
Divestiture	Private	Private	Private	Private	Indefinite	Private

1. Across the whole spectrum, including divestiture, it is usual for there to be government controls on tariffs.

2. "Traditional" outsourcing has similar features to management contracts, although the latter tend to be more comprehensive.

3. The main difference between leases and affermages is that under leases, the operator's remuneration depends on the customer tariff, while with affermages, the operator tariff is divorced from the customer tariff, even though the operator may be charged with collecting payments.

4. BOT is a particular form of concession in which ownership of a constructed operating asset effectively remains with the operator for a fixed term and is then transferred to the public authority for an agreed sum. In the short to medium term, it has the character of a privatisation.

Source: World Bank/PPIAF, 2006.

So, for purposes of discussion, liberalisation is seen as involving a measure of private sector participation (PSP), but not necessarily only by foreign interests, for reasons which will become clear. Liberalisation may in practice also involve a measure of development of consumer or customer rights and a greater degree of cost recovery, upon which the viability of a contract may depend. The latter two features need not and should not be incompatible with public ownership.

The goal of universal access

How are universal access goals defined in the water and sanitation services sector?

Targets for access are set with great difficulty for a variety of reasons, practical (*i.e.* what is physically feasible in the foreseeable future?) as well as methodological and political. To judge what constitutes access is bound to be arbitrary, even when bearing in mind local variations in geography, climate and culture. For example, the WHO *Global Water Supply and Sanitation Assessment 2000 Report* suggests that the low coverage figures for Latin America and the Caribbean may reflect comparatively narrow definitions of what is considered acceptable. This suggests a cultural bias that leads to under-reporting of access.

There are other reasons for the misleading nature of much of the existing data. Estimates of existing levels of service have often been made by service providers, rather than consumers' responses to local household surveys (see section 1.2 of the above-mentioned WHO report). They have often ignored private household wells for example, while surveys have been unable to estimate illegal theft of water from diversion of supply. These factors also lead to underestimates of access. Conversely, supply may be overestimated because providers assume that consumers use facilities when they do not, because of mechanical breakdown of pumps or refusal to use latrines. Furthermore, the low incidence of 24/7 or "round-the-clock" service in developing countries, described in the *2004 World Development Report* (WDR) as a "pipe dream" in many cities, poses a huge difficulty in terms of estimates of access, as does the difficulty of defining the safety of water available. So, even when an infrastructure actually exists, it should not be assumed to provide proper access. WDR reports that more of a third of *existing* rural infrastructure in South Asia is estimated to be dysfunctional.

Given the high profile debates over water and sanitation services, governments may well feel under pressure to present a positive face for reasons of prestige. The WHO report cited above reports individual country data showing "rapid and implausible changes in level of coverage from one assessment to the next". The only thing one can state with certainty about estimates of access is that they will be wrong; the issue is the range of acceptable error or the extent to which the right thing is being measured.

The WHO report describes the development of methodologies to render more accurate estimates for the 2000 assessment. The terms "safe" and "adequate" were replaced by "improved" to reflect these limitations, so that populations with access to improved water and sanitation services were considered to be covered. Household surveys were increasingly used to reflect real-life consumption patterns. But the assessment questionnaires did not allow for intermittence or poor quality water supply. The technologies considered by WHO to be improved are set out in Box 4.1.

Box 4.1. Definitions of access

The following technologies were included in the assessment as representing "improved" water supply and sanitation:

Water supply	Sanitation
Household connection	Connection to a public sewer
Public standpipe	Connection to septic system
Borehole	Pour-flush latrine
Protected dug well	Simple pit latrine
Protected spring	Ventilated improved pit latrine
Rainwater collection	

The following technologies were considered "not improved":

Water supply	Sanitation
Unprotected well	Service or bucket latrines (where excreta are manually removed)
Unprotected spring	Public latrines
Vendor-provided water	Latrines with an open pit
Bottled water*	
Tanker truck-provided water	

* Considered as "not improved" because of concerns about the quantity of supplied water, not because of concerns over the water quality

The assessment questionnaire defined access to water supply and sanitation in terms of the types of technology and levels of service afforded. For water, allowance was also made for other locally-defined technologies. Types of sources that did not give reasonable and ready access to water for domestic hygiene purposes, such as tanker trucks and bottled water, were not included in the "improved" category. The excreta disposal system was considered adequate for sanitation if it was private or shared (but not public), and if it hygienically separated human excreta from human contact.

Source: WHO, Annex A Global water supply and sanitation assessment 2000 Report.

Having defined what people should have access to in the water sector, definitions then revolve around volumes and distance from a fixed water point. "Reasonable" access is defined by WHO as at least 20 litres per person per day available from a source within one kilometre of the user's dwelling. This one kilometre standard would be considered shockingly low for Northern consumers. Yet 1.1 billion people do not even reach this standard (WHO) and 2.4 billion do not reach the improved sanitation standard. Therefore, almost one-fifth of the world's population is classified as not having access to improved water and most do not have access to piped water. In Chad, only 2.8% of households have taps in the home, and only 23.5% have reasonable access as defined above (CI, ROAF, 2004).

Given these extremely low minimum standards it is not surprising that national governments try to set higher standards and increase coverage accordingly. South Africa, for example, sets a minimum standard of a public standpipe within 200 metres of every village household and piped water to every home in cities with the first 25 litres per person per day free of charge. In practice, this translates to six cubic metres per household per month free of charge. The human right to water has been set out in the South African constitution. Of 15 million South Africans without such access in 1994, some eight million have now been connected according to these definitions (UNDP, 2003). (However, concern has been expressed anecdotally about the sustainability of these connections).

It is important to highlight four points. First, as the above definitions make clear, coverage levels alone do not tell the whole story. Coverage and standards clearly interact. Theoretically, all living people have access to water, otherwise they would be dead. But to argue from this that they have access would clearly be absurd. Coverage statistics are meaningless unless access is defined. This has practical implications when scrutinising the terms of contracts between companies and local authorities because they frequently specify numbers of new household connections or water points, but do not necessarily define access in terms of clear criteria (World Bank, 2004). So, theoretically, companies could increase the density of household connections and thus achieve a greater hook-up rate but still neglect unserved areas. Therefore, number of connections translated into a general percentage is a highly imperfect measure of coverage.

Second, local geography matters hugely. Identical distances from water points can mean very different things in practical terms if there are, say, extreme climatic conditions or dangerous social conditions. Distance also does not measure such factors as queuing time, which may depend on population density.

Third, the juxtaposition of Northern and Southern perspectives raises the vital question of whether developing country networks should ever become complete in the Northern sense. Highly engineered underground piping and sewer systems are extremely expensive to build and, by their very nature, take huge amounts of construction time. Even low-cost solutions take time as the Millennium Development Goals (MDGs) implicitly recognise (see Annex 4.A1). The MDGs aim to reduce by half the proportion of people without access to safe drinking water and sanitation by 2015.

There is a risk that access will be interpreted as simply meaning physical connection to or location within reach of a reticulated system. Yet reticulated systems may be undesirable for reasons not only of finance and time lags, but also because they require large amounts of water to function (for example, sewers have to be flushed). The requirements for waste disposal systems may be different from those for water distribution. Such systems may place demands on water supply and divert water from those as yet unserved, and may lead to an unsustainable level of abstraction from nature. There is a need not just to develop appropriate technology systems, but also to revive past traditions, such as the use of human manure in China, which will not lead to such an environmental or financial impasse.

In recognising that reticulation may not always be possible or desirable, one should perhaps not refer to those excluded from systems as *non-connected*, but rather as *unserved*. As an example, it is worth bearing in mind that in sparsely populated or isolated regions of rich countries, such as Canada, non-reticulated services serve consumers potable water by truck. Such users are unconnected but not unserved. One of the tricky questions that ISO is currently struggling with is how to develop standards for non-reticulated services (ISO TC224).

Fourth, for all the preceding reasons, there are dangers that the quantitative targets expressed in the MDGs may have perverse effects. They envisage that by 2015 the world will have only reached the half-way point in providing access to the unserved. Governments could invest heavily in reaching the 50% target while ignoring the needs of the remaining 50% still to be served (bearing in mind that changing demography is moving the target anyway). Of course, the ignored 50% will be the poorest. A more equitable policy would be one of "some for all, not more for some", a motto in wide circulation.

The impact of liberalisation

Many critics of liberalisation focus their attention on changes but pay little attention to the defects of the existing situation (Barlow and Clarke, 2002; Public Citizen 2002, 2003). Controversy thus focuses on PSP. Furthermore, the author's experience in working with consumer organisations has been that analysis tends to focus on price rather than coverage. It is argued here that for the poorest, *i.e.* the unserved, coverage is the more critical issue.

The poor pay more

To appreciate fully the changes brought about by liberalisation, it is important to look at the starting point. As mentioned above, poor consumers are often simply left out of network services, with little alternative organised provision. But they have to drink, and they generate waste. The common result, certainly for potable water, is that the poor pay higher unit costs than the better off, even though the volumes consumed are smaller.

According to the Consumers Information Network in Kenya, an example of this "poor pay more" syndrome is that the cost per litre of drinking water in Nairobi is ten times higher for customers of vendors than for those connected to a network (Odongo and Mungai, 2002). The ratios are similar in Latin America, as confirmed by a wide range of studies by academics, World Bank experts and local surveys carried out by consumer associations in the region. In the Caribbean region the contrasts are higher still with the differential reaching 100 in some extreme cases (de Moor, 1999).[4]

4. Such examples, notably from the Dominican Republic, featured heavily in the regional workshop of Consumers International in Buenos Aires in March 2002, which convened consumer organisations from throughout Latin America and the Caribbean.

Street-level prices for water

Table 4.2 shows the differences among various water sources in terms of the range of prices per cubic metre in US cents. It is based on a study of 47 countries and 93 locations derived from recent literature reviews (Brown, 2004).

Table 4.2. Street level prices for water

Type of supply	Low level of range	High level of range
Public utilities	0.02	0.79
Private networks	0.17	0.86
Point source vendors	0.34	3.60
Tanker trucks	0.45	6.32
Carters	0.76	11.00

The clear implication of this table is that, while it lends some limited support to the thesis that private networks tend to have higher tariffs than public networks, the ranges overlap and the difference is far less pronounced than the differentials between networked and non-networked sources. The point is rendered more dramatic on the ground by the fact that the informal sources are often in close proximity to the reticulated networks. It suggests that the really dramatic equalisation of prices will come from extending the networks. The differential between network and non-network services would be even greater if coping costs such as time spent queuing for or fetching water were included.

The poor-pay-more pattern is intensified when network prices are below cost, as is frequently the case. This means not only that the poor pay more, but also that the better-off receive a subsidy that is denied to the poor, resulting in a double disadvantage. This in turn leads to a further complication in which connection charges may go up to recoup revenue when running costs are below cost, or *de facto* connection charges are paid as bribes (Davis, 2004). This means that only those who have the capital to pay the connection fee get access to the service, a further (and triple) imposition on the poor.[5]

Can disadvantages become advantages?

Paradoxically, the above syndrome gives some grounds for optimism. The regrettable fact that the urban poor are used to paying very high unit prices suggests that there are reserves of revenue among the poor that could be channelled more efficiently than at present to raise standards and reduce unit prices. In contrast, the rural poor often pay through other coinage, such as their time, another area in which there are huge potential gains to be made. The efficient channelling of the capacity of the poor to pay is the holy grail of the water and sanitation services sector.

In theory, if the poor pay ten times more per litre now, then even if the network tariffs doubled, they would still be paying five times more. A doubling of the network revenue could be used to reduce existing service losses and concentrate subsidies where they are most needed to improve the lives of the poor, through extension of the drinking water

5. High connection charges have been described by the Cranfield University team as "Charging to enter the shop" (Franceys *et al.*, www.silsoe.cranfield.ac.uk/iwe/projects/connections).

system or development of sanitation systems. In practice this will not happen quite so simply, as raising tariffs does not necessarily increase revenue pro rata (evasion may rise and metered consumption may fall). Furthermore, raising network prices can have a knock-on effect on vendor prices, and, in any case, the extra revenue available from poor consumers may turn out to be modest as the factor of ten per litre does not mean that there is ten times the actual expenditure. The users of vendors consume less water, and so spend less in aggregate than the unit price differentials suggest (Komives *et al.*, 2000). Nevertheless, despite these caveats, the point is that there are resources available in the current expenditure of poor consumers. This is not a new element of household expenditure.

It is, however, frankly recognised that in terms of household expenditure, there are major problems in the sanitation sub-sector, because there is so little expenditure to channel. Governments seem very reluctant even to discuss sanitation issues, as was recently confirmed by a recent World Bank/CSO seminar in London, where WB task managers spoke of the reluctance of governments to set up sanitation programmes even when funds were available at below commercial rates (see also PPIAF/WSP, 2002, Preface). Introducing sanitation charges into household budgets would be a genuinely new element of expenditure, and this raises problems of a new order. It also suggests that subsidies should be diverted from drinking water to sanitation.

Poorer consumers are used (perforce) to paying regularly for current consumption, usually in relatively small amounts. This makes them potentially good network customers from the financial point of view. If the pattern of ready payment were carried over to networks after connection, it would mean that arrears would not build up as they have in the former Soviet Union, for example, where it is not uncommon for the majority of bills to be unpaid (OECD/International Water Association, 2001; Sivaev, 2002). Once bills are only paid by a minority, the service enters a downward spiral, as tariff increases are imposed to make up the shortfall but this in turn increases the incentive to evade payment. Evasion then becomes the norm and no longer a matter for disapproval. Under such circumstances, if many of the connected are simply not paying, it is not surprising that the non-connected may steal water from the distribution system or pay an illegal operator who siphons off water and sells it on. This way lies system failure, and everyone loses in the end. It may be that newly developed systems can avoid this downward slide if the habit of regular payment can be maintained and incorporated into the service once a network is up and running. For this to work, easy methods of payment need to be devised, and the prevailing evidence is that the poor prefer frequent small payments to staggered larger ones (Kariuki, 2002).

The above suggests that the task of extending networks on a cost-recovery basis, while difficult, is not an insurmountable task, although there are real problems in the area of urban sanitation. Have private sector operators been able to respond to these opportunities?

How has liberalisation – particularly in terms of eliminating barriers for foreign providers – affected access to services for the poor?

The answer to this question is inevitably mixed. In a paper for the World Bank, Foster *et al.* (2004) attempted to answer it. They provide in an appendix a summary of selected country studies on the impact of a wide range of utility reforms, especially in terms of the impact on poverty. Their assessment tends to be positive in spite of a tendency for prices to rise with liberalising reform in the water sector and concomitant moves towards cost recovery. They divide domestic customers as follows:

- *Existing paying customers* who will tend to see price rises for a service they receive already.
- *Potential customers* who may be connected for the first time, and who are therefore major gainers.
- *Clandestine customers* who currently obtain their water without official payment and who may therefore lose.

Although the first and last categories may lose in price terms, there may be gains in terms of service quality. Indeed, clandestine customers often have to pay middlemen anyway, and so may not even lose in terms of price. But despite some gains to most consumers from liberalisation, the results of Foster *et al.* (2004) show a repeated pattern of major gains accruing to the better off. This supports the author's repeated warning that domestic consumer interests should not be seen as monolithic (Simpson, 2002).

Table 4.3. PSP examples raised by stakeholders responding to global scoping review

Positive examples	Negative examples
Malindi, Kenya	
	Nairobi
Senegal	Senegal
Cote d'Ivoire	
	Gambia
	Ghana
Morocco	
Mozambique	Mozambique (Maputo)
South Africa: Nelspruit, Dolphin Coast	South Africa: Nelspruit, Dolphin Coast, Fort Beaufort, Stutterheim
Argentina	Argentina
Chile	Chile
Manila	Manila
Brazil: Manaus, Niteroi, Limeira, Cachoeira	Brazil: Manaus, Niteroi, Paranagua, Robeiro Preto
Bolivia: La Paz/El Alto	Bolivia: La Paz/El Alto, Cochabamba
France	France
United Kingdom	United Kingdom
United States	United States

Source: Urquhart and Moore in full report of the Global Water Scoping Process (now Water Dialogues) 2004.

Conflicting consumer interests

In the 2004 full Report of the Global Water Scoping Process (since renamed the Water Dialogues) (Urquhart and Moore, 2004), which makes a case for a full multi-level (global/national) stakeholder review of private sector participation in water and sanitation services, there is a most revealing table (see Table 4.3). On the basis of 312 interviews with experts and organisations in every continent, Urquhart and Moore list PSP projects cited as positive and negative examples by interviewees. Many projects are cited on both the negative and positive sides: Senegal, Mozambique, South Africa (Nelspruit and Dolphin Coast), Argentina, Chile, Manila, Brazil (Manaus, Niteroi), Bolivia (La Paz El Alto), France, the United Kingdom and the United States. While this appears paradoxical it contains two essential truths. First, because different groups have different interests, perceptions will vary, and this will colour the reporting. Second, it may indeed be true that there are positives and negatives within the same projects, involving as they frequently do very large populations.

Buenos Aires (see Box 4.2) and Manila are among the most commonly cited notorious examples.

Box 4.2. Buenos Aires

Literature reviews of the Buenos Aires concessions (Van den Berg, 2000; Foster *et al.*, 2004) suggest that "consumers are the big winners", although the various studies recognise that benefits accrued mostly to the high- and middle-income users. This is all the more disappointing in that, unlike in other locations where there were informal settlements, there was no legal obstacle to their inclusion, at least from the point of view of the water contractors (Gutierrez *et al.*, 2003). Indeed, the three private concessions all provided for universal coverage and were expected to include informal settlements in their network expansion plans.

The programmes therefore contained an inherent contradiction in mandating expansion while retaining high connection charges. Furthermore, legal ambiguities over land tenure remained a problem, all the more so as connection charges represented a sizeable investment by consumers, not to be undertaken lightly if rights of occupancy were uncertain. The expansion targets were not broken down by district, so local residents and consumer associations were unable to know what specific plans existed for their neighbourhoods.

Moreover, the agreements "cut off the branch they were sitting on" by reducing tariffs, initially by 27%[1] (see Chapter 6). Naturally, this was of no use to the poor who were not connected in the first place. In due course, renegotiation took place to reduce connection charges and raise tariffs, as well as to reduce expansion targets (WSP, 2001). Inevitably this was construed by many as an act of bad faith and the fact that one of the concessionaires, Azurix (a subsidiary of Enron), walked away from the contract was further pointed to as an indication of either bad faith or incompetence.

Yet despite these undoubted problems, some positive things happened. Capital investment rose ten-fold by some estimates, enabling a million people to obtain coverage during a five-year period (Van den Berg, 2000). But the imbalance of benefits and costs means that the criticisms were justified in equity terms.

1. There had been an increase of 62% before the contract was signed.

Van den Berg (2000) points to the strategic error of awarding the concession to the lowest tariff bidder while retaining a high connection charge for the unserved. She concluded from an analysis of draft contracts that newer smaller concessions in Argentina were unfortunately repeating the same mistake, so that "almost all the benefits for existing customers accrue to non-poor customers, because they form the majority of customers currently connected to the system". She points by way of explanation to the very high cost of water and sewerage connection, which can amount to more than USD 1 000 per household, far beyond the reach of the poor. Foster *et al.* (2004) point out that amendments were made to the contracts to correct some of these inequities. However, this was achieved in part by reducing connection targets to a level that was more easily financed and slowing down investment in sewage treatment.

WaterAid/Tearfund found that in Buenos Aires, as elsewhere: "communities are willing to contribute to the cost of the work" (of network extension). They found furthermore that for ongoing charges, "the prevalent fear that the poor will not pay is not based on experience. In reality, non-payment emerges when services are not provided – when public utilities refuse to provide services to informal settlements, populations like these had often connected themselves illegally. Studies in developing countries show that the poor are actually willing to pay more for their water once connected." (Gutierrez *et al.*, 2003)

Thus, it seems unwise for a contract to stipulate price reductions for existing users when large sectors of the population are still unserved. Yet, this is precisely what happened in Manila, too (see Box 4.3).

Box 4.3. Manila

The Eastern zone, the richer part of Manila, saw huge decreases of 74% on the award of the concession in 1997. The Western zone, a separate concession which contained the poorer population, saw an initial reduction of 43% (Rosenthal, 2001). Given that the Western concession also had to assume 90% of the USD 800 million of the Manila water service (denominated in dollars during a time of currency instability), the contract looks in retrospect like a disaster waiting to happen. Indeed it was described by WaterAid/Tearfund as a "dive bid" borne out of a desire to obtain the business although the distribution of the debt was not clear at the time of the bid (Esguerra, 2003). By the end of 2000, the Western zone concession was in "deep financial distress" according to WaterAid/Tearfund, and the concession was renegotiated in a way that "led to the cost of foreign exchange recovery being completely and immediately passed to consumers". It is this renegotiation which then led to severe price rises in pesos. Given the debacle, it is perhaps surprising that any progress was made at all in achieving better coverage. And yet this seems to have happened. Targets set out in the contracts were to achieve over 95% service coverage, and although the estimates are approximate, even severe critics of the operation acknowledge that coverage levels rose very significantly. Indeed, coverage levels role by about 15%, benefiting an additional 1.5 million people, although still short of the target and increasing the hours of service (Rosenthal, 2001).

These two cases illustrate the huge complexity of assessing the impact of liberalisation, and expert analysis has indeed been notably cautious (Foster *et al.*, 2004). It has been argued that while price tends to hit the headlines, impact should be assessed in the light of coverage, as the latter is of greater importance to the poorest.

Coverage

There has been remarkably little in the way of systematic comparative analysis dealing with the relationship, or lack thereof, of coverage to liberalisation. Clarke and Wallstern (2003) compare coverage for low-income households (using lack of education as a proxy) in the mid- to late-1990s for three categories of African countries: those with public operators, those with recently introduced PSP (within two years) and those with longer established private operators. Coverage was slightly lower in countries with public operators than in those with established private operators, and lower still than recently established PSP. While this indicates that PSP did not actually worsen the position of the poor, it is risky to read too much into the results, as the "public" sample consisted of 17 countries, while the other two categories consisted of only two each. Furthermore, if the hypothesis is that PSP improves coverage, it seems counter-intuitive that the recent PSP resulted in higher coverage than the longer-established PSP. Likewise, Clarke *et al.*

(2004) found the results in three Latin American countries inconclusive. Although coverage rose after the introduction of PSP, it also did in regions the authors used as a control. As in Africa, they concluded that PSP did not worsen the position of the poor.

Prices

As indicated in Table 4.2, prices have tended to be higher in the context of PSP. But claims about price increases are not always accurate for a variety of reasons. First, several of the big concession agreements, including for Buenos Aires and Manila, saw initial price *decreases,* largely as a result of the bidding process. If they were preceded by pre-contract price increases, as in Buenos Aires and Santiago, this increases the complexity of the claims and counterclaims. A further complication has been the effect of currency devaluation, a major reason why the Manila contract came to grief. The Argentine contracts also faced the difficulties inherent in the fact that consumers paid in pesos, but the contracts were denominated in dollars. This may or may not be reasonable, but denomination in a foreign currency is an additional risk for all parties. It also raises the possibility that prices may rise and fall at the same time depending on the currency in which they are denominated. To the extent that this is a feature of foreign-held contracts, this is an additional complication when multinationals are involved.

Table 4.2 shows also that differences in price between public and private systems are dwarfed by those between network and non-network prices. It is therefore argued here that price increases may well be justifiable, not just in cost-recovery terms, but also in terms of social equity. In terms of preventing access for the poor, prices below cost are part of the problem rather than part of the solution because the implicit subsidy which they represent diverts resources away from the non-connected.

The counterfactual – could improvements have occurred anyway?

So far, the answer to the question about the impact of liberalisation seems to be that access for the poor has improved somewhat, but nowhere near as much as might have been achieved with greater attention to such basic issues as connection charges. Furthermore, the question leads to an additional question: In the event of better access, could such improvements have been made without liberalisation given the same level of investment? The view taken here is that improvements could probably have been made without private sector participation, but they could not have been made without price increases. Some of the most successful increases in coverage or high levels of coverage are found in public sector services with high levels of cost recovery, such as Porto Alegre, (Brazil) (see Box 4.4) and Costa Rica.

Public sector reforms

So how does the evidence for public and private sector reform compare in terms of coverage? Foster *et al.* (2004) set out a spectrum of five types of utility reform — public-sector reform, private-sector participation, regulatory reform, sector restructuring and market liberalisation across all the utilities. They conclude that market liberalisation should reduce prices and improve access and quality in competitive conditions. But this poses the question of what to do when such conditions do not apply, which is more likely in the water and sanitation services than in the other utility sectors. The same analysis finds that prices *may* adjust up or down towards cost-reflective levels, and quality and access *may* improve under public-sector reform. In other words, across the spectrum of the utilities there are no certainties, only possibilities and even they are highly qualified.

Box 4.4. Brazil

Porto Alegre has become something of a test bed for citizens' participation as a form of public administration, and the results are widely admired and cited. The city has achieved high rates of coverage by world standards with 99.5% piped water for a relatively low price (including a social tariff), and 84% sewerage collection, though a lower level (one-quarter) of sewage treatment (Viero and Cordeiro, 2003). The water service is municipally owned, and the operator is a self-governing body whose management has to report to its Deliberative Council, which meets regularly and includes representatives of users and other stakeholders. The City Council operates a participatory budget system and authorises the necessary investment. The operational independence of the water operator is reinforced by the fact that it operates on a cost-recovery basis thus avoiding the need to bargain for a budget for current operational costs (Porto Alegre, 2004).

The **Sao Paulo** water service, said to be the largest public water utility in the world, embarked upon a major reform process in the mid-1990s, likewise raising its levels of cost recovery and reducing the costs to be recovered by 45%. Water service coverage increased from 84% to 91% and sewerage from 64% to 73%, and delinquency (non-paying accounts) fell by 8% (Hall, 2001).

The above evidence and consideration of the counter-factual question results in a frustrating lack of clarity. The analyses by Clarke and Wallsten (2003) and Clarke *et al.* (2004) for two continents confirm how difficult it is to attribute improvements to the presence or absence of PSP. Uganda perhaps suggests that scale could be relevant in developing countries (see Box 4.5).

Box 4.5. Uganda

The Ugandan National Water Utility the National Water and Sewerage Corporation embarked on an internal reform in 1997 which has resulted in water supply coverage rising from 54% to 63% between 1999/00 and 2002/3 with unaccounted-for water (leakage and theft) falling from 42% to 39% (Brown, 2004). These improvements which have resulted in one million Ugandans connected since 1998, have been achieved by contracting with small-scale independent providers. Barungi *et al.* (2003) conclude that PSP "has been a useful policy tool in expanding coverage", although they express concern about the sustainability of the programme in light of its hardware-driven nature and its reliance on foreign donors.

Micro-liberalisation

The Uganda case suggests that in poorer countries, where reticulation is still relatively undeveloped, the potential success of liberalisation may not be at the level of the large catch-all contracts, such as long-term concessions, but at a more flexible and local level. In many ways the truest examples of liberalisation come from developing countries in the unserved areas in the form of small-scale independent providers (SSIPs). The consequence of the failure of existing networks to serve their populations with an essential product has inevitably been that small-scale, even micro-operators, have stepped in, particularly in urban areas. Such operators may be seen as exploitative by some, but they vary enormously. Some water vendors are significant businesses in their own right and use very sophisticated techniques. They may become recognised by water companies or public authorities as providing a useful service, as in Uganda, Kenya and Ghana, and may end up operating as subcontractors, as in Manila (see Box 4.3) (Morel and Loury, 2004).

In some places, vendors are, in fact, members of the armed forces (Manila, Karachi) and use their authority, and the army's equipment, as a way of making money and distributing water. In Nairobi, municipal workers who had not been paid their wages simply developed water vending as a cottage industry, seizing opportunities to regain their lost wages by using their knowledge of the water sources to serve unserved populations (Brown, 2004). Others are people who happen to live close to water points and make a living from collecting water and selling it on. Finally, some are NGOs that have become local operators. Occasionally, they have begun as illegal tappers of water from mainlines intended for other districts while resident in illegal settlements (Alfonso *et al.*, 1997). There is a long history of local communities installing sanitation systems on a self-build basis as soon as rights of tenure are granted, as in Ciudad San Salvador in Lima, a peri-urban settlement of 300 000 cited as a model scheme by the UN.

Whatever the reasons for vendors to get into the business, it is doubtful if much purpose is to be served by branding them as exploiters. This is because the causes of the syndrome are structural, namely the failure, for whatever reason, of existing systems to serve their populations, a clear failure of either the government or markets to deal with demographic pressures and new patterns of demand. Vendors provide a service that is clearly essential in the short run, and in some cases is well delivered and with reasonable cost margins, being inherently more costly than mains delivery. In this sense, service liberalisation in the sense of licensing. or at least recognising, the role of vendors could be advantageous (Kariuki, 2002; Nickson and Vargas, 2002). In any case, if the existing monopoly provision has failed, criminalising its alternative is also doomed to fail. Indeed, vendors might resist service extension if they see that their livelihoods may be taken away. There is anecdotal evidence from locations as disparate as Jakarta and Tegucigalpa that vendors, or those acting on their behalf, have resorted to violence to prevent the extension of existing reticulated networks. The notorious case of Cochabamba saw resistance to the contentious scheme, also vigorously opposed for other reasons, from vendors. The outcome in Cochabamba has been that the scheme was cancelled, but the level of provision has remained stuck at around half the population (Gleick *et al.*, 2002; Holland, 2005; Nickson and Vargas, 2002).

Paradoxically, the greatest scope for "real" liberalisation may come from local providers operating on a small scale, rather than from the mega-contracts of the type developed during the 1990s. Interest in such contracts is declining anyway, owing in part to the scars resulting from conflict on all sides, both personal and financial. Private investment is now 11% of water and sanitation services investment, having fallen from a peak in 1996/97 and water and sanitation services is only 2% of private investment in infrastructure services. UNDP reports that the decline is expected to continue (UNDP, 2003). The level of such investment in volume terms is now well below half the 1997 peak (Brown, 2004).

Mechanisms for extending service

What sort of mechanisms, if any, have been used to encourage service providers to increase provision of services to previously unserved or under-served regions or consumers?

A central question in the debate on the evolution of the water and sanitation services industry is how to reconcile the industry's need to finance its operations with the ability of consumers to pay. As levels of cost recovery rise, the issue moves into focus. When the cost/affordability dilemma becomes so acute as to threaten the viability of access programmes, some kind of subsidy is needed. Subsidies can be divided into internal and external categories. Some utilities have enough reasonably well-off customers to be able to cross subsidise internally. Others are so poor (or so inefficient) as to need external help to extend the service.

There are broadly two types of internal subsidies used to extend provision. The first is through stipulations imposed on providers as a condition of contract. The second uses differential prices through which, in theory at least, better-off consumers (including commercial customers) cross-subsidise poorer consumers.

External subsidies involve support from taxpayers or donors. These include explicit targeted subsidies intended to be reserved for the poor to help them to pay the higher prices. While contract stipulations and explicit targeted external subsidies are distinct types, the varieties of differentiated pricing both internally and externally funded are in practice elided.

Contract conditions

Conditions of contract and market incentives are not mutually exclusive; indeed, in an ideal contract they would reinforce each other. In the West Manila concession, the obligations were expressed as overall population percentages broken down by municipal areas over five years (Rosenthal, 2001). This breakdown into discrete geographical zones would seem desirable to avoid the syndrome observed in Buenos Aires, *i.e.* local people were unable to obtain information about the rollout programme in their area. This requires considerable advance work on demographic and hydrological surveys.

If the rollout is several years away, what are people to do in the meantime? Even five years is a long time in the life of a child. It would be very rigid, indeed distinctly illiberal, if the concession were granted on a monopoly basis and any small-scale operators in the district were actively forbidden from meeting consumer demand, as has been reported in Kenya (Morel and Loury, 2004) and Latin America (Ugaz, 2004). In Manila, the concessionaires that operate on a monopoly basis have granted subcontracts to local operators to meet such demands, and this is widely considered to be one of the more successful aspects of the Manila story. Contractual rigidity appears to have inhibited development, especially in the poorer districts and with respect to sanitation.

Relying on contractual instruction, however, is easier said than done. If the tariff paid to the network by the new users is below cost, the operator will have every incentive to seek renegotiation or to leave the most difficult locations, often the poorest, to the last. Thus the command and control aspect of the contract could well pull in the opposite direction from the expansion targets unless the tariffs for the new customers cover costs. Even non-commercial mechanisms, such as expansion targets, end up rubbing against commercial reality sooner or later.

Dual pricing – operator and consumer tariffs

Differential pricing can distinguish between distinct categories of consumers or levels of consumption, and this is often attempted through social tariffs (see Box 4.6).

The notion of a subsidised tranche of consumption implies that above that level, the product will be charged at cost, or higher, in order to recoup the cost of the reduced price for the first tranche. This requires a certain degree of cost accounting which may be absent. Sometimes in consequence, sometimes as a principle, governments can decide to separate out consumer tariffs completely from operator costs and pay the difference as a more or less generalised subsidy. In other words, the operator may receive a tariff for service which covers cost plus a margin, but bears no relation to the lower price actually paid by the consumer. The difference can be made up by the commissioning authority, usually the municipality. That way there is an incentive for the operator to continue to connect and serve regardless of the consumer's income level. Such an arrangement is a feature of *affermage* contracts[6] (Brocklehurst 2001, 2003; Brocklehurst and Janssens 2004).

Box 4.6. Social tariffs[1]

Affordability is clearly an important part of access. To meet this reality many governments introduce tranches of free or cheap water in their service contracts. The South African example given above, is a national standard, which amounts to six cubic metres (m^3) per month per household. Other examples to be found within contracts are:

Senegal: social tariff below $20m^3$ over 60 days.

Gabon: social tariff up to $15m^3$ per month.

Cote d'Ivoire. social tariff up to 18 m^3 per month.

La Paz/El Alto: reduced tariff up to $30m^3$ per month.

Tangiers**:** subsidised tariff up to $8m^3$ per month.

Chile: reduced tariff up to 20 m^3 per household pr month.

Belgium/Flanders: free water for the first 15 m^3 *per person* per year.

1. In theory a social tariff is one which is explicitly subsidised, in other words that tranche of consumption is charged below cost recovery. If the bill is picked up by the government, as in Chile, then this is an external subsidy. If charged to other consumers as in Flanders, then it is internal. In practice, this distinction may be difficult to draw in accounting terms.

Source: For Belgium and Flanders, see Box 4.8; for the rest, World Bank/PPIAF (2006).

The regulator needs to take care to ensure that the relationship between the customer tariff and the operator tariff is rational. If the operator tariff is much higher than the customer tariff, then the sum of money contributed from the public purse may be so high as to starve the service (or the municipality) of much needed resources and thus lead operating subsidies to compete with capital for network extension. A way around this is to charge a transitional tariff after installation to help newly connected families to start budgeting for a different system with higher overall volumes of consumption. In theory, this can be cross-subsidised by customer tariffs in the already connected areas that are higher than the operator tariff so that there is in effect a cross-subsidy operating between newly served areas and previously served areas.

In practice, this proves difficult for three reasons. First, care needs to be taken to ensure that poor people in already served areas are not penalised by such a step. There is always a danger of geographical generalisations. While it is nearly always the case that unconnected households are poor, it does not follow that all connected households are *not* poor. Most of the world is not so segregated as to allow such easy assumptions. While

6. In contrast, concession contracts typically transfer greater risk to the company and require customer tariffs to cover operator costs.

this may be fortunate from the broader social point of view, it hugely complicates the social administration of the water and sanitation services. To allow for the existence of poor people in connected or even well-off neighbourhoods, it may be necessary to introduce individual subsidy mechanisms to ensure that they are not penalised by geographical transfers of resources.

Box 4.7. Senegal

The forerunner of Veolia Water *(Generale des Eaux)* was in place in Senegal at the time of independence in 1960, and the system was nationalised in 1971. In 1996 a ten-year enhanced *affermage* contract was signed with *Senegalaise des Eaux* (SDE, whose majority shareholder is SAUR of France) as the operator, with the assets still held by a state-owned asset-holding company SONES *(Societe Nationale des Eaux du Senegal)*. According to Brocklehurst and Janssens (2004), this division of responsibilities contributed to the positive performance of the water service in increasing the number of connections by 35% and the volume of water supplied by 20%. Consequently, leakage reduced from 31% to 22% and bill collection rose to the very high level of 97% (including the government as bill payer).

While the SONES/SDE split is quite commonly remarked upon as a formula worthy of emulation, of equal importance is the tariff formula which is bound up in the *affermage* contract. The central feature is the separation of the operator tariff from the consumer tariff. The operator does not set the tariff and SDE's income depends less on the tariff collected than on the volume of water delivered. This means that there is no need to discriminate against poor consumers on the basis of their inability to pay and their payment of only the lower social tariff. The system effectively limits the commercial risks assumed by the operator in trying to serve the poor and thus attempts to break away from the viability/affordability dilemma.

However, as the operator's remuneration is based on a proportion of the average tariff, there is a danger that a heavy skew in favour of social tariff customers would undermine its remuneration and indeed the revenue coming into the sector. This illustrates the common observation that social tariffs are often a useful device for reducing consumer resistance to inclusion in the water system for fear of being unable to pay the tariff, but they may outlive their usefulness in the long run. Gabon (Box 4.13), where use of social tariffs is declining, gives grounds for optimism in this respect (Tremolet *et al.*, 2002).

Second, in setting up transitional tariffs following initial connection it is expensive to allow such subsidies to remain in place indefinitely. They have a way of becoming permanent and may be captured by elites or extended to such a wide band of the population as to defeat their selective purpose. The classic example of elite capture is that of the special allowances made in the Former Soviet Union (FSU) for members of the armed forces and other functionaries, which in due course reached 40% of the population (Simpson, 2003).

Cases of indiscriminate subsidy are widely found, for example in Colombia (see Box 4.11) (Gomez-Lobo *et al.*, 2003; Clarke and Wallsten, 2003) This can produce results which are economically catastrophic for the industry and socially perverse.

Third, today's rehabilitated slum is tomorrow's desirable residential neighbourhood. Following installation of public utility services living standards rise, indeed that is one of the aims of the exercise. But at that point it is important for scarce resources to move on to other unserved neighbourhoods. If not, the water utility will find that it has to serve an ever larger customer base either at a loss to itself or at greater expense to existing customers who may object to such an indefinite cross subsidy (Brocklehurst, 2003).

Reluctant to face their anger, governments may instead insist on an indiscriminate subsidy.

There are instances in which the dual tariff strategy seems to have helped to extend access. Senegal is a notable case (Box 4.7).

Targeted subsidies

Have policies aimed at ensuring universal service used mechanisms aimed at the consumer (e.g. *subsidies, vouchers)?*

An alternative to subsidising the system is subsidising identified individual consumers, thus allowing the industry to function rationally while taking care of extraneous social problems on their own merits. Although theoretically poor consumers could be paid in cash, in practice, it is easier to administer the subsidy through the tariff and billing system or through physical distribution of a given quantity of water. Various examples are given in Boxes 4.8 to 4.10.

Box 4.8. Belgium – Flanders

Allocations of free or cheap tranches of water, based solely on households, treat small households much more generously in per capita terms than large households. In effect they discriminate against large families or those who occupy multi-occupied dwellings who are often the poorest. To avoid penalising large families, the Flemish scheme calculates the tranches on a per capita basis (unlike South Africa which converts its pledge of 25 litres per day per person to six cubic metres per month per household). The Flemish practice certainly reduces the bias but at the price of greatly increasing the "free" water provided. This necessitates a draconian increase in the marginal rate charged against the next tranche of consumption in order to recoup the resultant costs.

Since 1997, the first 15 m^3 per head per year of water consumed in each household in Flanders is provided free of charge. This was introduced in the context of rising expenditure due to environmental programmes. According to Peter Van Humbeeck of the Socio-Economic Council of Flanders, it: "has the virtue of being: small enough to ensure that very few households will face a zero price for their water, so there is still some incentive to conserve water; politically defensible by covering a certain core of basic (essential) water use in the home; equitable, especially between households of different sizes because the allowance is not based on the household as a unit but on the number of people in the household"

Source: *Water pricing in Flanders. The 1997 reform in the domestic water supply sector.* 1999 Sintra conference, Pricing Water: Economics, Environment and Society

Box 4.9. Chile

Chile has comprehensive urban supply and metering and the structure is simple: a standing charge and volumetric charges with no block tariff variation (Chavez and Quiroga, 2002). There is a seasonal tariff. For families below certain income levels, up to 85% of their fixed and variable charges are discounted up to a maximum of 20 m^3 per month. (In practice this means that roughly the first 15 m^3 are free out of an average consumption of about 23 m^3). The water companies send a bill minus the subsidy and they are compensated directly by the local authority. This means that the company receives all its revenue while indirectly providing a social subsidy for which it is reimbursed by national government via the municipalities. Chavez and Quiroga calculate that by the end of 1997 subsidy take-up covered about 17% of all families. In a variation of the scheme, some municipalities allow for vouchers or stamps to be taken up by consumers to pay for their rebate. The concept behind the scheme is that 5% of household income is considered to be a proxy for willingness to pay.

Box 4.10. The United Kingdom

The UK has gone even further down the selective road, following concerns about the effect of recently introduced metering on certain poor consumers. Metered customers who fall into the category of vulnerable groups pay the water company's average charges for their water and sewerage, and so are effectively subsidised by other customers if it is assumed that they would otherwise pay higher charges due to metering. Fewer than expected applied to the water companies to take up this option after its introduction under the 1999 Water Industry Act, *i.e.* less than a 1% take up rate. This is not 1% of all households, it is 1% of those within the very tightly defined group of households defined as eligible for assistance. Help is reserved for the neediest of the needy by virtue of being restricted to identified demographic groups (large families and people with medical conditions) who then have effectively to pass a means test (prior receipt of a means-tested benefit) and finally it is restricted to metered consumers. This triple test would be highly selective even with 100% take up of those eligible. Four years after its introduction, the system is a failure (NCC, 2002).

Even if it were affordable, it is difficult to see the Flemish scheme operating in developing countries. Indeed it might be difficult to operate outside of Belgium for it depends on local registration of residents, which is obligatory under Belgian law. It is hard to see this being acceptable to semi-legal or illegal settlement dwellers or to migrant workers or illegal immigrants.

So while the Flemish scheme universalises the free tranche, the Chilean scheme has the effect of reserving it for the poor, with external finance, rather than a rising marginal rate as happens in Flanders.

How have such schemes been targeted at the truly needy and have leakages to other groups been avoided, if at all?

The brutal answers to these questions are: *i)* badly and *ii)* leakage has not been avoided. This does not mean that the failures are due to incompetence. They are due to the intrinsic nature of the subsidies (see Box 4.11). Targeted help has been attempted in two ways, either through help in kind or through financial subsidy. In practice, targeting is extremely difficult both for subsidies in kind and in cash. Indeed it is impossible without extremely high administrative costs in all but the most segregated communities.

It is very hard to devise subsidies in the form of tranches of free water that do not leave out some poor consumers (errors of exclusion) and do not include non-poor consumers (errors of inclusion) (Komives, 2004; Brocklehurst, 2003). This is because geographical segregation by income level is not absolute in areas where services are available. There are some exceptions, such as smaller South African townships for historical reasons (the larger townships have internal social strata). However, generally speaking geographical districts are not an accurate surrogate for poverty, except for the unserved areas. There, in contrast, one can argue that almost by definition the unserved are poor. This means that for a public subsidy to ensure the simplest and most accurate targeting it should be focused on connecting the unserved rather than on holding down prices for the served.

Box 4.11. Chile and Colombia

A very illuminating study compares the Chilean and Colombian water subsidy policies (Gomez-Lobo and Contreras, 2003). The juxtaposition is apt, for, as mentioned above, Chile aims to target people while Colombia aims to target locations. In both cases the schemes are predicated on quite detailed registers, of dwellings in Colombia and of households in Chile. The funding for the Chilean scheme comes from the national government and for the Colombian scheme it comes in theory from cross-subsidies between better-off and poor consumers operating through geographical zoning as proxies for social groups; the idea is that the top two groups will subsidise the bottom three. In practice the survey found that only 1% of distributed benefits were funded by negative transfers (*i.e.* internal). In conclusion, the paper finds significant problems with both schemes: errors of inclusion in the Colombian scheme and errors of exclusion and inclusion in the Chilean one.

Gomez-Lobo and Contreras conclude that in Chile, about 25% of the population should receive the subsidy but does not. Furthermore the Chilean subsidy law defines beneficiary households as those in the first two income deciles, and yet "close to 70% of beneficiaries are not in this group".

The Colombian scheme escapes from the errors of exclusion, effectively by adopting a scheme which is so relaxed in eligibility terms that "close to 95% of households received some amount of subsidy". In other words the solution to errors of exclusion of a selective benefit is in practice to make it all but universal.

What were the administrative costs of any such assistance schemes?

To be effective, a means-tested (income-related) scheme depends on an existing and viable social security system. However, the costs of any means-tested scheme tend to be very high, for means tests are by nature labour-intensive. It is not a simple matter to define income, especially by household, as there may be more than one income. The poor often have irregular or highly variable incomes – that is part of the nature of poverty – and the income may be difficult to quantify precisely if it is informal or if wages are paid in kind.

However, even in countries with working social security systems, it should not be assumed that a means-tested system will function well. The administrative costs of mainstream means-tested systems in the United Kingdom for most of the post-war period have been around 13% of the money paid out (CPAG, 2004) for a relatively straightforward means tests (if that is not a contradiction in terms). However, benefit payments linked to water (or for any item of household expenditure) are not straightforward: the calculation is three-cornered because a means-tested benefit that is intended to provide a guaranteed minimum income pays the difference between actual income and a predetermined scale rate established by the public administration. This is complex enough, but if the payment is to take account of an expenditure item as well, then the administration has to take into account not only the scale rate and actual income but also the relevant (third) expenditure element for which proof will also be required.

If by some process of sympathetic magic, the technical problems could be resolved, there remain wider social issues which it would be foolish to ignore. These include the poverty trap, which causes recipients to lose benefits as their incomes rise, so that there is little net benefit. There is also the problem of stigma. The poor often hate to receive benefits, as these are considered to be the badge of poverty (CPAG, 2004). The author's evidence for this outside of the United Kingdom and the United States is essentially anecdotal, but is based on observations in countries as different from the above as Russia.

The reality of stigma cannot be ignored if it erodes the whole basis on which water-charging policy is constructed, *i.e.* the notion that the poor are being looked after.

The administrative costs of the Chilean scheme can be imagined from the description of the individual assessment that has to be carried out. Eligibility is determined by a score based on points derived from information gathered during a personal interview conducted at home. There are 50 questions in nine sections covering general information, environmental conditions, health, identification of family members, occupation and earnings, other subsidies, education and wealth, plus dwelling size and ownership of consumer durables (Gomez-Lobo and Contreras, 2003). It is hard to imagine that this can be done without implying an element of stigma and it must be very expensive in administrative terms. Foster, Gomez-Lobo and Halpern estimated that in Panama identifying low-income households cost USD10 per case, not an outrageous figure but more than the average monthly subsidy received by the lowest quintile. (see Walker *et al.*, 2000). De Moor (1999) reported that the high administration cost of the Flemish scheme contributed to the significant rise in expenditure on water borne by consumers.

How effective have all the above mechanisms been in extending service?

It is possible that the kinds of subsidy discussed above have helped extend provision in particular cases. The record of South Africa is particularly impressive, a combination of tariff subsidy and connection subsidy. However, if the objective was to concentrate subsidy on the poor then subsidies through the tariff system have been quite ineffective in all but the most segregated societies, where one can clearly earmark certain areas as poor. Study after study has found that errors of exclusion and of inclusion are endemic in block tariffs and social tariffs. Yet in political terms they are difficult to abolish precisely because so many people benefit. Indeed one might say that they are popular because they do not work.

An aspect that seems scarcely to have been researched is the opportunity cost of subsidies to drinking water and its effect on the sanitation sector. As mentioned above, sanitation is very neglected. Intuitively, drinking water subsidies will divert funds from sanitation as they are administered (if at all) from the same budget. To the extent that sanitation receives any tariff subsidy at all, it is usually based on water consumption which acts as a surrogate for sanitation (water in/water out). Yet over one billion people receive water services and yet are not connected to any sanitation service.

Furthermore, a scheme based on water consumption levels requires accurate metering at the household level. In many developed economies, including the United Kingdom, Ireland and Quebec, this is still not the case on a large scale. In the former Soviet Union, metering is done by block but hardly ever by household. In many countries many consumers are not metered and if they are, the meters often do not work as they tend to become faulty with interrupted supply. Yet without this most basic of tools social tariffs are difficult to apply other than at the physical point of distribution such as the Durban water tanks in South Africa or the water rationed by neighbourhood vendors.

Social tariffs are of course ineffective in the absolute sense for consumers who are not connected at all. Many studies have concluded that the best targeting of subsidies is to subsidise the cost of connection (Foster *et al.*, 2004; Brocklehurst, 2003; Komives, 2004). It should be recalled here that because sanitation does not yet figure in the household budgets of many, then whatever user subsidies are made available should be concentrated on that sector.

Great attention is paid in this chapter to the practice of subsidising people rather than systems, because in classical economic theory this is how things should be (Clarke and Wallsten, 2003). The theory is that industries should restrict themselves to doing what they do best – delivering services – while governments should deal with and provide for wider problems arising from social conditions. In practice, such elegant logic is defeated by the intrinsic inefficiencies of complex means-tested calculations and indiscriminate geographically based subsidies. As a result, a different classical economic precept, that of cost effectiveness is violated. The author concludes, in agreement with the WSP recommendation on tariffs in 2002, that "access, not consumption should be subsidised" (PPIAF/WSP, 2002).

Technological adaptability

Have the mechanisms or policies used encouraged providers to develop new or innovative solutions to universal service problems or have they focused on the use of existing technologies and solutions?

The sheer scale of the demographic crisis facing many developing countries has forced them to adapt to existing circumstances without waiting for full network rollout. This has necessitated improvising with low-technology solutions such as above-ground plastic pipe technology rather than underground pipes which take much longer to install and for which the logistics are difficult in dense urban areas. The advantage of plastic or rubber pipes is that they can be used flexibly and can be easily removed after more permanent installations are made. Some of these solutions have been found in private concessions, some have been pioneered as part of a drive to improve access. They have also featured in partnerships with neighbourhood associations (see Box 4.12).

Manila offers an example of a successful collaboration between a major concessionaire a local small company and local residents groups (see Box 4.12). Other local schemes have also developed under public ownership. Low-technology water distribution takes place under licence in Dhaka, Bangladesh, in partnership with local NGOs (Brocklehurst, 2003). The Durban public utility operates a system of water tanks which are used to facilitate the distribution of the "free" tranche of 200 litres per day in line with current government policy. Householders pay for the feeder pipe from the mains to the tanks, dig the trench and mount the tanks on concrete blocks (Brendan Martin, private correspondence).

Box 4.12. Manila

Perhaps the best known of these schemes is the Bayan Tubig scheme in Manila. Small private operators work in partnership with local community-based organisations which help with the community mapping process and the negotiating of "wayleaves" through the informal settlements. Water is delivered in conventional mains to the edge of a defined zone and then transported by above-ground pipe connections to meters from which each family makes its connection using low-cost plastic. The families are responsible for the upkeep. Connection costs are relatively high at USD 97 but as the current costs are some 25% lower than vendor costs for poor families it is worthwhile for them to connect (PPIAF/WSP, 2002; Rosenthal, 2001). A significant detail is that the concessionaire has also introduced a two-year interest-free payment scheme to enable the connections to be made. By the end of the Manila concession period it is intended that some 600 000 low-income households will be served in this way, and indeed, some of the small operators, notably Inpart Engineering, is no longer small.

Particularly widespread is the development of condominial water and sewerage systems, used in Brazil, South Africa and Pakistan (WDR, 2004). The difference between this and conventional systems is that instead of individual connections to the mains there is a common connection, the network runs through householders' dwellings and they take responsibility for upkeep. Such improvised low-technology systems will doubtless proliferate. The following points are worth noting.

First, in Karachi and Dhaka, neighbourhood associations have assumed the capital cost for the system as well as the running costs, even when, as in Manila, the connection costs are relatively high. Second, problems of exclusivity have been reported in both the public sector, in Kenya (Morel and Loury, 2004), and in the private sector, where exclusivity is seen as a way to protect concessionaires from competition for customers from low-cost producers (PPIAF/WSP, 2002). While this may be a customary reaction in commercial terms, it contradicts the point of PSP which is to improve access. Moreover, local low-cost producers seem to serve those unserved by the concessionnaires. To allow for such improvisation, the Manila and Cote d'Ivoire contracts recognise explicitly the potential role of third parties. However, the contracts for West Jakarta and Gabon, to take two examples, do not seem to envisage this (World Bank, 2004 draft).

The perverse consequences of exclusivity are shown by a study of latrine workers in Dar-es-Salaam, where the city used to have a monopoly of cesspit emptying (Kariuki and Wandera, 2000). As the service was unable to keep up with demand, richer clients operated a system of express payments for emptying the pits with vacuum equipment while the poor employed frogmen to empty the pits manually. They then dumped the ordure illegally, which led, predictably, to protests from those nearby. The monopoly then effectively suppressed the service, condemned informal workers to appalling working conditions and transferred the public health risk to others. The city then agreed to operate a licensing system for private operators with the result that charges have fallen and the numbers served increased. At Consumers International's regional conference for Africa in 2002, Mukami Kariuki advocated that municipalities relinquish such monopolies and allow alternative provision through a legal framework incorporating community-based organisations. She pointed to perverse aspects of the legislation such as the inability of public utilities to count alternative providers in coverage targets or business plans, as well as the monopoly provisions which in effect rendered alternative providers illegal. At times they were attacked, and their already unpleasant and dangerous work often had to be done under cover of darkness.

It is perhaps because sanitation has been such a neglected sector and so much harder to finance than drinking water, that, perhaps out of desperation, some of the most innovative small-scale schemes have developed. In Maharashtra, India's largest state with almost 100 million people, 45% of subsidised latrines were not actually used. A more localised scheme based on local competition bids (the Gadge Baba scheme) has produced a far better rate of use (WDR, 2004). An Indian NGO, Sulabh International, has developed low-cost, low flush toilets with dual leeching pits to allow one to be in use while the other is emptied (UNDP, 2003).

The common theme is that exclusivity risks stifling innovation, especially in the field of sanitation. In that sector, nothing is to be lost by abandoning it, for there is very little commercial competition to undermine anyway. The Water and Sanitation Programme recommends that: "Exclusivity provisions that create barriers to alternative providers whose services are orientated toward the poor should be avoided" (WSP, 2002). The issue again is not a public/private one, but liberalisation. The consequences of repressing small low-technology solutions can be severe.

Regulatory bodies

What sort of regulatory bodies exist or have been established to regulate the service in question?

It is widely accepted that introducing major PSP contracts in the absence of regulatory reform in the utility sector has been a mistake (Foster *et al.*, 2004; see also Chapter 6 in this volume). Theoretically, it should be possible to carry out regulatory reform even while the service is in the public sector, but this does not seem to happen very often in the water sector. Regulators frequently operate from a distance within central government ministries or local governments regulate themselves. It is becoming fairly common for the water sector to become a mixed economy, with PSP permitted under a loose national regulatory framework, with local governments deciding on the best model to adopt. Brazil is an example that comes to mind.

Another is Hungary, where, in 1995, the state-owned water industry gave way to municipal control in most cases (the state retained control of five regional companies) (Hall *et al.*, 2004). Municipalities make their own decisions whether to reform internally (as in Debrecen) or to adopt PSP (as in Szeged and Budapest) with the central government having only a supervisory role. As the result of decentralisation, the number of companies increased from 28 to 232. In such circumstances, one might argue that there is a need, not so much for control, as for supervision and support.

Interviews for the Global Water Scoping Review (Urquhart and Moore, 2004) detected a feeling that local administrations had come to regard newly contracted services as something over which they had relinquished responsibility, a headache that they had rid themselves of. They may indeed have relinquished *control* to all intents and purposes, but *responsibility* is another matter. There are dangers here, for there is an imbalance in experience between local governments that issue contracts and the companies with which they contract. Local governments may issue contracts for as long as 30 years with only occasional reviews, while multinational contractors draw up contracts on a regular basis. In discussions, industry representatives accepted the existence of this imbalance and also accepted the need for an expert body within the local government. Frequently this expert role is played by transaction advisors, but their role was criticised as being transitory and sometimes superficial, failing to take account of the complexities of a given location.

Failing a better balance of expertise on site, companies can end up almost self-regulating. Superficially one might imagine that some welcome this, indeed in the Netherlands this is almost the case (Mohajeri *et al.*, 2003). However, some companies have indicated that it is not in their interest since, when things go wrong, they are fully exposed to public discontent and thus to arbitrary changes by shifting local administrations. Consumers International's members in the Sahel region have drawn particular attention to this situation when water and electricity are produced and distributed by the same company as is customary in that region for reasons of local geography and hydrology (CI, 2001).

Without clearer regulatory oversight, in the words of Foster *et al.* (2004), "Regulation remains implicit or is incorporated into the contract for private participation." This becomes a sort of privatisation of the regulatory function or rather, the ceding of regulation to the ultimate power of the courts, where battle is joined by opposing lawyers. Judicial review or litigation undoubtedly has a place in the range of sanctions, but the record is one of bitterness and rancour.

There has been less movement towards autonomous public regulators in the water and sanitation services sector than in telecoms and energy. The clearest example of independent regulatory bodies in developing countries is the Latin American *Superintendencias* which may exercise a regulatory function (as in Chile) or a compliance monitoring function as in Colombia (where there is responsibility for public and private sectors alike).

In Chile it is worth noting that the *Superintendencia* was established before privatisation. From 1988 to 1990 state-owned enterprises were reformed into 13 state-owned corporations which covered 93% of the connected population by 1993 (with small private companies operating alongside) (Sanchez and Sanhueza, 2000). What followed was a substantial increase in prices, which enabled a fourfold increase in investment between 1990 and 1995 and marked increases in coverage to reach 99% urban water connection and 89% sewerage connection, with lower figures for rural areas (82% water). This took place during the period of public ownership. Some would argue that it was the prospect of private ownership which provided the spur to such reforms (critics describe this as a process of "fattening up" the industry for sale). Given that this often happens in utility sectors before privatisation there is undoubtedly some truth in the observation. Nevertheless, the fact is that reform took place under public ownership in Chile, under the supervision of a public regulator.

Public sector reform revisited

The discussion of regulation poses the old question: Can the public sector reform itself? Conventional wisdom has long been that it cannot. World Bank staffer John Nellis (1994) seemed to believe that even the exceptions proved the rule: "In the few cases where governments do establish and maintain the precedence of commercial aims, the results are very good. But they tend not to last. In most instances there is a pronounced backsliding. The common story is that bad times make for good policies... Ultimately, politics trumps economics."

Since then, attitudes to the public sector at the World Bank have become a little less judgemental, given some of the high profile failures of PSP contracts. Reforms of public sector services and their regulators are now enjoying a new lease on life, partly because the rate of private investment has slowed so dramatically, and partly because the sheer mathematics of the sector requires action by existing ownership. Even if the MDG targets are met, which is by no means guaranteed, it will take until 2015 just to halve the numbers of the presently unserved. What is to happen in the meantime?

The World Bank recognises that with over 90% of water and sanitation services in public hands, improvement of public sector performance is necessary regardless of PSP. Indeed, 70% of the Bank's lending goes to the traditional public sector and Jamal Saghir, Director of Energy and Water at the Bank, explicitly and publicly said during World Water Week 2004 that the Bank would lend irrespective of PSP if the scheme was sound, a policy he later described as "Engagement anywhere along the spectrum" (Saghir, 2004).

Foster *et al.* (2004) sum up the necessary reforms as follows:

> "A number of autonomy enhancing measures can be taken within the context of public sector service provision. These include the registration of the utility as a corporation, the establishment of a barrier between utility accounting and public administration, the signature of performance contracts with the executive, governance reforms aimed at increasing the independence of the utility board, and changes in the legal status of the enterprise (for example, through conversion to a public limited company that is freed from public sector procurement, employment and investment regulations)."

Recent work by the World Bank on a manual for public sector reform advocates moves in this direction (Baietti *et al.,* 2006). One might observe that the Bank is saying the public sector should be reformed to make it behave like the private sector. Indeed both critics and supporters would probably agree, especially in terms of cost recovery for example. This author, responding to an earlier draft by Kingdom and van Ginneken (2004), certainly accepted the need for many of the reforms listed. The danger, he argued during the consultation, was that the Bank's view was essentially unilinear, pushing the public sector in the direction indicated above but neglecting the possibility of other models, such as co-operatives, some of which could be nested within the more classical corporate structure.

So, *faute de mieux,* public sector regulators are having to reform public sector operators, come what may. In this context, it is not only liberalisation that holds promise for the future but also basic reforms of the present systems so that they operate in a more transparent way, even at the most rudimentary level. The need is for reform in the direction of a fuller customer base (fewer legal exemptions from payment), higher levels of payment (lower levels of delinquency), followed by higher cost recovery levels to promote sustainability. Would consumers not resist this? One should not assume that they would.

Some of the most effective public sectors operate under regulators with considerable public involvement, often by consumer organisations, some of them established for that purpose, as in the United States. This is increasingly the case in Africa where consumer associations are becoming involved with regulatory boards, sometimes as members, sometimes as interlocutors (CI ROAF, 2001). In Latin America, Porto Algre, discussed above, is an example. Costa Rica has perhaps the most elaborate of all mechanisms for consulting consumers, with no fewer than 1 600 consumer associations working with the public utilities (ADERASA, 2003). India's public participation programme in the Kerala water sector has been highly praised by the World Bank (Hall, 2000). It would appear that given the inevitable continued prevalence of the public sector for some time, there is no option but to reform it by exposing it to pressures from citizen-consumers.

Sometimes consumers surprise the public bodies by their capacity to take a long view. In 2001, the Russian Confederation of Consumer Unions issued a manifesto calling for public utility reform with preconditions for moving towards cost recovery, a move which they saw as both inevitable and, in due course, in the interests of consumers (Simpson, 2003). These were as follows:

> "Improving the regulatory and legal base of public utilities, especially the "transparency...of the regulatory system; relevant mechanisms for social security; creation of contracts (for consumers) and other mechanisms of responsibility, singling out in particular that consumers should pay only for services actually received".

In other words, moves towards cost recovery should be balanced by moves towards individual and collective consumer rights and state guarantees that the poor will be protected. Given the uncertainty of what was involved in moving towards cost recovery in practice, this was a courageous position for a consumer body to take.

Clearly consumers will become more demanding as prices rise. Indeed, this should form part of the feedback essential for sector reform. One should not assume a reflex resistance to price increases in all circumstances.

Individual consumer rights

The increasing articulation of consumer pressures in public arenas has led to renewed emphasis on another dimension of regulatory reform: resolving individual consumer disputes and complaints, and developing and protecting consumer rights. Sometimes these can be dealt with by improved complaint mechanisms and by codes of practice that auomatically compensate for service failures, as under the UK Guaranteed Standards Scheme. But there will always be the need for individual resolution of individual disputes. The problem of a judicial approach in this area is that the sums involved are frequently too small to justify court action but are nevertheless significant for the consumers concerned.

Some interesting developments are taking place worldwide. The Latin American *defensores del pueblos* (for example in Peru and Argentina) have acted as Ombudsmen dealing with individual consumer complaints about public utilities operated by local or national government. The Peruvian *defensor* has been particularly singled out for praise and has become something of a popular hero.[7] The idea is also developing in southeastern Europe, where the Macedonian Ombudsman already deals with water issues and district heating (CI, 2000) and consideration is being given to developing a consumer Ombudsman in Bosnia Herzegovina with jurisdiction over public utilities.[8] There could be scope for consumer involvement in resolving disputes. For example, one of the most intractable issues is how to deal with particular consumers who have not paid their bills, which may lead to collective sanctions such as block cut-offs. Consumer bodies may be able to establish the trust which the service provider has been unable to gain.

It is gradually being recognised that consumers are not simply a stakeholder interest to be assuaged. Satisfying their needs is, after all, the purpose of production, and they may have something to contribute to the regulatory process. There is a danger of placing too much weight on the technocratic relationship of the public regulator with the regulated industry. As most of the world's water and sanitation services sector is run at local level, it would be unwise and unfair to overlook the municipal dimension. Local decisions are often criticised as politicised, arbitrary and opportunistic, and this is doubtless sometimes true. But there is a danger of denigrating the proper role of politics, as Nellis (1994) seemed to do. Water and sanitation services are a political issue and rightly so. There are important decisions to be made at the political level.

How sustainable is the reform process in the long term?

We have already noted doubts about sustainability of public sector reform. There are in fact serious questions over the sustainability of liberalisation involving PSP. Indeed, a

7. Mr. Santistevan was spoken of as a future president of Peru.

8. Ongoing programme under the single economic space of Bosnia-Herzegovina.

salient feature of PSP contracts in water and sanitation services has been the high frequency of renegotiation.

Renegotiation

Van den Berg (2000) points out correctly that renegotiation of contracts is "difficult, time-consuming and risky". This is if anything an understatement. The rate of renegotiation is far higher for water and sanitation services contracts than for other infrastructure sectors. In a study of 1 000 infrastructure concessions in the Latin America/Caribbean region between 1985 and 2000, Guasch (2004) reported a renegotiation rate of 30%. Excluding telecoms raised the rate to 41.5%, while the average rate for water and sanitation services reached the extraordinary level of 74%. The instability that this signifies is continuing, and at a recent World Bank seminar it was reported that 45% of water and sanitation services contracts are in litigation or are financially distressed, that is, in danger of insolvency.[9] The damage done by renegotiation is huge as it invariably leads to accusations of bad faith and sometimes to calls for termination of the relationship. This was the case in Argentina's Santa Fe province where the Provincial Assembly for the Right to Water, a coalition of environmental, citizens and consumer groups (including CI's members in Argentina) organised a referendum in which 250 000 voters called for the revocation of the concession held by *Aguas Provinciales de Santa Fe* (whose main stockholder was Suez). Labour unions also point to the frequency of renegotiation as evidence of bad faith on the part of the companies (Hall *et al.*, 2004, for Public Services International Research Unit).

Of course, the competitive bidding process brings its own dangers. Azurix paid a very high "canon fee" (concession charge), which most observers considered excessive, burdening both itself and the consumers to whom the charge was inevitably passed on. Similar dangers appeared in the Manila concession (consciously modelled on Buenos Aires in light of its early apparent success). This led the author to suggest at a recent WB seminar that there is at least a case for bids to be published at the tender stage rather than be surrounded by secrecy, a practice which has some precedents. There is a separate and equally important issue concerning the publication of the final agreed contract.

With competitive tendering there is a risk that bidders, in seeking to outdo each other in submitting bids for both the lowest tariff and the highest rate of extension, may make unrealistic offers. Water Aid/Tearfund (2003), in a wide-ranging appraisal of PSP, concluded that the Manila concession involved just such a "dive bid", and the author has had anecdotal confirmation from company employees that such things can happen if companies are sufficiently keen to obtain a contract. On the other hand, one can well envisage situations in which renegotiation is not unreasonable. By definition, squatter or slum settlements have an uncertain cadastre and their populations are frequently undefined. The geography, hydrology and geology of a site may be very uncertain at the outset of a project and the physical state of the infrastructure almost undefined. The task of surveying the site in the detail required may be technically difficult and even dangerous, and factors with a huge bearing on utility company finances such as levels of non-payment and theft, are necessarily approximate. All of this adds up to arguments for pre-contract surveys, large tasks in themselves, before full contracts are entered. Yet the

9. A World Bank seminar in London in November 2004 indicated that the percentage of World Bank financed water and sanitation services projects "at risk" had declined since 1995, but the level remained at 17%.

delay that this would involve may be unattractive to a local administration which is understandably impatient to embark on a programme of reform.

It has been said that some systems, in particular the French, have a tradition of renegotiation for the above reasons.[10] Other traditions regard renegotiation as a sign of failure. If there is such legal/cultural ambiguity it needs to be dispelled at the start of the contract process and the possibility of renegotiation needs to be made known to the public. In the meantime high rates of renegotiation will continue to discredit the PSP process. Clearly there is something seriously wrong if there is a high level of renegotiation, litigation and distress.

Some PSP contracts do work, but it does not happen by "the magic of the market", it has to be underpinned by governance. Furthermore, as in Chile and in Gabon (see Box 4.13), such examples often follow on from public-sector reform. Gabon is interesting for a range of beneficial outcomes.

Box 4.13. Gabon

In 1997 *Societe d'Energie et d'Eau de Gabon* (SEEG) signed a 20-year contract with the Gabonese government for water and electricity services throughout the country. The contract was ten years in preparation, during which time the legal framework was adopted, tariffs were raised to levels that reflected costs and staff was reduced between 1989 and 1997. The system had expanded rapidly since nationalisation in the early 1960s. This puts into perspective Veolia's 2004 report that prices were reduced by 17.5% in 1997 and had since then remained below the rate of inflation.

From 1997 to 2004, the number of people served by SEEG increased by 68% for drinking water (Fonlladosa, 2005). A major element of the strategy was the cross-subsidy between the electricity sector and the water service. A further point of interest is that the government still carries out major investment. This is somewhat unusual for a concession agreement; such arrangements are more common in *affermage* contracts.

A further mechanism of cross-subsidy is the use of social tariffs (up to 15 m^3 of water per month). The coverage rate for reasonable access comes to about 90%. What may be of great significance is the fact that social tariff use is falling as consumption and incomes rise. If so this is encouraging as experience in other countries has shown how difficult it is to move away from consumption subsidies which tend to remain and thus to dilute the revenue needed to extend the service to the poorest.

This relatively successful record has been facilitated by adequate hydrological resources and the country's reasonable level of prosperity. Gabon has a per capita income four times that of most Sub-Saharan nations, ranking only below South Africa and Mauritius. This is of great help in the cost-recovery strategy for the prices, while low by European standards, are not negligible at about EUR 45 a month for the two services for about 60% of households and EUR 15 a month for a further 30%.

A major factor was the signing of a debt moratorium in 1999 with the government. Before then, the government, as in many countries, was a major debtor of the company. It has now undertaken to pay off its arrears by 2004. This of course raises the question as to whether consumers should also be allowed to make a fresh start of this nature.

Dividends rose from the contractually guaranteed 6.5% of the share price in 1997 to 20% in 2000. It has made 80% of the contractually required investments, all on a self-financing basis, and most local targets have been met (Tremolet and Neale, 2002).

10. The author is grateful to Ken Caplan of Building Partnerships for Development for this point.

At the time of writing, another major PSP contract has been terminated (La Paz/El Alto), which had been considered something of a model in terms of its public consultation procedures. The future of large-scale PSP contracts seems to be far less secure at this time than that of the public sector, which will always have to be the actor of last resort.[11] It may be that the water and sanitation services world is returning to traditional PSP in which private contractors operate under task-based contracts as has been the case over the past two decades. The irony is that some of the most celebrated municipal services, for example those of Porto Alegre and Stockholm, pay most of their receipts to private sub-contractors. The question is not: "Will PSP continue?", but in what form will it do so?

Summary

This chapter has addressed a number of questions.

How are universal access goals defined in the water and sanitation services sector?

The answer is: with difficulty and with great local variation. Access goals for water and sanitation services vary greatly between countries, inevitably, because global improved access goals as defined by the World Health Organisation (WHO) are extremely modest. Yet huge numbers do not have supply that meets even those standards. Coverage targets and standards are interdependent. Service coverage is not the same thing as access to a reticulated system. Chasing the MDG numerical targets without bearing in mind the needs of the total population may have perverse consequences. "Some for all not more for some" should be the guiding principle.

How has liberalization – particularly in terms of eliminating barriers for foreign providers – affected access to services for the poor?

The record is mixed, and one cannot necessarily demonstrate that improvements would not have happened under non-liberalised services, given the same level of investment. Broadly speaking; programmes operating under liberalised regimes have raised coverage (and also prices) but have not spread the service as widely as they could have, given better direction of subsidies. There are sound social reasons for network price increases when only a (usually better off) minority of a population is served by a subsidised network.

The poor pay more. Price differentials between different modes of supply hugely exceed those between public and private providers. Furthermore, the poor are excluded from the subsidy that is implicit in below-cost tariffs. The regrettable fact that the poor frequently pay more per unit of water than the better off, may, paradoxically, become an advantage for system expansion, as it provides a revenue base which may be channelled to more cost-effective methods of delivery. The same cannot be said of sanitation, unfortunately.

A recurrent theme in the design of major contracts has been that there is a conflict between keeping prices down (or even reducing them) and extending provision. The conflict is rendered more acute if connection charges are maintained for new customers.

---

11 At the time of writing, Suez was still running the El Alto system despite termination of the contract.

Liberalisation should not be equated either with privatisation or reform. Water and sanitation services reforms are possible without privatisation, but usually require moves towards cost recovery. In underdeveloped networks, a kind of liberalisation may happen at the micro level through recognition of small-scale alternative providers, rather than through their suppression; which may be counterproductive.

What sort of mechanisms, if any, have been used to encourage service providers to increase provision of services to previously unserved or under-served regions or consumers?

Command and control expansion targets may be circumvented if the new customers are loss makers for the companies. Rollout can be encouraged by separating consumer from provider tariffs, so that a cost-recovery tariff is paid to the provider but a lower tariff charged to the consumer, with the difference made up by the public authority. To prevent erosion of the revenue base, such a dual system should be time-limited to avoid regressive effects.

Have policies aimed at ensuring universal service used mechanisms aimed at the consumer (e.g. subsidies, vouchers)?

Such policies have been used on a large scale. A variety of policies aim directly at poor consumers either by allocating free or cheap tranches of water to all or by using means tests to concentrate them on the poor. Alternatively, they try to allocate cash or rebates to poor consumers to allow them the resources to pay the usual tariff. The more selective schemes are likely to encounter problems of take-up.

If so, how were these targeted at the truly needy and how were leakages to other groups avoided, if at all?

The brutal answers are: *i)* badly and *ii)* leakage has not been avoided. Consumption subsidies all encounter errors of exclusion (poor consumers fail to benefit), errors of inclusion (better-off consumers benefit) or both. The best solution in developing countries is to concentrate subsidies on the unserved, most likely through connection subsidies.

What were the administrative costs of any such assistance schemes?

Although there are few relevant data, it is likely that selective schemes aimed at individual consumers have high administrative costs on a per beneficiary basis. Gross costs may be kept down by poor take-up, which negates their purpose. Subsidies based on geographical zones have lower administrative costs but higher errors of inclusion.

How effective have all the above mechanisms been in extending service?

Such mechanisms have not been as effective as they could and should have been. They have been undermined by the attention paid to price rather than to connection charges. Targeted subsidies have been ineffective in terms of selectivity. By definition, the unconnected cannot benefit from network subsidies. The need for metering also handicaps consumption-based subsidies. Many studies have made the case for connection subsidies as the most cost-effective by far as the gains are permanent and the targeting the most accurate. Large-scale subsidies for drinking water probably compete with the resources needed to subsidise sanitation services.

Have the mechanisms or policies used encouraged providers to develop new or innovative solutions to universal service problems or to focus on the use of existing technologies and solutions?

Low-technology innovations have been applied and even fostered in the private and public sectors, sometimes in co-operation with local NGOs, and these innovations will be even more necessary if the MDGs are to be met. Exclusivity in service arrangements tends to militate against such innovation.

What sort of regulatory bodies exist or have been established to regulate the service in question?

Regulation is inevitable in a natural monopoly, and should be applied equally in the public and private sectors. It is intimately bound up with sectoral and structural reform. In promoting public-sector reform, care should be taken not to ignore models other than corporatisation. Local administrations should maintain a core of expertise for the commissioning process for contractors. Consumer rights should be developed and applied irrespective of ownership, and consumer organisations can be involved in developing good practice.

How sustainable is the reform process in the long term?

The current conventional wisdom seems too pessimistic about public-sector reform (although this may be changing) and too optimistic about the sustainability of PSP, especially for large-scale, long-term contracts, which carry a very high distress level. Disappointing results have led to renegotiations of contracts. Such renegotiations are at a disproportionate level in the water and sanitation services sector compared with other infrastructure sectors, and are hugely damaging to public perceptions of private-sector participation. Consideration might be given to open bids in competitive tendering procedures to avoid excessive "canon fees" or unrealistically low price undertakings.

Postscript

Water and sanitation services in general and the balance of public and private interests in particular have long been controversial, and the degree of liberalisation has ebbed and flowed. In London in 1818, the (private) Grand Junction Water Company rejected accusations of profiteering and issued notices rebutting "attempts to mislead and prejudice the public", stating that the company directors were in fact operating at great loss to themselves (Taylor and Trentmann, 2006).

In Helsinki, an invitation to tender was issued by the city in 1866 and a private concession agreement was signed in 1871 for 75 years. It was promptly abrogated and transferred to another private operator in 1872, and the system was municipalised in 1880 (Hukka and Katko, 2003). As these two episodes show, the current fierce debates come from a long tradition.

Annex 4.A1

Millennium Development Goals

In September 2000, the United Nations General Assembly adopted the Millennium Declaration, one of the goals of which was:

- To halve, by the year 2015, the proportion of people without sustainable access to safe drinking water,

In September 2002, the countries attending the UN World Summit on Sustainable Development in Johannesburg added the following aims to the Summit implementation plan:

- To halve, by the year 2015, the proportion of people without access to a basic sanitation system.
- Within five years, to get each country to set priorities for efficient water use as part of a comprehensive national water management plan.

Source: United Nations Development Programme.

References

ADERASA (2003), *Encuesta sobre la participacion de la sociedad civil en la regulacion de los servicios de saneamiento,* SUNASS, Lima.

Alfonso, O. *et al.* (1997), *Urban Development and People's Organisation in Bogota,* Institute of Developing Economies, Tokyo.

Baietti, A., W. Kingdom and M. van Ginneken (2006), "Characteristics of Well-performing Public Water Utilities", World Bank Series: Water Supply and Sanitation Working Notes, Note No. 9, February.

Barlow, M. and T. Clarke (2002), *Blue Gold,* Earthscan, London.

Barungi, A. *et al.* (2003), "Contracts and Commerce in Water Services in Uganda", WaterAid/Tearfund, London.

Brocklehurst, C. (2001), "Private Sector Participation and the Poor", paper delivered to WaterAid/WSP conference, Dar-es-Salaam.

Brocklehurst, C. (2003), "Can Subsidies be Better Targeted?", in *Water Tariffs and Subsidies in S. Asia*, WSP/PPIAF Series, Washington, DC.

Brocklehurst, C. and J. Janssens (2004), "Innovative Contracts, Sound Relationships: Urban Water Sector Reform in Senegal", World Bank, Washington, DC.

Brown, A. (2004), "The Reform Agenda for Urban Water Supply and Sanitation", paper delivered to CSO/WB Seminar, London, November, World Bank, Washington, DC.

Chavez, C. and M. Quiroga (2002), "Water Metering Successful Story: Chile", University of Concepción, Concepción, Chile.

Child Poverty Action Group (CPAG) (2004), *Poverty: The Facts*, ed. J. Flaherty *et al.*, Fifth edition, London.

Clarke, G.R. and S.J. Wallsten (2003), "Empirical Evidence on the Provision of Infrastructure Services to Rural and Poor Urban Consumers", World Bank/PPIAF, Washington, DC.

Clarke, G.R., K. Kosec and S.J. Wallsten (2004), "Has Private Participation in Water and Sewerage Improved Coverage? Empirical Evidence from Latin America", AEI-Brookings Joint Center for Regulation Studies, Washington, DC.

Consumers International (CI) (2000), *Vital Networks,* London, www.consumersinternational.org.

CI (2001), *The General Agreement on Trade in Services,* London.

Consumers International, Regional Office for Africa: CI ROAF (2004), "Water and Sanitation Program: Moving from Protest to Proposal", Harare.

Davis, J. (2004), “Corruption in Public Service Delivery: Experience from South Asia’s Water and Sanitation Sector”, *World Development*, Vol. 32, No. 1.

Esguerra, J. (2003), “Corporate Muddle of Manila’s Water Concessions”, WaterAid/Tearfund, London.

Fonlladosa, P. (2005), “Ouverture”, in *L’acces à l’eau et à l’energie,* P. Victoria (ed.), Lavoisier, Paris.

Foster, V., E.R. Tiongson and C.R. Laderchi (2004), *Poverty and Social Impact Analysis: Key Issues in Utility Reform*, World Bank, Washington, DC.

Franceys, R. *et al.* (undated), DFID Knowledge and Research Contract R8319, Cranfield University, www.silsoe.cranfield.ac.uk/iwe/projects/connections.

Gleick, P. *et al.* (2002), *The New Economy of Water*, Pacific Institute, Oakland, California.

Gomez-Lobo, A. and D. Contreras (2003), “Water Subsidy Policies: A Comparison of the Chilean and Colombian Schemes”, University of Chile, Santiago, Chile.

Guasch, J.L. (2004), “Granting and Renegotiating Infrastructure Concessions”, World Bank Institute, Washington, DC.

Gutierrez, E. *et al.* (2003), “Everyday Water Struggles in Buenos Aires”, WaterAid/Tearfund, London.

Hall D. *et al.* (2004), “Watertime: International Context”, www.watertime.org.

Hall, D. (2000), “Some World Class Questions”, Public Services International Research Unit (PSIRU), Greenwich.

Hall, D. (2001), “The Public Water Undertaking – A Necessary Option”, PSIRU, Greenwich.

Hukka, J. and T. Katko (2002), “Water Privatisation Revisited: Panacea or Pancake?”, International Water and Sanitation Centre, Delft.

ISO Technical Committee 224 (n.d.) “Service Activities relating to Drinking Water Supply and Sewerage”, Business Plan: ISO/TC 224 N 97.

Kariuki, M. (2002), “Making Space for the Urban Poor in Public-Private Partnerships”, paper delivered at the regional conference of CI-Africa, Nairobi,

Kariuki, M. and B. Wandera (2000), “Regulation of Cess-pit Emptying Services: A Case Study of Public Private Initiatives in Dar-es-Salaam”, in *Infrastructure for Development: Private Solutions and the Poor*, DFID, London.

Kingdom, W. and M. van Ginneken (2004), “A Guide to Using Private Firms to Improve Water Services”, in draft at the time of writing, World Bank, Washington, DC.

Komives, K. (2004), “Tariff Cross-Subsidies – Complicated Diversion or Valid Route to Cost Recovery?”, paper delivered to World Water Week, Washington, DC.

Komives, K., D. Whittington and X. Wu (2000), “Infrastructure Coverage and the Poor: A Global Perspective”, in *Infrastructure for Development, Private Solutions and the Poor*, DFID, London.

Mohajeri *et al.* (2003),. “European Water Management: Between Regulation and Competition”, Aqualibrium, Brussels.

Moor, A. de (1999), *Perverse Incentives*, Earth Council.

Morel, A. and M. Loury (2004), "Utility Sub-contractors for Local WSS Service Providers in Africa", paper presented to World Water Week, Washington. DC.

National Consumer Council (NCC) (2002), "Towards a Sustainable Water Charging Policy", NCC, London.

Nellis, J. (1994), "Is Privatisation Necessary?", in *Viewpoint*, FPD, Note No. 7, World Bank, Washington, DC.

Nickson, A. and C. Vargas (2002), "The Limitations of Water Regulation: The Failure of the Cochabamba Concession in Bolivia", *Bulletin of Latin American Research*, Vol. 21, No. 1.

Odongo, C. and W. Mungai (2002), "Empowering Vulnerable Consumers in Africa to Access and Influence Water and Sanitation Services: Case Study of the Korogocho Area", Consumers Information Network, Nairobi.

OECD/International Water Association (2001), *Water Management and Investment in the New Independent States*, OECD, Paris.

Porto Alegre (2004), *Orcamento participativo: Plano de Investimentos e Servicos 2003*, Prefeitura de Porto Alegre, PA.

PPIAF/WSP (2002), *New Designs for Water and Sanitation Transactions*, World Bank, Washington, DC.

Public Citizen (2002), *Profit Streams*, Washington, DC.

Public Citizen (2003), *Corporate Profits*, Washington, DC.

Rosenthal, S. (2001), "The Manila Water Concessions and their Impact on the Poor", Yale School of Forestry and Environmental Studies, New Haven, CT.

Saghir, J. (2004), "A Primer on the World Bank Group", WB/CSO dialogue, London.

Sánchez, M. and R. Sanhueza (2000), "La Regulación del Sector Sanitario en Chile", in S. Oxman and J.P. Oxer (eds.), *Privatización del Sector Sanitario Chileno: Análisis de un Proceso Inconcluso*, CESOC, August.

Simpson, R. (2002), "Should Consumers Demand Higher Water Prices?", *Consumer 21*, Issue 13, Consumers International, London.

Simpson, R. (2003), "Everyone Hates the Utility Company", paper delivered to the Russian Confederation of Consumer Organisations, Moscow.

Sivaev, S.B. (2002), "Tariff Regulation of Water and Wastewater Companies in the New Independent States", Moscow.

Sjolander Holland, A.C. (2005), The Water Business, Zed books, London.

Taylor, V. and F. Trentmann (2006), "From Users to Consumers: Water Politics in Nineteenth-Century London", pp. 53-73 in F. Trentmann (ed.), *The Making of the Consumer: Knowledge, Power and Identity in the Modern World*, Berg, Oxford and New York, 2006).

Tremolet, S. and J. Neale (2002), "Emerging Lessons in Private Provision of Infrastructure Services in Rural Areas: Water and Electricity Services in Gabon", World Bank, Washington, DC.

Tremolet, S., S. Browning and C. Howard (2002), "Emerging Lessons in Private Provision of Infrastructure Services in Rural Areas: Water Services in Cote d'Ivoire Aand Senegal", World Bank, Washington, DC.

Ugaz, C. (2004), "Consumer Participation and Pro-Poor Regulation in Latin America", United Nations University, Discussion Paper No. 2002/121.

UN *World Water Development Report* (UNESCO, updated 2002) www.unesco.org/water/wwap/.

United Nations Development Programme (UNDP) (2003), *Human Development Report*, New York and Oxford.

Urquhart, P. and D. Moore (2004), "Global Water Scoping Process: Is There a Case for a Multistakeholder Review of Private Sector Participation in Water and Sanitation?", Global Water Scoping Process (now Water Dialogues), London, www.waterdialogues.org.

Van den Berg, C. (2000), "Water Concessions, Who Wins, Who Loses? Public Policy for the Private Sector", Note 217, World Bank, Washington. DC.

Viero, O.M. and A.P. Cordeiro (2003), "The Case for Public Provisioning in Porto Alegre", WaterAid/Tearfund, London, 2003.

Walker, I. *et al*. (2000), "Pricing Subsidies and the Poor: Demand for Improved Water Services in Central America", World Bank Policy Research Working Paper No. 2468.

Water and Sanitation Program (WSP) (2001), *The Buenos Aires Concession,* WSP South Asia, New Delhi.

World Health Organisation (WHO) (2000), *Global Water Supply and Sanitation Assessment*, www.who.int/docstore/water_sanitation_health/Globassessment/Global1.2.htm.

WHO, *Water for Health; WHO Guidelines for Drinking Water Quality* (undated, post 2000).

World Bank/PPIAF (2006), *Approaches to Private Participation in Water Services: A Toolkit*, World Bank, Washington, DC.

World Bank (2004), *World Development Report* (WDR), World Bank, Washington, DC.

Chapter 5

Reflections on the Goal of Universal Access in the Water and Sanitation Sector: Lessons from Ghana, Senegal and Nepal

Dale Whittington
Departments of Environmental Sciences & Engineering, City & Regional Planning, and Public Policy, University of North Carolina at Chapel Hill

This chapter offers reflections on the goal of universal access, drawing on insights from experience in Ghana, Senegal and Nepal, as a way to help water and sanitation professionals see more clearly the nature of the challenges posed by a goal of universal access in the sector. The costs of providing improved piped municipal water and sanitation services are also examined.

Introduction

The community of official development assistance (ODA) experts likes to set quantity targets for the pursuit of development goals. It is now an established part of the development assistance culture for participants at international conferences to look at where they would like developing countries to be in 10-20 years in terms of progress towards a certain development goal and then calculate what is required in terms of additional financial assistance. The practice seems to be especially prevalent in the water and sanitation sector. The 1980s were designated the "International Water and Sanitation Decade", and the international community was to work with national governments to ensure that everyone in the world had access at least to basic water and sanitation services by 1990. These quantity targets were never met, and the global community has now made a commitment to a set of millennium development goals (MDGs), one of which is to cut the proportion of people in the world living without access to water and sanitation in half by 2015.

There are at least three good reasons for articulating development goals as quantity targets. First, these can provide a means of mobilising increased ODA from wealthy countries. They constitute a call for moral action to address income inequality. Poverty – and lack of access to water and sanitation services – is characterised as an assault on human dignity. Often using rights-based language, advocates of increased ODA seek to impose a financial obligation on wealthy countries to aid poorer ones. Second, quantity targets are an important form of agenda setting, raising the importance of some development goals while lowering the priority of others. Third, quantity targets may be accompanied by policy messages or new scientific evidence that the international community wants to communicate to developing countries themselves. In effect, the global community wants to realign national budget priorities to push a global consensus on the best way to reduce poverty.

As part of its global call to action, the international development community typically makes a variety of economic arguments to support its request for increased development assistance and national government budget realignment. Cost-benefit arguments predominate. For example, it is often argued that the economic benefits of water and sanitation investments exceed the costs by some amount. Such economic analyses are only one of numerous arguments made by proponents of increased technical assistance in general, and increased investment in water and sanitations services in particular, to promote progress towards quantity targets. Indeed, economic arguments are probably not overly important or persuasive in the minds of most ODA experts. Moral commitment to poverty reduction and reduction in income inequality seem to be more compelling reasons for action.

Still, it is important that the economic analysis of development policies and projects should be done carefully and the results presented honestly. At the most fundamental level, water and sanitation professionals need to know what business they are in, *i.e.* are they providing humanitarian relief (charity), or are they fostering economic development? Development projects that do not pass a cost-benefit test are likely to slow economic growth, and increased economic growth is one extremely important strategy for achieving both poverty reduction and meeting concrete quantity targets such as increased water and sanitation coverage. It is no coincidence that where progress is being made towards reaching the water and sanitation MDGs, economic growth is strong. Also, sound cost-benefit analysis can help proponents of moral action to better understand the financial (and political) obstacles in their path toward universal access. This is not to imply, of course, that cost-benefit analysis of municipal water and sanitation projects is simple or straightforward.

The aim of this chapter is to offer some reflections on the goal of universal access, drawing on insights from experiences in Ghana, Senegal and Nepal, with the hope of assisting water and sanitation professionals to see more clearly the nature of the challenges posed by setting a goal of universal access in the water and sanitations services sector. Most donors now recognise that, from an economic perspective, water and sanitations services projects have been among their most poorly performing investments. This should serve as a cautionary note for those wishing to expand investments in water and sanitations services.

The following pages first summarise three lessons from experience in Ghana, Senegal and Nepal. Some concluding remarks follow. Because an understanding of the costs of municipal water and sanitation investments is central to an appreciation of the challenges posed by the goal of universal access, Annex 5.A1 discusses the costs of providing improved piped municipal water and sanitation services.

The goal of universal coverage: three cautionary lessons

Lesson No. 1 (from Ghana): Providing access to improved water and sanitation services does not mean that such services will be used

During the 1990s both bilateral and multilateral donors were actively involved in rethinking the design and provision of rural water supply systems in Ghana. Rural water projects were designed with all of the latest "demand-driven" thinking about how to ensure sustainability:

- More active participation of communities.
- Transfer of facilities to community ownership.
- Provision of health education.
- Communities paid a (small) portion of the capital costs of the projects.
- Community responsibility for operation and maintenance.
- Community design and management of cost-recovery pricing systems.
- Involvement of women on village water committees; etc.

In a recent survey of several hundred households in 15 communities in the Volta region of Ghana, researchers found that 43% of households in communities with functioning, improved water systems did not use the new system as their primary water source. Moreover, many of those that did use the improved water system as their primary source supplemented their households' water use with water from traditional sources. Relatively few households in these communities restricted their water use to water from the improved source.

Households in these communities were paying only a small fraction of the real economic costs of the system. Capital contributions from communities amounted to only about 5% of the total capital costs, and household user fees were quite modest. Still, the researchers found that user fees discouraged some households from using the improved water system. Because many such community-managed water schemes in Ghana are falling into disrepair and are not being used, donors and government are studying ways of providing "post-construction support" in an attempt to keep such systems functioning. Such external support will require additional subsidies. The bottom line is that the cost of maintaining universal access in such rural communities is high and will require long-term infusions of capital from higher levels of government and/or donors.

Lesson No. 2 (from Dakar, Senegal): Cross-subsidising poor households from other water users in order to increase access is more difficult than commonly realized

Dakar's population numbers about 3 million, and about 90% of households have piped water service. Dakar privatised its water utility in 1996 using a lease-operate contract. Bills are rendered bi-monthly and the collection rate is high. The government uses three main policies to expand access to poor households:

- Public taps (borne fountains) provide water to households in new and informal settlements.
- Social connections are available for poor households in established neighbourhoods.
- An increasing block tariff (IBT) is used to calculate water bills for households with private connections.[1]

A social connections policy is based on the idea that if poor households have the choice between a low-cost, lower-quality service and a higher-cost, higher-quality service, they will choose the lower-cost, lower-quality service. For example, it is assumed that if households are given the choice between *i)* a water connection with a small diameter pipe with no connection fee, and *ii)* a water connection with larger diameter pipe with an associated full-cost connection fee, poor households will choose the small-diameter piped connection and non-poor households will choose the larger-diameter pipe. If this is true, one could use pipe diameter to identify poor households and target subsidised connections.

Lauria and Hopkins (2003) found that although the cost to households of ordinary and social connections differ in Dakar (social connections are free and ordinary connections cost more than USD 200), the levels of service are in fact the same. They found that social connections are made with a 15-mm diameter pipe and a 20-mm diameter lateral. Ordinary connections for households use the same diameters. Thus while the criteria for obtaining a social connection in Dakar are stringent (see Table 5.1), almost everyone in Dakar wants a social connection if they can get one, and in fact 70% of households have managed to do so.

Lauria and Hopkins conclude that households that pay for an ordinary connection do identify themselves as non-poor, but that it does not follow that households who wait for a social connection are poor. They conclude that many non-poor households get social connections, and that subsidies are not well targeted. The poorest households in Dakar are in fact not even eligible for social connections because they live in informal settlements. In established neighbourhoods, social connections serve both poor and non-poor households.[2] Lauria and Hopkins argue that another problem with the social connections

1. The initial block (or "lifeline") in Dakar is 10 m^3 per month

2. In Cote d'Ivoire, 25% of the households with connections use more than 15 m^3 a month and pay bills of more than USD 17 a month. Households that can afford to pay such water bills do not seem "poor".

policy is that once households receive a social connection, there is no attempt to reassess their eligibility. If they sell their house, the social connection passes to the next owner, its value capitalised into the market price of the house.

Table 5.1. Criteria for social connections in Dakar, Senegal

1	Applicants cannot be wealthy
2	A house must exist on the lot that is to be served by the connection
3	It must be a residence and not a business; the connection cannot be used for commercial purposes such as selling water to neighbours.
4	The connection cannot cross private property.
5	The applicant must have title to the house and land.
6	A pipe of the water network must be within 20 meters of where the house connection is made, or if a 100-meter extension is made of an existing pipe in the water network (not more than 100 mm in diameter), it can serve the houses of at least four applicants.
7	If approved for a social connection, the applicant must pay a security deposit of XOF 13 000 (USD 19) as security for future water charges. No charge is made, however, for the meter and lateral.

Source: Lauria and Hopkins, 2003.

Lauria and Hopkins also found that many households that get social connections thinking they can afford to pay the water bill find that they cannot and are disconnected. Households cannot easily monitor their water use to keep their water bill affordable.

In their study Lauria and Hopkins argue that the increasing block tariff actually hurts many of the poorest households. This perverse outcome occurs because water vendors typically obtain their water supply from ordinary connections. Because their bill is calculated based on an IBT, their large water use pushes them into the highest blocks of the IBT. These costs are passed on in the final price of the water sold to the poorest households in informal settlements. Lauria and Hopkins also note that this perverse result occurs when many poor households live in a multi-family dwelling and share a single water meter.

Lesson No. 3 (from Kathmandu, Nepal): Long-term infusions of donor capital and technical assistance do not necessarily lead to financially sustainable water and sanitation systems, nor do they ensure universal coverage

Today the Nepal Water Supply Corporation (NWSC) supplies piped water services to the five main municipalities in the Kathmandu Valley – Kathmandu, Lalitpur (Patan), Bhaktapur, Kirtipur and Madhyapur (Thimi). The total population in the NWSC's service area is approximately 1 million. Historically, households in the Kathmandu Valley have received water from an ancient system of 200-250 gravity-fed public taps, called "stone spouts", as well as their own private wells. The stone spouts capture mountain springs and transport water to public squares where people still come to bathe and collect water for their homes.

The late 19th and early 20th centuries witnessed the construction of the first piped distribution networks in Kathmandu. These captured local springs and distributed water to a small number of households. During the second half of the 20th century, the water supply system evolved in a symbiotic relationship between a public water utility in various guises and the international donor community. The first commercial water supply system was started in the 1960s with support from the Government of India. Binnie & Partners completed the first water supply master plan for the Kathmandu Valley in 1973. Subsequently, the World Bank played a major role in the municipal water sector, financing the First Kathmandu Water Supply Project in 1975 and the Second and Third Kathmandu Water Supply Projects.

Over 1975-87, the three World Bank projects financed expansion of the distribution network, sewers and wastewater treatment plants, water metering, groundwater production wells, new surface water supplies and a variety of "institutional strengthening" measures. Subsequently, the World Bank also indicated an interest in financing private-sector participation (PSP). However, the Private Sector Participation High-Level Committee (PSPC) in charge of private operator recruitment (assisted by the World Bank) was unable to award a contract. Then, the government and the World Bank agreed in 2002 to reallocate the World Bank funds that were originally earmarked for this PSP to other activities of national priority. The government, in turn, requested the Asian Development Bank (ADB) to assume the lead for the PSP scheme and associated institutional reforms and to identify other interested cofinancier(s).

A great deal of donor activity has also been focused on the need for new "out-of-valley" raw water sources. The 1973 master plan argued that in-valley water sources were inadequate to meet long-term needs and that out-of-valley sources should be studied. This process began in 1988 when Binnie & Partners conducted a prefeasiblity study of alternative raw water sources. From 1990 to 1992, Snowy Mountain Engineering Consultants conducted a large feasibility study of the Melamchi Water Supply Project (MWSP), funded by the UNDP and executed by the World Bank.

The MWSP has four main components. The first is raw water supply that involves an inter-basin transfer of 170 million litres per day (MLD). Much of the water from the Melamchi River located northeast of the Kathmandu Valley will be diverted into a tunnel 26 kilometres long. The water will be delivered to a new water treatment plant, the second component of the MWSP. The third component is a bulk distribution system (BDS) which includes primary transmission mains and ground storage reservoirs. The fourth component is rehabilitation of the water distribution network.

An influential environmental impact assessment in 1990 concluded that the environmental impacts of the MWSP would be lessened if its hydropower component was dropped, and the ADB and other donors accepted this recommendation. During the 1990s, several international consultants offered opinions on the water supply problems of Kathmandu Valley and the pros and cons of the MWSP. Finally, the ADB agreed to finance the majority of the costs of the MWSP.

After decades of donor investment, the population of the Kathmandu Valley currently faces chronic water shortages during the dry summer months. The NWSC produces about 120 million litres a day during the wet season, but only 80 million cubic meters a day during the dry season owing to limited water storage. Much of the water that is produced is lost before it reaches the NWSC's customers. Because many households have unmetered connections or connections with broken meters, it is difficult to estimate precisely how much of the water produced actually reaches NWSC's customers. However, it is estimated that some 40% is not accounted for. What is certain is that hydraulic pressure in the distribution system must be kept very low in many parts of the city to avoid massive leakage. The secondary and tertiary piped distribution system is now in such poor condition in some neighbourhoods that it is questionable whether the capital stock would have any residual value to a private operator; much of the distribution system must simply be replaced.

About 70% of the population in NWSC's service area have a private connection to the distribution system, but the quality of service is very low. Most households only receive water for a few hours a day. Intermittent water service means that the distribution system is subject to negative pressures and chronic contamination from groundwater infiltration. Because the water service from the piped distribution system is poor, many households with private connections also rely on alternative sources of water, such as private wells, and public taps and wells (Pattanayak *et al.*, 2005).

Households without a private connection may obtain water from a variety of sources. Some still collect water from the stone spouts that deliver water from nearby mountain springs to selected central locations in the five cities. Thus, after decades of donor investment, a substantial minority of households in the Kathmandu Valley still rely on contaminated traditional water sources as their main source of water for domestic use. Tanker trucks operated by the NWSC serve some outlying areas, filling household storage tanks for a nominal fee. Many unconnected households have dug private wells on their property; water from these is used largely for washing and bathing.[3]

In summary, the system delivers low volumes of poor quality water on an irregular basis. The only appealing aspect of the existing service from the households' perspective is that they do not pay much for it: average monthly water bills are of the order of NPR 100-158 (USD 1.39-2.19) a month. After decades of donor investment, Kathmandu has a fully depreciated capital stock that desperately needs replacement.

Most observers agree that a new raw water supply source is needed. It is estimated that this new raw water source (the Melamchi Water Supply Project) and rehabilitation of the existing system will require an investment of several hundred million dollars. In spite of the population's relatively high willingness to pay for water and sanitation improvements (Whittington *et al.*, 2002), under most plausible scenarios, the needed investments would not pass a cost-benefit test (Whittington *et al.*, 2004).

Concluding remarks

It is not technically difficult to provide universal access to piped water and sanitation services to urban populations; the former Soviet Union has made great strides in reaching this goal. The question is whether such a policy is financially sustainable in a specific country. In many of the countries of the former Soviet Union, the goal of universal access is receding because such services are simply not affordable at current income levels (Davis and Whittington, 2004).

If international donors wish to pursue a policy of universal access, they should acknowledge that the costs of improved services are far beyond the reach of many households and that many investments will be neither financially feasible nor pass a cost-benefit test. They should also recognise that there is little empirical evidence that municipal water and sanitation projects actually cause or induce economic growth. There

3. The ability of households to continue to rely on private wells is in doubt. The total sustainable yield of the groundwater aquifer is approximately 26 million litres a day. Total groundwater extraction is currently about 59 million litres a day. As a result the groundwater table is falling, and contamination is increasing.

is a great deal of evidence that most households want improved water and sanitation services, but their willingness to pay for such services is often much less than the cost.

Many water and sanitation investments are thus best viewed as humanitarian relief, and donors should be prepared to undertake a long-term financial commitment to make substantial progress towards a goal of universal coverage. This financial commitment is so large that many donors will probably not have the patience or perseverance to pay for water and sanitation services for the indefinite future. There will thus not be sufficient donor support to achieve a goal of universal access. Given this, it would be a mistake from both a humanitarian and economic perspective to spread available subsidies uniformly across communities currently without access to improved water and sanitations services. Priorities need to be set both for water and sanitations services projects designed for humanitarian relief and for water and sanitations services projects designed for economic development (*i.e.* projects that will pass a cost-benefit test). Unfortunately, the goal of universal access to improved water and sanitation services distracts water planners and policy makers from this hard task of priority setting.

Annex 5.A1

The Costs of Improved Municipal Water and Sanitation Services

Throughout the world, a preference for fresh, clean water for drinking and washing lies deep in people's collective subconscious and is reflected in all of the world's major religions. Some people still long for a lost world in which wandering nomads could visit an uncontaminated, refreshing spring. But in a world of more than 5 billion people, such places are few and far between, and even with the most stringent water pollution control measurements, there are very few places where people can expect to safely drink untreated water from natural sources. Nor do most households desire to do this on a daily basis. If they can afford it, most people want their water to be delivered directly to their homes. The treatment and delivery of water to households, and the removal and treatment of the wastewater generated are very expensive.

Of course, costs vary depending on the circumstances, and estimates of what it will cost to provide universal access (or to reach the water and sanitation MDGs) vary widely. Some rough calculations are, however, helpful. The approach here is to present a range of average unit costs of providing an urban household with modern water and sanitation services. First various unit costs per cubic meter for different components of water and sanitations services are presented. Second, some typical monthly quantities of water used by representative households are provided. Third, representative unit costs are multiplied by typical monthly household water use to obtain a range of estimates of the monthly economic costs of providing a household with improved, piped water and sanitation services.

The economic costs of providing a household with modern water and sanitation services are the sum of seven principal components:

- The opportunity cost of diverting raw water from alternative uses to the household (or resource rents).
- Transmission of untreated water to the urban area.
- Treatment of raw water to drinking water standards.
- Distribution of treated water within the urban area to the household.
- Collection of wastewater from the household (sewerage collection).
- Treatment of wastewater (sewage treatment).
- Any remaining costs or damages imposed on others by the discharge of treated wastewater (negative externalities).

Table 5.A1.1 presents an illustrative range of average unit costs for each of these seven cost components, expressed in USD per cubic meter. The upper bounds on the unit costs of these different cost components are not intended to represent an absolute upper bound, *i.e.* in many situations the upper bound unit costs could be much higher than indicated in the table. On the other hand, in a location with abundant fresh water supplies, for example, the cost of items 1 and 7 may in fact be very low. However, in more and more places opportunity costs associated with water diversion and the externalities from wastewater discharge are beginning to loom large.

Table 5.A1.1. Cost estimates: improved water and sanitation services

USD per cubic meter

No.	Cost component	USD per m3
1	Opportunity cost of raw water supply	USD 0.05-0.20
2	Storage and transmission to treatment plant	USD 0.15-0.20
3	Treatment of to drinking water standards	USD 0.15-0.20
4	Distribution of water to households	USD 0.50-0.70
5	Collection of wastewater from home and conveyance to wastewater treatment plant	USD 0.80-1.00
6	Wastewater treatment	USD 0.30-0.50
7	Damages associated with discharge of treated wastewater	USD 0.05-0.20
	Total	**USD 2.00-3.00**

Some cost components are subject to significant economies of scale, particularly the treatment of raw water to drinking water standards and the treatment of sewage. This means that the larger the quantity of water or wastewater treated, the lower the per-unit cost. On the other hand, some cost components experience diseconomies of scale. As large cities search farther and farther away for additional fresh water supplies and good reservoir sites become harder to find, the unit cost of storing and transporting raw water to a community increases. There are also tradeoffs between different cost components, *i.e.* one can be reduced, but only at the expense of another. For example, wastewater can receive only primary treatment, which is much cheaper than secondary treatment, but the negative externalities associated with wastewater discharge will increase.

The cost estimates in Table 5.A1.1 include both capital and operating and maintenance expenses. The opportunity costs of raw water supplies (item 1) are still quite low in most places at about a few cents per cubic meter. Even in places where urban water supplies are diverted from irrigated agriculture, the unit costs are rarely above USD 0.20 per cubic meter. Desalinisation and wastewater reclamation costs will set an upper limit of about USD 1.00 per cubic meter on opportunity costs of raw water, but the opportunity costs of raw water are nowhere near this level in most places.

Raw water storage and transmission and subsequent treatment (items 2 and 3) typically cost USD 0.30-40 per cubic meter. The distribution network for water within a city (item 4) is a major cost component, in many cases some USD 0.60-70 per cubic meter. The collection and conveyance of sewage to a wastewater treatment plant (item 5) is even more expensive than water distribution; it will cost USD .90-1.00 per cubic meter. The secondary wastewater treatment (item 6) will cost about USD 0.40-0.50 per cubic meter. The damages resulting from the discharge of treated wastewater are very site-specific, but environmentalists correctly point out that that they can be significant, even for discharges of wastewater receiving secondary treatment. It is assumed for purposes of illustration that these costs are of the same order of magnitude as the opportunity costs of raw water supplies (USD 0.05-0.20).

As shown, total economic costs per cubic meter are generally in the range of USD 2-3 per cubic meter. Again, these costs are not intended to represent an upper bound. For example, in the western United States costs of water and sanitations services are easily double or triple these amounts. Also, these cost estimates assume that financing is at competitive international market rates and that countries do not pay a high default or risk premium.

A reasonable question to ask is whether these costs would be significantly lower in developing countries owing to the lower labour costs. In fact, it is not obvious that total costs in developing countries will be much lower than in industrialised countries. Water and sanitation investments are very capital-intensive, and poor governance increases costs. Moreover, some cost components may be higher in some developing countries than in industrialised countries. For example, the transmission of raw water supplies to Mexico City is more expensive than comparable costs almost anywhere in Europe.

Table 5.A1.2 shows a reasonable lower-bound estimate of unit costs of piped water and sanitations services. In the table the opportunity cost of raw water supplies and the damages from wastewater discharges are assumed to be zero. Only minimal storage is included, and the only intake treatment is simple chlorination. The costs of the water distribution network assume the use of PVC pipes and shallow excavation. Wastewater is collected with condominial sewers and the only wastewater treatment is provided by simple lagoons. Given these assumptions, one can manage getting the unit costs of piped water and sanitations services down to about USD 1.00 per cubic meter.

Table 5.A1.2. Cost estimates: improved water and sanitation services for low-cost option for private water and sewer connections

USD per cubic meter

No.	Cost component	USD per m³
1	Opportunity cost of raw water supply (steal it)	USD 0.00
2	Storage and transmission to treatment plant (minimal storage0	USD 0.10
3	Treatment of to drinking water standards (simple chlorination)	USD 0.05
4	Distribution of water to households (PVC pipe)	USD 0.30
5	Collection of wastewater from home and conveyance to wastewater treatment plant (condominial sewers)	USD 0.35
6	Wastewater treatment (simple lagoon)	USD 0.20
7	Damages associated with discharge of treated wastewater (someone else's problem)	USD 0.00
	Total	**USD 1.00**

How much water does a typical household in a developing country "need"? The quantity of water used by a household will be a function of the price charged and household income. Currently most households in developing countries face quite low prices for water and sanitations services. One can look at typical water use figures from households around the world to see how much water one might expect a household to use for a comfortable and modern lifestyle. For households with an in-house piped water connection, residential in-door water use generally falls in the range of 125-250 litres per capita per day. For a household of five, this would amount to about 20-40 m^3 a month (Table 5.A1.3). At the current low prices prevailing in many third-world cities, such levels of water use among middle-income households are not uncommon. Other things being equal, households living in hot tropical climates use more water for drinking, bathing and washing than households in temperate climates.

Table 5.A1.3. Range of estimates of monthly water use

In-house, private connection

Per capita daily water use	Persons per household	Days per month	Monthly household water use
70 litres	5 persons	30 days	10 m^3
130 litres	5 persons	30 days	20 m^3
270 litres	5 persons	30 days	40 m^3

Assuming average unit costs of USD 2.00 per cubic meter, the full economic costs of providing 20-40 m^3 to a household (and then dealing with the wastewater) would be USD 40-80 a month (Table 5.A1.4), more than most households in industrialised countries pay for water and sanitation services, and far beyond the means of most households in developing countries.

Table 5.A1.4. Range of estimates of the full economic cost of providing improved water and sanitation services

In-house, private water connection; piped sewer

Monthly household water use	Average cost = USD 1 per m^3	Average cost = USD 2 per m^3	Average cost = USD 3 per m^3
10 m^3	USD 10	USD 20	USD 30
20 m^3	USD 20	USD 40	USD 60
40 m^3	USD 40	USD 80	USD 120

There is surprising little good empirical evidence on how poor households in developing countries with in-house water connections would respond to higher water and sanitation prices. It is possible that residential, in-door water use in developing countries might be as low as 65-70 litres per capita per day if higher prices were charged. For a household with five members, this level of residential, indoor use would amount to about 10 m^3 a month. The full economic cost of this level of water and sanitations services at this reduced quantity of water use (assuming that the unit cost of USD 2 per cubic meter remained unchanged) would be USD 20 a month per household. At entirely plausible levels of water use (130-140 litres per capita per day), the total economic cost would be about USD 40 a month per household. With the unit costs of the low-cost system depicted in Table 5.A2, the full economic cost of providing 10 m^3 a month would be USD 10 per household per month. This should be regarded as a lower bound on the full economic costs of piped water and sanitations services in most locations.

In both industrialised and developing countries, most people are unaware of the true economic costs of municipal water and sanitation services. There are several reasons why the economics costs of water and sanitations services are so poorly understood.

First, the capital costs are heavily subsidised by higher levels of government (and in developing countries by international donors), so that the households served do not see the capital costs reflected in the prices they pay.

Second, in many cities tariff structures are designed so that industrial water users cross-subsidise residential users; households thus do not even see the full operation and maintenance costs in the prices they pay.

Third, because many water utilities run financial deficits (in effect running down the value of their capital stock), water users in aggregate do not even see the full costs of operation and maintenance.

Fourth, most cities do not pay for their raw water supplies. The water is typically simply expropriated from water users in outlying rural areas.

Fifth, wastewater externalities are typically imposed on others (downstream) without compensation.

Sixth, the subsidies provided to consumers of water and sanitations services are not only huge, they are also regressive. It is thus often not politically "desirable" for most people to understand that middle and upper income households actually receive the most subsidies (Boland and Whittington, 2000). Many tariff designs are overly complex and appear to help poor households when in fact middle and upper income households receive the majority of subsidies provided to people with networked water and sanitation services (Whittington *et al.*, 2003). Most fundamentally, poor households are often not connected to the water or sewer network and so cannot receive the subsidised services. Even if they have connections, the poor use less water than the rich and thus receive lower absolute amounts of subsidy.

It is, of course, less expensive to provide intermediate levels of water and sanitations services such as public taps and communal sanitation facilities than the costs in Table 5.A2 would indicate. Monthly household costs for intermediate water and sanitation services are, however, often quite considerable, roughly USD 5-10 per month for small quantities of water and the use of on-site sanitation facilities. It is also important to appreciate that such intermediate services impose additional costs on households in terms of time spent and health. Indeed, there is reason to question whether intermediate water and sanitations services benefit health in any way at all (Esrey, 1996).

The high costs of both piped and intermediate water and sanitation services have important economic and political implications for the goal of universal access.

References

Boland, J. and D. Whittington (2000), "The Political Economy of Increasing Block Water Tariffs in Developing Countries", *The Political Economy of Water Pricing Reforms*, Ariel Dinar (ed.), Oxford University Press, pp. 215-236.

Davis, J. and D. Whittington (2004), "Challenges for Water Sector Reform in Transition Economies", *Water Policy* 6 (4), pp. 1-15.

Esrey, S. (1996), "Water, Waste, and Well-being: A Multicountry Study", *American Journal of Epidemiology*, Vol. 43, No. 6, pp. 608-623.

Lauria, D.T. and O.S. Hopkins (2003), "Pro-Poor Subsidies for Water Connections in West Africa: A Preliminary Study, A Report to the World Bank", August.

Pattanayak, S., J-C. Yang, D. Whittington and B. Kumar (2005), "Coping with Unreliable Public Water Supplies: Averting Expenditures by Households in Kathmandu, Nepal", *Water Resources Research* Vol. 4, No. 2, February, W02012, 11 pages.

Whittington, D., S. Pattanayak, J-C. Yang and B. Kumar (2002), "Household Demand for Improved Piped Water Services in Kathmandu, Nepal", *Water Policy*, Vol. 4, Issue 6, pp. 531-556.

Whittington, D., J. Boland and V. Foster (2002), "Water Tariffs and Subsidies in South Asia: Understanding the Basics", Water and Sanitation Program, New Delhi, India.

Whittington, D., D.T. Lauria, V. Prabhu and J. Cook (2004), "An Economic Reappraisal of the Melamchi Water Supply Project, Kathmandu, Nepal", *Portuguese Journal of Economics*, Vol. 3, No. 2.

Chapter 6

Efficiency, Equity and Liberalisation of Water Services in Buenos Aires, Argentina

Miguel Solanes
Regional Advisor, ECLAC/ONU*

This chapter traces Argentina's decision to privatise its water and sanitation services and describes in detail implementation of the privatisation scheme, including the many problems encountered with respect to the contract with the provider and regulatory issues as well as those attributable to the financial crisis, and the effects on access to water and sanitations services for the poor. Ultimately, the contract was rescinded. The experience offers useful lessons on pitfalls to be avoided.

* The author gratefully acknowledges Emilio Lentini, ETOSS Buenos Aires, and Daniel Azpiazu, Flacso-Coniset, Buenos Aires,for their help in answering questions, and the paper submitted by Suez in response to Macdonald's evaluation of Buenos Aires. Andrei Jouravlev of ECLAC made valuable comments on the original draft and Alejandro Vargas of ECLAC contributed socioeconomic data.

The context of privatisation

From 1912 to the 1980s, the National Water and Sewerage Corporation (*Obras Sanitarias de la Nación*) provided water services to Buenos Aires. Central authorities enacted regulations, designed rates and planned the expansion of service. Structural investment had the highest priority; the national treasury funded the system and guaranteed financing. Efficiency and economic and financial considerations were disregarded, and the setting of rates and tariffs was politically based (FIEL, 1999a, pp. 535-537). However, a policy of cross-subsidies made possible expansion to the less developed and populated areas of the country (Azpiazu and Forcinito, 2003, p. 7).

The system broke down as a result of recurrent fiscal crises at the national level, which constrained transfers of funds. From 1976 to 1982 Argentina maintained an artificial exchange rate, subsidised by the government with significant shares of national funds. Resources were reduced for other activities and the National Water and Sewerage Corporation suffered. Expansion was stopped, and maintenance and rehabilitation deteriorated. Water and sanitation services are an essential commodity but are especially vulnerable to financial shortages. They also constitute a natural monopoly and are the most capital-intensive of utilities, with a ratio of required capital per dollar of annual revenue ranging from 6:1 to 10:1 (Phillips, 1993, p. 15).

In 1982, a debt crisis occurred as a result of the financing of the artificial rate of exchange, and public financing became even more limited. The national water system was transferred to the provinces, and 161 service areas were transferred. At first, the provinces maintained the original national philosophy, but no alternatives to the previous national subsidies were provided (Azpiazu et Forcinito, 2003, p. 7). Water and sewerage was not a priority either for the national government or for the provinces and the system collapsed. Between 1970 and 1979 investment in the sector represented 0.31% of GDP. It decreased to 0.15% between 1980-89 and to 0.07% between 1990-91 (E. Lentini, personal communication). The state-owned utility lacked funds, owing to inefficient operation and declining real low water tariffs. Investment did not keep pace with population growth, and was not even enough to maintain existing assets. The deterioration of the system caused water shortages (Alcazar *et al.*, 2000, p. 4). There was no independent regulator capable of monitoring the state company and its practices and there were no regulatory standards. Quality and coverage, as well as policies, planning and regulation were affected.

In Buenos Aires it was clear that the state company was unable to meet investment and maintenance needs. In addition to the problems created by the debt crisis, sector-specific problems related to the vices and practices of an overmanned public company with strong, highly politicised labour unions and a short-term view of the social aspects of public utility water services.

At the time of the concession, 70% of the population of the Metropolitan Area (MA) had a water supply, and just 58% were connected to the sewerage system. Most of those unconnected lived in the poorer areas, where the percentages were 55% and 36%, respectively. The shortfall in the poorer areas had been rising by 5-6% per year, and involved 5.6 million people. On the other hand, city residents were almost all connected. The state company was unable to maintain the existing assets. Water tariffs were low and water that was unaccounted for reached 45%. Consumers had no incentive to conserve or to pay, since they could not be cut off if they did not pay. Rivers and groundwater were polluted by septic tanks, cesspools and direct discharge of untreated sewage and industrial effluent (Alcazar *et al.*, 2000, pp. 3-7).

The system has abundant and cheap raw water, and transport is cheap as well (Alcazar *et al.*, 2000, p. 3). It was deemed that favourable physical conditions, the professional type of management afforded by the private sector (FIEL, 1999, p. 538), and undertaking the postponed investments would improve service conditions. The concession was therefore launched with a sense of urgency (Alcazar *et al.*, 2000, p. 13). It was granted by a contract containing regulatory principles to a consortium of foreign and national private companies. The urgency of the situation affected the outcome.

At the time of privatisation for Buenos Aires (end 1992, beginning 1993) foreign currencies were kept artificially low in order to preserve currency stability (much as in 1976-82 and with even more disastrous results). The state intervened heavily in the currency market, borrowing and buying foreign currency and selling it in the local market. Debt and unemployment went up (Figure 6.1), and local production and fiscal revenue came down.

Figure 6.1. Urban unemployment during the period of the concession

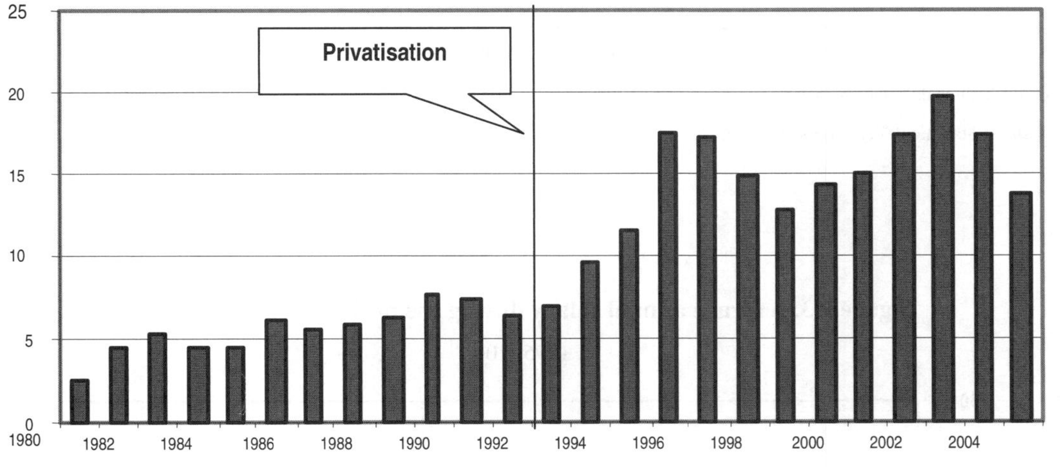

Source: BADEINSO, ECLAC, 2005.

By 2001, the year of the crisis, the external debt was unmanageable (Table 6.1 and Figure 6.2). Unemployment was rampant, and shops were looted by hungry mobs (Figures 6.3-6.5).

Table 6.1. External debt as a percentage of GDP during the period of the concession

				Privatisation	Argentina's national government gross public debt										
	1990	1991	1992	1993	1994	1995	1996	1997	1998	1999	2000	2001	2002	2003	2004 (p)
Total	-	-	-	29.4	31.3	33.8	35.7	34.5	37.6	43.0	45.0	53.7	145.9	138.2	126.3
Internal	-	-	-	-	-	-	-	8.9	9.8	13.1	15.2	20.9	54.2	60.0	52.0
External	-	-	-	-	-	-	-	25.6	27.8	29.9	29.8	32.9	91.6	78.2	74.3

Source: Secretariats of Budget and Financing. Ministry of Economics, Argentina (Preliminary Report. Last Data of June 2004.

Figure 6.2. The evolution of Argentina's GDP during the period of the concession

In constant USD 1995

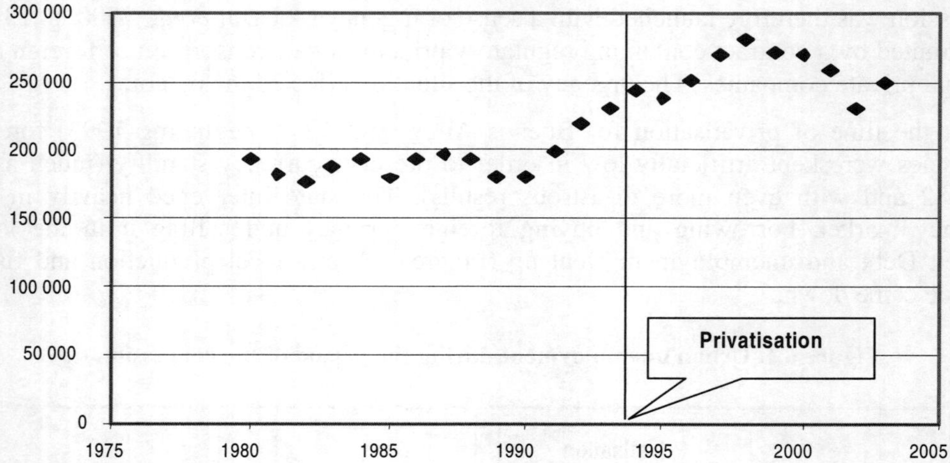

GDP: Values deflated by inflation index (1995=100).

Source: Statistical Year Book. ECLAC 2004.

Figure 6.3. Average annual salary during the period of the concession

1995=100

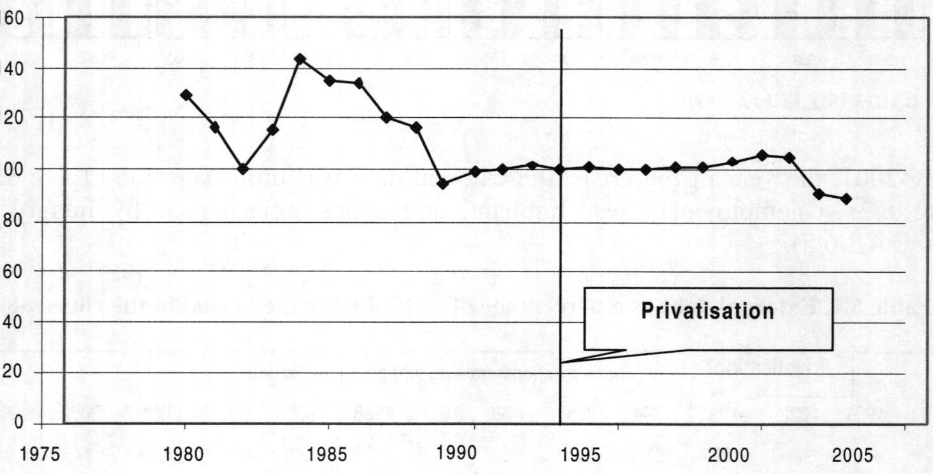

Note. Adjusted for inflation. Salary deflated by inflation index (1995=100).

Source: BADEINSO, ECLAC, 2005.

Figure 6.4. Poverty and indigence[1] during the period of the concession

% of total

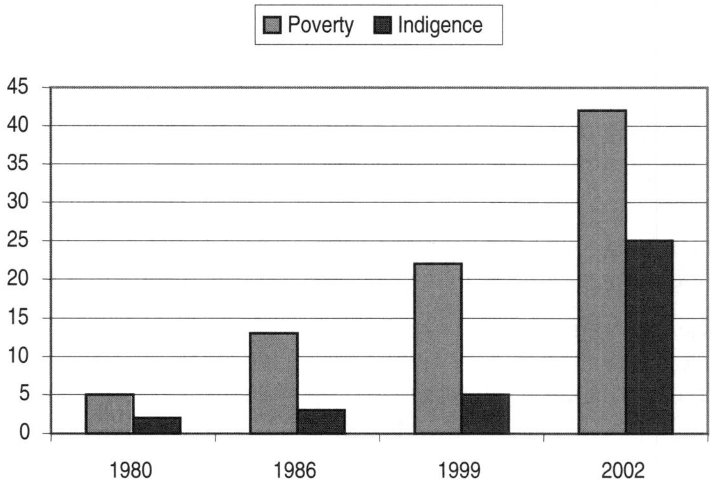

1. Indigents cannot afford to buy food. The poor can afford food, but can not fully satisfy their basic needs for clothing, food and recreation.

Source: BADEINSO–ECLAC 2005.

Figure 6.5. Gini index during the period of the concession

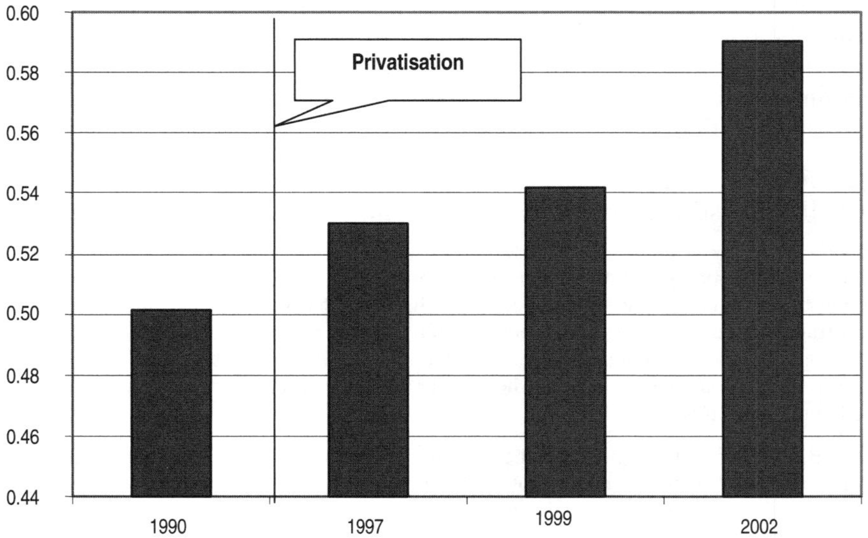

The Gini index is a measure of inequality of distribution, where 0 corresponds to perfect equality, and 1 corresponds to perfect inequality. Its application in the context of a paper on water supply and sanitation is helpful to illustrate the increases in inequality in Argentina at the time of the concession, therefore contributing to the understanding of lack of affordability by the poor.

Source: BADEINSO–ECLAC 2005.

The years of privatisation were a period of trust in private markets and distrust of governments. It was assumed that market competition, rate regulation with price cap mechanisms, light regulation and information substitutes would make up for the information asymmetries and for market, state and system failures:

- Distrust of government resulted in regulatory systems with weak information requirements (for examples, see Sappington, 1986).
- Overoptimistic assumptions, *e.g.* based on the idea that market contestability reduces the need for regulation, also affected regulatory quality.[1]
- It was assumed that, if competition is limited in the market, competition for the market creates some sort of substitute competition, theoretically reducing the need for regulation and information. Nonetheless, the exercise was fraught with difficulties.[2]
- In many cases, privatisation laws and regulations have applied theoretical price cap systems to regulate the earnings of providers. In practice, the system suffered from several problems, including the fact that a good deal of information was required in order to establish cost reduction potentials.[3]

The concession has been rescinded. Both sides are unhappy. The company requested that rates be adjusted to reflect devaluation (*La Nación*, 2005). The government claims that investments were not made as promised. Better understanding of the impact of the macroeconomic context and improved regulation and practices would have saved both parties a great deal of sorrow.

Implementation of the reform and universal service

In Buenos Aires, there was no liberalisation in the sense of ensuring competition. A private foreign monopolist provided the service. The provider won a bid based on an offer of a 26.9% tariff reduction (tariffs had increased by 62% prior to privatisation, and a value-added tax of 18% had also been added) associated with an expansion programme. New connections were to be paid for by the concessionaire. Yet, the high cost of infrastructure, relative to income, deterred prospective low-income new users.

The concession left an opaque and inefficient tariff system in place (Alcazar *et al.*, 2000, p. 21). Bills are issued every two months and most consumers were and are charged

1. Theoretically, efficient pricing and production can be forced on a supplier am much by the threat of competition as by actual competition. However, while the theory has gained considerable currency as an abstract construct: "its impact on regulatory policies in relation to natural monopolies has been much less significant, simply because the assumptions of perfect contestability on which it is based, notably that the entrant can leave the market, without costs, when it is no longer profitable to remain, are rarely encountered in practice" (Ogus, 1994, p. 33).

2. In the case of Buenos Aires it is argued that the bidding process encouraged the companies to offer the highest possible rate of discount, to be renegotiated later, if necessary. Furthermore, once the concession is awarded it becomes a monopoly enjoying an almost total advantage over potential competitors. The small number of actual bidders participating in the adjudication contest reinforced the inherently monopolistic nature of the concession process (Ferro, 1999). This is consonant with the data on limited number of bidders in most water supply and sanitation biddings provided by Vivien Foster at the "Primer Encuentro de Entes Reguladores de las Americas", Cartagena de Indias, Colombia, October, 2001.

3. In its initial British version it resulted in weak accountability and lack of procedural safeguards. This problem, the reliance of regulators on information provided by firms, and the history of bargaining between them all suggest that the system may not be as resistant to the influence of private interests as its proponents hoped (Ogus, 1994. p. 312/313).

a flat rate. There are two tariffs: metered and non-metered. Non-metered tariffs pay a flat rate. Metered rates consist of a relatively high fixed charge and a variable charge based on consumed cubic metres (m^3), starting at 20 m^3. Only 17% of users (36% of total billing) are metered. Both the flat rate of non-metered tariffs and the fixed charge of metered tariffs (50% of the flat rate) are based on built surface, age and quality of construction, location and 10% of total land surface. Therefore, most users pay a fixed charge that is independent of consumption, although individual billing varies according to the factors mentioned. The system contains cross-subsidies from metered to non-metered users and from non-residential to residential users. According to World Bank reports, this was an incentive to serve the areas able to pay more first. Flat rates did not encourage savings and expanded coverage in high-paying areas could have induced the company to slow expansion to other areas if returns did not justify the investment. According to some researchers, the option to meter consumption gave the company an incentive to meter poor households (because of the peculiarities of the local rates, it is profitable for the company to meter when the variable charge is more than half of the fixed rate) (Abdala, 1996). Returns in new poor areas did not in fact justify investment, since consumers there could not pay the infrastructure charge. It is also charged that the hybrid price cap system of the concession reduced incentives to keep costs down by allowing adjustments between periods, if the cumulative index of specific costs escalated beyond 7% (Alcazar *et al.*, 2000, pp. 27-29). In 2005, bills included a charge for universal service and environmental improvement (SUMA), which amounted to 27% of every average bill under the concession. Synthetically:

$$AB = BTT + (SUMA + CMC)$$

(in ARS)

- AB: Amount to be billed to residential unmetered users
- BTT: Basic two-months tariff
- SUMA: Charge for universal service and environmental improvement
- CMC: Maintenance and connection renewal charges

BTT is calculated as follows:

$$BTT = K*Z*TG*(SC*E+ST/10)$$

- K: Adjustment factor
- Z: Zone index (0.9-3.5)
- TG: General tariff
- SC: Covered surface (building surface)
- E: Construction index (0.64-3.88)
- ST: Land surface (plot extension)

Source: ETOSS-Gerencia de Economía del Sector (Regulatory Agency-Sector Economics Manager).

The original contract provided for sequential investments. Water coverage was 70% and was supposed to reach 90% by 2013 and 100% by 2023. Sewerage was supposed to increase to 73% by 2013 and 90% by 2023, from 57% at the beginning of the concession.

However, the contract did not provide incentives to reach the goals. Tariffs were globally estimated at mean long-term cost. Thus, tariffs were supposed to generate enough demand-related income to recover, within 30 years, operational costs, investment costs and the costs of capital outlays to make the investments. The estimates discounted in advance revenues required to pay for total concession costs. In practice this is tantamount to an incentive to delay investment, since once the company has collected the tariffs, it makes a profit by delaying investment. In the absence of adequate supervision and control, there was a perverse incentive not to comply with the investment plan. If penalties for non-compliance are lower than its benefits, a company has no incentive to invest. Chile has a different system: wastewater rates, for example, cannot be collected until treatment plants are operative. Rate increases are allowed only after investments are made and works and facilities are operational.

In 2003 Buenos Aires addressed the problem by implementing a trust fund that was created in 2001. The trust consists of funds accruing during the first five years after the rate revision, deposited into a bank. The regulator and the concessionaire agree on the programme of work, and the bank pays only after approval by the regulator.

There were other disincentives: *i)* rates paid in poorer areas were based on lower indexes than rates paid in other areas, since they were based not on consumption but on property valuation; *ii)* supply to such areas represents a higher investment in infrastructure, as well as relatively higher costs in transport, distribution and collection; *iii)* poorer areas represent higher commercial and collection risks; *iv)* the cost of connection discouraged users, who were accustomed to discharge into septic tanks; *v)* infrastructure charges were too high to be paid by the poorest sectors of the population; *vi)* the problems associated with a non-performing economy were not taken into account. Contract design and implementation had an impact on the incentives. In fact the rigid design of the contract created a barrier to implementation of reforms and regulations to solve problems (E. Lentini, personal communication 19 September 2005).

Aguas Argentinas chose a capital structure with a debt level higher than international standards. Debt levels were renegotiated in order to change the terms of the original bidding proposal. Financing was provided through debt and not through equity. With the depreciation of the Argentinean peso in 2002 the company's debt was USD 700 million (Table 6.2) and the level became critical.

Table 6.2. Profitability and debt level Aguas Argentinas S.A. (1994-2001)

Net income/sales	Net income/equity	Debt/equity
13%	21%	2.4

Source: ETOSS-Gerencia de Economía del Sector (Regulatory Agency-Sector Economics Manager).

Until 2000 the tools of choice for ensuring universal service were cross-subsidies for expansion, the infrastructure charge, later replaced by a universal service charge, and works by third parties. Works by third parties included connections and secondary networks paid for by new users or communities and neighbourhoods. Construction companies, working with municipalities with the authorisation of the concessionaire, negotiated with potential users to construct the works, which were paid for by users through long-term loans at high interest rates. The works, paid for, or mostly paid for, by users, then became an asset belonging to the concessionaire. This system operated before privatisation. It was a way to compensate for the dearth of public funding. Third-party works contracted and under construction before privatisation, and transferred to the concessionaire after the privatisation, facilitated compliance with some of the contract goals. They were accounted for as concessionaire investment. The system was not transparent, and the lack of clear rules regarding attribution has resulted in debate. Some argue that the concessionaire cannot legally claim to have financed third-party works, and therefore these cannot be counted as concessionaire investment. For others, third-party works were part of the risk assumed by the concessionaire, which stood to gain if they were significant in relation to contract goals, and to lose if they were negligible. It seems clear that the contract should have explicitly addressed this problem to prevent conflicting interpretations.

Table 6.3. Aguas Argentinas income statement, 1997-2004

ARS millions

	1997	1998	1999	2000	2001	2002	2003	2004
Revenues	419 998	536 722	510 958	514 246	566 037	59 9648	593 824	610 374
Operating expenses	349 300	366 903	389 854	359 739	409 575	457 874	489 427	637 675
EBIT: Earnings before interest and taxes	70 698	69 819	121 104	154 507	156 462	141 774	104 397	-27 301
Interest expense	-12 962	-19 774	-28 948	-33 393	-39 395	1 805 582	153 507	45 839
Income tax expense	-	-13 500	-30 037	-36 053	-43 188	11 727	-33 840	-4 699
Net income	57 736	36 545	62 119	85 061	73 879	1 652 081	224 064	13 839
Cash flow								
EBIT: Income tax expense	70 698	56 319	91 067	118 454	113 274	153 501	70 557	-32 000
Depreciation	66 251	51 465	72 413	70 440	71 982	-	-	-
Changes in working capital	1 740	-7 940	-21 412	-26 937	13 791	97 623	-82 802	-84 631
Capital expenditures	251 711	142 807	200 658	189 971	129 770	84 317	74 875	75 022
Free cash flow for the firm	-116 502	-27 083	-15 766	25 860	41 695	-28 439	78 484	-22 391
Balance sheet								
Current assets	123 114	131 312	150 418	203 877	121 717	194 839	239 345	129 352
Fixed assets	847 763	939 105	1 067 350	1 186 881	1 244 669	1 247 670	1 277 152	1 372 848
Total assets	970 877	1 070 417	1 217 768	1 390 758	1 366 386	1 442 509	1 516 498	1 502 200
Current liabilities	360 316	324 602	245 620	379 676	338 808	924 919	1 205 848	1 262 869
Long-term liabilities	337 136	453 845	638 059	612 932	582 549	1 758 744	1 327 739	1 156 083
Equity	273 425	291 970	33 4089	398 150	445 029	-1 241 154	-1 017 090	-916 752
Total liabilities and equity	970 877	1 070 417	1 217 768	1 390 758	1 366 386	1 442 509	1 516 497	1 502 200
Financial ratios								
Net margin (net income/sales)	13.7%	8.4%	12.2%	16.5%	13.1%	-275.5%	37.7%	2.3%
Return on equity	23.0%	12.9%	19.8%	23.2%	17.5%	415.0%	19.8%	-1.4%
Debt/equity	2.6	2.7	2.6	2.5	2.1	-2.16	-2.49	-2.64

Source: ETOSS-Gerencia de Economía del Sector (Regulatory Agency, Sector Economic Manager)

Table 6.3 presents the financial statement of Aguas Argentinas for the period 1997-2004. The 2002 crisis had a negative impact on its financial situation, since its debt was incurred in dollars and it suffered a loss as a result of exchange rates differences. Debt and losses resulted in negative equity. Profits increased however in the following years.

New programmes were implemented in 2001 and 2002: *i)* the Social Tariff Programme (PST) is a cross-subsidy to demand in which selected beneficiaries get targeted discounts, based on social polls; *ii)* the Programme for Poor Neighbourhoods (PPN) constructs secondary networks with municipal, beneficiary, and concessionaire contributions, and tariffs enjoy discounts.

The Programme of Social Tariff Beneficiaries is based on polls designed by the regulator. It will be audited to correct for mistakes. It benefits 80 000 households and 300 000 people. Poor neighbourhoods have location specificities that make leakage to non-targeted users difficult.

The costs of the new programmes for the poor are not significant for ETOSS (*Ente Tripartito de Obras y Servicios Sanitarios* – Tripartite Agency for the Regulation of Works and Sanitation Services) and AA (Aguas Argentinas, the concessionaire). For the Social Tariff Programme, municipal costs were high at the identification stage, since municipalities had to constitute special working teams. ETOSS spends ARS 110 000 a year, and the 18 participating municipalities spend ARS 350 000 a year to employ 69 people. The programme has a budget of ARS 4 million a year. The PPN's administrative cost to AA is ARS 500 000.

The concession did not have promoting innovative technologies as a main goal. The PPN's methods and supplies are adjusted to the needs of emergency neighbourhoods without compromising the quality achieved by the concession. Self-help is used, and sewerage utilises a system of "sewerage without solids".

Impacts of the change: the situation of the poor

The bidding proposal ensured a theoretically reasonable ratio of income to investment. The problem was that income did not match expectations. Total coverage increased by 4% for water by 1996/97 but decreased by 3% for sewerage (Azpiazu and Forcinito, 2003, p. 69; FIEL, 1999b).

According to Suez, Buenos Aires was a "sick system". The contract was prepared "with total inadequacy, or even absence of, of reliable information, data, records and measures" (Suez, undated, p. 2). Already in 1994 the company had taken a loan from the International Finance Corporation (IFC) that would only be repaid if there were rate increases or reductions in investment (Alcazar *et al.*, 2000, p. 41).. Both the paucity of data and the loan suggest that there was a reasonable expectation of renegotiation. This may justify the claim that the bidder was opportunistic and the offer predatory.

The context may not have favoured poor prospective users. Although the contract explicitly establishes that governments did not assume responsibility for factual accuracy (Alcazar *et al.*, 2000, p. 21), the information issue, among other factors, justified renegotiations (Suez, undated).

New users had to pay the costs of expanding the secondary network plus the costs of connection and modifications within the house. The average infrastructure charge was ARS 44 a month, for two years. New connections were a problem for the poor with a monthly income ranging from ARS 200 to ARS 245. The charge thus represents about 18% of the monthly or yearly income of a poor household, depending on the time period considered. Some 85% of those unconnected were either poor or low income. When the pipes and connection are available to a household, the owner is obliged to connect to the service. If the owner does not, the contract allows the concessionaire to start billing even if no service is provided (Abdala, 1996). Tariffs and connection and infrastructure charges for both water and sewerage were increased in 1994.

Problems of affordability affecting the infrastructure charge prompted contract renegotiations. The infrastructure charge was eliminated in 1997 and the universal service and environmental charges were established in 1997 (SUMA), The universal service charge was ARS 2.01 per service every two months (water and sanitation). The environmental charge was ARS 0.99 per service every two months, starting in December 1998. Both charges were to be paid by all users. Lower connection charges for new users were implemented (ARS 120 per service, to be paid in 30 bi-monthly instalments). Expansion was cut (by 15% for water and 13% for sewerage for the first five years). The average water bill of customers already connected rose by 19%, while for new consumers it declined by 74%. SUMA was paid in advance, which reduced the government's leverage for ensuring completion of the works in a timely manner (Alcazar *et al.*, 2000, pp. 36-39). While expansion was reduced, tariffs, based on the promise of expansion, were not lowered. According to some researchers, the ARS 700 million not invested mostly affected the poor of greater Buenos Aires.[4]

One of the problems of the concession was the lack of an agreed methodology for establishing compliance with targets. The concessionaire counted as compliance works done by third parties and the legalisation of existing informal connections. Others argued that such expansion should not be credited to the concessionaire. If legalised connections and third-party works are counted, the rate of compliance during the first five years of the concession would be 70% of contracted works, for both water and sewerage. It not, the rate of compliance falls to 40% for water and 20% for sewerage. Thus non-compliance, seven years after initiating the concession, would be 41% for water and 56% for sewerage (Arza, 2002, p. 17). There are also claims that average water bills increased by 63% as of January 1999, although increases were banned during the first ten years of the concession (Table 6.4).

Table 6.4. Evolution of the average residential bill, with SUMA[1]

Concept	Date	Average bill in ARS	Avg. bill, May index 1993 = 100
OSN	May 1993	19.40	133
Bidding Aguas Argentinas	May 1993	14.56	100
1st tariff revision	June 1994	16.53	114
Universal service incorporation	November 1997	20.55	141
2nd tariff revision	May 1998	21.65	149
Environmental charge incorporation	January 1999	23.73	163
Increase 2001 five years and annual revision	January 2001	26.25	180
Increase 2002 five years and annual revision	January 2002	27.40	188

1. Prices are nominal market prices and are not adjusted for inflation.

Source: ETOSS-Gerencia de Economía del Sector (Regulatory Agency-Sector Economics Manager).

4. Maria Elena Corrales, comments in Peter Rogers IADB paper, Fortaleza.

The original tariff adjustment was 0.731, against the state company's tariff base of 1. It was adjusted in 1994 (13.5%). The universal service and environmental charges, explained above, were added later, together with a fixed connection charge of ARS 120 to be paid by new users. In 1998 ETOSS authorised an increase of 1.61%. The K factor increased to 0.8434 (Table 6.5 and Figure 6.6). The company appealed to the executive, which authorised an increase of 5.31%. The K factor increased to 0.8741.[5] There were K increases of 4.5% (2001), 4.4% (2002) and 3.9% (2003). A fixed charge of 1.5% of the tariff, not reflected in K, was also approved in 2003. Tariff amendments were approved by the executive branch and not by the regulator.

Table 6.5. The K factor

Details	Date	Evolution of K
O.S.N.	May-93	1.0000
Bid AASA	May-93	0.7310
1º tariff review	Jun-94	0.8300
2º tariff review	May-98	0.8741
Increase 2001 five years and annual review	Jan -01	0.9169
Increase 2002 five years and annual review	Jan -02	0.9572

Source: ETOSS-Gerencia de Economía del Sector (Regulatory Agency-Sector Economics Manager)

Figure 6.6. Evolution of the K factor

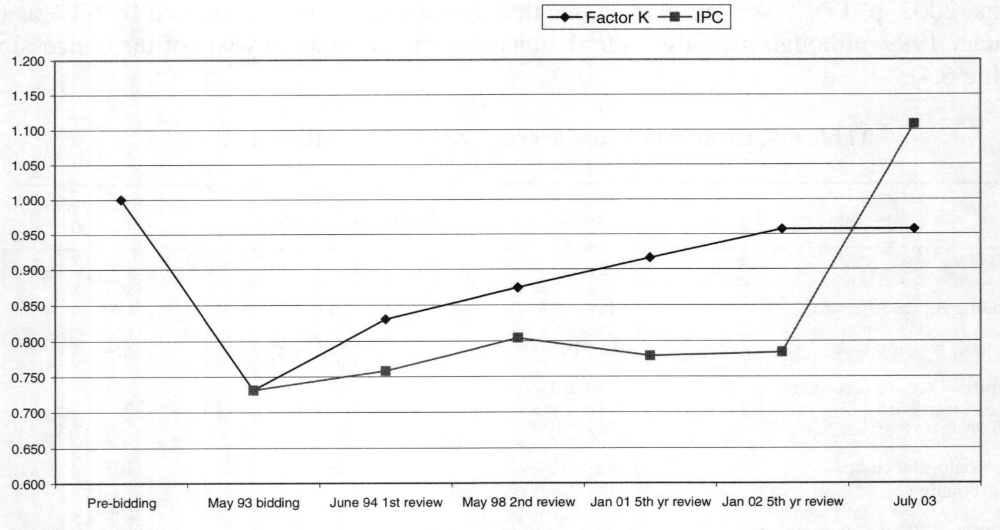

Source: ETOSS-Gerencia de Economía del Sector (Regulatory Agency-Sector Economics Manager).

"K" is a multiplier, whose value was 1 at the time of bidding for the concession. The base to which the K factor was applied was the existing rate. The concession was won

5. Truly independent regulators are not subject to administrative appeals. Appeals go to court. Administrative appeals destroy independence from the political establishment.

with a bid to reduce tariffs by 26.9%. Therefore, the concession bid that won proposed a K multiplier of 0.731 which was accepted by the government.

K is similar to a price cap and is adjusted every five years, based on the investment plan. It is the result of a composite index, consisting of ten categories of cost, such as fuel, chemicals, electricity, labour, debt service, etc. The complexity of the index allows for opportunistic behaviour, by both the company and the regulator (Alcazar *et al.*, 2000).

The increase in the K factor was generally above the national consumer price index. For a service whose users depend on a depressed national economy to be able to pay, this creates a gap between income and service costs. When recession and devaluation hit the country the concession became unsustainable. In Chile, where the privatisation process has been very successful, researchers stress that high investment rates and ensuing high tariffs can only be paid when there is a process of continuous national economic growth (Peña *et al.*, 2004, pp. 12-13).

As of 2001 only 39% of the households of the Conurbano had water and sewerage. Only 66% had water. Just 40% had sewerage and 33% had neither. Thus, 56% of households in the poorest decile had neither water nor sewerage, and 83% had no sewerage (Navajas, 2001;[6] Rogers, 2002).

There were no direct subsidies to the poor until 2001, although the poorest households with service access spent 1.1% of their income on water and sanitation, while the richest decile spent 0.3% (Arza, 2004, p. 34). As of 1985-86 the lowest quintile of the population had a rate of access to water supply of 44.8% and the second lowest had a rate of access of 67%. As of 1996-97 the rates had increased to 51.9% and 70.5%, respectively. The same quintiles had a rate of access to sewerage of 30% and of 54.2%, respectively, in 1985-86. These rates dropped to 27% and 45.5% in 1996-97 (Arza, 2004, p. 52, based on FIEL, 1999a). The original design and regulations did not include subsidies for the very poor (Arza, 2004, p. 54). This was a major oversight on the part of the government. In Chile, the system focused subsidies on the poor to accompany the privatisation process. Every water bill in Chile informs the user that it is possible to resort to the local municipality to seek financial assistance in paying it (Peña *et al.*, 2004, p. 51). Obviously this major failure is not attributable to the concessionaire, but to the concession design process.

New programmes for the poor were started in 2001 and 2002. They give some satisfaction, but they do not allow for compliance with universal service objectives. There are now 1.8 million people without water and 3.5 million without sewerage. Only 10% of effluent is treated. A comparison of the agreed results and the effective achievements of the concession shows that, after nine years, water coverage reaches 79% of the population (against a target of 88% and thus a deficit of 800 000); sewerage reaches 63%, short of the target by 11% and a deficit of 1 million; primary sewage treatment is 7%, against a target of 74% and a deficit of 6.2 million people; and investment has been ARS 1 342 000 million against a target of ARS 2 202 200 million, a deficit of 859 400 million (E. Lentini, personal communication). As explained, new consumers were unable to pay the high infrastructure charge, which was therefore replaced by the universal service charge, which in fact was a cross-subsidy. However, the firm could collect it in advance, with a view to future investments, rather than after investments were made. Other programmes that could have helped the process of expanding services to the poor,

6. According to information from Maria Elena Corrales, consultant.

such as third-party works, were not successful either, owing to a lack of transparency in negotiations between construction companies and local authorities.[7] The problems originate in the structure of relationships between construction companies and municipalities.

Renegotiations, inadequate initial data and imperfect evaluation of the economic capacity of the population served, plus the crisis of 2002, resulted in non-compliance with agreed targets. Measures such as the STP and PPN, while effective, do not make up for the lack of investment commensurate with the magnitude of the problem.

Conflicts between equity and efficiency: conflict resolution and sectoral characteristics

In a social and economic sense equity may be understood as the balance in the distribution of costs and benefits between providers and consumers (fairness), including access by the poor to water and sanitation services.

Systems with a long-standing history of private provision of public utility services have often seen conflicts between private and public interests. One aims to maximise profit while the other seeks adequate service at the lowest possible price (Phillips, 1993, pp. 5-6). Thus, in the absence of competition, such a balance hinges on regulation and contract design so that both economic efficiency and social equity are sought and achieved.

In technical regulatory terms, equity can also be understood, by opposition to debt, as the part of the capital structure of the company provided by stockholders (shared capital/property). Inadequate ratios of equity (property) to debt, in capital structures, affect social equity and efficiency.

In the past utility rate structures aimed at promoting usage but they now look to efficiency. "The shift in emphasis moreover highlights an underlying conflict in objectives – specifically, fairness versus economic efficiency (Phillips, 1993, p. 20; Zajac, 1978). Fully distributed cost pricing may be defended on grounds of fairness, but only incremental cost pricing can be defended on grounds of efficiency and competitiveness (Phillips, 1993, p. 20). Regulators cannot regulate without knowing about investment activities, transfer prices, debt and other items, which necessitate specific accounting systems. These, and many other issues, make regulation an analytically demanding activity.

Buenos Aires' problems have structural and regulatory roots. The structural assessment of the sustainability of both the national economy and the concession was flawed, and appropriate regulation was not in place.

In 2000, before the Argentinean debacle, the World Bank had warned that: "The Buenos Aires privatisation of water utility services, their information shortcomings, lack of transparency in regulatory decisions and *ad hoc* nature of executive branch interventions, make it difficult to reassure consumers that their welfare is being protected, and that the concession is sustainable." (Alcazar *et al.*, 2000, front cover)

In similar terms, but with hindsight, *The Economist* stated that: "In Argentina it has been said that privatisations were sweet deals, with public utilities becoming private,

7. Personal Communication, ETOSS, Office of the Economic Manager of the Sector, 24 September 2005.

rather than public monopolies. Rates in long-term contracts were updated on the basis of US inflation, even if prices in Argentina were falling. Dollar interest rates were high, even if in theory risk was low." (*The Economist*, 2002, p. 27)

Regulation did not properly address the conflicts between equity and efficiency in the relationship between society and the company or the complexities of capital structure and adequate ratios of property to debt. Neither regulation nor contract design addressed properly the needs of the poor. Regulation and control were weak, and political authorities routinely bypassed the regulator, as in the 1997 renegotiation.[8]

Regulation and contract negotiations lacked a key technical tool for enhancing social equity as they did not ensure that the level of equity (property invested/shared capital of stockholders) was commensurate with the magnitude of the operation. Public utilities may finance their investment through equity or through debt. If debt is too high, fixed charges are high and have to be paid by consumers. Likewise the cost of capital increases financial risks and therefore costs (Phillips, 1993, p. 233). Users pay these costs. That is why the debt-capital ratio is closely controlled. In the United Kingdom, for example, the maximum theoretical debt is 1:1 or 50% debt and 50% equity (Ofwat, 2002). In Buenos Aires, it was 2.4:1. The strategy of having a debt/equity (shared capital) ratio well above what is technically acceptable in advanced regulatory systems affected both economic efficiency and social equity (in the relationship between company and users). Costs were higher than they might have been and were transferred, through rates, to users.

Transfer pricing also affects efficiency. Companies may buy their inputs from associates, eventually increasing costs and therefore tariffs. Social equity (in allocation of costs and benefits) is again affected.[9] In addition, privatisation did not originally provide subsidies for the poor, and the charge system did not encourage expansion to poor areas. Equity was not properly embedded into the concession design.

The conflicts associated with regulation require a regulator with independence, impartiality and technical knowledge to ensure equity in conflict adjudication processes. Yet, political authorities often bypassed the Buenos Aires regulator in both rate regulation processes and contract renegotiation (Alcazar *et al.*, 2000, p. 37).

The global economy and its institutional framework, in addition to internal regulations and institutions, can affect the equity aspects of the concession. As a foreign investor, the provider was entitled to use the state arbitration procedure. In state arbitration cases investors usually attempt to keep a tariff level commensurate with contractual arrangements and agreed adjustment provisions, even if adjustments are in foreign currencies and the national economy is in crisis. Because of the 2002 crisis, Aguas Argentinas submitted an emergency plan which suspended all non-emergency investment, with the company to receive dollars at the old 1:1 exchange rate, in order to serve the debt and buy inputs.[10]

8. As of 1 January 2005, Maria Julia Alsogaray, the Secretary of State responsible for renegotiation was in jail, accused in eight cases of corruption, although none is specifically related to Buenos Aires concession, Clarin, Buenos Aires, 1 March 2005.

9. In the case of Aguas Argentinas, an audit carried out by Halcrow on 15 August 1997 concluded that the works in the first three years of the five-year plan, were generally contracted to companies related to Aguas Argentinas. Prices could have been lower if contracts had been grouped. Comparing prices with similar waterworks, budgets were generally higher than the references.

10. Memo from Carlos Ben and Juan Carlos Cassagne, January, 2002, to the National Secretary for Water Resources.

Aguas Argentinas signed an agreement that put arbitration on hold until 31 December 2004. Then, the concession was rescinded and the company sued the government, requesting that tariffs be adjusted in line with devaluation. Such adjustments may well go beyond the carrying capacity of the country and the paying capacity of users. Elsewhere, previous cases of national economic crisis of the magnitude of Argentina's have consistently ruled that tariffs cannot increase above the rate of national economic growth.[11] Otherwise some economic actors would not be affected by the crisis and be a regressive factor. It may be argued that differential protection is not equitable.

The practice of guaranteeing exchange rates is questioned. World Bank analysts have pointed out that such guarantees can wipe out the benefits of privatisation by dampening incentives to select and manage programmes and projects efficiently (Gray and Irwin, 2003). Chile does not allow adjustments according to exchange rate variations. As a result companies seek financing in local capital markets to avoid the risk of currency fluctuations.

The regulator

Buenos Aires did not have a regulator prior to the concession, when ETOSS was created to control it. Almost every empirical and theoretical principle regarding the organisation of regulators was disregarded. The Buenos Aires regulator ETOSS is a political body, with representatives from three levels of government, and its decisions may therefore be influenced by political considerations. Its board consists of two representatives of the Presidency of Argentina, two from Buenos Aires Province and two from Buenos Aires Municipality. They represent different political jurisdictions and different political parties. Although members are chosen for six years, most have lasted only two years. The different levels of government have put pressure on the regulator to take politically motivated decisions (Alcazar *et al.*, 2000, p. 30). For example, in 1994 the mayor of Buenos Aires wanted to build a highway and resettle the residents of a shantytown located on the chosen route. He pressured Aguas Argentinas to build water and sewerage and then ETOSS to approve the tariff increase requested by the company to finance the construction. Some observers believe that the increase was too large, and that the change in responsibilities and tariffs violated the concession contract. Disputes arose among board members, resulting in paralysis. The opposition party governed the city, and the province was President Menem's main opponent in the governing political party. "This situation raised the risk that regulatory decisions would be based on partisan conflicts, and reduced the credibility of the concession." (Alcazar *et al.*, 2000, pp. 30-31) Moreover, the regulatory framework, approved by decree, was easily manipulated and changed, as compared to a regulatory body with regulations based on laws.

11. In the United States, at the time of the Depression, the courts recognised a decline in interest rates and business earnings throughout the country, and was willing to accept lower rates of return (Phillips, 1993, p. 378, and cases quoted there). In addition: Wilcox vs. Consolidated Gas, 212 US 19, 48-49 (1909); Lincoln Gas and Electric Light vs. Lincoln, 250 US 256 (1919); Missouri ex-real Southern Bell Tel Co. vs. Missouri Public Services Commission, 262 US 276 (1923); McCardle vs. Indianapolis Water, 272 US 400, 419 (1926), Alexandria Water Company vs. City Council of Alexandria, Supreme Court of Virginia, 163 Va. 512;177 S.E. 454 (1934); State *et al.* vs. Lone Star Gas Company, Texas (July 1935); Lexis 1935; Daytona Power 1934; Chesapeake and Potomac 1935; Driscoll, 1939.

The regulator was staffed with people from the former government agency.[12] It thus had divided loyalties, was inexperienced, had to work on a one-to-one basis with a single regulated company, and lacked a basis of comparison. Because of the theoretical underpinnings of the regulatory approach applied in Buenos Aires it was also weak, in terms of powers, capacity and information.

It is, however, well financed through a surcharge on bills. While some authors have criticised the procedure, it reflects international practices. In the United States, financing comes from a percentage tax on each utility's gross revenues, although six states finance from general revenues (Phillips, 1993, p. 37). The total budget of ETOSS is ARS 12 million and compares favourably with the budgets of state regulars in the United States (Phillips, 1993, pp. 138-139).

ETOSS has 130 employees, and there are no programmes to reduce costs. There have been some training courses, but not a full-fledged policy to create a fully capacitated, competitive, world standard regulator. Directors are not generally appointed on the basis of experience and training relevant to the regulation of the sector. Its structure is affected by information asymmetries. Some personnel have developed skills beyond their initial capabilities, but it is more the result of personal effort and of the regional impact of ADERASA (South American Association of Water Regulators) than of a coherent national policy.

Institutional adaptation

Regulation was initially affected by rushed privatisation, ideology and the idiosyncrasies of the government of the time. Comparing the Buenos Aires privatisation with those of Lima and Santiago, a World Bank Report says that: "The Buenos Aires privatisation went forward as part of the block of transactions because the political net benefits to Menem appeared to be larger than the net benefits from similar actions in Peru to Fujimori, or in Chile to Pinochet." (Alcazar *et al.*, 2000, p. 14) Emphasis on speed affected information (Alcazar *et al.*, 2000, p. 20). The privatisation "left in place" (it did not change with the privatisation) a tariff system that was opaque and not transparent. "Once again, the Government actors did not think they had time to develop a more transparent regime." (Alcazar *et al.*, 2000, p. 21)

Light regulation was the approach taken for public utilities at the time of privatisation. As a result, several important issues were disregarded. Transfer price, regulatory accounting, information requirements, minimum conditions of capital structure, were among the regulatory tools omitted. In issues such as rates of indebtedness, too much flexibility was allowed.

The regulatory regime was set by decree and therefore could be changed at any time by the national government. As a result a secretariat of the national government was the authority for the application of the contract and bypassed the regulator when taking decisions, as in the 1997 renegotiation of the contract (Alcazar *et al.*, 2000, p. 37).

Over time, the regulator, civil society and the company developed important tools: a user commission was set up, public audiences on tariffs were instituted, public directorate meetings were planned, a social tariff programme and a poor neighbourhood programme were created, and a trust fund for expansion was implemented. Other developments were

12. Although some of them, who were also union members, such as Carlos Ben, served AA (as a Director) and not the regulator.

regulatory accounting, permanent auditing of billing, procurement regulations, related services and suppliers regulations, separation of concession accounting and accounting books (E. Lentini, personal communication).

Conclusions and lessons

Conclusions to be drawn from the Buenos Aires concession include:

- Public utility services, generally, and water services, specifically, are not sustainable without adequate rates of economic growth, income and employment.
- Water services were not a priority for the national government. It did not put any funds into the concession after the privatisation.
- The main priority of the Argentinean government was to ensure an artificially stable exchange rate. Resources were allocated accordingly. The impact of such policy on growth and governance was not evaluated. This should have been done and should be considered in future privatisation processes.
- The poor were not a priority. Funds were not provided to cover their needs.
- The socioeconomic context and affordability were not properly evaluated.
- The regulator was weak, politically designated, and not independent. It did not have all the necessary regulatory tools.
- A number of decisions and renegotiations of the national authorities, which were favourable to the concessionaire, eroded the regulator's authority.
- The regulatory framework was weak, affected the sustainability of the concession (Alcazar *et al.*, 2000, p. 55), and did not take into account relevant experience, such as that of the United States and the United Kingdom.
- Conflict-solving mechanisms, *i.e.* international courts of arbitration, have not yet developed criteria for addressing conflicts resulting from general economic crises.
- Contractual and legal protection of concessionaires is not enough at times of economic crises. Moreover, some protection, such as guaranteed exchange rates, may be counterproductive, since it gives a false sense of security and does not encourage economic efficiency.
- The Buenos Aires regulatory system was mostly based on contract regulation. In accepting contract regulation, the parties ignored the fact that contract regulation affects regulatory quality. This type of regulation is disqualified by mature regulatory systems, such as that of the United States (Phillips, 1993, p. 130).

Lessons

- Countries, financing institutions and service providers should carefully analyse the socioeconomic context, the quality of macroeconomic policies, national priorities and the sustainability of economic growth before embarking on public or private development of water services. Services are costly and stagnating economies may be unable to afford them.

- Governments striving to expand and enhance water services, including control of environmental externalities, will not be successful unless policy priority is given to the sector, resources are adequate and subsidies are provided for the poor.
- Rushed decisions should be resisted. Adequate physical, economic and social data are crucial to good decision making and to the sustainability of services, state-owned or privatised.
- Public utility services are not independent of the socioeconomic mores of their environment. Their sustainability is affected by overall economic performance. Privatisation is a formal procedure that does not, by itself, ensure sustainability, since success depends on the quality of overall economic policies, public priorities and economic growth.
- Future regulatory design should put in place the basic regulatory instruments necessary for good regulation, based on relevant experience, enacted through regulatory law and separate from the contract. [13]
- Future regulatory efforts should rely less on theory and be aware of, and regulate for, proper management of critical regulatory issues.
- International courts of arbitration dealing with controversies associated with public utility services should apply the principles and rules accepted by civilised nations when legislating, regulating and adjudicating conflicts associated to the utilities sector.
- Countries with a tradition of private provision of utility services, such as the United States and the United Kingdom, have developed such principles. They include reasonable returns, linking rates and tariffs to growth and performance of national economies, controlling transfer prices, requiring expenses to be reasonable, controlling company debt, setting regulatory accounting, having independent regulators, connecting returns to actual investment, providing subsidies and protection for the poor, requiring efficient companies that transfer efficiencies to customers, providing regulators with broad information powers, penalising improvidence and non-compliance, etc.
- Governments and lending organisations should carefully consider the impact of special guarantees, such as rates of exchange, on the efficiency of service providers, macroeconomic national balances, contingent national liabilities, and equitable apportionment of national resources.
- Bidding mechanisms, and other measures such as price cap systems, are no substitute for adequate regulation. There is a need to refine competition mechanisms for awarding monopolies in order to avoid bid offers with predatory tariffs (to win now and negotiate later) and provide for a capital contribution from the successful bidder that represents a level of risk appropriate to the venture undertaken.
- Initiating a privatisation process with faulty data and inadequate public information is a prescription for conflict.

13. See for example, Phillips (1993) for the United States; Cour des Comptes (1997), for France, and Ogus (1994) for the English experience.

Postscript

In 2002 the Argentinean government enacted emergency legislation to cope with the collapse of the official exchange rate. The macroeconomic shock was intense. The artificial exchange rate of one peso to the dollar changed to four pesos to the dollar and then, as of September 2006, to three pesos to the dollar. Public utility rates were kept at the pre-devaluation levels, along with a prohibition to transfer the devaluation to the rates or to adjust them according to any indices.

Aguas Argentinas and the government discussed and negotiated various alternatives for coping with the situation throughout 2003 and 2004. In 2005, the situation became critical when the parties failed to agree to continue negotiations. Faulting the government, Aguas Argentinas requested rescission of the contract, but the government rejected its claim. Aguas Argentina then sued the Argentine Republic, at the International Centre for the Settlement of Investment Disputes (ICSID). Aguas Argentina claimed that:

- The Argentinean government had violated its obligations under international treaties for the protection of investments.
- The company's property had been expropriated without compensation.
- The government had dealt with the company and its investors and stockholders in an unfair and non-equitable manner.

Specifically, two claims were made: one initiated by the company and other, subsidiary to the first, by the stockholders, with the exception of the International Finance Corporation (IFC), requesting compensation from the Argentinean government. The claim initiated by the company was subsequently withdrawn, but the claim by the stockholders remains.

On 21 March 2006, the Argentinean government rescinded the concession, arguing that the concessionaire did not fulfil its obligations. In particular it cited:

- Failure to comply with obligations in terms of expansion and quality.
- High levels of nitrates in the water supplied.
- Non-execution of waterworks including the Lanus-Temperley aqueduct and the Lanus plant.
- Non-compliance with water pressure obligations.

ICSID has not, at the time of writing, issued its decision.

The government has created a new company, which is funded by the government and which owns 90% of the stock. The other 10% is owned by the company's labour union. The president of the new company was previously a member of the Direction of Aguas Argentinas representing labour-owned stock. While the new company is state-owned, it is governed by the rules of private corporations. The new utility is therefore likely to require significant regulation; applying rules applicable to private corporations to a public company or managing public funds under private corporation arrangements can create important challenges.

Before privatising its water utilities, Chile improved the performance of state-owned utilities through appropriate regulation. By the time the utilities were privatised they had achieved high standards of performance.

External advisors encouraged the Argentinean government to strengthen the regulator in order to cope with the new situation; to enact stringent efficiency requirements; to enact precise rules for regulatory accounting; to facilitate public control, participation and monitoring; to create a national system that would allow for comparing companies, both private and public; to enable the regulator to draw on foreign data and information to evaluate the company; to create a national system of regulators of public utilities; and, very importantly, to create a system of stringent penalties for companies and employees that do not carry out their duties. Advisors also suggested making efficiency not only a regulatory requirement but also a personal duty of managers and employees, with violations subject to stiff penalties.

Members of the government, the regulator, the management of the company and labour are, at the time of writing, discussing the contents of the new regulations.

References

Abdala, M. (1996), "The Welfare Effects of Buenos Aires Water and Sewerage Services Privatization", unpublished manuscript, World Bank, Washington, DC, December.

Alcazar, Lorena *et al.* (2000), "The Buenos Aires Concession", The World Bank Development Research Group, Regulation and Competition Policy, April, Policy Research Working Paper 2311.

Arza, C. (2002), "El Impacto Social de las Privatizaciones: El caso de los servicios publicos domiciliarios" Flacso, Documento de Trabajo Proyecto Bid 1201/OC-AR PICT99-02-O7523, March.

Azpiazu, D. and K. Forcinito (2003), "Historia de un Fracaso: La Privatizacion del Sistema de Agua y Saneamiento en el Area Metropolitana de Buenos Aires", paper presented at the special session of the Third world Forum on Water, held in Kyoto, April.

Cour des Comptes (1997), "La Gestion des services publics locaux d'eau et d'assainissement", January.

Ferro, G. (1999), "El Servicio Publico de Agua Potable y Saneamiento en Buenos Aires, Privatizacion y Regulacion" , Buenos Aires.

Fundación de Investigaciones Económicas Latinoamericanas (FIEL) (1999a), "La Regulacion de la Competencia y de los Servicios Publicos", *Teoria y Práctica de la Experiencia Argentina Reciente*, Buenos Aires.

FIEL (1999b), "La Distribucion del Ingreso en Argentina, Fundacion de Invesigaciones Economicas Latinoamericanas, Buenos Aires.

Gray, P. and T. Irwin (2003), "Allocating Exchange Rate Risk in Private Infrastructure Projects", *Public Policy for the Private Sector*, Number 266, December, World Bank, Washington, DC.

La Nacion (2005), 24 January, Buenos Aires.

Levy, B. and P. Spiller (1993), Comment on David Sappington, *Proceedings of the World Bank Annual Conference on Development Economics*, www.eclac.cl/samtac/noticias/documentosdetrabajo/8/23318/DrSam00203.pdf.

Navajas, F. (2001), "Mirando el Nivel de Cobertura en Agua y Saneamiento en la Argentina. Datos preliminaries", June.

Ogus, A. (1994), *Regulation, Legal Form and Economic Theory*, Clarendon Law Series, Oxford.

Peña, H. *et al.* (2004), "Water, Development and Public Policies", Samtac-Gwp, Santiago, Chile.

Phillips, C.F., Jr. (1993), "The Regulation of Public Utilities", Public Utilities Reports, Inc. Arlington Virginia.

Rogers, P. (2002), "Water Governance 2002", prepared for the Interamerican Bank Annual Meeting, Fortaleza, Brazil, March.

Sappington, D. (1986), "Comments to Regulatory Bureaucracy", *Information Economics and Policy* 2 (4), pp. 243-58.

Suez (undated), "An Informed Appraisal of the Document Published in South Africa by Municipal Services Project Titled "Lessons from Argentina-The Buenos Aires Water Concession.

The Economist (2002), "Special Report on Argentina's Collapse", 2 March.

Zajac, E.E. (1978),"Fairness or Efficiency: An Introduction to Public Utility Pricing", Ballinger Publishing Co., Cambridge.

Part III

Financial Services

Chapter 7

Universal Access to Financial Services: A Review of the Issues and Public Policy Objectives[1]

Stijn Claessens
Senior Adviser, World Bank and Professor, University of Amsterdam

This chapter reviews the evidence on the importance of finance for economic well-being, provides data on the degree of access by households and firms to basic financial services across a sample of countries, assesses the desirability of more universal access and summarises the macroeconomic, legal and regulatory obstacles to access using general evidence and case studies. The data show that universal access is far from prevalent in many countries, especially developing countries. At the same time, universal access should not be a public policy objective and is surely not easily achievable in most countries. Countries can, however, undertake action to facilitate access to financial services, including by strengthening their institutional infrastructures, liberalising and opening up their markets and facilitating greater competition, and encouraging innovative use of know-how and technology. The chapter draws attention to some of the risks and costs associated with attempts to broader the provision of access to finance and points out that intervention carries a significant risk of missing the targeted groups. The chapter ends with possible actions aimed at improving data on access and further analysis to help identify the constraints to broadening access to financial services.

1. Prepared for the Fifth Services Experts Meeting on Universal Access, organised by the WTO and the World Bank, Paris, 3-4 February 2005. This chapter draws on material from Stephen Peachey and Alan Roe, and presentations by Priya Basu, Thorsten Beck, Patrick Honohan, Anjali Kumar, Tova Solo and others at the World Bank working on access to financial services. Thanks to Ying Lin for useful research assistance. The opinions expressed do not necessarily represent those of the World Bank.

Introduction

Finance has been shown to matter for countries' economic development. There is much evidence for a strong and causal relationship between the depth of the financial system (as measured, for example, by the supply of private credit, stock market capitalisation or other financial measures relative to GDP), on the one hand, and investment, growth, poverty, total factor productivity, etc., on the other. Indeed, by many empirical tests, initial financial development is one of the few robust determinants of countries' subsequent growth. Finance matters for the well-being of people beyond overall economic growth: it can help individuals smooth their income, insure against risks and more generally broaden investment opportunities. It can be particularly important for the poor; indeed, recent evidence has shown that a more developed financial system can help reduce income inequality and poverty.

The evidence has focused attention on the importance of overall financial development. Yet, and especially in many developing countries, the financial system at large does not appear to cater to the needs of all customers. Banking systems and capital markets are often skewed towards those already better off, mainly large enterprises and wealthier individuals. It has been found that some segments of the enterprise and household sector suffer from lack of access to finance, hindering their growth and welfare. This raises the question of whether more general availability of financial services should be a public sector goal and, if so, what the best means of achieving this are.

This chapter reviews the evidence on the importance of financial development for economic well-being, provides data on the degree of access across a sample of countries and an assessment of the desirability of more universal access to financial services, summarises the macroeconomic, legal and regulatory obstacles to access to financial services, and reviews the risks and costs associated with attempts to broader access to finance. The chapter addresses the following topics: Why the recent attention to access? What does access to finance mean? What is the evidence on access and who has access? What do we know about constraints on access and what can be done by governments in this respect? What are possible international actions?

Access to finance: relevance

Access to financial services has received greater attention lately and seems to have become a more important part of the overall development agenda, probably for a number of reasons. For one, evidence that "finance" – as in financial development – matters for growth has been accumulating over the last decade. Second, based on changes in economies and economic production, finance may have moved up in the ranking of barriers to growth. Third, there is an increasing perception that access of households and enterprises to finance has been skewed. The evidence on these three aspects is reviewed briefly.

Today, the empirical evidence that finance causes growth is very robust and available at the level of country, sector and individual firm, and households. Various statistical techniques are used. Financial deepening has been shown to "cause" growth (Rajan and Zingales, 1998; Demirgüç-Kunt and Maksimovic, 1998; Beck *et al.*, 2000; Wurgler, 2000; for an extensive review of the evidence, see Levine, 2005). Finance helps growth by raising and pooling funds, thereby making it possible to undertake more, and more risky, investments, by allocating resources to their most productive use, by monitoring the use of funds, and by providing instruments for risk mitigation. It is less the forms taken by these services – banks or capital markets – than the fact that they are provided in an efficient manner, *i.e.* supported by a proper institutional and competitive environment, as this matters for growth (Demirgűç-Kunt and Levine, 2001; see also World Bank, 2001). As such, it is difficult to assert that particular types of financial systems are more conducive to growth or perhaps more conducive to facilitating access to financial services.

Finance also helps improve income distribution and poverty reduction through several channels. First, it helps through economic growth, by raising overall income levels. It can help more specifically by distributing opportunities more fairly. There is evidence that finance matters especially for poor households and smaller firms. In a cross-country study on the link to poverty, Beck *et al.* (2004a), controlling for reverse causality, find that financial development causes less income inequality. Clarke *et al.* (2002) also find that inequality decreases as finance develops. Since the more concentrated the income, the greater the degree of poverty, finance can help reduce poverty.

Honohan (2004a, 2004b) shows that financial depth explains poverty (people with income of less than USD 1 or USD 2 a day). He also finds that the degree of penetration of microfinance, often thought to be specifically useful for the poor, has no special effect on poverty (see, however, Morduch and Hayley, 2002). Development of the financial sector has been found to help reduce poverty by alleviating credit constraints, reducing child labour and increasing education, including the opportunity cost of foregone child labour, and by insuring against shocks (see Morduch, 2003, for the importance of micro-insurance for poverty). More generally, with one or two exceptions, the direct access of poor people to financial services can strongly affect the attainability of each of the millennium development goals (MDGs),[2] including those that chiefly require upgrading of public services in health and education, as these also require poor households to be able to afford access.

Second, as economic production changes and countries liberalise their real economies, it has become clearer that the degree of financial development significantly influences the ability of countries, firms and individuals to make use of (new) growth opportunities. The fact that finance matters for firms' growth opportunities is especially clear for SMEs. Beck *et al.* (2005) show that, while large SME sectors are characteristic of successful economies, SMEs do not "cause" growth nor do they alleviate poverty or decrease income inequality. Rather they show that the overall business environment – ease of firm entry and exit, sound property rights and proper contract enforcement – influences economic growth. Finance, however, accelerates growth by removing constraints on small firms more than on large firms. It allows firms to operate on a larger scale and encourages more efficient asset allocation (Beck *et al.*, 2004b). Financial and institutional development thus helps level the playing field among firms and countries, and this is especially important in a global economy with rapidly changing growth opportunities.

Third, while financial development in general is beneficial for growth and for reducing poverty, this does not mean that finance is available on an equal basis. The allocation of finance can be skewed or even perverse. While hard to "prove" for a large sample of countries, there is increasing evidence that finance often benefits the few, especially in developing countries. In normal times, this has meant that not everyone has

2. See IMF/World Bank (2004) on the MDGs and progress in achieving them.

had a fair chance at obtaining financing for their projects. Loans are allocated on the basis of connections and non-market criteria. During financial crises, this has meant that the brunt of the costs has fallen on the poor. Halac and Schmukler (2004) show that during crises financial transfers are large and are expected to increase income inequality and to be very regressive. For more discussion of the uneven distribution of finance and the impact of financial reform on inequality, see Claessens and Perotti (2004) and references therein.[3]

These three aspects already suggest that there may be a case for making financial services more generally available. It is necessary to analyse what access means, what the data show, what the impediments to access are, how access can be improved and whether there is a residual role for government in encouraging greater and more equal access.

What does access to financial services mean and what do the data tell about access to finance?

To analyse the issue of access requires a definition of what access to finance means. There are various dimensions to access to financial services (see Bodie and Merton, 1995, for a general review of the functions of finance). First is the question of availability: Are financial services available and in what quantity? Second is the question of cost: At what price are financial services available, including all costs, as well as the opportunity costs of, say, having to wait in line for a teller or having to travel a long distance to a bank branch? Third, what are the range, type and quality of financial services being offered? Following Morduch (1999), these dimensions can be defined as: reliability (is finance available when needed/desired?); convenience (what is the ease of access?); continuity (can finance be accessed repeatedly?); and flexibility (is the product tailored to the need?). Other variants of these dimensions are also used in other studies.[4] The point is that access has various dimensions, thus making it more difficult to establish the degree of (lack) of access.

This discussion already shows that there is no easy definition of access. One also needs a clear objective of the desirable degree of access. Universal access is not

3. The following are examples of such analyses. La Porta *et al.* (2003) find for Mexico that related lending in the 1990s was prevalent (20% of commercial loans) and took place on better terms than arm's-length lending (annual interest rates were four percentage points lower). Fisman (2001) for Indonesia and Johnson and Mitton (2003) for Malaysia find large financial value from political connections, suggesting that politics rather than economics (alone) determined access. For Indonesia, Leuz and Oberholzer-Gee (2003) find that corporate transparency and political connections are substitutes: firms with ties to then President Suharto are significantly less likely to issue foreign securities. Connected firms have lower rates of return during the 1997-98 crisis than transparent firms, but did receive considerable support during this period. Faccio (2006) reports that connected companies enjoy easier access to debt financing, lower taxation and higher market shares. She finds that benefits are particularly pronounced when companies are connected through their owner, a seasoned politician, or a minister and when the connected firm operates in a country with a higher degree of corruption. Also, stock prices increase by 2.59% upon announcement of a new connection, but only in highly corrupt countries. Khwaja and Mian (2004 and forthcoming) have much evidence that finance is perversely allocated in Pakistan and that capital markets are used to benefits insiders.

4. For example, Kempson *et al.* (2000) distinguish between five types of exclusion from financial services: *i)* access exclusion: *e.g.* through risk screening; *ii)* condition exclusion: product design inappropriate for the needs of some people; *iii)* price exclusion: financial products too costly; *iv)* marketing exclusion: some people effectively excluded by targeting of marketing and sales; *v)* self-exclusion: persons not applying in the belief that they would be refused.

necessarily the goal, as it may be for basic health services, primary education, clean water, etc. There are number of reasons. For one, demand for financial services may not exist. Many households, even in developed countries, choose not have a bank account as they have too few financial transactions, *e.g.* write no checks, collect wages in cash or cash their checks, yet the lack of access may not be a burden. Firms without access to credit may choose to remain so as their rates of return on capital are too low to justify formal finance or because they are unwilling to provide the necessary information on their business to banks, and by implications to others, including tax authorities. Equally important, and even in the best financial systems, financial services providers may not wish to provide access to all customers because it is not profitable or sustainable to so. This does not reflect a market failure, but rather that finance, like other services, has its own demand and supply.

To decide whether there is a case for more universal provision of financial services, it is necessary to know more about the benefits of access and the costs to society of providing greater access. This raises a number of issues, the first of which involves the limited data across countries on the degree of access to financial services.[5] While there is much data on financial sector development, there is very limited data on access for both households and firms. There is consequently limited analysis on the dimensions in which access may be deficient. It may be deficient geographically (access to branches and outlets). Or it may be socio-economically deficient (access only for some population segments). Or it may be deficient in an opportunity sense (the deserving do not have access). Data are insufficient in all respects so that it is hard to judge the relative benefits of access.

Some countries have data on households' use of basic financial services, such as having a bank account, often obtained using data from commercial banks and central banks. More recently, following efforts by the Consultative Group to Assist the Poor (CGAP) and the Microcredit Summit, data have been collected on the spread of microfinance. These cover the number of people with access to a savings account. Some countries have data from household surveys, such as Living Standard Measurement Surveys (LSMS). Of these surveys, about 27 have covered some dimensions of households' use of financial services (Honohan, 2004c). Still, and with the exceptions of some developed countries such as Sweden, many of these data are very basic and limited in terms of the various dimensions of use and access (quantity, costs, quality). Access to credit, although it represents only one-quarter of the access to savings in terms of numbers, is equally difficult to document at the household level. Many countries, for example, do not even have data on the aggregate level of consumer credit.

Data on firms' use of and access to financial services are equally limited. While there is much information on listed firms' financial structure and their access to (some forms of) external financing, there is much less on unlisted firms; information on small firms' access to finance is especially limited. Mostly data come from surveys, such as those conducted by the World Bank (World Bank Economic Survey [WBES], Investment Climate Assessments [ICAs]), or by the US Federal Reserve Boards, the Bank of England, the EU, etc. Some come from central bank statistics and advocacy groups (*e.g.* US Small Business Administration, chambers of commerce and equivalents). Again, the data are basic and limited in terms of various dimensions of access (quantity, costs, quality). Access to credit dominates the data collection efforts, with access to savings

5. See Honohan (2004c) and DFID (2005) on data availability and deficiencies.

services less of an issue, although payment services are important as well. Most data are collected on use of and access to banking services; data on other financial services, such as insurance, leasing, factoring and the like, are much more limited.

Although weak and often not comparable, available data show that access of households to banking services varies greatly. In developing countries, many households do not have a bank account. Bank facilities dominate the supply of financial services. Table 7.1 provides data on the degree to which households use a basic financial service from a formal financial institution, *e.g.* have a checking or savings bank account, across a number of countries. It shows that usage is nearly universal in most OECD countries, with many percentages above 95% and with an average of 90%; in developing countries, usage is much lower, and the average is only 25% (the highest usage of a formal financial institution is 57% in Jamaica). Other high numbers may not be representative as they apply to the population of the capital city only (Mexico) or specific cities (in China, Colombia and India) or urban areas (Brazil). For most other developing countries, access to a basic bank account does not exceed 30%, and in the lowest-income countries, access is less than 10%.

Individuals obtain financial services through other means, however, including non-financial institutions, as the comparison for some Latin American countries shows (Table 7.2). The Microcredit data also show that there is access to other forms of financial services. As such, these numbers underestimate access to financial services, but they show the large differences between developed and developing countries in terms of use of financial services from formal financial institutions.

The next question then is which are the unbanked households and how do they differ, if at all, between developed and developing countries? To the extent that they are known, the profiles are as expected, although it must be recognised that this often reflects households' choice, as only revealed demand is observed (given costs, quality, ease, etc., many do not bother to seek access from formal financial institutions). Socioeconomic characteristics such as income, wealth and education play the largest roles in explaining access. Financial exclusion is often part of broader exclusion in terms of education, jobs, formal training, etc. Credit access for households has a different profile from banking account and savings access and is more affected by income and wealth, as it tends to be the richer that borrow.

The comparison between the United States and Latin American countries shows some similarities between otherwise very different countries in terms of why people do not want to bank (Table 7.3). Convenience, trust and savings are important for whether households seek financial services from banks. Unbanked households also display very similar characteristics in the United States and Mexico, two countries otherwise at different levels of development, with the exception of home ownership (Table 7.4). The costs of being unbanked vary considerably, however, as the alternatives are much fewer and more costly in Mexico. The costs in the United States for being unbanked are estimated to be only 2.5% of median income in the lowest income segment, whereas in Mexico they are estimated at 5% (Solo *et al.*, 2004).

Table 7.1. Share of households with access to a bank account or using financial services

Country	Source	Date of survey	Number	% saving money in past 12 months	% using formal financial institutions to save	% using informal finance to save	% borrowing money in past 12 months	% using formal financial institutions to borrow	% using informal finance to borrow
Armenia	LSMS	1996	4 920	17.13	8.86	0.203			4.51
Bosnia and Herzegovina	LSMS	2001	5 400				21.78	6.22	15.83
Bulgaria	LSMS	2001	2 633				5.43	5.43	
China (Hebei and Liaoning)	LSMS	1995-97	787	82.47	41.93	13.34	28.08	5.21	24.65
Côte d'Ivoire	LSMS	1988	1 600	88.13	24.81		23.81	3.19	21.06
Ghana	LSMS	1998/99	5 998	11.97			39.08	3.27	32.03
Guatemala	LSMS	2000	7 276	18.13	17.77	0.38	31.75	23.47	7.42
Guyana	LSMS	1992/93	1 819	15.67	13.74	3.63	4.67	1.32	2.53
Jamaica	LSMS	1997	2 020	68.12	59.41	17.82	10.54	1.88	5.89
Kyrgyz Republic	LSMS	1998	2 979	11.35	1.34	10.14	6.08	0.34	5.3
Morocco	LSMS	1990-91	3 323	15.53			22.03	3.55	19.32
Nepal	LSMS	1996	3 373				57.04	12.93	49.96
Nicaragua	LSMS	1998-99	4 209	6.53	4.73	0.19	22.52	7.58	7.75
Pakistan	LSMS	1991	4 800	23.58	12.21	14.52	30.31	1.1	29.42
Panama	LSMS	1997	4 945				1.52	0.83	0.79
Peru	LSMS	1994	3 623	25.23			16.64	2.07	14.52
Romania	LSMS	1994-95	24 560	94.28	22.53	1.36	15.88	6	11.41
South Africa	LSMS	1993	9 000				44.76	4.94	42.58
Viet Nam	LSMS	1997-98	6 002	89.85	8.7	12.81	49.1	26.12	30.44
Brazil (11 urban areas)	SAFS	2002	2 000		42.7	45.45			
Colombia (Bogotá city)					41.2				
India	AIDIS	1991	57 031				26.9	11.8	19
India (UP and AP)	RFAS	2003	6 000		47.5				
Mexico (Mexico city)					25				
Botswana	FINSCOPE	2003	530		46.98	25.66		11.70	29.06
Lesotho	FINSCOPE	2003	534		17.04	11.05			5.99
Namibia	FINSCOPE	2003	810		28.40	0.86		5.31	15.19
Swaziland	FINSCOPE	2003	604		35.26	19.54		4.14	16.06
South Africa	FINSCOPE	2004	2 988		46				
Kenya	Estimate				10.00				
Tanzania	Estimate				5.00				
Uganda	Estimate				< 5				
United States	SCF	2001	4 449		90.9		75.1		
Denmark					99.1				
Netherlands					98.9				
Sweden					98				
Finland					96.7				
Germany					96.5				
France					96.3				
Luxembourg					94.1				
Belgium					92.7				
Spain					91.6				
United Kingdom					87.7				
Portugal					81.6				
Austria					81.4				
Ireland					79.6				
Greece					78.9				
Italy					70.4				

Source: The main sources are household surveys, the Living Standard Measurement Surveys. Here individual household responses on questions of usage of financial services liberalisation are averaged for each country. Second main sources are the surveys conducted by FINMARK in a number of southern African countries. Again, these are household surveys, but more specifically aimed at usage of financial services. The source for the EU countries is Pesaresi and Pilley (2003). For the United States, it is the Survey of Consumer Finance (2004). For Brazil, Colombia, India and Mexico the recent estimates are from Kumar *et al.* (2004), Basu *et al.* (2004), Solo *et al.* (2004) and Caskey *et al.* (2004). The earlier India numbers are from the regular Indian household survey. The Kenya, Tanzania and Uganda estimates are from Peachey and Roe (2004). Questions on financial services usage vary across the household survey and numbers are not necessarily comparable. Some numbers are only rough estimates.

Table 7.2. What (other) savings and deposit facilities are being used?

Distribution of deposits	Brazil	India	Colombia	Mexico
Banks	95% (54% private; 41% public)	90% (30% rural regional banks)	85%	96%
Co-operatives	0%	7%	14%	
Post office	n.a.	2%		
Family/friends	4%	n.a.		
Others	1%	1%	1%	4%

Source: Kumar *et al.*, 2004.

Table 7.3. Why don't the unbanked use banks?

	United States	Mexico	Colombia	Brazil	India
Demand limitations: no need/no savings	53%	7%	16%	n.a.	75%
No awareness					18%
Supply limitations: bank barriers/(*e.g.* high costs, minimum balances; documentations)	45%	70%	78%	42%	n.a.
Perceptions of service/safety/mistrust:	18%	16%	3%	25%	
Lack of documentation	10%	3%			
Privacy	22%	2%			
Inconvenience: location and hours	10%	2%			
Other reasons			3%	33%	

Source: Kumar *et al.* 2004.

Table 7.4. Who are the unbanked? United States and Mexico

Similarities: lower income groups; below median income	
United States	79%
Mexico	90%
Less educated: less than high school	
United States	56%
Mexico	51%
Marginalised in socio-economic terms	
Mexico (informal sector)	60%
United States (Latino and Afro-American)	90%
Differences: percentage of unbanked	
Mexico (Mexico City)	75%
United States	9.1%
Home ownership of unbanked	
Mexico (own home in Mexico City)	63%
United States	7.8%

Source: Solo *et al.* 2004.

The answer to the question about unbanked firms is somewhat similar. To the extent known, profiles are as expected, with the size and age of the firm especially important. For a large sample of countries, size affects access to credit most (Beck *et al.*, 2004b). For Brazil, size is more important than performance and other variables, suggesting quantitative limitations to credit access (Francisco and Kumar, 2004). For Brazil as well as for many other countries, the impact of size on credit is greater for longer-term loans. Public financial institutions in Brazil are actually more likely to lend to large firms, as they seem easier to lend to, negating the idea that public banks fill market gaps.

Size may, however, reflect not only profitability, financial and legal collateral but also political collateral. This is particularly so in developing countries where lending is often done on the basis of relationships and connections, often political. Indeed, in countries with well-developed financial systems, size can be overcome. Many banks in developed countries, for example, lend to small, single proprietary firms without requiring collateral, financial statements or other justification. Thanks to technological advances such as automated credit scoring, banks in developing countries are also becoming active in these forms of financing. In the most developed financial markets, universal access to basic financial services is essentially available for households, as the above data show.

Access can thus be based on opportunity and need. Since this does not seem to be the case in many countries, the question is what constrains access in general and in some countries in particular? Before asking whether there is a need for intervention, one needs to address the question of whether there is in fact a market failure.

Explanations of lack of access and barriers to access

Explanations for the lack of access fall into two categories: financial institutions' specific constraints and barriers arising from the overall institutional environment. In the terminology of Beck and de la Torre (2005), this means that one can group options to expand access into individual financial institutions' solutions (what they call moving towards the country's access possibilities frontier) and government action (what they call expanding the country's access possibilities frontier). The following discussion first looks at these two aspects and the relevant evidence and then considers the associated policy actions.

Individual financial institutions' constraints. Consumers, both households and firms, often state that they restrain their demand because the right types of financial services are not provided. Households often mention problems of high minimum deposits and high administrative burden and fees. Getting a loan can be very cumbersome and too costly for many borrowers given the small amounts desired and often high rejection rates. Financial institutions may also demand collateral, which poor borrowers typically lack. Formal financial services provision may also entail other, non-pecuniary barriers, such as a (greater) literacy requirement. Instead, households and firms do not seek financial services from formal financial institutions and rely on informal forms of finance for deposit, lending and payment services. Individuals wanting to transmit payments to relatives, for example, may rely on informal networks, despite the higher costs. This is obvious in the transmission of international remittances, where unit costs can be very high when more informal mechanisms are used. A USD 100 wire from New York to Mexico costs USD 9 plus an unknown exchange rate spread for the banked, whereas it costs USD 19 plus an unknown exchange rate spread for the unbanked (Solo *et al.*, 2004). Yet, these informal mechanisms are often preferred.

Lack of demand is thus a very important reason why access is not universal: many households and firms may not have a demand for financial services. Banks may also consider some households and firms as less attractive customers. When demand is there, though, and the environment is sufficiently competitive, banks can be expected to try to provide financial services. One common reaction by financial services providers as to why they do not serve poor households and small firms is that these are too high-risk, too high-cost propositions. In other words, financial institutions find it not attractive enough to provide financial services to these segments.

There may be a variety of reasons for the lack of provision of appropriate products and services. Banks may have problems providing financial services to all households and firms given the population density, *e.g.* it may be too costly to provide the physical infrastructure in rural areas. In some areas where there is a lack of security for cash transfers, branches cannot be operated profitably. High transactions costs for small volumes are often mentioned as constraining financial services providers from broadening access. Small borrowers borrow frequently, for example, and repay in small instalments. They consequently do not want financial products with high per unit costs, yet the bank's costs are often similar regardless of transaction size. Households and firms in developing countries may seek financing or insurance for specific purposes (major life events such as marriage, health, or crop insurance) for which contracts are difficult to design. Firms may be underserved for the same reasons. Small firms seek different products from large enterprises, *e.g.* payment services for small amounts, and banks may therefore not consider these firms sufficiently attractive as clients.

For financial services providers, the fixed costs in financial intermediation make it hard for small institutions and in small markets to provide services to small clients. At the same time, economies of scale lead to decreasing unit costs as transaction volume increases, making some specialisation attractive. While better cost management can lower unit cost and thereby lead to higher outreach to low-income clientele, there are limits to cost management at the level of an individual institution. Evidence on microfinance institutions shows this. The proliferation of microfinance institutions in many countries has not necessarily benefited final clients, as few institutions have reached the scale necessary for efficient provision. Similar constraints arise at the country level if many financial systems are very small (less than a few billion dollars, which is less than a very small bank in most developed countries), hindering effective financial services provision. This suggests that in many countries the scale required for effective provision may not exist.

Banks can innovate, however, and move closer to the access frontier. Sometimes, prodded by government and public opinion, they make their products more suited to low-income households. In South Africa, the country's major banks launched in November 2004 a low-cost bank account aimed at extending banking to the black majority. The country's four big retail banks along with the post office's Postbank launched the "Mzansi" account. The account, set up under a financial-sector charter agreed on by the industry in 2003, requires a minimum deposit of ZAR 20 (about USD 4) and is aimed at providing some 13 million low-income South Africans without prior access to bank accounts access to financial services. Whether this will be profitable and sustainable is to be seen.

Institutional environment constraints. For many of the mismatches between potential demand and supply, it is not clear if there is a market failure and if so its exact source. Why would financial institutions not offer these products if feasible? Or why would financial institutions that operate at the right scale and with the right technology not enter certain markets? The fact that they do not must mean that it is not profitable to do so given current technology and the institutional environment (legal, regulatory and other requirements) they face in a particular market. The question is whether these mismatches between demand and supply need to be and can be remedied. While there is much (relevant) analysis on what affects financial sector development and the role of the institutional environment (*e.g.* World Bank, 2001), evidence on what affects households' and firms' access to financial services across countries is so far very limited, although the information available gives some insight on the most binding constraints.

Across countries, it appears that the poor or the near-poor have less access to microfinance in countries with higher GDP per capita, in countries with better "institutional" quality and a larger market size (Honohan, 2004a; 2004b). This suggests that there is some element of overall general development, including greater use of advanced technology, that allows more developed countries to offer financial services profitably to lower segments. Of course, the lower segment in these more developed countries represents a higher income level, so it does not mean that with the same technology the lower segments in developing countries would also be reached. The same analysis shows that a higher-quality main banking system discourages the spread of microfinance institutions. Countries with higher spreads and higher profitability in their main banking system have fewer microfinance institutions. This suggests that more competition in the banking system can foster greater access to financial services by microfinance institutions.

It also appears that access to savings can be a function of the financial services distribution networks (postal and saving banks and others). In Brazil, for example, the size and scope of some branch networks, as well as the split between public and private banks as well as domestic and foreign banks, play a role in the degree of access (Kumar *et al.,* 2004). In other markets, more specialised financial institutions such as savings banks and other proximity banks which have, besides profitability, an objective of providing financial services, have had some impact on broadening access (Peachy and Roe, 2004).

These findings suggest that what drives households' access is not purely a function of the scope for profitable banking, but that the overall institutional environment and level of development also play a role. Recent evidence on the access of small firms across countries suggests even more than for households that the institutional environment matters. This is particularly so on the credit side, as can be expected. The absence of credit information, the lack of collateral that can be registered and enforced, difficulties in general contract design and enforcement can all make lending difficult. Credit services may consequently be limited to entrepreneurs with a credit history, (political) connections or immovable collateral, such as real estate. Even when a business is viable, there will often be a lack of formal reliance on past records and little regard for expected future performance. In many countries, there is often the additional problem of uncertain repayment capacity arising from volatile income and expenditure. New and smaller firms especially often have high exposure to these systemic risks (*e.g.* macroeconomic volatility, financial crises, default by governments, arbitrary taxation and other risks).

There is empirical evidence on the importance of these channels. The quality of legal systems and property rights enforcement and the presence of mechanisms for reliable information have been found to be especially important for small firms (Beck *et al.*, 2004c). Small firms and firms in countries with poor institutions use less external finance, for example, especially less bank finance. Better protection of property rights increases the external financing of small firms significantly more than that of large firms, mainly owing to more bank and equity finance. It also appears that substitutes for bank finance are imperfect, *e.g.* small firms do not use disproportionately more leasing or trade finance than larger firms (see Beck *et al.*, 2004b; and other papers presented at a World Bank SME conference (World Bank, 2004).

Analysis at the individual country level has been more limited to date but does provide some insight into what may be driving access. It is clear that banking system regulations can hinder access. There may be minimum or maximum interest rate policies, for example, which make it hard for financial services providers to offer saving or lending instruments profitably. Other regulations may include usury laws, lending restrictions and requirements, and high compliance costs. Households may face high transactions costs and barriers when dealing with formal financial institutions owing to administrative regulations and procedures. The procedures for opening a bank account can be complex, for example, requiring among other things proof of identity, address or income. Many countries have customer identification requirements, so-called "know your customer" rules, which limit the ability to offer simple banking products. The recent focus on anti-money laundering and counter-terrorism financing (AML/CTF) has led to laws that can adversely affect the provision of financial services, as in South Africa (Genesis Analytics, 2004). Some countries have other costly or distortive rules (*e.g.* in some African countries permission from the male household head is necessary for a female member of the household to open a bank account). More generally, government interference can distort risk-return signals, making it hard for formal financial institutions to offer attractive products.

In addition to hindering the activity of existing financial services providers, regulations can also hinder the emergence of financial institutions more suited to the needs of lower-income households or smaller firms. Rigidity in chartering rules, (high) minimum capital adequacy requirements (in absolute terms), limited degrees of freedom in funding structures, excessive regulation and supervision, too strict accounting requirements and other rules can hinder the emergence of microfinance and smaller financial institutions. In South Africa, regulation and supervision were extended to microfinance institutions and reduced their capacity to offer financial services profitably to the lower segments of the population (Glaessner *et al.*, 2004). Separate charters may be useful, with the required structures based on whether the institution borrows, takes deposits, is owned by its members and only caters to them, etc. (Van Greuning *et al.*, 1999).

With these and other regulatory and supervisory requirements, tradeoffs arise, however, as the requirements are meant to serve other public policy purposes, such as financial stability and financial integrity. There are also tradeoffs in terms of facilitating the mainstreaming of microfinance institutions. Jansson *et al.* (2004) argue, for example, that one does not want to create new and distinct institutional forms for microfinance unless: *i)* there are several mature and well-managed non-profit organisations ready to become such financial intermediaries, and *ii)* the existing institutional forms, such as banks or finance companies, for all practical purposes cannot be used (owing to high minimum capital requirements, for instance) or carry important operational restrictions (such as the inability to mobilise deposits).

There is consequently a need to evaluate regulatory approaches from the perspective of overall welfare. Although they have to strike the right balance, regulations can at times be adjusted to enhance access (Honohan, 2004b). In many countries, for example, anti-predatory lending rather than usury laws are needed, as the latter ultimately hurt small borrowers who cannot obtain credit, even at high interest rates. Also adopting "truth in lending" requirements for small-scale lending, rather than the extensive "small print" regulations which many countries have, can help ease access.

Adapting regulations can also mean facilitating multiple forms of financial services provision. In many cases, this will involve considering savings separately from credit. Many households are interested in savings and payment services but not in credit services. It may be that these different types of financial services require different forms of regulation and supervision. Specific frameworks for microfinance institutions and the small-scale activities of commercial banks may be useful. Finally, much regulation is aimed at protecting savers and borrowers against misuse and risks, yet may not be effective in developing countries given the lack of supervisory capacity, independence and effective checks and balances (Barth *et al.*, 2005) and may still end up hindering access. Consideration also needs to be given to educating people about the risks of (new) financial services and the different types of financial services providers, so that they themselves strike the right balance between risk and benefits. More generally, it will be necessary to increase financial literacy, as is actively being done in the United Kingdom and some other countries. The best approaches in these areas will vary greatly from country to country.

Improvement in institutional infrastructure is an area in which progress can obviously be made to further access in many developing countries. Better legal, information and payment systems, and better distribution and other infrastructures are often needed. The agendas of many governments, multilateral financial institutions and others already address this issue, but it will take time. Evidence on the profitability of the main banking system suggests that one important way to enhance access is by improving competition in banking systems. This is often easier than improving the institutional environment. Increasing competition and market opening can also bring in more and newer technology and know-how.

Competition can be increased in all segments. One can, for example, allow smaller and non-bank financial institutions access to existing networks (payment system, information). In many countries, access to the payment system is limited to a group of large banks, or the pricing structure of access is such as to preclude smaller financial institutions from having effective access. In many countries information sharing is restricted to incumbent banks and formal financial institutions. As Miller (2001) has shown, this hinders smaller financial institutions from providing financial services to low-income people. Few countries, for example, allow non-bank financial institutions and entities such as department stores to access non-payment information, thereby making it more difficult for them to provide financial services to low-income households. Yet, such non-financial institutions are often where lower-income people get credit. In Mexico, for example, close to 50% of credit for those with no banking relationship comes from department stores (Solo *et al.*, 2004).

Although some of these changes can be adopted relatively easily, competition policy remains a very complex area, especially in small markets with little institutional capacity. It requires establishing a credible competition agency, for which the institutional requirements are quite high. Furthermore, even in developed countries, questions arise as to how to deal with the many network properties in financial services (access to the payment system, credit bureau, distribution networks, etc.). The answers are not obvious.

One does not want to undermine the incentive to provide accurate information, for example, by opening up a credit bureau to any new party. Nor does one want to have financial institutions disclose all types of information as this can undermine their willingness to enter into relationships with their clients out of fear that competitors will take their business.

In addition to the general evidence that competition can help access, there is ample evidence that allowing greater entry of foreign banks can enhance access. (General evidence on the effects of the entry of foreign banks is reviewed in Clarke *et al.*, 2003.) A study on borrowers' perceptions in 36 countries found that reported financing obstacles were lower in countries with high levels of foreign bank penetration (Clarke *et al.*, 2004). The same study found strong evidence that even small entities benefited and no evidence that they were harmed by the presence of foreign banks. The channels appear to be competitive pressures by foreign banks on the domestic banking system, forcing local banks to go downscale, as well as direct provision of financial services by foreign banks. A study on Latin America found that foreign banks with a small local presence do not appear to lend much to small businesses, but that large foreign banks often surpass lending by large domestic banks (Sanchez *et al.*, 2002).

There are plenty of examples of the effects of the entry of foreign banks. For instance, Mongolia has a per capita income of less than USD 500 and a very rural economy. In 1990, after many years of operating deficits, loan losses and a failed attempt at privatisation, the government-owned Agricultural Bank of Mongolia ("Khan" Bank) was placed in receivership. Today it is the financial institution posting the highest return on equity of any Mongolian bank. In March 2003 HS Securities of Japan bought Khan Bank from the Government of Mongolia for USD 6.85 million. Khan Bank now operates a network with 379 points of service throughout Mongolia, many more than any of the other 16 banks operating in the country (and up from 269 when the new management took over). One out of every two Mongolian households today is a client of Khan Bank and it continues to expand its branch network and services.

Specific interventions and the role of the government

Some specific improvements can accelerate access, as a number of recent country experiences have shown. In India, for example, experiments are under way to use existing networks (*e.g.* the postal system) to allow the delivery of new financial services by many other public and private providers. The idea is that the technology and information backbone of existing public or other networks need not be limited to a single entity. There is little reason, for example, not to allow multiple financial services providers to offer their products using the same distribution network and the same outlets. Many countries have large networks of post offices and one might envision, for example, an electronic "kiosk" in every post office where various financial institutions offer their services to customers on line. In South Africa's post offices, a platform is being developed to allow customers to use e-finance services to apply for loans from any bank. Brazil has another model with the post office present in 1 738 out of more than 5 000 municipalities that lack a bank outlet. In 2001, the government auctioned off the exclusive right to distribute financial services through post offices. A large private bank won. While this may quickly improve the quality of services, it does carry the risk of creating a local monopoly.

New technology, including the Internet, smart cards and mobile phones can also help broaden access (see BIS, 2004, for a general overview of e-finance developments). On one end of the income spectrum, payment for parking fees in Vienna and payment at vending machines in Finland can be made by mobile phone. In many developed countries, mobile payments can now be made through voice access, text messaging (SMS) or WAP (as a gateway to the Internet). Another arrangement in developed countries allows customers to pay using the prepaid value stored on the mobile phone or pay *ex post*, with payment for goods/services added to the customer's phone bill. Use of mobile phones for financial services might also facilitate access in lower-income developing countries, as mobile phones are often more widespread and may have a lower threshold for users.

In some developing and transition countries, banks have offered prepaid cards (Bolivia, Brazil, China, Ghana, India, Lithuania, Malawi, Malaysia, Mexico, Nigeria, the Philippines, Russia, Turkey and Venezuela). The use of prepaid cards can facilitate payment services for low-income households. Often though, this will require regulatory changes, as prepaid cards may be considered deposit instruments and fall under some form of banking regulation. Technology can help in other ways. In Uganda, over the past two years, Hewlett-Packard and a group of seven leaders in the microfinance industry have been working to achieve a breakthrough in the scale of microfinance. The team has developed, tested and is implementing a new technology solution. It involves a remote transaction system using handheld devices, which capture transaction data and use a GSM network to transmit the data back to a head-office server and, in turn, to a management information system. While the technology needed to be adapted to local practices, it did show promising results. Hand-held tools are being used more generally by several microfinance institutions to provide on-the-spot loan applications and approvals (see Microsave.org for other examples).

Mexico has adopted an innovative means of trade finance using reverse factoring. The programme, developed by Nafin, a government development bank, allows many small suppliers to use their receivables from large creditworthy buyers, including foreign multinationals, to obtain working capital financing, effectively transferring that creditworthiness to allow small firms to access more and cheaper financing. What makes Nafin special is that it operates an electronic platform that provides Internet-based, online services, thereby reducing costs, increasing transparency and improving security. In the short run, overhead costs are subsidised, but by lowering costs for working capital for small and medium-sized enterprises (SMEs), it expects to generate more business and become sustainable (Klapper, 2004).

Paulson and McAndrews (1998) provide a case study of how Standard Bank of South Africa tried a new way of addressing an unbanked population. Already in 1993, Standard Bank set up E-Bank. It was a simple savings product offering card-only access, supported by dedicated staff speaking a mix of relevant local languages and operating out of dedicated outlets to help overcome problems of illiteracy and concerns about security in a high crime environment. It had high start-up costs, but provided financial services to a low-income segment. Since then E-Bank has been absorbed into the bank's more general provision of financial services to low-income households.

These are examples of specific market approaches and government interventions that can enhance access. Many others exist. More generally, there has been much emphasis recently on facilitating the mainstreaming of microfinance institutions, and the scaling up of new initiatives on access. These initiatives can be the result of specific interventions, as the above examples and work under way in India (see Basu *et al.*, 2004) and other places shows, but how to generalise is a lesson still to be drawn.

Government interventions to broaden access

Universal access, as will be clear by now, should not be the goal and trying too forcefully to broaden access raises some concerns. Access to credit may be a problem when it leads to impoverishing indebtedness, as the poor may over-borrow, often on unfavourable terms. The fact that the poor and disenfranchised lack access may be more a problem of poverty than a problem of access. Although data are weak and do not allow for a definitive assessment, the percentage of those with potential "bankable" demand for financial services but no access in poorer developing economies may well be similar to the percentage of exclusion in richer advanced industrial economies. Since there is evidence that access rises with per capita income and wealth, although with complex causality links, the focus should arguably be primarily on poverty-reducing growth and programmes to enhance overall inclusion (jobs, social participation). Greater access to financial services would follow as corollary. In fact, even when there is a case for trying to extend provision of financial services to a larger segment, the costs of general public or public-induced provision may outweigh the benefits.

Broader public interventions may nevertheless be useful in some cases, but need to be very carefully introduced. Given political economy factors, broadening access may not relax credit and savings constraints if there is a selection bias, *i.e.* households or firms with good prospects apply for credit anyway. Subsidies may not only distort the markets, evidence is also mounting that subsidies are captured by the relatively well-off who often already have access. Priority lending requirements are not the solution and can divert resources away from the lowest segments and towards the less needy. Furthermore, there may not be any additionality, as clients that already have access move to new providers that are subsidised. For example, much of the emphasis on improving the supply of housing finance (by providing tax breaks, requiring minimum lending shares for commercial banks or establishing specialised financial institutions that rely on implicit government support) ends up being a subsidy for the middle class. Enhancing access can then ultimately hurt the truly needy as the costs are borne by all. In Brazil, for example, the cost of the housing finance programme is one of many factors behind the generally high financial intermediation spreads, which hurt borrowers and depositors, presumably especially those who are less well off, through higher lending rates and lower deposit rates,.

Another example relates to microfinance institutions. Much emphasis has been placed by donors and others, including multilateral financial institutions, on microfinance institutions, including by providing subsidies for setting them up (sometimes also with subsidies for operating costs, but this has been less accepted in recent years). Such subsidies can work perversely as they can lead to higher subsequent spreads in order to recover the fixed costs (Hoff and Stiglitz, 1998). There is thus a need to keep direct and indirect subsidies minimal, and for any programme, costs and risk co-sharing are an essential (partial) market test.

There is some evidence that demand for and supply of financial services may be stimulated in other, less costly ways. Many employers prefer to deposit their payroll and wages electronically, and would be willing to stimulate use of formal bank services by providing some form of subsidy (for example, facilitating a branch on the premises, encouraging the establishment of a credit union, or facilitating private savings schemes). Governments can also do this. They can, for example, try to encourage more bank access by making social security, tax and other individual-oriented payments electronically.

In 1999, the US Treasury Department initiated a programme for paying all federal benefit payments, such as social security benefits, by electronic transfer accounts (ETAs). One impediment was the large number of benefit recipients without a bank account, who cashed their checks instead of depositing them in a bank account. Using subsidies, banks were encouraged to open bank accounts and recipients were encouraged to switch to electronic payments. The Treasury offered to pay banks USD 12.60 for each ETA account they established for benefit recipients, and the Treasury specified a minimum set of characteristics that these accounts must meet (the accounts could not cost account owners more than USD 3 a month and they could not levy a fee for the electronic deposits coming in). The switch would benefit the government as supplier (lower costs), but could also help the recipient by giving access to financial services. In the end, the take-up was less than expected, suggesting again that lack of access to financial services is part of a broader issue of social exclusion. Similar experiences exist for encouraging tax payments and tax returns to be made electronically; here again, usage is often concentrated among those who already have access and are otherwise better off.

Besides these methods, governments have other options for stimulating households' access to banking and other basic financial services. For one, the regulatory system can be used to direct, although not mandate, banks to address the problem. This might be described as the US Community Reinvestment Act (RCA) model. Second, authorities can mandate all banks to provide minimum banking services ("basic accounts") for otherwise excluded market segments. Third, governments can rely on banks with a social commitment (their legal form may be public bank, co-operative, foundation, the postal network or proximity bank such as a local savings bank) offering very restricted retail services. Each of these approaches has its advantages and disadvantages.[6]

The US Community Reinvestment Act (CRA) enacted by the US Congress in 1977 and revised in 1995 aims to improve financial access. It aims to help meet the credit requirements of communities in which banks operate, including low- to moderate-income neighbourhoods. Each bank is rated every three years on its performance in making loans to people with low and moderate incomes (rather than its process for complying with CRA), which allows the general public to apply pressures for non-compliance. Ratings focus on the areas of lending, services and investment, with lending carrying the greatest weight. Claims of its success are contested although neither side has established a strong position; still its lengthy existence is a sign of success. The CRA model is very specific and has not been followed elsewhere, which suggest that its replicability is limited. Moreover, the CRA should not be seen in isolation.

The United Kingdom, France, Sweden and Ireland, among others, have tried by legal means to broaden access. In France, for example, anyone seeking to open an account but rejected by a bank can contact the Bank of France which will provide a named bank (often the postal bank) which will be obliged to open an account for that person. In some other countries, postal banks (often government-owned) have been given the task of providing basic cash and banking services. There is little review of experience with these schemes, in terms of their effects and efficiency. Experience with "proximity" banks is reviewed by Peachey and Roe (2004) who find some support for a positive effect of increased presence of such banks on access. Also, credit unions and other non-for-profit financial institutions can make a difference for access.

6 The following draws extensively on Peachey and Roe (2004).

Experience with credit lines, especially for SMEs, is extensive, in both developed and developing countries, suggesting a large public need for them. The efficacy of these interventions is doubtful, however (a general review of credit lines is found in World Bank, 2005; Caprio and Demirgüç-Kunt, 1997, provide some empirical evidence on subsidies and review general experiences). The means for distributing credit to these groups are generally distortive. Credit often does not reach the intended target group but rather the well-connected, and institutional development is undermined, as banks do not develop their credit analysis skills. The case for direct and indirect intervention in access to credit is therefore less clear than for access to basic savings, payment and transaction services.

Conclusions

Over the last decade, finance has been recognised as an important driver of economic growth. More recently, access to financial services has been recognised as an important aspect of development and more emphasis has been given to extending financial services to low-income households. Although analysis is still subject to caution, given the weakness of the data, there is some evidence that access is improving. On the household side, data on the access to microfinance suggest that access for households has expanded. The data should be interpreted with care as the increase may represent better coverage over time rather than expansion. There is also evidence in terms of more mainstreaming of access by commercial banks as competition compels and technology allows them to go to the lower income segments. Examples of good practice in developing countries include ICICI bank and SHG Bank Linkage, South African banks that have made it a priority to reach out to lower segments.

For firms, the evidence on access to credit is more mixed. It appears to be increasing in some countries, but mostly in the form of consumer finance rather than for SMEs. Some have argued that recent trends in banking systems may have adverse consequences. Consolidation of the banking system in many countries increases the distance between borrower and lender, making lending more based on hard information and reducing the role of relationship lending which can be especially useful for new and small firms. Yet, part of the increased consolidation is the consequence of increased competition, which in general helps to increase access.

More definite conclusions will have to wait for better data on access. This will require national and international actions to develop more comparable data. Data on access will have to come from different sources: providers of financial services (using national statistics), users of financial services (on the basis of surveys), and experts (to identify constraints). Each of these data sources has its tradeoffs, so simultaneous actions will be needed, but without good data, little progress can be made in terms of policy recommendations.

Better data will allow for benchmarking (across and over time) and more solid analysis of what is driving access. Furthermore, it will allow analysis of the success of different models, possibly with more controlled "experiments" and rigorous evaluations of successes of failures. This will help private financial institutions deliver financial services profitably and guide national and global policy interventions. It may also be useful for international and national agencies to develop "models" for various aspects of access, *i.e.* advice on regulations for microfinance institutions and their activities, rules on consumer protection and "know thy customer", and guidance on what data to collect, who should collect them and how they should be collected.

References

Barth, J., G. Caprio Jr. and R. Levine (2005), *Rethinking Bank Regulation and Supervision: Till Angels Govern*, forthcoming, World Bank, Cambridge University Press.

Basu, P. *et al.* (2004), "Scaling-up Access to Finance for India's Rural Poor", World Bank, draft report.

Beck, T., A. Demirgűç-Kunt and R. Levine (2004a), "Finance and Poverty: Cross-Country Evidence", World Bank Policy Research Working Paper 3338.

Beck, T., A. Demirgüç-Kunt and V. Maksimovic (2004b), "Financial and Legal Constraints to Firm Growth: Does Firm Size Matter?", *Journal of Finance*, 60, February 2004, pp. 137-177.

Beck, T., A. Demirgűç-Kunt and R. Levine (2005), "SMEs, Growth, and Poverty: Cross-Country Evidence", *Journal of Economic Growth*, September, 197-227.

Beck, T. and A. de la Torre (2005), "Broadening Access to Financial Services: Risks and Costs", unpublished presentation, World Bank, Washington, DC.

Bank for International Settlements (BIS) (2004), "Survey of Developments in Electronic Money and Internet and Mobile Payments. Information on Current and New Innovative Products", Consultative Report, Bank for International Settlements, Basle.

Bodie, Z. and R. Merton (1995), "A Conceptual Framework of Analyzing the Financial Environment", in D.B. Crane, Z. Bodie, K.A. Froot, A.F. Perold and R.C. Merton (eds.), *The Global Financial System: A Functional Perspective*, Harvard Business School Press, Boston.

Caprio, G. Jr. and A. Demirgüç-Kunt (1997), "The Role of Long Term Finance: Theory and Evidence." Policy Research Working Paper 1746. World Bank, Washington, DC.

Caskey, J.P., C. Ruiz Durán and T.M. Solo (2004), "The Unbanked in Mexico and the United States", unpublished, World Bank, Washington, DC.

Claessens, S. and E. Perotti (2004), "The Links between Finance and Inequality: Channels and Evidence", background paper for the 2005 World Development Report, World Bank, University of Amsterdam

Clarke, G., L.C Xu and H. Zou (2002), "Finance and Income Inequality: Test of Alternative Theories", World Bank, June.

Clarke, G., R. Cull, M.S. Martinez Peria and S.M. Sánchez (2003), Foreign Bank Entry: Experience, Implications for Developing Economies, and Agenda for Further Research, *World Bank Research Observer* 18, pp. 25-59.

Clarke, G., R. Cull and M.S. Martinez Peria (2004), "Does Foreign Bank Penetration Reduce Access to Credit in Developing Countries? Evidence from Asking Borrowers", World Bank Working Paper 2716.

Demirgüç-Kunt, A. and R. Levine (eds.) (2001), *Financial Structure and Economic Growth: A Cross-Country Comparison of Banks, Markets, and Development*, MIT Press, Cambridge, Massachusetts.

Demirgüç-Kunt, A. and V. Maksimovic (1998), "Law, Finance and Firm Growth", *Journal of Finance*, Vol. 53, No. 6, pp. 2107-2137.

DFID (2005), "Financial Access Indicators Stocktake", prepared by Emerging Market Economics for the Department for International Development, London.

Faccio, M. (2006), "Politically connected firms", *American Economic Review*, Vol. 96(1), March, pp. 369-386.

Fisman, R. (2001), "Estimating the Value of Political Connections", *American Economic Review*, 91(4), pp. 1095-1102.

Francisco, M. and A. Kumar (2004), "Enterprise Size, Financing Patterns and Credit Constraints in Brazil: Analysis of Data from the Investment Climate Assessment Survey", September, World Bank.

Genesis Analytics (2004), "A Survey of the SADC Region: South African Financial Institutions, Regional Policies and Issues of Access", mimeo.

Glaessner, T., N. Anamali, S. Claessens, K. Furst, D. Klingebiel, L. Klapper and R. Schware (2004), "South Africa: Technology and Access to Financial Services: Lessons from Experience", mimeo, The World Bank. Washington, DC.

Halac, M. and S.L. Schmukler (2004), "Distributional Effects of Crises: The Financial Channel", World Bank Working Paper 3173.

Hoff, K. and J.E. Stiglitz (1998), "Moneylenders and Bankers: Price-increasing Subsidies in a Monopolistically Competitive Market", *Journal of Development Economics* 55, pp. 485-518.

Honohan, P. (2004a), "Financial Development, Growth and Poverty: How Close Are the Links?", World Bank Policy Research Working Paper 3203; also in C. Goodhart (ed.) *Financial Development and Economic Growth: Explaining the Links*, Palgrave, London.

Honohan, P. (2004b), "Financial Sector Policy and the Poor: Selected Findings and Issues", Working Paper No. 43, World Bank, Washington, DC.

Honohan, P. (2004c), "Data on Microfinance and Access: Thinking about What Is Available and What Is Needed, mimeo, World Bank, Washington, DC.

IMF and World Bank (2004), *Global Monitoring Report: Polices and Actions for Achieving the Millennium Development Goals and Related Outcomes*, Washington, DC.

Jansson, T., R. Rosales and G.D. Westley (2004), *Principles and Practices for Regulating and Supervising Microfinance*, Inter-American Development Bank, Washington, DC.

Johnson, S. and T. Mitton (2003), "Cronyism and Capital Controls: Evidence from Malaysia", *Journal of Financial Economics* 67:2, pp. 351-82.

Kempson, E., C. Whyley, J. Caskey and S. Collard (2000), "In or Out? Financial Exclusion: A Literature and Research Review", London Financial Services Authority.

Khwaja, A.I. and A. Mian (2004), "Do Lenders Favor Politically Connected Firms? Renting-seeking in an Emerging Financial Market", mimeo, University of Chicago.

Khwaja, A.I. and A. Mian (forthcoming), "Unchecked Intermediaries: Price Manipulation in an Emerging Stock Market", *Journal of Financial Economics*.

Klapper, L. (2004), "The Role of Reverse Factoring in Supplier Financing of Small and Medium Sized Enterprises", mimeo, World Bank, Washington, DC.

Kumar, A., T. Beck, C. Campos and S. Chattopadhyay (2004), Assessing Financial Access in Brazil, World Bank Working Paper 50, Washington, DC.

La Porta, R., F. Lopez-de-Silanes and G. Zamarippa (2003), "Related Lending", *Quarterly Journal of Economics*, Vol. 118, Issue 1, pp. 231-268.

Leuz, C. and F. Oberholzer-Gee (2003), "Corporate Transparency and Political Connections", mimeo, Wharton School, Philadelphia, Pennsylvania.

Levine, R. (2005), "Finance and Growth: Theory, Evidence, and Mechanisms", in *Handbook of Economic Growth*, P. Aghion and S. Durlauf (eds.), North-Holland Elsevier Publishers, Amsterdam, forthcoming.

Miller, M. (2001), *Credit Reporting Systems and the International Economy*, MIT Press, Cambridge, Massachusetts.

Morduch, J. (1999), "The Microfinance Promise", *Journal of Economic Literature*, 37(4), pp. 1569–1614.

Morduch, J. (2003), "Microinsurance: The Next Revolution?", New York University, mimeo.

Morduch, J. and B. Hayley (2002), "Analysis of the Effects of Microfinance on Poverty Reduction", NYU Wagner Working Paper No. 1014.

Paulson, J.A. and J. McAndrews (1998), "Financial Services for the Urban Poor – South Africa's E Plan", World Bank Working Paper No. 449.

Peachey, S. and A. Roe (2004), "Access to Finance: A Study for the World Savings Banks Institute", Oxford

Pesaresi, N. and O. Pilley (2003), "Retail Banking, Social Exclusion and Public Service", EU Directorate-General – Competition, Brussels.

Rajan, R.G. and L. Zingales (1998), "Financial Development and Growth", *The American Economic Review* 88, pp. 559-586.

Sánchez, S.M., G. Clarke, R. Cull, and M.S. Martinez Peria (2002), "Bank Lending to Small Businesses in Latin America: Does Bank Origin Matter?", World Bank Working Paper 2760, forthcoming in *Journal of Money, Credit and Banking*.

Solo, T.M., J. Caskey and C. Durán (2004), "The Unbanked in Mexico and the USA: Five Questions Addressed", World Bank, Swarthmore College, Universidad Nacional Autónoma de México.

Van Greuning, H., J. Gallardo and B. Randhawa (1999), "A Framework for Regulating Microfinance Institutions", Policy Research Working Paper No. 2061, World Bank, Washington, DC.

World Bank (2001), *Finance for Growth, Policy Choices in a Volatile World*, Oxford University Press and World Bank, Washington, DC.

World Bank (2004), Conference on Small and Medium Enterprises, Washington DC, October 14 and 15, 2004, papers available at econ.worldbank.org/programs/finance

World Bank (2005), Review of World Bank Lending For Lines of Credit, January 6, Operations Evaluation Department, Washington, D.C.

Wurgler, J. (2000), "Financial markets and the allocation of capital", *Journal of Financial Economics* 58, pp. 187-214.

Chapter 8

Provision of Financial Services in South Africa

Mark Napier
Chief Executive Officer, FinMark Trust

This chapter explores the extent to which South African retail financial markets can truly be considered "liberal" and the factors that have contributed to the development of more liberalised markets. The main focus is on two sub-markets – transaction banking and credit – which appear relevant to a discussion of universal service provision. Both have been the subject of prominent initiatives in South Africa

Introduction

In the second half of 2004, ten years after South Africa's first democratic elections, two events took place which may have a profound impact on the shape of South African financial markets in the years to come.

First, it was announced on 23 September 2004 that Barclays, the UK banking giant, intended to acquire a majority shareholding in South Africa's largest retail bank, ABSA. This signalled its return to retail banking in South Africa after economic sanctions and political instability forced it out of the country in 1986.

Second, on 25 October 2004, the four largest banks in South Africa, together with the Postbank and some smaller players, announced the launch of a basic banking product specifically aimed at low-end consumers. Known as Mzansi, the product offers an ATM card and basic, but limited, bank functionality at lower cost to the consumer than other bank accounts.

These events, while very different, are the clearest indicators yet of the process of liberalisation that has been taking place in South Africa's financial markets since 1994. It involves both the reintegration of the domestic economy into the global environment, as evidenced by a gradual relaxation of exchange controls, and the democratisation of the provision of domestic financial services in order to reach the poor, typically non-white, population that was, in practice, excluded from formal financial services in the apartheid era.

That these events took place only very recently undoubtedly shows the scale of the challenge facing the newly elected government and the financial services sector in 1994. But it also begs the question as to whether more could, or should, have been done, or done differently, to accelerate the pace of liberalisation as defined here. The answer to this question depends to a great extent on an analysis of the relationship between government and the private sector in financial services, a relationship that has warmed and cooled and warmed again as the parties have moved towards accepting their roles and obligations.

Overall, significant progress has been achieved, as is evidenced by the widespread discussion today about "banking the unbanked", but progress has not been uniform across the various financial sub-markets. While the Financial Sector Charter (the "Charter"), to be welcomed for its vision and clarity of purpose, will be successful in channelling efforts towards providing much greater access to financial services, targeted government intervention may yet be required if its goals are to be achieved.

This chapter explores the extent to which South African retail financial markets can truly be considered "liberal" and the factors that have contributed to the development of more liberalised markets. The main focus is on two sub-markets – transaction banking and credit – which appear relevant to a discussion of universal service provision. Both have been the subject of prominent initiatives in South Africa and are therefore worthy of particular scrutiny. Insurance has a different story to tell and, for reasons of space, is largely omitted here. The chapter draws extensively on Porteous and Hazlehurst (2004), an excellent and detailed study of how South Africa's financial markets have developed since 1994.

Definition of "liberal" and "universal"

For the purposes of this chapter, a liberal market is defined as one in which the particular service is provided largely by the private sector and effective competition takes place between domestic and non-domestic providers, with the latter free to carry out their business in the absence of exchange controls or tariff systems. Such a market should be characterised by price competition, innovation and choice for the consumer.

However, it is possible for a liberal market to work well for only part of the population, for example, if it requires a high income to access that market or if legislation specifically excludes part of the population. Universal service provision surely implies that most people, if not all, in the relevant part of the population, have physical access to, and can afford, a particular service. In a liberal market, where private-sector interests compete to provide the service, the number of users of that service should increase over time as product choice and price competition extend the natural boundaries of the market by bringing more consumers within reach (Porteous, 2004).

Consumers beyond the reach of the market (typically the very poor), in what Porteous (2004) has called the "supra-market zone", will therefore be excluded from use of the particular service, unless the state intervenes to extend the natural limit of the market. It can achieve this through redistributive techniques such as direct state provision, outsourcing to the private sector, voucher systems, subsidies or legislation to require providers to cross-subsidise extension of the service or, indirectly, by creating an enabling environment (as regulator or in support of innovation) to extend the access frontier.

Therefore, when a market is dominated by private sector providers, as is the case for South Africa's financial services sector, it is critically important to be able to measure reliably, and over time, people's access to, and use of, a service to determine how well that market is functioning for the wider population and to determine what role the state should play in making the service truly universal.

State of access to financial services in South Africa

Access is an elusive concept which embraces, as suggested above, not just physical access, but also affordability, product features (appropriate to a consumer's needs) and choice. To date, demand-side surveys in the financial sector that have addressed access take usage as a proxy for access because there are as yet no established procedures for measuring access itself. Usage data are likely to understate access if it assumed that people may have access to a particular product or services but choose not to use it.

FinMark Trust's FinScope survey is recognised as the most comprehensive household survey of financial services in South Africa. The survey is co-ordinated by FinMark Trust and its cost is syndicated to private sector organisations. This distinguishes it from traditional donor surveys. First run in 2002, FinScope takes usage as a proxy for access, as does the other major source of consumer information on use of financial products, the All Media & Products Survey (AMPS). Alongside usage, FinScope assembles data to consider the wider dimensions of access, such as geographic proximity, associated cost, fees paid and so on.

AMPS is especially significant in the South African context as the only major source of longer-term trend data and its development of the Living Standard Measure (LSM) segmentation model which is commonly understood and accepted across society and also defines access targets for the Financial Sector Charter (see below). AMPS is a biannual survey carried out by private-market research firms for the South African Advertising Research Foundation (www.saarf.org).

LSM 1-5s are the poorer people in society. In 2005 there were approximately 19.3 million LSM 1-5s in South Africa (FinScope SA, 2005), or 63% of the adult population (30.7 million over 16 years of age); 63% of the adult population earns less than ZAR 1,000 (USD 145) a month.

FinScope SA 2005[1] data confirm that, with the exception of financial services provided through retailers and the advent of cell phone banking, the landscape of access to financial services in South Africa has not changed materially from 2003 (Figure 8.1). In particular the proportion of banked people in the LSM 1-5 category (32%) has not changed since 2003, reflecting the numbers of young people coming into the 16+ category. As the figures shows, provision of financial services is far from universal, albeit reasonably extensive by peer standards.

Figure 8.1. Landscape of access, 2003

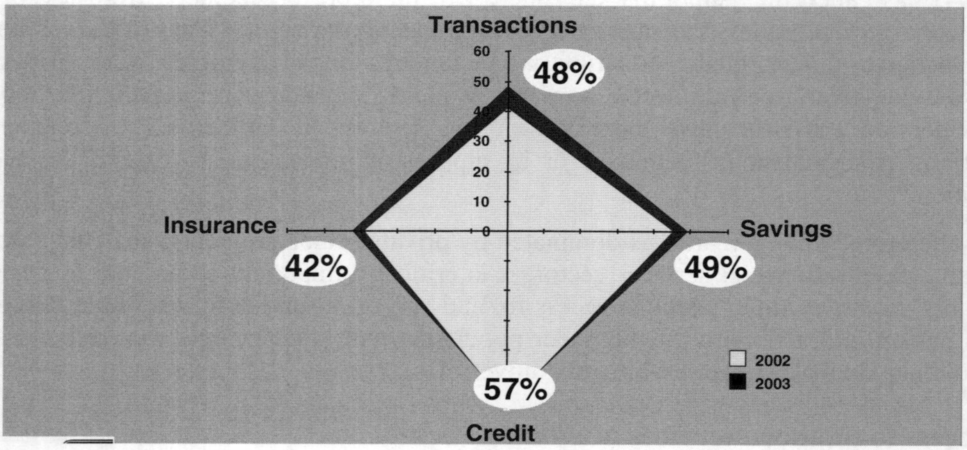

Source: FinScope SA (2003).

Highlights from FinScope SA 2005 include:

- 53% of the adult population are unbanked and 41% have never had a bank account.
- Overwhelmingly, the unbanked cite lack of job or money as the reason for not having a bank account.
- Physical access to banks is a major issue for the rural poor: while 56% of people in "urban formal" areas say they have a bank "nearby", only 11% of those in tribal rural areas say they do.
- Only 13% have some form of formal life insurance product although only 4% in LSM 1-5.

1. See www.finscope.co.za.

- Retailers provide a major possible outlet for financial services: 38% of LSM 1-5 have a store card or a store account.

- Access to a cell phone is increasing rapidly; 49% had access to a cell phone (either they own one or have access to a friend's).

In short, despite progress since 1994 in drawing those previously excluded into the financial mainstream, there is still plenty to do. Through surveys such as FinScope, however, there is greater understanding of the needs of those who still do not, or cannot, use formal financial services. Where such surveys are regularly carried out, as is the case with FinScope, they provide a credible framework within which to measure progress towards access targets, such as those defined in the Charter.

Black economic empowerment and the Financial Sector Charter

Black economic empowerment (BEE) has been one of the core unifying themes in South Africa's legislative development since 1994. It aims to ensure broader participation of black people and women in the economy through transfer of the ownership, management and control of the country's financial and economic resources to previously disadvantaged individuals (PDIs) in order to achieve sustainable development and prosperity.

The Broad-Based Black Economic Empowerment Act, signed in January 2004, provides the legislative framework for BEE. The process has been evolving since 1994, at first somewhat chaotically but now in a more formal way, especially with the publication of a number of sector-based charters that set out targets and timelines for equity transfer, employment and procurement from PDI companies.

It is central to government thinking in South Africa that broad-based BEE cannot happen unless PDIs, and especially the poor, are able to access financial services in order to borrow to invest in small businesses, to save and to protect themselves against risks. Government pressure on private-sector financial services providers to ensure that the poor have effective access to financial services has been a central feature of the relationship between government and the private sector referred to above. Who should provide those services, who should take the risk and who should bear the cost?

To date, the government has almost entirely avoided competing directly with the private sector. although, in an effort to stimulate provision, it has established a number of wholesale finance organisations in housing and enterprise finance, as well as a massive subsidy programme in housing. It has also refrained from legislation to compel the private sector to provide services that that might have been seen as risky or less profitable, although it has come close to doing so at times.

In some sense, the government and the private sector have shadowboxed since 1994, debating their roles and obligations, although this came to a provisional end with the signing of the Charter in October 2003 (Porteous and Hazlehurst, 2004, pp. 8-10). In some ways the Charter is a pre-emptive strike against the possibility of unpalatable legislation, but it is a nevertheless a voluntary commitment by the financial services sector to transformation and BEE. It is a document that is remarkable for its vision and for the clarity with which many of its goals are expressed. The signatories are the private-sector representatives of the financial services industry (for example, the Banking

Council of South Africa, the Life Offices Association and the Association of Black Securities and Investment Professionals).

The Charter (available from www.banking.org.za) has set detailed targets for the industry in terms of ownership (*i.e.* proportion of black shareholding), management representation and procurement policies but also, crucially, access targets, to be achieved by 2008, for the provision of "first-order retail financial services products" to poorer people.

The Charter access targets (together with actual usage figures, which are not directly comparable but instructive to consider) can be summarised as indicated in Table 8.1.

Table 8.1. Access targets under the Financial Sector Charter

Percentage of LSM 1-5s with effective access to:	2008 access target	2003 actual usage
Transaction accounts	80%	32%
Bank savings products	80%	28%
Life assurance products	A percentage to be defined	5%
Collective investment savings products	1% plus 250 000	Negligible
Short-term risk insurance products	6%	Negligible

Source: www.treasury.gov.za/press/other/2003101701.pdf.

Although these access targets are for the private sector to achieve, it is recognised that the government is able to influence how successfully the private sector achieves them. In the key areas of housing finance, agriculture, infrastructure and the financing of black small and medium-sized enterprises (SMEs) (the so-called "targeted investments" under the Charter), negotiations are under way between government and the private sector on how government can intervene to mitigate risk as the private sector explores hitherto uncharted territory.

Much rests on the Charter succeeding and it is by no means clear what will happen if the targets are not met. While the Charter represents an imaginative alternative to government coercion of the private sector, the threat of coercion remains. As to whether the Charter offers a credible template for other transitional economies, it is certainly possible to speculate that the moral suasion successfully exercised by the government in South Africa may only have been successful as a direct response to the particularly grotesque imbalances wrought by the apartheid system.

How liberal is the South African financial services sector?

The previous paragraphs have described how far removed the South African financial services sector is today from being able to be considered a universal service provider under the definition given above. The discussion of the Financial Sector Charter described the roadmap on which government and the private sector have agreed for moving towards establishing a more universal service.

If the present definition of a liberal market is applied to South African financial markets, it is clear that they qualify, but also fall short, on a number of counts. The following describe how far the liberalisation process has gone and help to explain why access levels remain obdurately low:

- ***Role of the state***: As regards the role of the state, the South African government has tended to facilitate and regulate, rather than provide financial services directly. In fact, direct provision of financial services by the state is negligible. Since financial markets in South Africa are dominated by private sector players, they can be said to be liberal, at least in this respect. The main areas in which government does provide finance directly are addressed below.

  Certain political constituencies have argued that the state should assume a more muscular role in driving the provision of basic services in order to accelerate the process of economic democratisation, but the state has remained largely non-interventionist.

- ***Macroeconomic policy***: As summarised in a speech by the Minister of Finance in 2002,[2] policy has aimed to: "[ensure] that appropriate macroeconomic fundamentals are in place, that a sound and well-regulated financial system exists to promote financial stability, including prudential regulation, and that social safety nets are in place to protect the poor against the potential social costs of globalisation. At the centre of the range of policy choices that our Government faces lies the principle that South Africa is an open economy."

  A raft of new legislation has been introduced since 1994 to shape this vision of an "open economy". Policy development has been notable for its consistency in this respect, despite pressures arising from the negative impacts associated with global influences, notably exchange rate volatility.

- ***Regulatory burden***: While the broad thrust of macroeconomic policy has tended towards a liberal or "open economy", the regulatory burden has arguably increased. Improved access can conflict with regulatory control objectives such as consumer protection and systemic stability, and these tensions are not easily resolved.

  South Africa continues, for example, to impose interest rate cap on consumer loans despite evidence that this discourages providers from entering the market and therefore stunts competition, to the ultimate disadvantage of the consumer. The cap has survived a major overhaul of credit legislation introduced in 2006.

  Establishing the right balance between greater service provision and regulatory control is also central to the effectiveness of the tiered banking legislation made public in November 2004.[3] This legislation creates a space for new types of organisation, including retailers and cell phone operators, to apply for limited forms of banking licence. At the same time, a new legislative framework has been created for member-based, or co-operative, financial institutions. The regulations governing the new laws will have to address key issues, such as the way the payments system is to be accessed; which may have a major impact on whether the legislation achieves the purpose for which it was intended.

  Hawkins (2003) points out that the greater commitment to international standards (around corporate governance, market conduct and consumer protection, for

2. Closing remarks by Trevor Manuel, South Africa's Minister of Finance, to the Commission of Inquiry into the rapid depreciation of the Rand, 24 May 2002.

3. The Dedicated Banks Bill and the Co-operative Banks Bill are available through the National Treasury website at www.treasury.gov.za.

example) has also led to an increased regulatory burden which could affect the extension of service provision. One example might be the introduction of the Financial Advisory and Intermediary Services (FAIS) Act which has imposed a significant additional burden on insurance brokers, causing many to leave the market. Anti-money laundering legislation in particular will have a severe impact on access if it is insensitively enforced given that many people in South Africa live on tribal land without conventional postal addresses.

In a sense South Africa's financial markets, as they adopt these international regulatory standards, are no less liberal than their developed world counterparts. However, raising an already well-developed financial system to international standards could make it harder for policy makers to achieve the goal of universal service provision across a market which remains in many respects that of a developing country.

- ***"Complex monopoly"***: The April 2004 Competition in South African Banking report (Falkena *et al.*, 2004), which was not officially published but was leaked later in the year, found evidence that the "big four" South African banks collectively "behave as a complex monopoly". The report highlighted in particular the material financial and procedural difficulties faced by organisations wishing to access the national payment system which is owned and controlled by these banks. The government has not yet indicated what action it intends take in response to the report's findings, although it is actively considering a number of relevant issues.

  The four banks' economic concentration is substantial (although in line with other emerging markets such as Brazil) (Falkena *et al.*, 2004), with collective market shares at 90% and higher in certain categories such as credit cards, mortgages and instalment finance.

  Profitability in retail banking in South Africa remains consistently high, generating a return on assets in excess of the world's top 100 banks in every year in the past decade;[4] some 80% of those active in the retail banking segment regard their business as "very or exceptionally profitable", yet a similarly high 83% also regard it as "intensively" competitive" (PricewaterhouseCoopers, 2003).

  It therefore appears that the market is not being contested from outside (which would place downward pressure on profit margins) and that the barriers to entry are either real or perceived as such. Competition appears only to emanate from those already in the market and is not eroding banks' profitability.

- ***Lack of non-bank deposit-taking alternatives***: As described below, there is a lack of non-bank alternatives to give poor, and especially rural, populations a credible alternative to formal financial services.

  The effect of this absence of choice is to ensure that accessing financial services remains both inconvenient and expensive for poor people, as they are typically forced to rely on what the major banks, and some niche players, offer. Generally this means a full banking service but often in locations that are inconvenient for them and always accompanied by an array of bank charges the structure of which is unique to South Africa (Falkena *et al.*, 2004). For poor people, such charges undermine the

4. Dr. Penelope Hawkins, in a presentation to the South African Savings Institute annual symposium, October 2004, quoting *The Banker 2003/4.*

value of having a bank account at all. The Mzansi initiative (discussed below) purports to address this issue.

To conclude, South Africa's financial services sector are overwhelmingly private-sector in character and are nurtured by macroeconomic policies that are consistently supportive of an "open market". They may appear outwardly liberal but the dominance of retail banking by the four major banks, the lack of choice especially in the non-banking sector and, arguably, excessive regulation in some areas all conspire to create an environment that has failed to cater for the needs of the wider population.

Member-based financial services and the informal sector

The informal sector plays a significant role in the economic lives of those who use it, and it would be natural for policy makers seeking to achieve broad access to financial services to support the informal financial sector with financial incentives and a supportive legislative and regulatory framework. In fact, as regards non-bank deposit-taking entities, there has until recently been practically no direct financial support from government for member-based financial services institutions or for their regulators. Such regulatory development as there has been has been by way of exemption notices. No new direct legislation for non-banks has been passed since 1994. Perhaps as a result the non-bank financial sector today remains underdeveloped (ECI*Africa*, 2003). Postbank partially fills the gap for savings and transaction accounts but does not offer credit.

South Africa has no building societies. Following legislation in the late 1980s, when apartheid was still in force, building societies were required to be capitalised on a basis similar to banks with the result that many were forced to access equity capital and therefore demutualise. Although the Mutual Banks Act 1993 was designed to reverse some of this damage and add greater depth to the financial system, there are in fact today only two mutual banks. The reasons cited include the fact that they cannot mobilise external capital and onerous reporting and disclosure requirements (ECI*Africa*, July 2003).

Use of "stokvels", rotating savings and credit associations (ROSCAs), is fairly widespread, especially among black women living in tribal or informal urban areas. In all there are approximately 2 million stokvel members in South Africa (FinScope SA, 2005), out of a total adult population of 30.7 million. Interestingly, although stokvels rely on trust among members, levels of trust are not especially high and the vast majority (some 80%) of stokvel members also have bank accounts (FinScope SA, 2003, 2004) so this form of financial instrument should be seen as complementary, rather than substitutive, to the formal banking system. Although an estimated ZAR 5 billion flows through stokvels each year there is clearly a limit to the role they can perform and to the role that their members would like them to have.

Burial societies are similar in structure to stokvels. Although some 6 million people "save" into burial societies (FinScope SA, 2004, pp. 52-54), this should really be understood as a form of insurance rather than savings in the conventional sense and, because they are dedicated to providing funding for funerals, they cannot underpin other forms of financial service, such as the extension of credit.

Credit unions are marginal players with only 31 savings and credit co-operatives (SACCOs) registered (Falkena *et al.*, 2004). There are 62 village banks, or co-operative financial institutions, operating in rural areas and linked to a formal bank which acts as a deposit taker. Village banks and SACCOs together have an estimated deposit base of only

ZAR 37 million, less than 0.005% of the banking industry's total deposit base (ECI*Africa*, 2003).

Leaving aside stokvels and burial societies, with their long-established cultural roots, it is clear that recent attempts to stimulate a viable third tier have been unsuccessful.

The government's contribution has been confined largely to legislation. In particular, it introduced in 1994 a "common bond" exemption to the Banks Act 1990 to allow member-based groups, including SACCOs, stokvels and credit unions, to take deposits but only from their members. A similar exemption was introduced for village banks in 1998. The recently published Co-operative Banks Bill will provide the legislative space for successful member-based non-banks to graduate in time into banks although, as has been seen, very few organisations would be able to make that transition today.

Eschewing direct intervention to regulate or support member-based organisations, the government's preferred route has been to allow self-regulation (ECI*Africa*, 2003). Established with donor support, the two apex organisations for village banks, FSA and FINASOL, collapsed through lack of funding, capacity or expertise. SACCOL, the SACCOs' self-regulator, continues today, although with only 31 credit union members, one may question whether SACCOL has the capacity, in view of its size, to promote the industry as well as regulate it or indeed whether it is appropriate for it to play both roles at the same time.

There has also been a duplication of regulatory responsibility (ECI*Africa*, 2003) with cooperatives required to submit to at least three controlling bodies: the Registrar of Co-operatives, the Registrar of Banks (through the self-regulator) and, for credit activities, the Micro Finance Regulatory Council, all of which imposes a considerable compliance burden on financial co-operatives.

Following the collapse of FSA and FINASOL, the National Department of Agriculture assumed responsibility in 2002 for developing rural co-operatives, in part through the establishment of a co-operative development fund (ECI*Africa*, 2003). This is a "fund of funds" intended to meet the credit needs of member-based organisations as they strive to achieve critical mass.

Thus, government funding, if only for rural co-operatives, has finally become available. Regulation remains complex. There is little doubt that the government recognises the potential for member-based organisations to deliver financial services to the underbanked, especially in rural areas. Indeed this point was reinforced in the competition in banking report referred to above, which mentioned the need for the government to play a faciliatory and regulatory role and, if the market cannot provide services, to consider subsidising a banking product or state-supported institution, such as the Postbank.

Direct government intervention in financial markets

Three areas in which the state has become involved as a direct provider of finance are worth highlighting. These are:

- ***Postbank***, a division of the SA Post Office, is a deposit-taking institution but does not lend. Operating through more than 2 000 post-office outlets across the country, it provides a variety of savings products and a card-based transaction account known as Flexi Card (www.sapo.org.za/postbank). Because Postbank is a participant in the Mzansi basic bank account initiative, Mzansi Flexi Card users have access to the

12 000 automatic teller machines (ATMs) of all the major banks at reduced Mzansi rates.

The government has announced its intention to restructure and corporatise Postbank and to expand its product range to include insurance and other financial services. Many observers (*e.g.* Falkena *et al.*, 2004) would see a positive role for the Postbank, if it were transformed into a state-owned bank, given the extent of its branch network and its ability to reach the poor, especially in rural areas. For poorer people, having a Postbank savings account features highly as a preferred location for their savings (FinScope, 2003).

- ***Retail savings bonds*** were introduced by the government in May 2004. At mid-2006 the interest rate on offer is up to 9% (www.treasury.gov.za). Since the minimum investment is ZAR 1 000, this is not an initiative aimed at the poor; in order to receive interest from the bonds, a holder must have a bank (or Postbank) account. This excludes the millions who lack one. It has been a success, however, and had raised some ZAR 1.5 billion as at mid-2006. In addition, this has forced the banks to increase their deposit rates in response. New products are likely to be introduced which may be directed towards poorer savers.

- In ***housing and SMME finance*** the government provides subsidies and wholesale finance, as well as business services, through a number of parastatal development finance institutions (DFIs).

  In small, medium and micro enterprise (SMME) finance, there has been considerable institutional change (see Porteous and Hazlehurst, 2004). The National Small Business Act 1996 established the National Small Business Council (NSBC) to represent the interests of small business as well as Ntsika, a provider of non-financial support services to small businesses. The NSBC closed amid allegations of mismanagement in 1997/98. Khula Enterprise Finance, a provider of guarantee finance to retail finance institutions (RFIs) was established by the Department of Trade and Industry in 1996. The landscape changed further with the establishment, by Act of Parliament in 1998, of the National Empowerment Fund, whose purpose was to finance BEE transactions, and, in 2001, of the Umsobomvu Youth Fund which makes strategic investments to create opportunities for young people to acquire skills and access job opportunities. At the end of 2004, Ntsika was merged with the National Manufacturing Advisory Centres (NAMAC), another governmental non-financial support entity, to form the Small Enterprise Development Agency (SEDA). Finally, the government launched a new Apex Fund, to provide wholesale funding to institutions serving micro-enterprises, also at the end of 2004.

  Though well-intentioned, these various state-sponsored initiatives have had a chequered history, owing to confusion over their respective mandates, mismanagement and management change. Khula, in particular, suffered from a lack of capacity in the RFIs it supported, with over half of the 32 RFIs it funded closing down during the period.

  In housing finance, a credit-linked subsidy programme has been a central plank of government housing policy since 1994. Some 2 million subsidies were delivered over the decade to 2004 (Porteous and Hazelhurst, 2004). Those qualifying for subsidies were first-time buyers earning less than ZAR 3 500 a month (in September

2004 the ceiling was lifted to ZAR 7 500). The subsidy programme has succeeded in housing millions of the poorest South Africans but it has not succeeded in driving the supply of private housing finance down to households earning materially less than ZAR 7 500 a month, the level at which conventional mortgage finance would become available.

To provide wholesale finance to non-bank housing finance providers, the government established the National Housing Finance Corporation (NHFC) and its sister fund, the Rural Housing Loan Fund (RHLF). There are considerable constraints on the NHFC's ability to fulfil its mandate: it cannot deploy the funds it has because the retail network through which its funds are supposed to be deployed is limited in size and a number of these retailers are in distress; second, it has an exposure limit (partly self-imposed, partly prudential) of ZAR 100 million per client and so cannot wholesale finance in sufficient volume (Porteous and Hazelhurst, 2004).

The direct provision of finance has been supplemented in the housing arena by the threat of new banking legislation. The Home Loan and Mortgage Disclosure Act was passed in 2000 to ensure better information on lending by area. In this way the practice of redlining could at least be highlighted and tackled. The regulations giving effect to this Act have yet to be passed, however. Further, a US-style Community Reinvestment Bill was tabled in 2002 which required banks to meet certain low-income lending targets or face a fine. This was shelved in favour of the Financial Sector Charter under which banks have committed to substantial additional funding targets for low-income housing. However, the mechanisms by which these targets are to be achieved remain unclear.

Macroeconomic progress, exchange controls and liberalisation

The process of reintegrating South Africa into the global economy since 1994 has been accompanied by a gradual easing of exchange controls, starting with the abolition of the financial rand system in 1995. It has long been the case that foreign companies (or individuals) wishing to invest in South Africa would not be prevented from repatriating their profits. As recently as October 2004 exchange control limits on South African corporates wishing to invest abroad were effectively removed. In the financial markets, South African banks were able to establish businesses outside South Africa and become competitive on a global level; in return, multinational financial institutions would be granted unrestricted entry into South Africa.

Exchange rate volatility has been a feature of this gradual easing of exchange controls although it is probably true that this has had limited direct impact on the provision of domestic financial services.

According to the South African Reserve Bank, as at 30 June 2004, there were six foreign-controlled banks registered in South Africa (as against 17 locally controlled), 15 foreign banks with registered branches in South Africa and a further 30 with representative offices. Although this amounts to a sizeable presence of foreign banks, they have had practically no impact, either positive or negative, on mass retail markets in South Africa as they have tended to focus on corporate and merchant banking and treasury and capital markets activities. Where there has been activity in the retail market it has targeted a high-end customer base, in Internet banking (as with Standard

Chartered's TwentyTwenty initiative) or international personal banking (Falkena *et al.*, 2004.

The completion of the Barclays/ABSA transaction could in theory herald a shake-up in the competitive landscape of South African retail banking, with Barclays able to take advantage of economies of scale, its experience in other emerging markets and its technological skill. It is too early to say how aggressive Barclays might be in tackling South Africa's mass market opportunities.

As to whether other foreign banks would follow Barclays in looking to acquire a domestic South African player, there has been speculation but nothing more, although Standard Chartered has publicly stated its intention to be an active player in retail banking. The regulator's attitude towards foreign ownership appears to rest on the premise that there should be four domestic "pillars" (*i.e.* four local banks) to retail banking in South Africa. However, Barclays/ABSA has perhaps redefined this premise.

Transaction banking

One of the more positive features of the development of financial markets in the past decade has been the growth in the number of users of low-end bank accounts.

Porteous and Hazelhurst, 2004, (p. 22) quote AMPS records which show that the number of people with a bank account increased from 7.8 million in 1994 to 11.4 million in 2004. FinScope SA (2005), which, unlike AMPS, also includes over a million Postbank customers, estimates that 14.3 million people have a bank account, or 47% of the adult population over 16 years of age.

The increase has been driven by a number of factors, such as increased use of ATM cards and the move by employers to automate their payroll systems to save costs and avoid the risk of crime (Porteous and Hazelhurst, 2004). A number of banks experimented with new brands and banking models to capture a new market. While some were successful (such as Standard Bank's E-Plan), others were not, but they at least helped to create the perception that there was a sizeable market to address.

However, the relationship between poorer or less sophisticated customers and the banks is not straightforward. For one, many individuals who became bank account holders found that they were unable to maintain their accounts. FinScope SA 2005 estimates that around 12.3% of the adult population, or 3.8 million people, are "previously banked"; they have dropped out of the system for reasons largely related to poverty (*e.g.* they have lost their regular income) and can no longer afford the cost of maintaining a bank account. Further, approximately 1.6 million bank account holders withdraw their entire salary as soon as it is paid which means that they incur bank charges but are not active users of the financial system in any sense.

Under any definition, a transaction bank account is a "first-order financial product" and so it was appropriate for the Charter to focus on effective access to a bank account as one of its core objectives. As noted above, the banks have undertaken to increase the number of poorer people (LSM 1-5s) with effective access to a bank account from 32% today to 80% in 2008.

Much of the debate around Mzansi, the low-cost banking product which the banks have launched at a collective cost of ZAR 25-30 million, according to press reports, has centred on the reduced charges that Mzansi offers consumers for specific features. In South Africa, banks levy a wide range of charges for services such as electronic transfers, cash deposits, ATM withdrawals, balance enquiries and so on, which appear to make banking expensive for the consumer when compared with countries such as the United Kingdom where banking is generally free if the account stays in credit. Indeed, Mzansi does charge significantly less for the individual transactions a consumer is able to carry out on the account but the range of transactions is limited; for example, the consumer cannot (as yet) make electronic payments by way of debit order to cover loan repayments or insurance premiums and there is no credit facility. Further, if an account holder becomes an "active" transactor beyond a certain threshold, penalties are levied and costs escalate.

By pooling infrastructure, the eight participating banks have made 12 000 ATMs available to every individual with a Mzansi account. At the insistence of the minister of finance, pricing is competitive but, for 12 months, the product features are common to all participating banks.

Within the first six weeks Mzansi had attracted 180 000 users, according to the Banking Council of South Africa, thereby exceeding many people's expectations. These early successes need to be maintained if the Charter target is to be achieved by 2008, but it is clear that Mzansi is a material step forward towards the delivery of a universal service and has been achieved without government subsidy, legislation or interference, except for its insistence on competitive pricing.

Micro-credit

The 1992 exemption to the Usury Act, which removed the interest rate cap on small loans, ushered in an era of extraordinary growth in micro-credit (Porteous and Hazelhurst, 2004). Intended to promote the development of small businesses as a response to an unemployment crisis, the exemption mainly stimulated consumption borrowing and led to public concern over exploitative business practices by commercial micro lenders.

The post-apartheid government therefore inherited a situation in which there was virtually no consumer protection and no regulation, although micro lending was now legal. As a result considerable numbers of commercial micro lenders joined the existing not-for-profit lenders, some of which were commercialised. Significantly, the major banks also developed micro lending strategies and came to dominate the sector as they do to this day. Banks account for 50% of outstanding loans in micro lending with retailers and cash lenders together accounting for 48% (MFRC; Porteous and Hazlehurst, 2004).

Micro lending volumes grew dramatically, trebling between 1995 and 1997 from ZAR 3.6 billion to ZAR 10.1 billion,[5] and government unease over the apparent exploitation of low-income borrowers led to re-regulation of the sector through a revised Usury Act Exemption Notice 1999. This gave rise to the establishment of the Micro Finance Regulatory Council (MFRC), with which all lenders operating under the "unrestricted interest rate window" are required to register, in order to operate legally. The Notice also outlawed the card-and–PIN collection under which borrowers were forced to surrender their ATM cards to lenders.

A further measure introduced by the government was the elimination in June 2000 of payroll deduction facilities (Persal) for civil servants on unsecured loans (and insurance policies) which meant that lenders had to find alternative collection methods overnight.

5. Du Plessis, cited in Porteous and Hazelhurst, 2004.

One bank in particular, Saambou, suffered a loss of investor confidence as a result of the bad debts it incurred following the withdrawal of Persal and failed in 2002, triggering a major banking crisis. This is a clear reminder of what can result from ill-considered, though well-intentioned, government intervention.

The government's role in micro-credit has been to dampen the market's enthusiasm for micro-credit but also to legitimise the sector through the operations of the MFRC, by introducing a measure of consumer protection and providing for much better information on the sector, for example through the setting up of a National Loans Register.

A review of consumer credit legislation, starting in 2002, has led to a revised legislative framework for credit (the proposed Consumer Credit Bill), the establishment of a new National Credit Regulator under the Department of Trade and Industry (into which the MFRC has been subsumed) and a National Credit Register. Perhaps inevitably, providers have criticised the bill as imposing a heavy regulatory burden on the industry. However, the bill introduces certainty into credit law, normalises the regulation of the various credit markets and addresses the problem of reckless lending. If this encourages providers to enter the market and compete despite the perception of heavy regulation, the bill could give borrowers improved access to credit over time.

Summary

Ten years after South Africa's first democratic elections, a large proportion of the country's population still does not have effective access to financial services. As such a key objective of the government's commitment to broad-based black economic empowerment has not been fulfilled.

The provision of financial services remains dominated by the private sector and especially by four major retail banks. The government has not sought to increase its provision of financial services although it continues to provide wholesale finance in housing and enterprise finance and offers subsidies to homeowners in an effort to stimulate private sector provision.

There has been a flurry of financial sector legislation, much of it (for example, tiered banking legislation and credit law reform) in the very recent past. It has been enabling, rather than coercive, in character. The government has been content to accept the private sector's commitment under the Charter to deliver broad-based access by 2008.

South Africa's informal banking sector is particularly weak compared with the formal sector, offering the poor very few alternatives in the way of banking services.

In transaction banking and credit there have been significant changes to the landscape since 1994, which indicate the capacity of the private sector to adapt to, and take advantage of, changing circumstances.

The government has been consistent in its macroeconomic policies in moving towards the creation of an "open economy", by gradually dismantling exchange controls and exposing the financial sector to foreign competition, although this has had little impact as yet on the provision of domestic financial services.

The outwardly liberal characteristics of South Africa's financial sector belie practices which have been described as those of a "complex monopoly". Bank profitability has been high by international standards; by contrast, there has been limited progress towards making basic services generally available to the wider population. However, early indications from the Mzansi initiative give grounds for considerable optimism and appear to be a positive conclusion to ten years of active experimentation by banks in the transaction banking arena.

The next few years will be crucial in determining whether recent legislative developments bear fruit in terms of extending access to financial services. For the Charter to succeed by 2008, a significant number of new initiatives will have to be agreed upon and set in train over the next couple of years.

References

ECI*Africa* (2003), "Third Tier Banking Report", July, available at: www.finmarktrust.org.za/documents/2003/SEPTEMBER/ThirdTierBanking.pdf.

Falkena, H., P. Hawkins, G. Davel, E. Masilela *et al.* (2004), "Competition in South African Banking", Task Group Report for the National Treasury and the South African Reserve Bank, April.

FinScope SA (2003, 2004, 2005), available at www.finscope.co.za

Hawkins, P. (2003), "South Africa's Financial Sector Ten Years On: The Performance of the Financial Sector since Democracy", FEASibility (Pty) Ltd, August.

Porteous D. (2004), "Making Financial Markets Work for the Poor", October, available at www.finmarktrust.org.za.

Porteous, D. and E. Hazlehurst (2004), *Banking on Change – Democratising Finance in South Africa 1994-2004 and Beyond*, , Double Storey, Capetown and available through FinMark Trust's Web site at: www.finmarktrust.org.za.

PricewaterhouseCoopers (2003), "Strategic and Emerging Issues in SA Banking".

Chapter 9

Regulatory Aspects of Universal Access to Financial Services in India

Bindu Ananth
Manager, ICICI Bank
and
Nachiket Mor
Deputy Managing Director, ICICI Bank, Chairman, Managing Committee of IFMR [1]

This chapter focuses on access to finance for the rural and urban poor in India. It provides a brief overview of the current situation, including some measurement issues. It discusses various dimensions of access relevant to universal access and describes India's current regulatory approach. Some policy initiatives that might have an impact on universal access are suggested.

1. The views expressed are those of the authors and do not in any way reflect the views of the institution to which they belong.

Introduction

Economic theory has long argued that one of the most powerful ways to break the "poverty trap" is to make available to the poor as near a complete set of financial markets as feasible. This allows them to protect themselves from adverse shocks and to make investments in high-return activities in a manner that is not limited by their current low income. These investments could include borrowed money in high-return service enterprises (such as dairies, tea-shops, eateries and grocery stores), financing migration from low-productivity rural to high-productivity urban sectors/occupations, or investments in improved education and health care through retained earnings.

If theory predicts large gains from improvement in access to financial services, why is it that there has been little progress? Market failures in credit and insurance markets arise from limited information and limited enforceability. The problem is compounded when dealing with the poor owing to their inability to provide collateral. Peer lending models that use local information and the threat of credit denial as leading strategies have been popular since the 1990s.[2] However, smooth access to financial services continues to be a challenge for various segments. In India the underserved segments for financial services include state governments, public-sector units, local urban bodies, mid-to-low quality large companies, small and medium-sized enterprises (SME), rural households and enterprises, and urban low-income households. This chapter focuses principally on access to finance for the rural and urban poor.

A discussion of universal access would encompass issues of institutional structure and incentives, product and contract design, and the regulatory/policy environment. This chapter only highlights certain regulatory aspects and policy initiatives that can contribute to achieving universal access. The following discussion first provides a brief overview of access to financial services for the poor in India, including some measurement issues. It turns next to various dimensions of access relevant to a discussion of universal service and then to India's current regulatory approach in this area. A final section suggests policy initiatives that could have significant impact on universal access and concludes.

Access to financial services for the poor in India

The degree and implications of diminished access to financial services are often difficult to discern and cannot be derived from stated demand and supply gaps alone. In many instances, the behaviour of the poor is influenced by the anticipation of limitations on access. For instance, Morduch (1995) finds that less well-off households in the ICRISAT [International Crop Research Institute for the Semi-arid Tropics] villages will make production choices with an eye to reducing the likelihood of difficulties. Similarly, the over-diversification of economic activity observed by Hess *et al.* (2001) is another manifestation of reduced access to insurance-like services which, over time, prevents households from deriving benefits from specialisation and scale. Banerjee and Newman (1998) develop a framework that tries to explain India's low rates of migration from less productive rural occupations to highly productive urban occupations in terms of constrained credit access at urban locations. Therefore, the pernicious effects of constrained access may often be better observed indirectly in *ex ante* sub-optimal

2. These include the Grameen replicators and the Self-help Group Commercial Bank Linkage models in India.

production and consumption choices among the poor rather than in survey/self-reported demand data.

However, even according to overall data, the achievements are negligible. The banked population in India, as defined by population above the age of 15 with a bank account, is a mere 20%.[3] Even here, there are disparities between rural and urban populations in terms of access to bank accounts. Against an estimated demand for credit of between USD 3 billion and USD 9 billion annually by poor households in India, the formal sector is barely able to provide USD 200 million to USD 300 million. There is a high degree of reliance on informal provision of savings facilities and insurance arrangements in rural areas. Especially among the poor these arrangements tend to be informal and mutual in nature and do not offer sufficient protection against systemic shocks.

Access to financial services and dimensions of access

It is useful to describe the various dimensions of access to financial services and understand what universal access means in this context.

Several authors have discussed the attributes of access that are important for the poor. For example, Morduch and Rutherford (2003) summarise it thus: "Poor people want what many of the less poor already enjoy: reliable, convenient and flexible ways to store and retrieve cash and to turn their capacity to save into spending power, in the short, medium and long term. And they want it on a continuing, not a one-off, basis."

Access has to be distinguished from mere physical proximity to the source of the service. Owing to various historical factors, including the nationalisation of banks, India has a large network of formal financial institutions which includes rural branches of commercial banks, regional rural banks (RRBs), co-operatives and non-bank financial institutions and local area banks.[4] However, this by itself has not always ensured sustained or universal access.[5] The incentives of staff working in these organisational formats represent a challenge that needs to be addressed.

3. In Germany, the figure is 98% (Commonwealth Business Council and Visa, 2004).

4. Formal financial services are available to low-income families through the 33 000 rural and 14 000 suburban branches of the major banks and RRBs and through 94 000 co-operative outlets, either bank branches or village-level societies (Sinha, 2003). This needs to be viewed against the fact that India has more than 550 000 villages. Relevant issues involve both the extent of outreach and the quality of access that the existing network affords to the rural poor. Access to a bank branch, which may observe a traditional 9 to 5 schedule, may involve significant explicit and implicit costs (*e.g.* lost income for the time spent commuting to the bank). From the provider's perspective, however, providing a larger network of branches is difficult since high transaction intensities, combined with low per-transaction values, mean that bank branches serving very small communities are not viable. A similar situation prevails even for the most basic of insurance products – life insurance. Total insurance premiums paid annually in India represent only 2.7% of GDP, compared to 14.2% for the United Kingdom (Swiss Re, Economic Research & Consulting, Sigma No. 6/2002). However, owing to the existence of a wide network of insurance agents (use of agents is not permitted in banking, particularly where savings are concerned) availability may be far greater than for banking.

5. There is some empirical evidence to show that the presence of a branch has some implications for access. Pande and Burgess (2003) use state-level data to show that rural branch expansion in India was associated with significant reductions in rural poverty. In addition, household data demonstrate that, during the years of the social banking programme, bank borrowing among rural households (manual labour) was higher in states which saw more rapid expansion of rural branches. They also show that the programme increased access of lower caste and tribal households to bank loans.

Mor and Ananth (2004) observe that availability often refers to a problem of access unrelated to price. It refers to restrictions on availability irrespective of the rates that users are willing to pay.[6] This could also be a result of organisation and service characteristics. For instance, in India, a commonly cited problem is that opening hours of bank branches are not suitable to the rural context and that this limits access. There is also a more subtle concern that while specialised institutions cater to the needs of some segments (for example, microfinance institutions [MFIs] for the poor and urban co-operative banks for small businesses), there are no mechanisms for smoothly graduating these segments from one level of funding to another and there are often large gaps in credit availability at the intermediate levels. The "transaction costs" to the customer of obtaining a loan or opening a savings account are often not examined comprehensively enough. Repeat visits to bank branches, long group meetings for MFIs, documentation requirements, etc., drive these costs up.

Another key aspect is the range of financial services available. Although policy makers and donors pay much attention to credit, other financial services such as savings, investment, remittances, insurance (life, health, accident, weather) and derivatives are equally important in the overall discussion. In several cases, especially among the very poor, insurance services might be more relevant than credit. Even as regards credit, while MFIs have made small loans (USD 10-300) available for consumption and working capital, enterprise finance or housing finance for the poor, which entail larger per capita amounts of credit, continue to be gaps that are inadequately addressed. Therefore, universal access also entails designing services in each of these categories and making them available at scale.

Continuity in access to financial services has been an important challenge in the Indian context. The failure to pursue commercial models capable of scale partly explains why there have been more financial services "schemes" than permanent institutional designs that respond to the needs of the poor. If one were to examine the leading rural credit programme in India, the Self-help Group Bank Linkage programme, the emphasis is on obtaining one loan for the group from a commercial bank branch, and this is in fact the metric that is tracked when measuring the programme's success. It fails to analyse the mechanisms through which the individual/group may access credit and savings services on an ongoing basis.

It would be useful to think of universal access in terms of an environment of continuing and cost-effective (including direct and indirect costs to the customer) access to a range of financial services for all "eligible" customers and enterprises, recognising that the financial service providers are profit-maximising entities. This tension – between profitability and outreach – is often highlighted in the specific context of microfinance. It also nuances the role of regulation.

Regulatory approach to universal access in India

The dominant regulatory approach to access in India has been what is popularly known as "directed credit". Through a series of measures including "priority sector norms" for credit and insurance and special schemes for identified population segments,

6. Several anecdotes point to the existence of credit rationing among the rural and urban poor in India; rationing is defined (by Stiglitz and Weiss, 1981) as a state in which, with a given supply of credit, identifiable groups of individuals in the population are unable to obtain loans at any interest rate.

the regulator has sought to address the issue of formal providers in rural and underserved markets.

The main regulatory policy in this regard is the priority sector obligation, which requires all commercial banks in India to advance 40% of their net bank credit in a given year to certain defined sectors, including agriculture, small enterprise, micro-credit, rural infrastructure and others.[7] The same approach is taken in the insurance industry, which has a mandate to insure a specified number of lives (in the case of life insurance) and to receive a proportion of premiums from the rural and socially vulnerable population.[8] The Reserve Bank of India's report, *Advances to Agriculture and Weaker Sections* (2004, available at www.rbi.org.in to public-sector and private-sector banks reveals that only four out of 30 private-sector banks and seven of 27 public-sector banks met the target for lending to "weaker sections". Shortfalls in meeting priority sector obligations may be compensated for by investing in Government of India bonds. The data on lending reveal that this policy alone does not give commercial banks sufficient incentive to expand their role in this market.

Another policy tool prevalent in India has been the specification of price ceilings in lending to some of these sectors. Price ceilings may themselves act to limit availability of financial services on a sustained basis. For example, in the case of loans of less than INR 200 000 to farmers, where interest rates are capped, even providers that would be willing to make these loans (but only at higher rates that reflect underlying transaction costs and risks) may refrain from doing so. A similar effect is observed when subsidised products (for example, life insurance products for the poor, crop insurance policies and auto insurance policies) are introduced in the market through a limited number of government-owned entities or through the imposition of artificial price caps. The subsidised rate effectively acts as a price cap and leads to diminished supply (few players) of these products. It also deters new players and does not allow market forces to have free play. Regulation in India exempts microfinance from price caps when undertaken through self-help groups and microfinance institutions. It may be argued that this has contributed in no small measure to the rapid growth of these delivery channels. However, even the microfinance movement faces pressure from state governments and local politicians on the issue of interest rates and supervision under usury laws. The sustainability of these institutions and their clients depends on how successfully these pressures can be navigated.

At some level, there appears to be a conflict between the role of the regulator as responsible for "financial stability" and the goal of universal access. Nowhere is this more evident than in the debates on deposit mobilisation. Deposit mobilisation remains a very highly regulated activity in India given concerns about the safety and liquidity of public deposits. Entities other than banks and approved non-bank finance companies cannot collect deposits. In the current scenario, providing access to savings facilities for the poor appears difficult. Concern is often voiced by microfinance organisations which view savings as crucial for allowing the poor to smooth consumption. Bank branches will find it a huge challenge to provide access to small savings accounts with high transaction

7. See RBI Master Circular of 1 August 2001 for a detailed description of the priority sector norms at www.rbi.org.in.

8. For the rural sector, in respect of a life insurer the obligation starts at 5% of total policies in the first financial year and goes up to 15% of total policies in the fifth year. In respect of a general insurer, the obligations begin at 2% of gross premium income in the first year and represent 5% from the third year onwards.

intensity in a viable manner, given that returns on deposits have to be uniform across all accounts. Transaction costs for clients are also likely to be high because of the rigidities implicit in transacting with a formal provider (see the above discussion on branch opening hours and employee incentives). In this scenario, MFIs are demanding the right to offer savings facilities on their own. While this seems to be a response to an observed market failure, it is fraught with risks. Owing to their inability to achieve asset diversification and their low capital base, MFIs are less suited to be providers of savings facilities. The dilemma that India faces is the fact that banks are not expanding their branch networks in rural India (for deposit mobilisation or otherwise) while institutions whose presence in these regions are growing are not permitted to accept deposits because of their local and semi-formal character.[9]

Direct subsidy has been used in this sphere in the past in the form of subsidised loans through programmes such as the Integrated Rural Development Programme. While such programmes have largely been discontinued in the case of credit, re-financing made available to banks for lending to self-help groups and co-operatives is an indirect form of price subsidy. Over the longer term, this discourages banks from making pricing decisions based on estimated risk and undermines the scope for innovation. The absence of segment-wise reporting for banks does not reveal the true profitability of rural branch operations. Other functions of the banks, such as trading, are also aspects of cross-subsidisation. This again creates a credit culture which tolerates lack of viability.

Regulation implicitly requires all banks to be "direct originators" irrespective of their comparative advantage. Facilitating the emergence of a secondary market for new asset classes such as microfinance may be a move towards bank specialisation whereby banks with relative strengths in origination supply assets to other banks.[10]

The challenge raised by a vitiated credit culture is often alluded to with respect to expanding access, especially in rural India. Among certain segments, large farmers for instance, a history of loan forgiveness programmes has resulted in a credit culture that does not act as a strong deterrent to default. The absence of shared credit histories further erodes the credibility of the threat of denial of credit. Thus, the perceived credit risk in these markets is high owing to low enforceability of contracts. Cole (2004) finds evidence of political capture of agricultural credit in India.

With the advent of financial sector reforms, new participants have entered the banking, insurance and mutual funds industries. While this has corresponded to an increase in credit availability for certain segments in urban areas (see the above discussion of growth in mortgage markets) and has affected financial markets (for instance, the derivatives market) positively, the reforms have had no real impact on the

9. A related issue is the limited scope for the emergence of non-traditional competitors. For example, money market mutual funds (MMMF) in India are not permitted to offer checking facilities to account holders except for redemption by the investor. If this were not the case, MMMFs could substitute savings bank accounts. MMMFs should be in the nature of drawing accounts, distinct from any other account, with clear limits for withdrawals, number of cheques drawn, etc., as prescribed by MMMF/MF. They should not be used as a regular bank account and cheques drawn on these accounts should only be in favour of the investor (as part of redemption) and not in favour of third parties. No deposits can be made in the account. Each withdrawal by the investor should be consistent with the terms prescribed by the MMMF/MF and treated as redemption of holdings in the MMMF/MF to that extent. See www.rbi.org.in, DBOD.FSC.No. 56/24.01.001/2003-04.

10. A positive development in this regard has been the recognition of pass-through certificates with underlying agricultural assets as qualifying for priority sector status.

rural and poor segments. It may be argued that the current regulatory approach has not contributed to rapid growth in outreach. It may be that greater domestic deregulation, which encourages existing players to expand access through market-based mechanisms, has greater potential than entry of additional players or even privatisation.[11]

Elements of an enabling environment for universal access

This section discusses specific policy initiatives for universal access to financial services. It argues for a role for the regulator that is much more focused on pro-actively creating a facilitative financial infrastructure and, to a lesser degree, reliance on instruments of subsidy (either directly for products or indirectly through refinance to lenders). In terms of allocation efficiency and equity, outlays of the former type seem less prone to capture by some groups than the latter.

India requires a large number of local financial institutions (LFIs). It is a very large and diverse country, with only about 33 000 branches (see note 4). Local financial institutions provide appropriate and available financial services and they help to overcome information asymmetry in various ways. They can create a low-cost local distribution capability that can be leveraged to deliver many financial services to groups and individuals.[12] They may take various organisational forms and may be for-profit or not-for-profit. However, their principal contribution is in evolving models of outreach that are scaleable and sustainable. The fact that local financial institutions have limited geographical outreach (unlike commercial banks) gives them an incentive to address the financial service needs of their constituencies comprehensively. Because the staff of these organisations are recruited locally, they can overcome some of the "cultural" issues observed among managers of commercial bank branches (see Thorat *et al.*, 2003, for further detail). Supporting the emergence of these institutions then becomes an important strategy for universal access. While models for scale-up are largely commercial in nature, there is space for government and donor participation to support training initiatives and meet the start-up expenses of these institutions.

In addition to increasing the number of local financial institutions, a set of initiatives to improve India's financial infrastructure is crucial. Some of these are described below:

Unique identifier: A unique identifier is a basis for implementing initiatives such as credit history tracking and targeting for services such as health insurance. The unique

11. This comment is specific to the scenario of access to finance for the poor. For infrastructure finance, instead, liberalisation might have near-term benefits in terms of making available the volume of funds and expertise necessary in that sector.

12. In the United States, community development financial institutions (CDFIs) are a class of local financial institutions. They do not supplant conventional financial institutions. Since CDFIs and banks share a market-based approach to serving communities, CDFIs often work in partnership with banks to develop innovative ways to deliver loans, investments and financial services to distressed communities. Often, they jointly fund community projects, with the CDFI assuming the more risky subordinated debt. Mainstream financial institutions also invest their own capital directly in CDFIs and receive credit under the Community Reinvestment Act (CRA). See www.cdfi.org.

    ICICI Bank's own vision for universal access is the existence of 200 LFIs serving a million clients each and providing a range of financial services. ICICI Bank will seek to work with these LFIs by providing scaled amounts of debt and mezzanine finance, technology, training and a comprehensive product suite.

    Banerjee *et al.* (2003) make a similar recommendation for the creation of finance companies linked to bigger corporations which would have detailed information and lend to firms in a particular industry as a way to overcome insufficient lending in some segments.

identifier is best developed by the government so that it can be used for other services as well. It is the first step towards creating a centralised credit database.

Credit bureau: Credit information tracking and sharing enables lenders to provide incentives to those with good credit history and is a strong deterrent to wilful default. This can also facilitate the transition to individual lending programmes over time. Banerjee (2001) argues that helping the poor develop credit histories and centralising credit histories render credit markets less segmented and therefore give borrowers access to cheaper sources of credit. Similarly, Rajan and Zingales (2004) emphasise the role of initiatives like credit bureaus in expanding access to finance, especially for those who cannot afford to provide collateral. In its 2002 report on strengthening financial systems infrastructure, the World Bank stated that more than half of the institutions participating in a credit bureau reported decreases of 25% or more in defaults, costs and processing time for lending decisions.[13.]

Promoting better disclosure instead of price caps: Imposing price caps that do not take into account the true cost of operating a credit programme can have adverse effects on sustainability. Assuming that the regulator's concerns are the existence of monopoly pricing and ensuring consumer protection, initiatives that promote transparency seem more promising than price caps. For example, the regulator could prescribe a format for all MFIs and banks operating in these markets to report interest rates in a consistent and standard manner. This information could then be published to enable benchmarking of rates across institutions.

Rural infrastructure: Investment in certain kinds of rural infrastructure will enable providers to offer financial services with superior design and convenience for the client. Such investment is likely to be beyond the means of any one provider and should have the character of a public good. Relevant examples include computerised weather stations that provide real-time weather data and Internet connectivity at the village level to enable ATMs and other payment devices. In some cases, this infrastructure will spur more sophisticated product design. For example, real-time availability of village-level rainfall data makes it possible to offer index-based rainfall insurance contracts.

Presence of payment infrastructure, either through the Internet or through cards can facilitate financial transactions in rural areas. Wireless technologies can expand the range of electronic payment systems and provide critical "last mile" access. Certain environments can be connected via wireless point of sale (POS) products and reduce cash handling needs. Cash handling contributes significantly to total transaction costs.[14]

13. State Bank of India (SBI), Housing Development and Finance Corporation (HDFC), Dun and Bradstreet Information Services India Private Ltd. (D&B) and TransUnion International Inc. (TransUnion) have joined hands to establish a Credit Information Bureau of (India) Limited (CIBIL). However, it appears to be principally designed to serve urban middle- to upper-income markets and not rural markets.

14. The total costs of a cash payment system are not always readily apparent. Merchants have labour costs, for counting, bagging and transporting cash to the bank, and for reconciling accounts. Errors and pilferage by employees raise these costs further. At the central bank level, cash is cheap to print, but expensive to manage. Cash is expensive to transport, insure and distribute. Large volumes of cash enable shadow economies to thrive, depriving the government of tax revenues. And cash economies can support criminal activities such as counterfeiting, as well as encourage a culture of bribes and special favours. Some observers estimate that the total cost to an economy of maintaining a cash-based payment system can be as much as 5% of GDP (Commonwealth Business Council and Visa, 2004).

Regulator support for hybrid models: Creative responses to the challenge of access to financial services will require experimentation with several delivery formats.[15] Regulators (including the RBI, the Securities and Exchange Board of India, and the Insurance Regulatory and Development Authority of India) must encourage providers to carry out pilots in order to better address the challenges. Lessons learned from these pilots can be actively disseminated. As discussed above, a specific policy aspect that is a constraint in the Indian context is that handling of cash related to a bank account can only be done by bank employees. In other countries acceptance and withdrawal of cash are permitted at third-party locations including grocery stores. Some countries (South Africa, Brazil) have responded to this challenge by treating cash handling as a function distinct from providing savings accounts to clients. Where third-party entities accept and dispense cash, agent norms have been adopted. The bank continues to be responsible for safety, liquidity and privacy of contract issues. This is an interesting approach to increasing access to savings facilities which has not been tried in India and might be a strategy for breaking the impasse in a manner that is consistent with regulatory prudence.

Discontinuation of direct subsidies and recognition of risk and capital issues: Subsidising financial services directly (through interest rate caps or premium caps) blunts providers' incentives to innovate in product design. A case in point is the subsidised government crop insurance programme, which has resulted in very limited private-sector participation. Subsidies may be best channelled towards public goods, as mentioned above. Regulation must encourage banks and financial institutions to recognise the risks inherent in various kinds of lending and deal with this through market-based mechanisms such as derivatives in the case of commodity risk.[16]

Conclusion

Greater access to financial services for the poor is not only an important objective in its own right but may also have the potential to encourage growth in the economy by signalling resource allocation. Universal access to financial services calls for a regulatory and policy environment that permits experimentation. It requires a transition from an interventionist approach characterised by price subsidies and licensing to a facilitative

15. ICICI Bank is experimenting with the use of village-level transaction points, typically Internet kiosks, for the delivery of a range of financial services. The emergence of connectivity and transaction devices increases the scope for agent-based models. For example, Internet connectivity enables third-party agents to offer "transaction fulfilment" at a non-bank provider location. For instance, a person desirous of purchasing an insurance policy can obtain it from an authorised agent of the insurance company in a village. The process is as follows: client chooses the relevant policy and makes payment to agent; agent accepts cash and remits the money through the payment gateway from his/her account. The agent also updates the database of the provider (in this case the insurance company) on a real-time basis. The provider issues the policy on line; the agent prints it and hands it to the customer. In this manner, the entire transaction loop is closed at the agent location without a time lag and without the client having to travel or interact directly with the provider. The distinction between the process outlined above and a traditional agent model is the fact that transactions costs are reduced and that Internet connectivity is leveraged to reduce potential for fraud (agent has to update provider databases on line and make payments immediately. Lags in this process increase agent risk (agent is responsible for entire transaction, not parts of it). Similarly devices such as ATMs enable the provider to disburse and collect cash at a non-provider location while minimising the risk of fraud. The ATM can authenticate the customer and update the transaction on a real time basis.

16. Regulation in India prohibits banks from hedging commodities. This forces lenders to largely ignore the commodity as collateral both pre- and post-harvest, significantly increasing the cost of finance and excluding several potential borrowers whose primary collateral base may only be a commodity.

approach in which investments are made with a view to creating the system's ability to respond to the needs of underserved segments. A key feature of building access, evident from the Indian experience, is the role that local financial institutions can play in concentrated geographical areas to address financial services needs of clients comprehensively. Efforts aimed at creating a national unique identifier, credit information sharing and improvement in critical rural infrastructure will further strengthen the system's capacity to service this objective.

References

Bandyopadhyay, T. (2003), "How Good Are Our Banks?", *Business Standard Banking Annual.*

Banerjee, A. (2001), "Contracting Constraints, Credit Markets and Economic Development", MIT Working Paper Series 02-17.

Banerjee, A., E. Duflo and S. Cole (2003), "Bank Financing in India", www.imf.org.

Banerjee, A. and A. Newman (1998), "Information, the Dual Economy and Development", *The Review of Economic Studies*, Vol. 65, No. 4.

Cole, Shawn (2004), "Fixing Market Failures or Fixing Elections? Agricultural Credit in India", mimeo, MIT, December.

Commonwealth Business Council and Visa (2004), *Payment Solutions for Modernising Economies*, White Paper published by the Commonwealth Business Council and Visa.

Hess, U., R. Kaspar and A. Stoppa (2000), "Weather Risk Management for Agriculture and Agri-Business in Developing Countries", The World Bank, Washington, DC.

Mor, N. and B. Ananth (2004), "Issues in Access to Finance", www.icicisocialinitiatives.org.

Morduch, J. (1995), "Income Smoothing and Consumption Smoothing", *Journal of Economic Perspectives*, Vol. 9.

Morduch, J. and S. Rutherford (2003); "Microfinance: Analytical Issues for India"", Essay for the World Bank, South Asia Region – Finance and Private Sector Development.

Pande, R. and R. Burgess (2003), " Do Rural Banks Matter?: Evidence from the Indian Social Banking Experiment", London School of Economics, Discussion Paper Series No. DEDPS/40.

Rajan, R.G. and L. Zingales (2004), *Saving Capitalism from the Capitalists*, Princeton University Press, Princeton, NJ.

Singhal, A. and B. Duggal (2002), "Extending Banking to the Poor", www.icicisocialinitiatives.org.

Sinha, S. (2003), "Financial Services for Low Income Families: An Appraisal", *IIMB Management Review.*

Stiglitz, J. and A. Weiss (1981). "Credit Rationing in Markets with Imperfect Information", *American Economic Review*, Vol. 71.

Thorat, Y., H. Jones, M. Williams and A. Thorat (2003), "Attitudes of Rural Branch Managers in Madhya Pradesh, India Towards their Role as Providers of Financial Services to the Poor", *Journal of Micro Finance*, Vol. 5.

Part IV

Electricity

Chapter 10

Power Sector Liberalisation, the Poor and Multilateral Trade Commitments

Peter C. Evans
Laboratory for Energy and Environment
Massachusetts Institute of Technology

This chapter examines how the application of liberal trade principles can complement domestic reform programmes that seek to improve the performance of electric power supply. It argues that trade commitments can strengthen domestic reform initiatives designed to improve the efficiency and performance of electric power systems. With certain caveats, it also finds that trade disciplines in the GATS do not constrain the ability of governments to pursue pro-poor policies intended to improve affordability and access to electricity. The findings suggest that WTO member countries can benefit from trade commitments with ongoing domestic electricity sector reform programmes, if they are made part of an integrated set of policies that include market-based reforms, consumer protection and well targeted safety nets.

Introduction

Rising energy costs are refocusing attention on the energy sector. Higher prices not only challenge policy makers to make energy delivery systems as efficient and productive as possible but also complicate efforts to make modern energy services available and affordable for the poor. In light of these developments, ongoing trade negotiations present countries with questions about whether to deepen services trade commitments that apply to the energy sector, including services involved in the provision of electricity. Members of the World Trade Organization (WTO) are drawing on the framework provided by the General Agreement on Trade in Services (GATS) for this purpose. An important goal of the current round of negotiations is to achieve the broadest possible market access, national treatment and regulatory transparency commitments affecting access to service markets.

Both theoretical and empirical work shows that the introduction of private-sector participation in electricity and other basic services is more likely to benefit consumers and the economy as a whole when competition is maximised and regulatory commitments are sustained (Zhang *et al.*, 2002; Pollitt, 1997; on the significance of regulatory commitment, see Spiller, 1997, p. 64). Trade rules can support this outcome when countries accept obligations that foster free and fair trade and avail themselves of the WTO's independent dispute resolution mechanism. However, the prospect of using international trade rules to bind and reinforce liberalisation has generated concern about what will happen to vulnerable consumers and those without access. Given their limited purchasing power and lack of access, particularly in rural communities, reform has raised concerns about the likelihood of achieving the universal service goals set forth in domestic mandates and international targets such as the Millennium Development Goals.

This chapter examines how the application of liberal trade principles can complement domestic reform programmes that seek to improve the performance of electric power supply. It argues that trade commitments can strengthen domestic reform initiatives designed to improve the efficiency and performance of electric power systems. With certain caveats, it also finds that trade disciplines in the GATS do not constrain the ability of governments to pursue pro-poor policies intended to improve affordability and access to electricity. The findings suggest that WTO member countries can benefit from trade commitments with ongoing domestic electricity sector reform programmes, if they are made part of an integrated set of policies that include market-based reforms, consumer protection and well-targeted safety nets.

The chapter takes up the issue of trade rules, domestic power sector reform and measures to improve affordability and access in two parts. The first part examines diverse ways in which the private sector now participates in the electric power industry. It reviews the experience of liberalisation and presents strategies that countries have adopted to sustain access and affordability under more competitive market structures. The second part turns to the linkages between electricity reform and trade policy. It briefly reviews how the GATS may apply to the electricity sector before examining the issue of access and affordability and how concerns can be mitigated. The chapter concludes that it is in the interest of WTO members to make market access, regulatory and transparency commitments to at least match the level of domestic reforms and to adopt regulatory and institutional reforms that better target resources to the truly needy.

Private sector participation in electricity

With privatisation, vertical unbundling (separation of generation from transmission and distribution) and regulatory reform occurring in the electricity sector in many countries, opportunities for private-sector participation have expanded. Few countries have fully opened all segments of their markets to competition (ABS Energy Research, 2004). However, as shown in Figure 10.1, a significant number of countries have begun the process. Even partial liberalisation means that private generation, distribution, retailing and end-user service companies increasingly perform functions that were once the exclusive domain of state-owned electric utility monopolies. These services involve new market entry and competition by domestic as well as foreign energy companies. Because market structure and the extent of liberalisation in a particular country or region matter greatly for how private service providers can participate, it is useful to briefly review four major segments of the electricity sector: generation, supply, trading and marketing, and associated services.

Figure 10.1. Scope of global electricity market restructuring

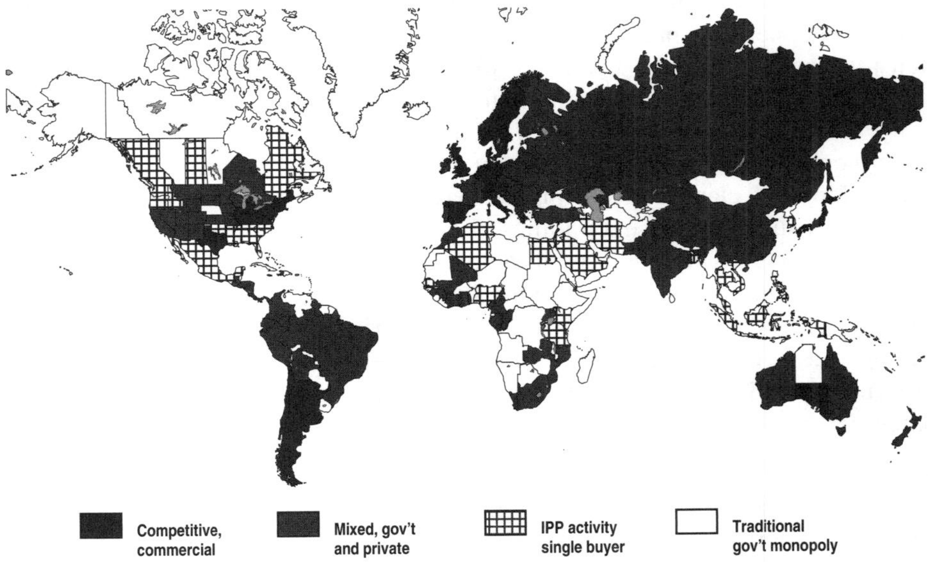

Source: Cambridge Energy Research Associates, "Markets where restructuring and/or privatisation has occurred or is pending but government remains an important direct player in the industry either through direct ownership of assets or strong regulatory control." 50422-4.

Generation services

Generation services are the most significant segment of the electricity supply chain that was opened to private sector participation in the 1990s. The manner in which the private sector participates in services related to power generation depends on the extent of market liberalisation. Some countries have adopted very liberal models that offer extensive opportunities for private participation in the generation sector whereas others have established more restrictive conditions. Private generators, often called independent power producers (IPPs), can participate in building and/or may enter the generation market by buying privatised or divested generating assets or by building new greenfield generating plants. These generation plants may be connected to the main power grid or may be situated off the main grid in so-called off-grid or mini-grid applications.

In the most restrictive case, private-sector generators are limited to selling electric output on a wholesale basis to one or more distribution companies. This can happen in a number of ways. One model involves sales to a single buyer, typically a government- or investor-owned utility company. In this case, prices are determined on the basis of competitive bids and long-term contracts negotiated with the monopoly buyer. This rather restricted approach was common in Asia during the 1990s and led to nearly USD 70 billion in new capacity. A more advanced form of wholesale electricity supply involves supplying into a power pool. Here, an independent system operator, responsible for matching electricity demand at the least cost, purchases power. Competitive power pools require a more advanced regulatory framework and attention to issues such as counteracting the effects of market concentration, which has been an issue in Europe, North America and some Latin American countries. The single buyer and wholesale pools are partial forms of regulation since the market entrant has no access to final consumers. This approach can also run into trouble if wholesale prices paid to generators are not reflected in retail prices.

More extensive liberalisation permits IPPs to sell power directly to final consumers. This can also happen in a number of ways. One way is to permit generators access to the electricity network. However, even if grid access is permitted, private generators may only be permitted to access certain final customers. Many reform programmes have begun by restricting competitive sales of electricity to the largest consumers in the system, typically steel, chemical and other large industrial consumers. If liberalisation proceeds, additional classes of customers may then be open to choice, beginning with commercial consumers (office buildings, large retail stores, hospitals) and eventually household consumers, who are large in number but consume relatively small amounts of electricity on an individual basis. Progressive opening of the retail market has been a staple of the reform process in Europe, North America and Japan. To be effective, open access, regardless of the classes of customers permitted choice, requires significant market structure and regulatory changes including guarantees of grid access on fair and transparent terms.

Private sector participants may also provide generation services by locating adjacent to the final consumer. Distributed generation – also called auto-generation or decentralised generation – can have advantages over centralised power provision (Pepermans *et al.*, 2003). This form of market entry can offer consumers cheaper, more flexible power and sometimes more reliable electricity. It can also provide benefits to utilities and distribution companies by reducing congestion and lowering transmission and distribution losses. Diesel engines are currently preferred by some users because they are more economical; however micro-gas turbines are gaining market penetration for environmental reasons, especially in markets with developed gas pipeline networks. In some markets there is a relatively small but growing market for electricity generation based on renewable fuels, including small hydro, biomass and solar applications, in areas where grid extension is high. Examples of private participation in off-grid generation are limited but can be found in Africa, Latin America and South Asia (*e.g.* Krause and Nordström, 2004).

Electricity supply services

Supply services are associated with owning and operating downstream segments of the electricity supply chain. Both transmission and distribution are natural monopolies and thus present fewer opportunities for competition than generation. Reforms have therefore focused on improving performance by shifting ownership from the public to private sector and by instituting various forms of incentive regulation such as price-cap regulation (Joskow, 1997). While some countries have experimented with high voltage transmission franchises it has been more common for the private sector to participate in downstream segments of the industry by owning distribution companies. Distribution companies play an important role by carrying out such functions as maintaining and extending the low voltage portion of the power grid, metering usage, consumer billing and revenue collection.

Liberalisation and the ability to trade have opened new opportunities for intermediaries to facilitate transactions between buyers and sellers. These intermediaries pay a fee to one or more generators from which they purchase the power and a fee to the transmission and distribution companies to transport the electricity to end users. Unlike a generator or distribution company, marketers do not necessarily own physical assets. Instead they build a business around selling to certain market segments or concentrate on selling certain types of power such as green power.[1] While the scope for electricity brokers is large, incomplete liberalisation in most electricity markets and regulatory uncertainty have limited their role (*Platts Retail Energy*, 2002, p. 1).

It is worth noting that, if permitted, private energy companies can combine generation and supply services to serve specific customers. A project developed by Rolls-Royce in Turkey provides an example (Rolls-Royce Power Ventures, undated). In the late 1990s the company formed a joint venture to build, own and operate a 36 megawatt (MW) cogeneration facility at Bilkent University in Ankara. The university's existing 4 MW cogeneration facility was insufficient to meet the growing energy demand from the university and its affiliated manufacturing business. The completed plant began operations in early 2000, supplying steam and power to the university campus, a paper mill, a gypsum board manufacturing company, a furniture manufacturing company, a construction company as well as other commercial and residential properties. Where permitted, market access provides opportunities for energy companies to integrate generation and distribution services.

Associated services

In addition to the generation and supply of electricity, private firms provide services that support the provision of electricity. Consulting is one such service. Maintenance and repair of power plants and transmission lines is another. Services aimed at improving demand-side efficiency (load reduction) to factories, hospitals and other final consumers provide yet another. There are several ways in which end-user services can be organised. One approach is to use consultant engineers who perform energy audits and other services. Another is provided by energy service companies (ESCOs), which are compensated on the basis of their ability to meet explicit targets (Goldman *et al.*, 2005; Bertoldi *et al.*, 2006). In performing their services, ESCOs typically provide full project

1. For information on green power in the United States see the Green Power Network run by the National Renewable Energy Laboratory for the US Department of Energy at www.eere.energy.gov/greenpower/markets/marketing.shtml?page=2.

responsibilities, including engineering design, arranging financing, construction management and monitoring project performance, energy equipment and supply.

Since associated services support the provision of electricity, market access is not as directly tied to key structural changes. Associated services do not require network access or consumer choice. Even under a monopoly structure, companies providing associated service providers can perform useful activities. However, the scope of their activities is often expanded by privatisation and de-monopolisation of the sector. Liberalisation opens up new opportunities for associated services as greater competition in core electricity functions generates incentives for companies to scrutinise more carefully which functions it should keep in house and which functions it should contract out to reduce costs and improve service.

Table 10.1 summarises opportunities that electricity liberalisation provides for market access and competition under alternative industry structures.

Table 10.1 Market access and competition under alternative industry structures

Industry structure	Monopoly Monopoly at all levels	Single buyer Competitive bidding for new power plants	Wholesale competition Competition in generation; choice for distribution companies	Retail competition Competition in generation; choice for final users
Generation services	No	Yes	Yes	Yes
Distribution services	No	No	Yes	Yes
Marketing services	No	No	Yes	Yes
Associated services*	Limited	Limited	Limited	Yes

* End user services, maintenance and repair, consulting, upgrades and other services associated with investment, operation, upkeep and utilisation of the electric power system.

Experience with private sector participation

Experience with private sector participation in electricity markets has varied across countries. Many countries have experienced positive welfare gains. Examining data from 19 OECD countries from 1987 to 1996, Steiner (2000) found that capacity utilisation rates in electricity generation were positively and significantly correlated with both private ownership and unbundling of generation and distribution. These findings suggest that privatisation and vertical de-integration can improve efficiency and reduce prices, particularly for large industrial customers. Zhang *et al.* (2002) examined data for 51 developing countries from 1985 to 2000 and found that privatisation significantly improved performance, measured in terms of capacity, output and labour productivity, but only when accompanied by competition and independent regulation. Other studies on the experience of specific countries have also found positive effects of reform on productive efficiency in both developed and developing country contexts (Plane, 1999).

At the same time, gains from privatisation and the introduction of competition are not certain. One reason is that electricity production and supply has characteristics that make designing competitive markets particularly challenging. This is due in part to the technical and economic characteristics of electricity systems. Power systems involve not only large sunk capital costs but require matching supply and demand in real time. Since it is not feasible to store electricity, avoiding price volatility and disruptions in service is a greater challenge than in most industries. It is also due to the political and institutional issues associated with large-scale network industries. As a product that is critical for modern economies, electricity is essential to both industry and households. Together, these characteristics make the power industry susceptible to technical disruptions and active political interference.

Many countries have experienced difficulty in establishing regulatory regimes that extract the full benefits of private-sector participation. The specific problems vary from market to market, but an important factor has been the state of a country's power sector prior to reform and how reform was approached. As might be expected, countries with more favourable pre-reform conditions have been more successful and have captured greater benefits. These conditions include the financial state of the utilities, the size of capacity reserves, the prevalence of cost-reflective pricing, and the strength of regulatory traditions.

Pricing has been one the most significant stumbling blocks, particularly in developing countries, where electricity tariffs may be set high enough to cover the average cost of supply but not high enough to cover the cost of new capital investment. Consumers quickly adjust to and come to expect subsidised pricing and lax payment procedures. This means that before privatisation can become economically viable or market-based competition can take hold, consumers face upward price adjustments. It also means that non-paying customers, which cost utilities enormous amounts a year in lost revenue, face service termination or other enforcement measures for non-payment (for further detail, see Smith, 2004).

The transition to a commercially run and financially sound power sector can be politically difficult. As has been shown in cases as diverse as India, the Republic of Georgia and the Republic of Mali, not all governments have been able to meet the challenge of sustaining a credible commitment to the reform process. Many reform programmes have suffered from indeterminate outcomes, as governments vacillate between attempting to create sufficient incentives to attract private-sector investment on the one hand and responding to political pressure to retain subsidised prices on the other. While policy failures are not inevitable, price volatility and power service disruptions, caused by missteps in market design and implementation, have contributed to clouding the public's perception of what liberalisation can achieve.

In spite of the challenges, many countries continue to introduce policy measures to expand private-sector participation in their power sectors. Privatisation and market restructuring continue to advance, albeit at different rates. Outside the OECD area this is the case of Bulgaria, China, India, Indonesia, Nigeria, the Philippines, Russia, Romania and South Africa. A key driver is the vast scope of the investment requirements needed to keep pace with growing electricity demand. Global forecasts predict very large investment requirements even under conservative growth assumptions. To meet electricity needs under a conservative estimate of growth in demand of 1.7% a year over the first three decades of the 21st century, the International Energy Agency (IEA, 2003) estimates that the sector will require a total of USD 9.84 trillion in electricity infrastructure (see Figure 10.2). Approximately USD 4 trillion of this investment will be needed in OECD countries to keep pace with growth of demand. The power sector in non-OECD countries will require even more. The IEA estimates that developing countries will require investments exceeding USD 5.7 trillion. Two-thirds of the total investment, some USD 3.5 trillion, will be required to support power infrastructure in developing Asia. China's requirements alone are expected approach USD 2 trillion.

Figure 10.2. Total world power sector investment requirements, 2001

USD billions

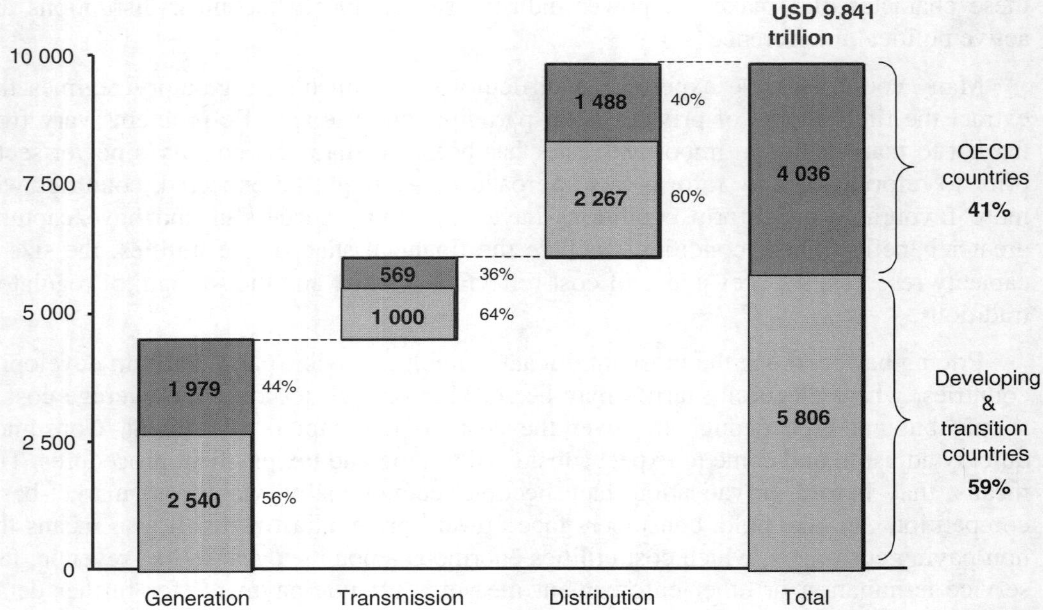

Source: International Energy Agency, *World Energy Investment Outlook 2003*, OECD/IEA, Paris.

Without concerted attention to improving the performance of electric power systems, capital investment may be insufficient to meet demand. There is also a risk that whatever funds are raised may be allocated inefficiently. This is of particular concern for significant areas of the world where access capital is limited and per capita consumption of electricity is well below the world average.

Liberalisation and the poor

Universal service in the electricity sector has two basic components: physical access and affordability. Among the advanced industrial countries that are members of the OECD, access to electricity is a policy goal that has been successfully accomplished. Electrification rates in these countries now approach 100%. Even very remote areas generally have access to the network. However, affordability remains an issue in many countries. It is of special concern in countries with higher rates of poverty and less encompassing welfare and income support programmes. In the United States, the affordability of home energy is calculated with reference to the federal poverty line. By this measure, 29 million households were eligible for federal fuel assistance in 2001, although only 4.6 million low-income households actually received it.[2] In the United Kingdom, the definition of affordable warmth is the level at which a household can

2. Households with annual incomes under 150% of the federal poverty level or 60% of state median income are eligible for fuel income assistance in the United States through the Low Income Home Energy Assistance Program (LIHEAP) (LIHEAP, 2004).

achieve the temperatures needed to maintain health and comfort for an expenditure of less than 10% of net household income. By this measure, official estimates of the number of households in fuel poverty range between 2.8 million and 3.9 million, depending on whether or not housing subsidies are taken into account (Department of Trade and Industry, 2002).

In the developing world both access and affordability present difficult policy challenges (Figure 10.3). Significant progress has been made in expanding access to electricity among non-OECD countries over the past three decades. In Latin America, electrification increased from 45% in the 1970s to nearly 90% in 2000. In East Asia the rate has climbed from just 30% to 87% over the same period. China has achieved one of the most impressive performances. Despite its size and large population, an estimated 98% of the population now has access to electricity (Yang, 2003).

Figure 10.3. World population without access to electricity

Millions of people

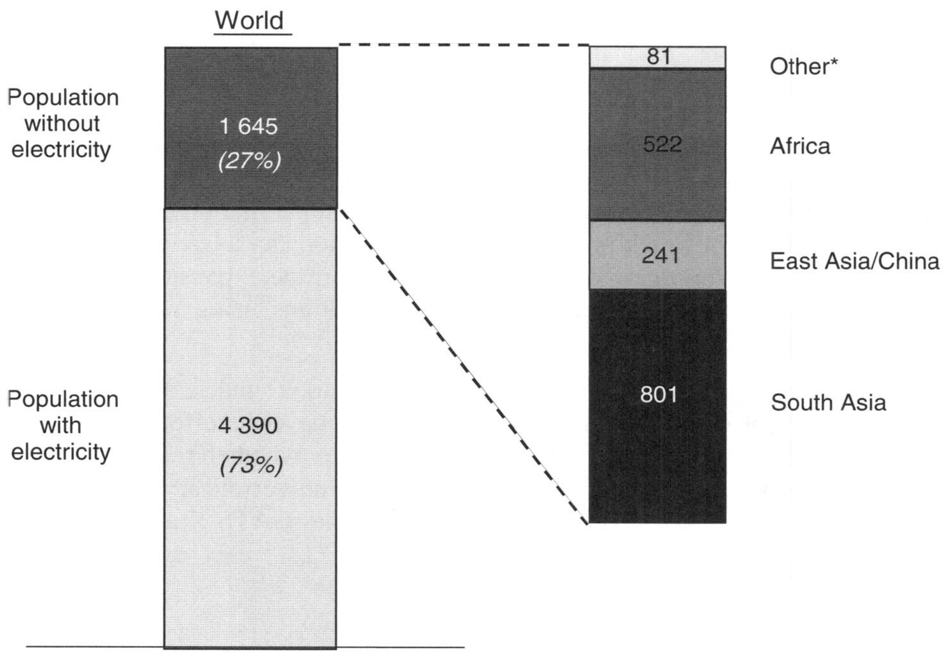

*Includes Latin America (56 million), Middle East (15 million), OECD (9 million) and transition economies (2 million).

Source: International Energy Agency, *World Energy Outlook 2002*.

Despite this progress, the number of communities and household without electricity remains significant in some regions. In South Asia, over 800 million people are estimated to be without access to electricity. In India, the electrification rate is only 43% of the population. Africa continues to have some of the lowest electrification rates in the world; in Sub-Saharan Africa the vast majority of the population has no access to electricity. In Ethiopia, only 3 million of the country's 64 million residents have access to electricity. In Angola, D.R. of Congo, Kenya, Madagascar, Malawi and Mozambique, less than 15% of the population has access to electricity. Even if the investments projected by the IEA are made, large segments of the world's population will still be without electric service well into the future. Without concerted action by governments, the IEA estimates that 1.4 billion people, or 18% of the world's population, will still not have access to electricity in 2030 (IEA, 2003, p. 33).

Liberalisation of electricity supply and the resultant competition are likely to lead to lower prices, greater availability and improved quality of services. In so far as the poor are consumers of these services, they are likely to benefit. But there is a twist. Frequently, as noted above, prices prior to liberalisation are not determined by the market but are set administratively and are kept artificially low. This pricing structure is often sustained through cross-subsidisation within public monopolies or through government financial support. New entrants may focus on the most profitable market segment (redlining), such as urban areas, where the cost of service may be lower and incomes higher. Without the ability to cross-subsidise, utilities will lose the wherewithal to subsidise grid extension programmes.

Critics of power sector liberalisation often make strong assumptions about how regulators responsible for the sector will behave. They typically assume that regulatory authorities have little power to or interest in controlling the sequencing of reforms or in shaping the timing and extent of liberalisation with an eye to how it will affect vulnerable groups. They assume that regulators will expend little time or resources to understand the needs of the poor, their location and the particular barriers they face in accessing adequate services. They assume that regulators will not monitor the impact of market liberalisation on the distribution of income and wealth. Finally, they assume that regulators will fail to grasp the different ways in which private sector participation can advance the interests of the poorest, either through programmes designed to support the expansion of the national grid or through programmes that promote off-grid solutions using strategies such as distributed generation technologies.

If these assumptions hold, trade commitments do look undesirable. If true, the beneficial "lock-in" for competition and efficiency could have the effect of harming the poor since they would be unprotected. Before turning to whether trade commitments necessarily make it more rather than less difficult to meet universal service aspirations in the power sector, the next section briefly reviews the GATS framework and its underlying principles.

GATS trade rules and electricity liberalisation

Like trade rules for goods, services rules provide a way for sovereign countries to strengthen the legal framework under which foreign firms participate in their markets. The rules seek to guard against unnecessary discrimination and to ensure that foreign companies participate on an equal footing with domestic firms in whatever competitive market evolves. The GATS provides specific rules in the context of international trade in services.

The GATS achieves these objectives through a legal framework consisting of general and specific obligations. It has more than a dozen general obligations that apply to all WTO members. Two of the most important are most-favoured-nation (MFN) treatment and transparency. GATS members must meet these general obligations, with certain caveats and exceptions, as part of their WTO membership.

In addition to the general obligations, the GATS includes provisions for specific commitments. The basic GATS framework lists two: market access (Article 16) and national treatment (Article 17). Those obligations come into effect only when they are explicitly listed in the member's schedule of specific commitments. Articles 16 and 17 do not apply unless a member has positively affirmed that the sector will be bound by these disciplines.

Market access is a requirement to grant services and service suppliers of other members the treatment specified in their schedule. A schedule can grant full or partial market access. Full access means that a government has agreed not to apply limitations which restrict or require specific types of legal entity or joint venture or limitations on: the number of suppliers in the market; the total value of transactions or assets; the total number of operations or the total quantity of service output; the total number of employees permitted in a sector or by a supplier; and foreign equity participation. Other measures not included in this list fall outside the scope of this market access definition.

National treatment requires a government to treat foreign firms as it treats national firms in relation to all laws, measures and practices. Exceptions are granted only to the extent that they are clearly listed in its schedule.

The GATS principles focus on making market entry and competition work better. Energy service providers operating internationally value commitments to market access because they clarify the rights of foreign firms and provide legal standing in a trade dispute. From the standpoint of encouraging fully open and competitive electricity markets, the GATS has important limitations (Evans, 2002, pp. 23-25). By far the greatest barrier facing international trade in energy services arises from the lack of structural reform. To enter and compete in electricity markets, for example, distributed generators need both non-discriminatory access to transmission and distribution systems and the right to sell to eligible customers. The request-offer process creates a forum for reciprocal market opening; however the GATS does not require countries to undertake market restructuring. It does not restrict the right of WTO members to maintain monopolies at the national or local levels. This right holds unless a member country decides to make a commitment not to impose monopolies or other market access limitations.

The GATS does not prescribe how to address the social dimensions of liberalisation. Instead, it leaves these decisions to individual members by recognising their sovereign right to regulate. GATS obligations do not restrict the ability of governments to establish, maintain and fully enforce domestic laws protecting consumers, health, safety and the environment. With respect to the social dimensions of liberalisation, the GATS leaves the responsibility for formulating and implementing social policy to members.

In the context of energy services negotiations, the GATS has been the subject of two criticisms. One is that the GATS should take on some of these responsibilities. Global trade rules should be used as instruments to secure social objectives such as universal service. The other is that social concerns should be left to sovereign states but that GATS commitments are too constraining. By accepting GATS obligations member governments run the risk of tying their hands and restricting the range of useful policy interventions they have available to develop their power sectors in the public interest.

Before examining the specific criticisms and the policy prescriptions that flow from them, the following section reviews the many and varied policy instruments that states can adopt to address social concerns over access and affordability in the context of opening the sector to greater private sector entry and competition.

Consumer safety net and access arrangements

The shift from public to private provision of a basic service like electricity not only requires reforms in market design but also changes in how regulatory functions are performed. Independent regulatory authorities provide a means to separate policy functions from regulatory functions and to enhance procedures for transparency. Another institutional change concerns how consumers are protected and social welfare considerations are addressed. Here the approaches are more diverse, since a variety of policy mechanisms exist to improve affordability and access under more competitive electric power market structures. These mechanisms include consumer protection rules, service and price guarantees, and targeted transfer payments.

Consumer protection

As in other markets, electricity consumers require protection against adverse industry behaviour. Such behaviour may be economically rational but objectionable from the perspective of justice and fairness. The practice of redlining – price or service discrimination such as unjustified disconnection of the elderly, the unemployed or the handicapped – is one example (Sharam, 2001). Such behaviour may also be economically irrational, as in the case of denial of service to ethnic groups who can pay for the service. In either case, consumers require protection and reasonable legal or administrative recourse. Since consumer protection may have been implicit or customary under monopoly provision, restructuring requires establishing explicit rules for minimum customer service standards which electric utilities must respect when providing electric service to the public. This includes articulating rules for payment of bills, late payment and non-payment.

Rules are also needed to define who is eligible for special treatment, when they are eligible and for how long. For example, special dispensations may be justified for such factors as medical conditions, age (elderly or infants in the home) and times when temperature conditions are extreme. More lenient contractual or financial terms may also be justified. For example, it may be reasonable to waive security deposit requirements and certain fees if these have the effect of excluding certain households from accessing electric service.

Countries have introduced such protection in a variety of ways. One is to make it a part of the licensing conditions that permit domestic and foreign electricity service providers to operate in the market. For example, in Texas, the Texas Public Utility Commission promulgated detailed customer protection rules that apply to market participants.[3] Market participants may create codes of practice which may be voluntary or may be submitted to regulators for review and approval. Finally, consumer protection measures can be ensured by articulating more clearly the applicability of customer protections available under more general commercial law, as in Australia.

Service and price guarantees

Given the importance and value of electricity, governments have made service guarantees a part of the regulatory safety net. These guarantees take both temporary and

3. Public Utility Commission of Texas, Chapter 25. Substantive Rules Applicable to Electric Service Providers, Subchapter B, Customer Service and Protection, at www.puc.state.tx.us/rules/subrules/electric/index.cfm.

permanent forms. Temporary guarantees of service with price caps have been extended as part of many retail competition programmes to protect customers from various market risks, including price volatility that may occur in the transition to the new marketplace. It also ensures that retail consumers who do not choose to switch suppliers retain service at an affordable price. As the market deepens and becomes more robust and predictable, the expectation is that these price controls will eventually be lifted.

The permanent guarantee is intended to ensure service to customers who are not served by the new market either temporarily or permanently (Oppenheim, 2002, p. 34). It applies more narrowly to low-income and other vulnerable customers so that they are not excluded from service. The guarantee is executed by assigning to at least one company, usually the incumbent distributor, the obligation to provide "default service". Depending on the country, guaranteed service is also referred to as the "provider of last resort (POLR)" (United States), the "standing offer" (United Kingdom and Australia), and *grundversorgungspflicht* or basic supply duty (Germany).

A critical regulatory issue is the pricing of this guaranteed service (Tschamler, 2000, pp. 75-82). To set the price, regulators have used at least three different approaches: fixed administrative price, market-based regulated price and wholesale spot price pass-through. From the standpoint of establishing a competitive market, a fundamental issue is whether the default price set by regulators provides sufficient retail margins to encourage widespread competitive offers. In many cases it has not. In many jurisdictions, there has been pressure on regulators to set low default rates in order to win political acceptance of liberalisation and to ensure that consumers who choose not to switch obtain reasonable rates.[4]

If the gap between the regulated price and the best price competing electricity service providers can offer is too narrow, service suppliers will have difficulty achieving the scale and profitability necessary to remain viable. Consumers will also have little incentive to switch suppliers (Figure 10.4). The rational residential consumer will only switch from the regulated incumbent utility's default service when the default price plus the cost of switching suppliers is below the price offered by competitors. If the default service price is set low and competitors are unable to offer significant price reductions, the incentive to switch is also low (Joskow, 2003, p. 45). The result is an encompassing safety net which consumers rationally take advantage of but also one which undermines competition and distorts price and investment signals.

Transfer payments

Even when electricity is affordable for the public at large, some segments of the population will find the price an extreme financial hardship. To address this issue such customers need to be identified and a payment mechanism established that makes it possible for them to have electricity. The most common mechanism is bill assistance. These are recurring price subsidies that make electricity more affordable for low-income and vulnerable consumers. Bill assistance programmes include discount programmes (block or lifeline tariffs), percentage of income payment plans and arrearage management programmes. They may also include emergency assistance to forestall service disconnection or ease the burden of short-term energy price spikes or extreme weather.

4. This has been particularly true in the United States. In Massachusetts, the guaranteed prices were set below market prices giving consumers little incentive to switch and making it nearly impossible for new service providers to maintain a business presence in the small retail market.

Figure 10.4. Relationship between best price reduction and network switching rates in six power markets open to retail competition

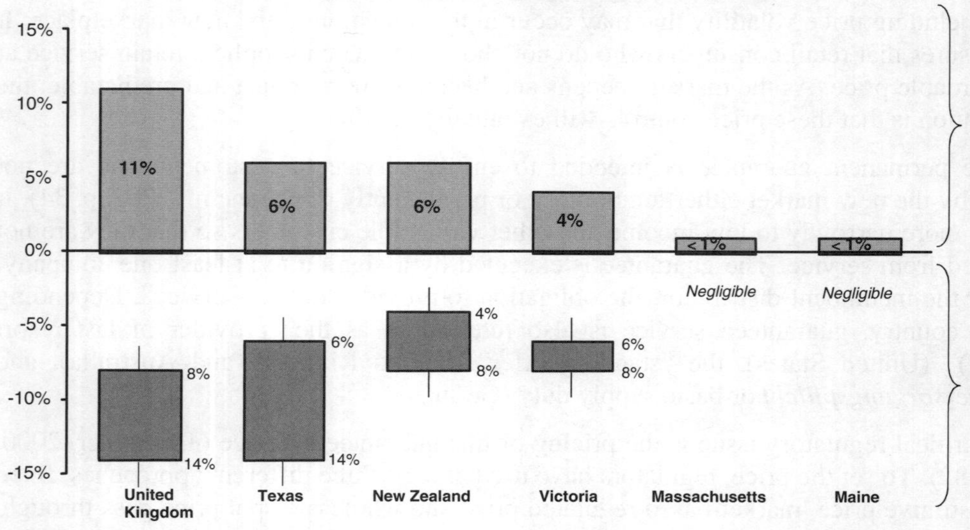

Source: TXU, FRC Effectiveness Review, Essential Services Commission, Melbourne, 2 February 2004.

Competitive markets can support special price programmes for vulnerable customers, but only to a point. Private electricity suppliers can offer lower prices to these groups by accepting lower profit margins but not by offering prices below cost. This may represent a prudent business decision, but it may also be prohibited on competition grounds. In the UK market, for example, licensed suppliers may not cross-subsidise or receive a cross-subsidy from any other business unit or business affiliate since this could be used as a predatory practice and may distort competition (Office of Gas and Electricity Markets, 2004). As a result, if bill assistance programmes are to involve substantial discounting of rates below cost, mechanisms must be established to compensate electricity service providers through public funds in ways that do not put one market participant at a competitive disadvantage in relation to others (see Box 10.1).

The poor not only have lower incomes but often live in lower-quality housing. They may also have older heating/cooling systems and less efficient home appliances. Housing investment subsidies offer a way to address these problems. Programmes designed to help reduce home energy-cost burdens may pay for conservation measures that increase the home's energy efficiency. Weatherisation programmes are attractive because they generally yield benefits that extend beyond poverty alleviation, such as environmental gains from reduced energy consumption, health benefits and improved revenue collection (Oppenheim and MacGregor, 2000).

Box 10.1. **Funding transfer payments in liberalising markets**

Since it is inconsistent to impose non-economic obligations on incumbents while removing barriers to entry, alternative funding mechanisms must be established in competitive markets (Heald, 1997). There are several possibilities in the electricity sector.

Welfare payments. In some countries, the power industry is bypassed and subsidies are paid to low-income and vulnerable groups through the country's welfare system. In Germany low-income bill assistance is provided as part of the general welfare programme know as *Sozialhilfe*. In 2003 3.7% of Germany's 39 million households received assistance under this programme, which includes a special subsidy for heating and electricity costs. It is based on a general calculation of current expenses for nutrition, household needs, etc., including personal needs for daily life. In each case, the amount of the subsidy is specified annually by the responsible regional social administration and can vary substantially among regions and categories of people.[1]

The allocation of energy subsidies to low-income households is a matter of general redistribution policies within the tax system, organised by the central and local governments and unrelated to the liberalisation of the electricity market.[2] In 2002, electricity represented less than 2% of the total subsidy of EUR 25 billion spent on all services included in the Federal Social Welfare programme for poor or low-income households (*Bundessozialhilfegesetz*).

System charges are also a way to fund public service objectives. They involve establishing a system-wide levy that is applied to the regulated distribution of electricity. A number of countries undergoing electricity restructuring have established or expanded ratepayer taxes. In January 2003 the French government modified and extended the compensation mechanism for the cost of public service missions assumed by electricity suppliers by introducing a system of "contributions to the electricity public services" (CSPE), which replaced the previous "public service of electricity production" (FSPPE). These fees are applied to all electricity consumers whether or not they are eligible to choose their supplier and are redistributed to electricity suppliers to compensate them for the costs of public services.

The scope and application of system charges range widely among countries.[3] In the United States, 30 states use system charges and raise from less than USD 1 million to as much as USD 120 million, which is used to pay for social programmes and a variety of other public interests ranging from energy R&D to helping low-income households pay for energy efficiency investments.[4]

Special budget allocations. Governments can also draw on public budgets (tax the general public). The funds come from regional taxes (state or province) or national taxes. In Australia, the state of Victoria's Network Tariff Rebate is one example of a special budget allocation This is a transfer funded from general tax revenues to provide a discount to customers located in rural, regional and outer metropolitan areas who use less than 160 megawatt hours of electricity a year (Essential Services Commission, 2004, p. 29).

Special budget allocations have also been used to establish special financial vehicles that can lower the cost of borrowing for public benefits. Energy funds have been established which combine tax revenue bonds: low-cost, tax-exempt financing to implement energy conservation projects under performance-based energy efficiency contracts. The special budget allocation is used to "buy down" the interest rate of the revenue bond and extend the term of the loan (Kaiser *et al.*, 2005).

External subsidies for power sector investments and institutional reform remain an important source of financing for a large number of developing countries. Between 1988 and 2001 bilateral donors in OECD countries provided USD 12.6 billion for electricity transmission and distribution projects. This represents roughly 30% of the total energy-related official development assistance provided during this period. The World Bank and regional multilateral development banks are a significant source of grants and low interest loans for electrification and institutional development associated with power sector reform. These external sources remain an important source of funding, especially for the poorest developing countries.

1. See Willkommen auf den Seiten des SobI e.V. Sozialhilfe at www.sozialhilfe-online.de.

2. Thanks are due to Jens Weinmann, Repsol YPF-Harvard Kennedy School Fellow, 2004-05, John F. Kennedy School of Government, Harvard University, for this information.

3. See "Project de loi de finances pour 2005: Energie, Chapitre III: Les Évolutions des Marchés Électrique et Gazier et La Poursuite du Mouvement de Libéralisation," Sénat, France, at www.senat.fr/rap/a04-076-6/a04-076-6_mono.html.

4. "State Public Benefit Funds: Expanding Support for Low-Income Weatherization and Rehab," Weatherization, Rehab and Asset Preservation Partnership, Issue Brief, August 5, 2004, at www. energyprograms.org/html/EPC_IBP.htm.

Rural electrification

Electrification of rural and remote areas presents a particularly difficult challenge for many countries. The capital cost of extending power networks is generally high and revenues are often poor. Historically, most subsidised rural electrification programmes have been run by centralised state-owned monopolies. Subsidies are generally necessary to fund service extension into these areas. In the past, state-owned power companies were mandated to undertake rural electrification to meet political and social objectives to alleviate poverty. However, these mandates were often unfunded or underfunded and lacked sufficient incentives for least-cost connections to the main grid and off-grid solutions where appropriate. The breaking up of public monopolies and the introduction of competitive private participation have generated the need for new approaches. In the past decade WTO members have experimented with a number of different approaches to encourage private service providers to expanding access to electricity (Table 10.2).

Table 10.2. Alternative approaches to rural electricity provision using private providers

	Gabon	Mozambique	Chile
Award	1997	Pilot beginning 2004	Annually (1994-2004)
Concession scope	National (generation and distribution)	Regional (generation and distribution)	Regional (non exclusive)
Concession period	20 years	Generation 10 yrs; distribution 20 yrs.	–
Subsidy source	Cross-subsidies within concession	Central government and donors	Central government, distribution companies
Subsidy allocation	Concessionaire based on performance mandates	Payment per connection once verified	Lump sum award
Monitoring/ regulation	Contractual/ Central government	Contractual/ central government	National Energy Commission and local community
Competition	One time competition for the exclusive right to generate, distribute and sell electricity for the country	One time competition for the exclusive right to generate, distribute and sell electricity in a fixed area*	Annual competition for subsidies between communities and among distribution companies seeking to expand their networks

* If cheaper electricity becomes available, the concessionaire has an obligation to pass some benefits on to consumers.

Non-exclusive concession with competition for subsidies

Chile provides an example of a competitive, non-exclusive model for funding rural electrification. In the 1980s Chile privatised the state-owned electricity companies and restructured the market. A new electricity law permitted open entry and competition in generation, a non-exclusive concession system for distribution and a cost-reflective tariff system. Distribution companies were sold off on the basis of the regions they served but were not granted exclusive rights. Foreign companies now own and operate some of these distribution companies.[5] However, in the early 1990s almost half of the rural population or approximately 1 million people (240 000 households) had no access to electricity.

5. For example, two American energy companies, Sempra Pipelines & Storage and PSEG Global (Public Service Electric and Gas Company), jointly own Chilquinta Energía S.A., the third-largest electricity distributor in Chile. Chilquinta Energía and its affiliates serve 509 000 customers in central Chile.

In 1994, the central government began a new programme of funding grid extension. The goal was to achieve complete national electrification within ten years. The scheme required the capital costs of rural connections to be shared among users, private distribution companies and the central government. The central government initially contributed 70% of the funding but its share later fell to 60%. To minimise project costs, encourage innovation and reduce rent seeking, resources from the central government were allocated to projects through an annual bidding system. Awards were allocated on the basis of technical merit, amount of investment contributed by private companies and social impact. This approach created competition both among rural communities seeking financing for grid extensions and among private distributions companies seeking funds to implement grid extensions.

The programme is credited with helping to expand the level of access to electricity in rural areas by nearly 50% in the first five years of the programme (Jadresic, 2000). Although the subsidy costs are nearly USD 2 000 per extension, the programme has succeeded in supporting over 110 000 new connections. By 2006 over 90% of the country is expected to have access to electricity service compared to 53% in 1995.

Exclusive regional concession with performance-based subsidies

Mozambique provides an example of contracting rural electrification services by awarding an exclusive regional concession supplemented with targeted subsidies. This approach centres on competition for the right to an exclusive right to serve a designated area (Cockburn and Low, 2005). Mozambique has a population of 18.3 million, of which two-thirds in rural areas. Less than 6% of households have access to electricity supplied either by the national utility, Electricidade de Moçambique (EdM), or to smaller isolated grids operated by municipalities. In 1997 the government revised its basic electricity law to permit privately operated electricity concessions.

A consortium of companies from Mozambique and South Africa won the contract to expand electricity services. The concession included exclusive generation rights for ten years and exclusive distribution rights for 20 years. However, there is a provision that if cheaper electricity becomes available from the central grid or another source, the concession holder is obliged to pass part of the benefits on to consumers. Under the terms of the concession, the wining companies are granted the freedom to determine how to develop the power system most cost effectively. Following physical verification of the work, the concessionaire receives USD 400 per household to offset the capital costs of establishing a connection. No subsidies are paid for connections to business customers. It is still too early to fully evaluate the effectiveness of Mozambique's pilot scheme since the concession was only signed in mid-2004. However, the initial goal of providing 3 000 connections in four villages has already been exceeded.

Exclusive national concession with cross-subsidies

Finally, Gabon encourages rural electrification services and improvements in the entire national utility by awarding an exclusive national concession. As a result of its rich endowment of natural resources and small population of 1 million, Gabon's per capita income ranks third in Africa after South Africa and Mauritius. However, its basic electricity and water supply network was poorly developed. To improve and expand the provision of basic utility services, Gabon embarked on Africa's first privatisation of the water and electric utility. In 1997 the government awarded a 20-year concession to the French firm, Vivendi, to run SEEG (Société d'Énergie et d'Eau du Gabon), as an exclusive national concession to operate the country's electricity and water services. SEEG offered water and electricity services, with cross subsidies between electricity and the less developed water services and between urban areas and rural areas where access was limited. Performance reviews indicate the approach has been successful in meeting or exceeding performance targets. The contract sets out a number of targets including an obligation to increase electricity coverage in regions not yet served from 0 to 54% by 2015 and invest USD 135 million (Cho and Dubash, 2003, p. 15). Within the first five years SEEG had invested more than this amount and substantially increased service in previously unserved regions (Table 10.3).

Table 10.3. Gabon's electricity concession: targets and performance

Region	1993 observed	2000 targets	2000 actual	2015 targets
Libreville network	68.5%	73%	74%	83%
Franceville network	63.5%	67%	90%	80%
Louetsi network	49.6%	54%	76%	66%
Port-Gentil	81.0%	83%	91%	91%
Isolated centres served in 1996	33.0%	65%	89%	60%
Isolated centres to be served	0.0%	15%	0%	54%

Source: Tremolet and Neale (2002), p. 36.

Modify the GATS?

Power market reform can raise social concerns and there have been calls for re-evaluating and even changing the provisions of trade rules. Does the international framework of services law need to be altered to better address electricity's role as an essential service in modern economies? There are several options. Comparing these options suggests that the existing GATS framework would benefit from clarification but does not need to be fundamentally altered.

Rights-based approach

One set of proposals seeks to have electricity recognised as a basic right in trade law. In the United Kingdom, consumer groups have issued manifestos demanding that the government recognise and act on a basic right to fuel, including electricity (National Right to Fuel Campaign, undated). In South Africa, legal defence groups have issued reports arguing that electricity is a basic right and justifies a national policy for the free supply of sufficient electricity to meet basic human needs (Roux and Vahle, 2002). Other consumer groups have attempted to define this right: "[the] minimum level of service to which all people are entitled is that which enables them to enjoy their basic rights as enshrined in the Universal Declaration on Human Rights and other international statutes covering rights to specific service access" and have recommended imposing public service obligations on private suppliers through a reference paper or annex to the GATS (UNDP, 2003, p. 278).

Establishing a rights-based approach to electricity through trade law presents a variety of difficulties. It assumes that electricity is a merit good, or a good (or service) that is intrinsically desirable or socially valuable to consumers, independently of their actual desires or ability to pay (Musgrave, 1959, pp. 13-14). While few would disagree that electricity is an extremely valuable service, closely linked to living standards, there is little consensus that electricity consumption ought to be provided at public expense, irrespective of the social cost. For example, the Asian Development Bank (ADB) states categorically: "Electric power is not a merit good or a public good. It is a service provided to clearly identifiable consumers for a charge that must cover the full cost of supply." (ADB, undated)

At the very least, a rights-based approach leaves unanswered key questions such as how much electricity is required to satisfy basic human needs, how it should be paid for, and whether assigning such rights may not create distortions in the allocation of resources that outweigh their social benefit.

Expand policy autonomy

Another set of proposals centres on the view that internationally negotiated trade disciplines reduce the "policy space" available to policy makers to pursue effective, if not orthodox, economic policies for the electricity sector. Cho and Dubash (2003, p. 19) cite Gabon as an example of how the GATS may undermine effective strategies to expand affordable utility services. They conclude: "The transition to private management in Gabon has worked well in the absence of specific GATS commitments in the electricity sector. Indeed, successful reform in Gabon depended largely on the government's freedom to structure foreign investment in ways consistent with its development priorities."

However, Gabon is hardly representative. Gabon's power system is extremely small by international standards. When the franchise was tendered in 1997, the country only had a total installed generation capacity of 300 megawatts. The Philippines and Egypt have an installed generating capacity of 17 600 and 13 400 megawatts, respectively.[6] Gabon's total installed capacity is smaller than a medium-size power plant in these systems. Power sector experts have long argued that competition is unlikely to be viable or recommended for very small power systems (Bacon, 1995).

The exclusive national concession approach involves tradeoffs. On the one hand it can increase service coverage by allowing the concessionaire to capture certain economies. In Gabon, for example, combining water and electricity services made cost reductions possible through the sharing of resources. Cross subsidisation helped bring the water sector up to speed with the electricity sector and made it possible to undertake investments within the overall scope of the concession that would have been difficult if the two had remained separated. However, this approach also has costs, as it precludes small-scale operators from entering the market. "Granting exclusivity to the main operator may exclude small-scale operators where they could provide valuable solutions for expanding service coverage more quickly." (Tremolet and Neale, 2002, p. 60) It could also preclude efficiencies gained from cross-border trade.

Other countries with very small power systems may want to follow Gabon's lead and tender an exclusive national concession that combines electricity and water. In that case, the country would want to withhold GATS market access commitments in services incidental to energy distribution since such commitments would conflict with the terms of a long-term concession. Countries that have adopted a strategy of establishing exclusive regional franchises will want to make specific commitments but then list reservations for

6. US Energy Information Administration, EIA Country Analysis Briefs, available at http://eia.doe.gov/.

rural areas. Countries that have adopted a competitive bidding process and have non-exclusive distribution franchises can make full market assess and national treatment commitments since such programmes do not depend on exclusivity.

Indeed, for most countries it would be unwise to adopt a national concession model for power sector reform. To the extent possible electricity reforms should encourage, not discourage, competitive entry. This is the conclusion of a recent United Nation report concerning the role of energy in meeting Millennium Development Goals. It is worth quoting at length:

> "Low cost services should be emphasized in policies for meeting the poor's energy needs… Reforms to energy markets should focus on removing obstacles to the efficient functioning of these [energy] markets. These reforms should include providing for efficient entry and exit to these markets for energy suppliers and users, eliminating restrictions or bottlenecks on the import and distribution of modern fuels and electricity, removing market distortions that unfairly favour one supply source over another and pricing energy to cover the cost of both operations and investments incurred in the delivery of energy services. They should establish sound regulation of these markets with specific provision for rural and off-grid areas, various types of private providers of energy services, and promotion of regional energy production and supply cooperation under market conditions." (United Nations, 2005)

Build on the existing legal framework

A third approach is to develop universal service obligations based on the existing GATS framework. Trade law should balance the rights of WTO members to place reservations on commitments against the need for clarity and transparency in the pursuit of universal service goals. The danger of using universal service obligations to mask protectionism cannot be ignored.

Although it involved a dispute over goods, there are lessons for the energy services negotiations in the dispute over reformulated gasoline. In 1995, Venezuela brought a complaint against the United States for imported gasoline (Shenk, 1996). Venezuela (later joined by Brazil) claimed that the United States violated the national treatment principle by applying stricter standards on imported gasoline than it did for domestically refined gasoline. The Appellate Body of the WTO's Dispute Settlement Body ruled against the United States. The panel found that the United States had in fact established higher standards for gasoline of foreign than of domestic origin, and noted that the legislative history explicitly mentioned congressional intent to provide favourable treatment to domestic producers. The panel asked if the different treatment was necessary for the United States to achieve the legitimate objective of improving air quality, but concluded that it was not. On 19 June 1996, the United States informed the WTO that it would take measures to end the discriminatory practice.

The case was controversial. Critics portrayed the case as evidence of the willingness of the WTO to sacrifice domestic social regulation to defend an open global economic order. However, the outcome of WTO panel ruling is more circumscribed than popularly portrayed. The WTO did not void or weaken US clean air laws but ruled that the United States could not require foreign refineries to adhere to a higher standard than it required of US refiners. Had the United States not made a commitment to national treatment, both US consumers and Venezuelan exporters would have been worse off, with no benefit to the environment.

The case illustrates the dangers of according domestic regulators too much discretion and denying foreign competitors legal recourse. International trade commitments can help by recognising the right of governments to withhold commitments in the name of public interest goals, but also by providing a legal basis that ensures that countries adhere to "least trade-restrictive" standards. The lesson of the Venezuela case, as one observer noted, is that, "trade agreements can help improve domestic regulatory policies because they can highlight rent seeking that is masquerading as consumer or environmental protection" (Vogel, 1998). The same holds for policies aimed at achieving important social objectives. Weakening the existing framework by creating more policy space on top of the flexibility that already exists in the GATS would be a step backwards that WTO members should avoid. Although power sector liberalisation is a relatively recent phenomenon, sufficient experience has accumulated to recognise that, to be successful, it requires a mix of policy responses from governments. Table 10.4 summarises some of the key policy instruments in order to show that trade policy measures should not be considered in isolation. Trade commitments are more productively viewed as an element in an integrated package of reforms.

Table 10.4. Integrating policy instruments for improving efficiency and equity

Key policy instruments

Market-based reforms	Consumer protection	Targeted subsidies	Trade rules (GATS)
Privatisation	License private suppliers	Welfare payments paid by tax payers	General obligations MFN (Article 2); Transparency (Article 3)
Commercial pricing (cost-reflective tariffs)	Market oversight and enforcement	Energy fund paid by consumer charges	Market access (Article 16)
Market restructuring (vertical unbundling)	Price caps on default service (providers of last resort)	Special budget allocations (rural and peri-urban electrification)	National treatment (Article 17)
Independent regulation	Rules regarding consumer credit	Donor funding for specific programmes	Additional commitments[1] (Article 18)

1. These additional commitments may include but not be limited to guaranteed access to the grid; market transparency; competition safeguards and independent regulation.

Source: Author.

Integrating domestic reform with trade policy measures

First, private providers cannot be expected to operate at a loss (Kessides, 2003). Privatisation and market restructuring measures such as the introduction of competitive wholesale markets are not feasible without a commitment to cost-reflective tariffs. One set of policy instruments should be devoted to setting and maintaining appropriate electricity prices. At the same time, private companies cannot necessarily be expected to pursue the interest of consumers. It is therefore appropriate for governments to strengthen consumer protection measures, including licensing provisions, and ensure strong oversight and enforcement. Likewise, if market prices are introduced, certain vulnerable and low-income groups may not be able either to gain access or afford the service once they do. This requires establishing appropriate safety nets, to be paid for either through general welfare, universal service funds or special budget allocations.

Finally, governments cannot be expected to treat domestic and foreign market participants equally. Political pressures can cause governments to adopt policies that are discriminatory towards foreign entrants. Liberalisation should create opportunities for market entry for both domestic and foreign service providers. This is where trade commitments can play a useful role and serve to reinforce and support governments' credibility among both the domestic and the international community.

As scholars have shown, elevating commitments to the international level has positive implications. The acceptance of treaty obligations raises expectations about behaviour that, once made, are costly, in terms of reputation, for governments to violate. An international legal commitment is one way for governments to seek to raise the costs of reneging on commitments, with important consequences for their behaviour (Simmons, 2000, p. 819)

Thus, power market reform is most usefully thought of not as a single act of government but as an integrated set of policy instruments with particular objectives. At the very least, electric power reform should include market-based reforms, consumer protection measures, targeted subsidies and, as this chapter has argued, international trade commitments.

Conclusion

Given the critical role of electric power in modern economies, governments are understandably reluctant to restructure without a clear understanding of the benefits and risks. At the same time, there is significant potential for technological and commercial innovations that bring better services within reach of the poor (Brook and Smith, 2000, p. 104). Experience has shown that countries that adopt more flexible regulatory regimes generally make it possible for companies to bundle energy services in more innovative and efficient ways.

Making legally binding commitments at the international level for measures already in force at the domestic level can increase competition and prevent measures that that overtly or covertly discriminate against foreign suppliers. Discrimination can create market distortions that increase costs and reduce sector performance, with negative implications for productivity, growth and economic opportunity. The GATS does not obligate domestic energy reform but, when it does take place, scheduling commitments can reinforce the benefit of well-crafted liberalisation. Trade commitments should be viewed as one instrument in a package of policy instruments.

In many ways, power sector reform reflects the broader challenge that policy makers face in establishing the right balance between market and non-market measures. Mrinal Datta-Chaudhri of the Delhi School of Economics captured the challenge well when he wrote: "The important question for developing societies is how to develop a mutually supportive structure of market and non-market institutions, which is well-suited to promote economic development." (Datta-Chaudhuri, 1990, p. 38) Policy makers should recognise that trade commitments can play an important role in building these mutually supportive structures, particularly when made as part of an integrated package of measures that yield reforms that are both pro-competitive and pro-poor.

References

ABS Energy Research (2004), *Electricity Deregulation Report Global*, 3rd ed, August.

Asian Development Bank (undated), "Bank Policy Initiatives for the Energy Sector: Energy Policy Issues: Energy Pricing", at www.adb.org/Documents/Policies/Energy_Initiatives/energy_ini332.asp.

Bacon, R. (1995), "Privatization and Reform in the Global Electricity Supply Industry", *Annual Review of Energy and Environment*, Vol. 20, pp. 119-143.

Bertoldi, P., S. Rezessy and E. Vine (2006), "Energy Service Companies in European Countries: Current Status and a Strategy to Foster Their Development", *Energy Policy*. Vol. 34, Issue 14, September, pp. 1818-1832.

Brook, P.J. and W.P. Smith, "Better Energy Services for the Poor", in World Bank, *Energy Services for the World's Poor*, World Bank, Washington, DC.

Cho, A.H. and N.K. Dubash (2003), "Do Investment Rules Shrink Policy Space for Sustainable Development? Evidence from the Electricity Sector", World Resources Institute Institute Working Paper, September.

Cockburn, M. and C. Low (2005), "Output-based Aid in Mozambique: Private Electricity Operator Connects Rural Households", *OBApprаches,* Note No. 3, January.

Datta-Chaudhuri, Mrinal (1990), "Market Failure and Government Failure", *The Journal of Economic Perspectives*, Vol. 4, No. 3 (Summer), pp. 25-39.

Department of Trade and Industry (2002), "Fuel Poverty in England in 1999 and 2000", London, January.

Essential Services Commission (2004), "Special Investigation: Review of Effectiveness of Retail Competition and Consumer Safety Net in Gas and Electricity, Final Report to Minister, Essential Services Commission, Melbourne, June.

Evans, P.C. (2002), *Liberalizing Global Trade in Energy Services,* AEI Press, Washington, DC.

Goldman, C.A., N.C. Hopper and J.G. Osborn (2005), "Review of US ESCO Industry Market Trends: An Empirical Analysis of Project Data", *Energy Policy*, Vol. 33, pp. 387-405.

Heald, D.A. (1997). "Public Policy Towards Cross Subsidy", *Annals of Public and Cooperative Economics*, Vol. 68, No. 4, pp. 591-623.

International Energy Agency (IEA) (2003), *World Energy Investment Outlook 2003*, OECD/International Energy Agency.

Jadresic, A. (2000), "A Case Study on Subsidizing Rural Electrification in Chile", in *Energy Services for the World's Poor, Energy and Development Report*, Energy Sector Management Assistance Program, World Bank, Washington, DC, June.

Joskow, P.L. (1997), "Restructuring, Competition and Regulatory Reform in the U.S. Electricity Sector", *The Journal of Economic Perspectives*, Vol. 11, No. 3 (Summer), pp. 119-138.

Joskow, P.L. (2003), The Difficult Transition to Competitive Electricity Markets in the U.S." paper presented at the conference Electricity Deregulation: Where from Here?, Texas A&M University, May.

Kaiser, M.J., W.O. Olatubi and A.G. Pulsipher (2005), "Economic, Energy and Environmental Impact of the Louisiana Energy Fund", *Energy Policy*, Vol. 33, No. 7, pp. 873-883.

Kessides, I. (2003), "Infrastructure Regulation: Promises, Perils and Principles", AEI-Brookings Joint Center for Regulation Studies, July.

Krause, M. and S. Nordström (eds.) (2004), *Solar Photovoltaics in Africa: Experiences with Financing and Delivery Models,* United Nations Development Programme, New York, May.

Low Income Home Energy Assistance Program (LIHEAP) (2004), *LIHEAP Databook: A State-by-State Analysis of Home Energy Assistance, Campaign for Home Energy Assistance*, Washington, DC, January.

Musgrave, R.A. 1959), *The Theory of Public Finance* McGraw-Hill, New York.

National Right to Fuel Campaign, London (undated), "What We Want—Manifesto of the National Right to Fuel Campaign" at www.righttofuel.org.uk.

Office of Gas and Electricity Markets (2004), "Supplying Low Income and Vulnerable Customer Groups", Ofgem Report No. 272/04, London, December, at www.ofgem.gov.uk/ofgem.

Oppenheim, J. (2002), "Assuring Electricity Service for All Residential Customers After Electricity Industry Restructuring", *Electricity Journal*, Vol. 15, Issue 7, (August/September).

Oppenheim, J. and T. MacGregor (2000), "Low Income Consumer Utility Issues: A National Perspective", at www.liheap.ncat.org/pubs/liutilj&t.doc.

Pepermans, G., J. Driesen and D. Haeseldonckx (2003), "Distriubuted Generation: Definition, Benefits and Issues", University of Leuven Energy Institute, August.

Plane, P. (1999), "Privatization, Technical Efficiency and Welfare Consequences: The Case of the Côte d'Ivoire Electricity Company (CIE)", *World Development*, Vol. 27, No. 2, pp. 343-360.

Platts (2002), "Wholesale Trading Shakeout Offers Mixed Blessing for Retail Suppliers", *Retail Energy*, 18 October, p. 1.

Pollitt, M. (1997), "Impact of Liberalization on the Performance of the Electricity Supply Industry: An International Survey", *The Journal of Energy Literature*, Vol. 3, No. 2, pp. 3-31.

Rolls-Royce Power Ventures (undated), "Creating Partnerships in Power", Rolls-Royce Power Ventures Limited, London, available at www.rrpv.com/about/brochure.pdf.

Roux, T. and R. Vahle (2002), "Electricity Rights in Soweto: An Analysis of Possible Legal Arguments, Law and Transformation Programme, Center for Applied Legal Studies, University of the Witwatersrand, October.

Sharam, A. (2001), "From Universal Service to No Service? The Redlining of Vulnerable Electricity Customers in Victoria", Energy Action Group and Essendon Community Legal Centre, Melbourne.

Shenk, M.D. (1996), "United States—Standards for Reformulated and Conventional Gasoline", *The American Journal of International Law*, Vol. 90, No. 4 (October).

Simmons, B.A. (2000), "International Law and State Behavior: Commitment and Compliance in International Monetary Affairs", *American Political Science Review*, Vol. 94, No. 4 (December).

Smith, T.B. (2004), "Electricity Theft: A Comparative Analysis", *Energy Policy*, Vol. 32, Issue 18 (December), pp. 1993-2088.

Spiller, P.T. (1997), "Regulatory Commitment and Utilities' Privatization: Implications for Future Comparative Research", in *Modern Political Economy: Old Topics, New Directions*, Jeffrey S. Banks and Eric A. Hanushek (eds.), Cambridge University Press, New York.

Steiner, F. (2000), "Regulation, Industry Structure and Performance in the Electricity Supply Industry", OECD Economics Department Working Papers, No. 238, OECD, Paris.

Tremolet, S. and J, Neale (2002), "Emerging Lessons in Private Provision of Infrastructure Services in Rural Areas: Water and Electricity Services in Gabon, World Bank/PPIAF, Washington, DC, September.

Tschamler, T. (2000), "Designing Competitive Electric Markets: The Importance of Default Service and Its Pricing", *The Electricity Journal*, March, pp. 75-82.

United Nations (2005), "The Energy Challenge for Achieving the Millennium Development Goals", UN-Energy, New York, at http://esa.un.org/un-energy.

United Nations Development Programme (UNDP) (2003), *Making Global Trade Work for People*, Kamal Malhotra (ed.), Earthscan Publications.

Vogel, D. (1998), "Social Regulations As Trade Barriers: How Regulatory Reform Can Also Help Liberalize Trade", *The Brookings Review*, Vol. 16, No. 1 (Winter), pp. 33-36.

Weatherization, Rehab and Asset Preservation Partnership, (2004), "State Public Benefit Funds: Expanding Support for Low-Income Weatherization and Rehab", Issue Brief, August, at www. energyprograms.org/html/EPC_IBP.htm.

Yang, M. (2003),"China's Rural Electrification and Poverty Reduction", *Energy Policy*, Vol. 31, Issue 3 (February), pp. 203-297.

Zhang, Y., D. Parker and C. Kirkpatrick (2002), "Electricity Sector Reform in Developing Countries: An Econometric Assessment of the Effects of Privatization, Competition and Regulation", Aston Business School Research Institute, November; Working Paper No. 31, Centre on Regulation and Competition, Institute for Development Policy and Management, University of Manchester.

Chapter 11

Power Sector Liberalisation and Access to Energy in the Philippines

Romeo Pacudan
Risøe National Laboratory, Roskilde, Denmark

This chapter describes the process of liberalising access to electricity services in the Philippines with a view to universal access. It discusses the efforts made by government to deal with access issues, availability of reliable services and affordability, notably to rural areas, through the use of private distribution utilities and electric co-operatives. Details are provided on the instruments adopted to achieve this goal and the means of addressing continuing challenges, notably for service to remote areas, are considered.

Liberalisation of the Philippine electricity supply industry

The Philippine electricity supply industry consists of three main grids: Luzon, Visayas and Mindanao (Table 11.1). The grids are interconnected at various islands with varying transfer capacities. The total installed capacity of the generation sector reached more than 15 GW in 2004 and peak demand was recorded at over 9 GW. The transmission sector, which is responsible for high-voltage transport, comprises around 21 000 circuit-kilometres. Transport of low-voltage electricity is ensured by 146 distribution utilities.

Table 11.1. Philippines power sector, 2004

Generation, transmission, distribution

Grid	Installed capacity	Dependable capacity	Peak demand
	MW		
Luzon	12 377	11 086	6 728
Visayas	1 721	1 520	1 063
Mindanao	1 665	1 402	1 278
Total	15 763	14 008	9 069

Plant type	Installed (MW)	% share
Oil-based	3 669	23
Hydro	3 217	20
Geothermal	2 147	14
Coal	3 967	25
Natural gas	2 763	18
Total	15 763	100

Distribution utilities	
Electric co-operatives	119
Private distribution utilities	17
LGUs	10
Barangay electrification, as of 9/04	
Number electrified	38 350
Number remaining	3 595

T/L length = 20 773 ckt-kms

Leyte-Luzon (440 MW)

Leyte-Cebu (200 MW)

Cebu-Negros (180 MW)

Negros-Panay (100 MW

Leyte-Bohol (100 MW)

Source: Department of Energy.

Prior to the liberalisation process, the Philippine electricity supply industry was a vertically integrated industry in generation and transmission. The National Power Corporation, a wholly government-owned corporation, was the sole organisation responsible for generation and high-voltage electricity transport. Electricity distribution in major cities was undertaken by private distribution utilities and by electric co-operatives in rural and less urbanised cities.

The country's first step towards liberalisation of the electricity market was the government's issuance of Executive Order 215 in 1987, which facilitated the entry of independent power producers into the wholesale electricity market. The next most significant event was the passage of Republic Act No. 9136 or RA 9136, the Electric Power Industry Restructuring Act in 2001. The Act embodied two major reforms, namely, the restructuring of the electricity supply industry and the privatisation of the National Power Corporation.

The first of these called for separation of the different functions of the power sector (generation, transmission, distribution and supply), the establishment of the wholesale electricity spot market (WESM) and the introduction of retail competition. Generation and supply represent the competitive segment of the industry while transmission and distribution constitute the natural monopoly segment. The privatisation of the National Power Corporation involved the sale of the state-owned power firm's generation and transmission assets (*e.g.* power plants and transmission facilities) to private investors. These reforms aimed at encouraging greater competition and attracting more private-sector investment in the power industry. A more competitive power industry results in lower power rates and a more efficient delivery of electricity supply to end users. The new electricity supply industry structure is shown in Figure 11.1.

Figure 11.1. New Philippine electricity supply industry structure

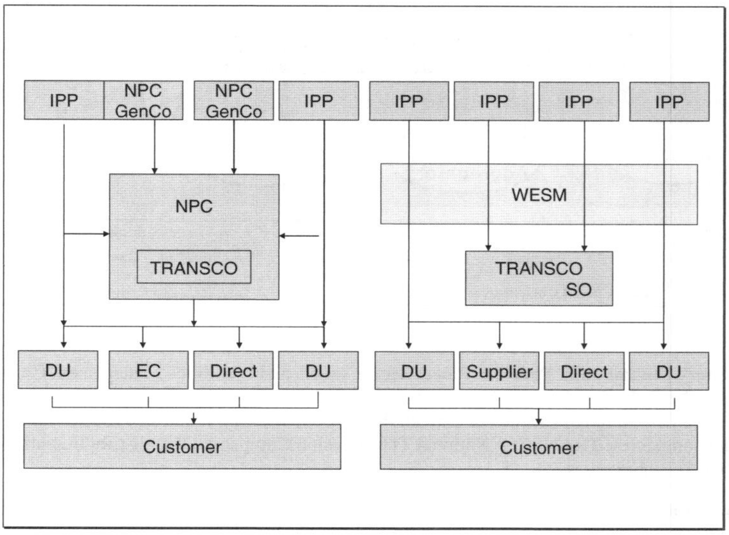

Note: The figure on the left represents industry structure during the transition phase. The National Power Corporation (NPC) and independent power producers (IPPs) are the main producers of electricity. At the wholesale level, NPC is the main buyer of electricity though some distribution utilities (DUs) source directly from IPPs. The electricity generated by these entities is transported through the high-voltage transmission network system operated by the National Transmission Company (TRANSCO). Electricity distribution and supply are undertaken by distribution utilities (DUs) and electric co-operatives (ECs) through their low-voltage networks. These utilities sourced their wholesale power mainly from NPC. Some customers with high demand purchase electricity directly from either NPC or IPPs. The figure on the right shows the industry structure envisaged by the Electric Power Industry Act. The generation and supply functions are competitive segments of the industry while the transmission and distribution functions represent the natural monopoly segments. The generation function will be in the hands of the private sector (the generating assets of NPC will be privatised). The transport of high-voltage electricity will be through the privatised TRANSCO networks, which will be also responsible for operation of the network system. Electricity exchange will be facilitated by the wholesale electricity spot market (WESM), which will be managed by a non-profit market operator. Distribution utilities operate the low voltage network systems. Customers with high electricity demand (contestable customers) are free to select their electricity suppliers while those with relatively low demand (captive customers) will remain captive to the distribution utilities.

Source: Holopainen (2004).

Six government bodies are responsible for the transition and the governance of the restructured power industry (Figure 11.2). These are the Joint Congressional Power Commission for guidelines and overall framework; the Department of Energy for policy; the Energy Regulatory Commission for economic regulation; the Power Sector Assets and Liabilities Management Corporation for the privatisation programme; the National Power Corporation through its Small Power Utilities Group for missionary electrification; and the National Electrification Administration for rural electrification promotion. The Energy Regulatory Commission and the Power Sector Assets and Liabilities Management

Corporation were created by the Electric Power Industry Restructuring Act, Additional functions were defined by the same law for the remaining agencies.

Figure 11.2. Governance of the electricity supply industry reforms

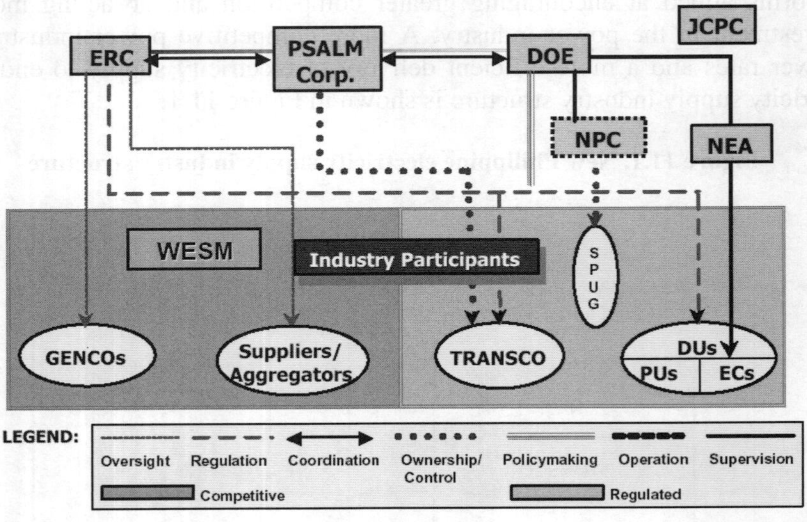

ERC: Energy Regulatory Commission; PSALM: Power Sector Assets and Liabilities Management Corporation; DOE: Department of Energy; NPC: National Power Corporation; JCPC: Joint Congressional Power Commission; SPUG: Small Power Utilities Group; NEA: National Electrification Administration; WESM: Wholesale Electricity Spot Market; GENCOs: generating companies; TRANSCO: National Transmission Company; DU : distribution utilities ; PU : private utilities ; EC: electricity co-operatives.

Source: Department of Energy.

To implement the Electric Power Industry Restructuring Act, the integrated assets of the National Power Corporation were broken down and its generating assets were prepared for privatisation by the Power Sector Assets and Liabilities Management Corporation. In 2004, five small hydropower plants (total installed capacity of 8.5 MW) and a large coal-fired power plant (600 MW capacity) were successfully sold. The remaining generating assets were scheduled for privatisation in 2005-06. The National Transmission Company was created by the law to carry out high voltage transmission and sub-transmission functions. The National Transmission Company will be privatised through concession, a 25-year lease of all transmission assets which is automatically renewable for another 25 years.

Distribution utilities, consisting of private distribution utilities and electric co-operatives, will retain their functions and will be required to provide open and non-discriminatory access to users of distribution wires and charge wheeling rates to be determined by the Energy Regulatory Commission. The Philippine Electricity Market Corporation was established in 2003 to prepare for the operation of the wholesale electricity spot market. Given the current pace of technical preparation, the earliest commercial operation of the wholesale electricity spot market in the Luzon Grid was anticipated for December 2005. The implementation of retail competition and distribution network open access in the Luzon Grid was set for July 2006 by the Energy Regulatory Commission. The level of initial demand in the contestable market is 1 MW peak demand, which will be reduced to 750 kW after one year. Thereafter, ERC will review and determine the appropriate level of demand of contestable consumers. The Commission has not yet issued guidelines concerning the licensing of electricity suppliers and aggregators.

Energy access and liberalisation

Access goals

Access in the electricity sector refers to access to affordable and reliable electricity services. Most developing countries have embarked on centralised and decentralised electrification programmes to broaden access to electricity, particularly in rural and remote communities. In the past, many rural electrification programmes in developing countries were mainly grid extension projects, though decentralised approaches have been introduced more recently. Access programmes are driven by various country-specific goals, and the two most common objectives are to promote sustainable economic development and social equity.

In the Philippines, the rural electrification programme aims to support the overall objective of the government to improve the quality of life for all citizens by providing adequate, affordable and reliable energy services. This objective is addressed by the electricity supply industry reforms while broadening electricity access is the focus of the government electrification programmes. During the period 2000-03, the Department of Energy adopted the O'Ilaw Programme which integrated the efforts of several government agencies to increase electricity access to all of the country's villages and encouraged increased participation of private organisations, business communities and civic organisations in the electrification of marginal villages. Since 2003, the Department of Energy has implemented the national Expanded Rural Electrification Programme, the goal of which is to strengthen and integrate all rural electrification efforts of the government and the private sector. The new programme aims to further widen electricity access to small communities and households in rural villages.

Electricity access programmes are gauged by their success in improving the country's level of electrification, which is measured in terms of the percentage of municipalities, villages or households with access to electricity; governments often define electrification level targets. In 2004, 90.8% of all villages had access to electricity and the government projects 100% electrification by 2008 (Table 11.2). The government's ambitious target is to increase the percentage of households (not only villages) with access to electricity to 90% in 2017.

Social equity goals and efficiency

As presented above, access goals are based on the government's socioeconomic and developmental goals. Various evaluations of rural electrification projects in developing countries have shown that the provision of electricity services in rural areas has indeed resulted in the development of productive activities and helped to develop health, education, commerce and ICT (information and communication technology). A 2003 UNDP/World Bank study of the Philippines quantifies the "non-measurable" benefits of rural electrification and shows that the benefits derived from better electricity services outweigh the costs of extending the service.

Table 11.2. Electrification programme (2004-08)

Number of villages to be electrified

Agency/Office	2004 (Jun-Dec)	2005	2006	2007	2008	Total
NEA/Ecs	250	200	200	200	200	1050
NPC-SPUG	116	116	116	116	116	580
DOE	180	80	80	80	80	500
PNOC-EDC	86	100	100	100	100	486
IPPs/QTPs	489	403	-	-	-	892
Total	1121					3508
Energisation level	93.5%	95.6%	96.8%	98.0%	99.2%	
Remaining unenergised villages (as of May 2004)						3860
Balance (to be offered to QTPs; NPC-SPUG as last resort)						352

NEA: National Electrification Administration. This government agency was responsible for establishing electric co-operatives. It acted as a conduit for government funds intended for rural electrification. Under the Electric Power Industry Restructuring Act, its licensing function had been transferred to the Philippine Congress and its role has been reduced to providing financial guarantee to electric co-operatives in the wholesale electricity market.

ECs: Electric co-operatives. These are utilities involved in electricity distribution in rural areas and operate as private entities. Under the Reform Act, they are to be transformed either into a stock corporation or stock co-operatives.

NPC-SPUG: Small Power Utilities Group. A unit of the National Power Corporation tasked by the Electric Power Industry Restructuring Act to provide electricity services in remote (missionary) areas not covered by electric co-operatives. Its operations are subsidised by ratepayers through the mandatory universal charge.

DOE: Department of Energy. Under the Reform Act, The Department is responsible for policy making. It administers the trust fund created under the Energy Regulation 1-94 (Benefits to Host Communities), which is partly used to improve electricity access in rural areas.

PNOC-EDC: Philippine National Oil Corporation – Energy Development Company. This government agency is responsible for the exploitation of geothermal (and recently wind) energy resources. The agency is also involved in providing electricity access in areas adjacent to their power generation sites.

IPPs: Independent power producers. These are private entities involved in electricity generation (not distribution). IPPs are however required by Energy Regulation 1-94 to contribute PHP 1 for every kWh (USD 1 = PHP 55) it generates to be used to improve the welfare of communities hosting their power plants. Under the Expanded Rural Electrification Programme, the government encouraged the IPPs to be proactive and be involved in increasing electricity access by using their financial contribution to Energy Regulation 1-94 in advance.

QTPs: Qualified third parties. These are private entities which are allowed to participate in NPC-SPUG's operations in remote villages. NPC-SPUG is opening the missionary areas to private investors under various contractual arrangements such as leasing, participation in generation, asset divestiture, etc.

Source: Department of Energy.

The above-mentioned access goals are strategically pursued by government-owned electricity utilities or financed electricity co-operatives. Such utilities need to maintain a certain level of operational efficiency in order to remain financially viable and competitive. The conflict between efficiency and equity goals is driven by the following factors: rural households have lower income levels and their ability to pay for energy services is relatively low; for social equity reasons, electricity tariffs are fixed by governments at rates below the real cost of providing the electricity service; and grid extension, mini-grid development or even an off-grid option are all capital-intensive.

Capital investments for access programmes are therefore not easily recouped by distribution utilities through revenues derived from electricity sales. These are among the main reasons why many utilities in developing countries involved in access programmes have weak financial performance. Other factors include high system losses (technical and non-technical), ineffective rate collection systems, poor management accountability, etc.

Public sector financing and subsidies are often required (and provided) to sustain the financial efficiency of electric utilities and to attract private investors to participate in the provision of energy services, particularly in remote and unviable areas. In the Philippines, rural electrification is mainly funded by government-secured loans extended to electric co-operatives through the National Electrification Administration.

Implications of liberalisation on energy access

Liberalisation in the electricity supply industry opens up the electricity market to private companies, including foreign firms. The main difference between a public and a private enterprise is that the former pursues social goals in addition to the standard corporate and efficiency objectives. Socially oriented investments such as access programmes, unless mandated by the government, would not be supported by private or privatised electric utilities. On the other hand, the liberalisation of the electricity supply industry in most developing countries is coupled with industry restructuring and the introduction of competitive electricity markets. To remain competitive and efficient, utilities will not continue to invest in programmes that do not result in acceptable benefits. Liberalisation and competition therefore slow investments in socially oriented programmes such as electrification programmes.

Access issues, availability of reliable services and affordability are among the most contentious areas of the Electric Power Industry Restructuring Act. Lawmakers ensured that provisions to address these issues were integrated in the reform law. Regulatory mechanisms and measures integrated in the Act as well as other policies elaborated by the government to address access and affordability issues are discussed below.

Policy measures to improve electricity access

One of the main goals of the Electric Power Industry Restructuring Act is to provide universal access to electricity services. To meet these objectives, the Act mandates distribution utilities to provide universal service within their franchise areas and designates the National Power Corporation to provide services in remote areas outside the franchise areas of distribution utilities. The Energy Regulatory Commission elaborated specific rules for implementing the universal service regulation, and the Department of Energy designed innovative policies that accelerate the provision of electricity services through greater private sector participation. Various provisions of the Act ease the financial burden of electric co-operatives and have enhanced their capacity to provide energy services in unserved areas. The Act also institutionalises the mechanism that provides funding for various socioeconomic and environmental activities of communities hosting power generation units.

Universal service regulation

The Electric Power Industry Restructuring Act requires distribution utilities to provide universal service within their franchise areas, including unviable areas, as part of their social obligations. The utility is, however, allowed to charge different rates in unviable areas to recover its investment costs and sustain its economic viability, subject to the approval of the Electricity Regulatory Commission. In electricity rate setting, the Commission allows inclusion of capital expenditures and reinvestment for service expansion in the rate base of the private distribution utilities and electric co-operatives, respectively.

To facilitate the implementation of the universal service obligation, the Electricity Regulatory Commission promulgated the Magna Carta for Residential Electricity Consumers in July 2004, which spelled out the basic rights of electricity end users as well as their obligations. The guidelines for its implementation were issued in October 2004. Two guidelines issued relate to reducing cost barriers to the provision of electricity service: the refund of the service deposit (equivalent to estimated billing for one month) within one month of the termination of the service or after diligent payment of electricity bills for three consecutive years; and the exemption of payment for electric meters since utilities have incorporated these costs in the electricity rate base. A third guideline relates to customers' right of line extension. Utilities are required to finance the line extension or installation of additional facilities if the applicant customer is within 30 metres of the utilities' existing secondary low-voltage lines. The customer may initially fund the investments and request a refund if he/she is located beyond that distance.

Since the enactment of the Electricity Industry Reform Law in 2001, no review has been undertaken to determine whether distribution utility investments to improve access in remote areas were carried out by utilities in response to the universal service regulation or as part of their previously planned investments under the distribution development plan. In this respect, distribution utilities are required to submit an annual five-year Distribution Development Plan to the Department of Energy. Private distribution utilities submit directly to the Department of Energy while electric co-operatives submit through the National Electrification Administration, which first consolidates the plans into a National Electric Co-operatives Distribution Development Plan.

Unviable areas and qualified third parties

The Electric Power Industry Restructuring Act allows the opening up of remote and unviable areas to qualified third parties if the franchise holder distribution utility is unable to serve before June 2004 (three years from when the Act took effect). In June 2004 the Department of Energy issued a circular prescribing the qualifications of such third parties. In March 2005, the Department of Energy issued a public notice declaring 428 villages as unviable areas and open for provision of electric service by qualified third parties and/or through private sector participation. Currently, the Department of Energy is finalising another circular prescribing participation guidelines, which include subsidy policies. To attract private investors, the Department of Energy developed a cluster of villages lacking electricity as "market packages" to create a critical mass of base customers.

Currently, two qualified third-party projects are being implemented. One is the pilot electrification project of PowerSource Philippines, Inc., in Palawan Province. The company employs a distributed generation technology and provides not only energy services but also other services such as water purification, communication and entertainment. The company will transfer ownership of the system to the local community after ten years, and it will tap village associations to help collect service payments. The pilot site is actually an isolated village with fishing, mining and agricultural industries. The second is the Philippine Rural Electrification Service (PRES) Project in Masbate Province. It is a consortium of French and Filipino companies with loan financing from the French government. The company will use a mini-grid powered by diesel engines to provide electricity in clustered communities and solar home systems for isolated households.

Improvement of electric co-operatives' performance

Various mechanisms implemented under the Act seek to improve the financial performance of electric co-operatives and their ability to provide reliable and affordable services. These include transformation of electric co-operatives, debt relief and investment management contracts. These have a positive indirect effect on electric co-operatives' ability to provide services to unserved areas.

Under the new liberalised industry, electric co-operatives have the option to convert to either stock co-operatives or stock corporations. Co-operatives that choose to become stock co-operatives will be governed by the Co-operative Code of the Philippines; those that opt to become stock corporations will be covered by the Corporation Code; those that opt to retain a non-stock co-operative status will remain under the supervision of the National Electrification Administration. These changes may strengthen the overall performance of electric co-operatives.

The new liberalisation law shifts the outstanding debt of electric co-operatives incurred for the purpose of financing rural electrification to the National Electrification Administration and other government agencies. The Power Sector Assets and Liabilities Management Corporation is mandated by law to assume these financial obligations. A recent audit shows that the total relevant debt amounts to PHP 13.57 billion. The electric co-operatives are however not allowed to transfer ownership or control of their assets, franchise or operations within five years; otherwise they will be required to pay the total amount plus accrued interest. This may indirectly improve electric co-operatives' ability to provide services within their franchise areas.

The Department of Energy recently issued a circular, allowing electric co-operatives, particularly those performing poorly in the recent years, to enter into investment management contracts with the private sector. The Department of Energy defines an investment management contract as a contractual relationship between an electric co-operative and an investor-operator for the infusion of risk capital and provision of management expertise to provide for sustainable electric co-operative recovery based on improved efficiency, lower costs and reduction of system losses. With improved efficiency, electric co-operatives could provide affordable and reliable universal service within their franchise areas. In 2004, the Department of Energy and National Electrification Administration assisted three electric co-operatives in preparing an investment management contract. Due diligence studies were undertaken and submitted to a transaction advisor. Requests for pre-qualification of investors were planned at the end of 2004.

Electrification fund for host communities and independent power producers

Prior to the enactment of the reform law, the government created a fund to provide financial benefits to communities hosting power generation plants (Energy Regulation 1-94 of 1992). The granting of benefits to host communities was subsequently institutionalised by the Electric Power Industry Restructuring Act. Generating companies are required to set aside PHP 0.01/kWh of electricity sales for the benefit of their host communities. In regions that are not highly urbanised, half of the benefits are allocated to the electrification fund (EF) while the other half is evenly divided among a development and livelihood fund (DLF) and reforestation, watershed management, health and/or environment enhancement fund (RWMHEEF). In highly urbanised area, the funds are distributed as follows: PHP 0.075/kWh for EF, and PHP 0.00125/kWh each for DLF and RWMHEEF. From January 1997 to October 2004, the Host Communities Fund generated

PHP 1.5 billion and the EF granted 1 400 grid extension projects amounting to PHP 608.42 million covering 663 villages and 737 sub-villages.

To accelerate investment in rural electrification, the Department of Energy encourages independent power producers to be involved in grid extension projects in rural areas. Their investments can be recovered from the electrification fund of the benefit granted to host communities by electricity generators (including the independent power producers). As of the beginning of 2005, eight independent power producers had implemented or committed to implement grid extension projects involving around 2 000 villages and small communities.

Missionary electrification and private participation

The Electric Power Industry Restructuring Act prescribes that geographic areas not covered by the national transmission system are to be served by the National Power Corporation through its unit, the Small Power Utilities Group. Based on the Missionary Electrification Development Plan developed by Department of Energy and Small Power Utilities Group, the latter could petition the Electricity Regulatory Commission for a subsidy through the universal charge. In 2004, the Small Power Utilities Group received a total of PHP 772.85 million to support its missionary electrification activities while the National Power Corporation received a disbursement of PHP 61.89 million for the maintenance and rehabilitation of watershed areas.

To promote private investments in electricity services in missionary areas, the Department of Energy issued a circular prescribing the rules and procedures for private sector participation in Small Power Utilities Group areas. The Small Power Utilities Group has recently identified eight provinces as the first group to be opened for private investments. More recently, the Department of Energy, Power Sector Assets and Liabilities Management Corporation and National Power Corporation have engaged a transaction advisor to assist in the development of an appropriate privatisation programme and the selection of new power provider. As of 2004, the transaction advisor had undertaken*:* *i)* project preparation, review of the regulatory framework and industry policies, and conduct of due diligence; *ii) preparation* of a model Power Sales Agreement (PSA); *iii)* consultation with the Energy Regulatory Commission on the regulatory framework; and *iv)* marketing of the project and the advantages of PSAs to electric co-operatives. Among the first target areas, the Department of Energy, in consultation with the transaction advisor, has identified three pilot areas for implementation: Tablas Island, Romblon and Marinduque.

Policy measures to reduce electricity prices

As already noted, one of the contentious issues of the reform is its impact on electricity prices. To ensure that the reforms would avoid increased electricity rates, the Electric Power Industry Restructuring Act mandates a rate reduction for all residential customers and prescribes a lifeline rate for marginalised end-users. To further mitigate rate impacts, the government pursued other measures such as review of the franchise tax and renegotiation of contracts with the independent power producers. The absorption by the government of electric co-operatives' debt, which was intended to alleviate their financial difficulties, was found to have a positive impact on electricity rates. Measures designed to make rates transparent and fair, such as rate unbundling and removal of cross-subsidies, have had mixed effects. On the other hand, measures to obtain funding from ratepayers to finance reform costs and other socioeconomic goals, such as the universal charge, lifeline rates, subsidy for renewable energies, etc., tend to negate the positive gains from the reduction of electricity rates.

Mandated rate reduction

One of the main goals of the liberalisation of the power industry in the Philippines is to reduce electricity tariff rates. In early 1990s, the Philippines ranked second (after Japan) in terms of highest average electricity rate in Asia. To ensure that the rates would decline as a result of liberalisation, the Electric Power Industry Restructuring Act spelled out a mandatory reduction of PHP 0.30/kWh to all residential end users. The reduction was implemented in 2001. Currently, the Philippines has the fourth and seventh highest average electricity rates for residential and commercial customers, respectively (Figure 11.3). Electricity rate changes are affected by various factors such as the continued devaluation of Philippine peso against the US dollar, higher imported fuel supply costs and higher costs of power contracts.

Independent power producers' contract renegotiation

One of the main sources of high electricity rates in the Philippines is the take-or-pay contracts entered into in the early 1990s by the National Power Corporation and the independent power producers. It was during this period that the country experienced a massive electricity supply shortage. Through build-operate-transfer arrangements, the government was able to attract foreign investments in the power sector. Almost a decade later, some of these contracts were found to be disadvantageous. Owing to pressure from consumers, the government was forced to review and renegotiate some of these contracts.

As of the first half of 2005, the Power Sector Assets and Liabilities Management Corporation and the National Power Corporation had resolved 20 of the 35 contracts with private investors. The renegotiation has resulted in an estimated reduction of USD 1.03 billion of stranded contract costs (in present value terms). This translated into savings of around PHP 0.098/kWh for 2004 (USD 1 = PHP 57 in 2004). The renegotiation of the remaining contracts was to be completed at the end of 2005.

Franchise tax review

The Electricity Regulatory Commission has recently submitted a position paper to the Department of Finance to reduce the franchise tax on distribution utilities. These utilities currently pay a tax rate based on gross receipts, which covers distribution wheeling and captive market supply revenues as well as generation, transmission and distribution loss charges. The Commission recommended that the system loss charge should not be considered part of a utility's revenue and its removal will lower the base for the computation of the franchise tax and may translate into lower electricity rates. The Department of Finance is currently reviewing the Commission's position paper.

Impact of debt relief

As discussed above, in order to prepare the electric co-operatives for the new electricity market structure, the Electric Power Industry Restructuring Act relieves these utilities of the debt of incurred for financing rural electrification. As a result, rates of the electric co-operatives have declined owing to the removal of amortisation payments for their loans. The reduction of utility rates ranges from PHP 0.012 kWh to PHP 0.7642/kWh.

Figure 11.3. Regional electricity rates

A. Comparison of residential electricity rates in selected Asian economies, US cents/kWh

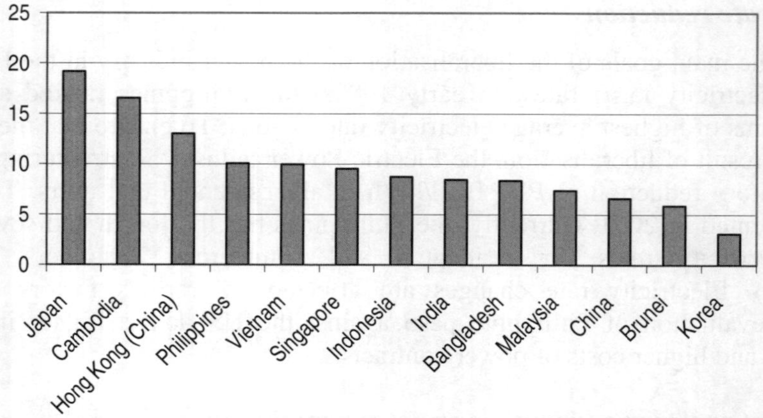

B. Comparison of commercial electricity rates in selected Asian economies, US cents/kWh

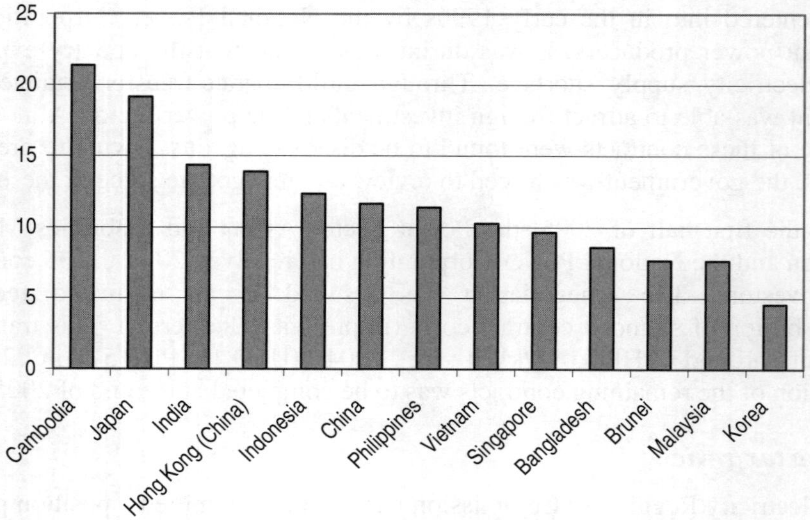

1. Electricity price data of selected Asian countries were taken from the actually electricity bills of Philippine embassies and embassy staff for the billing period June 2004 (Source: DFA), except China and Singapore.

2. Philippine electricity data based on actually residential and commercial milling of Meralco for June 2004.

3. Rates from China Energy Research Institute

4. Rates from Singapore Power website.

5. Exchange rates used were provided by each embassy, except for Hong Kong (China) and India which were taken from OANDA.com.

6. Residential rates assumed the same as commercial rates.

Rate unbundling

To make the rate transparent and easy to understand, the Electric Power Industry Restructuring Act requires the unbundling of rates and a breakdown of specific components of the power bill (*e.g.* generation, transmission, distribution and supply). As a result, rates in some utilities decreased and others increased. Based on the overall average tariff adjustment approved by the Energy Regulatory Commission in March

2004, rates of 24 distribution utilities have declined by PHP 0.3538/kWh to PHP 0.00481/kWh and those of 84 have increased by PHP 0.00481/kWh to PHP 1.7855/kWh.

Removal of cross-subsidies

Before the passage of the law, three types of electricity price cross-subsidies existed in the Philippines: *i)* price cross-subsidies between customers of a utility (the industrial and commercial customers subsidise the residential and public customers); *ii)* price cross-subsidies between wholesale electricity customers of the National Power Corporation in the Luzon grid; and *iii)* price cross-subsidies between the three national grids. The Electric Power Industry Restructuring Act requires the gradual phase-out of these cross-subsidies within three years from the establishment of a universal charge but may be put off for another year by the Energy Regulatory Commission if a material adverse effect upon the public interest is found, particularly for residential end users, or if there is an immediate, irreparable and adverse financial effect on the distribution utility. The inter-regional cross-subsidy was removed in 2002 when the National Power Corporation unbundled its rates. In 2003, the Energy Regulatory Commission started to implement intra-regional cross subsidy removal. One-third of the original subsidy was removed in September 2003, another third in September 2004, and the final third in September 2005. For inter-class cross-subsidy removal, the Commission approved a two-phase removal scheme for customers of the Manila Electric Company: 40% of the subsidy was removed in October 2004 and the remaining 60% in October 2005. The Energy Regulatory Commission calculations show that residential rates will increase by PHP 0.2852/kWh during the first phase and will increase by a further PHP 0.4278/kWh in the second phase. Based on the residential impact study commissioned by the Department of Energy, the removal of the cross-subsidy increases residential electricity rates. The mandated reduction of PHP 0.30/kWh will slightly mitigate the impact of the removal of the cross-subsidy. However, with the introduction of a competitive market, prices are expected to approach the long-run marginal cost of electricity production. The long-run marginal cost of electricity plus the stranded asset recovery of the industry (estimated at PHP 0.30/kWh) is expected to be lower than current electricity prices.

Universal charge

The universal charge is an obligatory charge imposed by the Electric Power Industry Restructuring Act for the following purposes: *i)* recovery of stranded debts of the National Power Corporation and stranded contract costs of the National Power Corporation and qualified distribution utilities; *ii)* missionary electrification fund; *iii)* equalisation of taxes and royalties between the indigenous or renewable energy resources and imported energy fuel; *iv)* environmental charge for the rehabilitation and maintenance of watershed areas; and *v)* mitigation fund for the removal of cross-subsidies.

At present only two components of the universal charge are being levied on all electricity end-users: the missionary electrification fund and the environmental charge. The Small Power Utilities Group of the National Power Corporation petitioned for a missionary electrification subsidy of PHP 0.0831/kWh during the first petition period but the Electricity Regulatory Commission only approved an amount equivalent to PHP 0.0373/kWh. The environmental charge was fixed by the Electric Power Industry Restructuring Act at PHP 0.0025/kWh.

Lifeline rates

The Electric Power Industry Restructuring Act also sets a social pricing mechanism for marginalised users. A lifeline rate is set separately by each utility subject to approval by the Electricity Regulation Commission. Lifeline rates therefore vary. A lifeline rate is defined as the subsidised rate given to low-income captive end-users who cannot afford to pay the full cost. In various distribution rate petition hearings, the Commission calculated the lifeline rate based on the load requirement of a typical low-income household with two lighting facilities (20 Watts each) and a 50-Watt radio used for a reasonable number of hours. The Commission adopts a graduated scale for the lifeline discount and adjusts the minimum level of consumption to maximise the benefit to low-income end-users while keeping the subsidy costs borne by other end-users between PHP 0.05/kWh and PHP 0.10/kWh. Lifeline rates and subsidies for selected private distribution utilities are given in Table 11.3.

Table 11.3. Lifeline rates and subsidies for selected private distribution utilities

Distribution utility	Lifeline level and discounts	Subsidy of lifeline borne by other end-users (PHP /kWh)
Manila Electric Company (MERALCO)	*Lifeline level:* 100 kWh *Discounts* 50 kWh and below = 50% 51-55 kWh = 45% ... 96-100 kWh = 5%	0.0679
Visayas Electric Company (VECO)	*Lifeline level:* 55 kWh *Discounts* 50 kWh and below = 35% ... 55 kWh = 10%	0.0912
Cagayan Electric and Power Company (CEPALCO)	*Lifeline level:* 100 kWh *Discounts* 20 kWh and below = 50% 21-30 kWh = 45% ... 91-100 kWh = 20%	0.0507
Davao Light and Power Company (DLPC)	*Lifeline level:* 100 kWh *Discounts* 40 kWh and below = 50% 41-50 kWh = 45% ... 91-100 kWh = 10%	0.0720

Solar photovoltaic systems subsidy

The Department of Energy considers solar photovoltaic (PV) systems as a cost-effective and environmentally friendly technology for providing electricity service and other community services to sparsely populated, remote, unserved and dispersed areas. In this regard, it recently issued a circular rationalising the grant of subsidies to missionary electrification using PV systems. The beneficiaries are the end users in a non-energised, remote, dispersed and unviable area that is suitable for solar PV systems. The Department of Energy circular also identified the missionary electrification component of the universal charge as a main source of the PV subsidy. The amount of the subsidy remains to be determined, although the circular specified that the following factors will be taken into account in the calculation: electricity consumption of consumers; size/capacity and number of installations of solar PV systems; cost of solar PV systems; consumers' willingness to pay; potential contribution of household electrification to community development; innovative delivery mechanisms of solar PV systems such as, but not limited to, direct dealership and fee-for-service schemes; and cost of developing and marketing solar PV systems.

Energy regulatory body

Both policy and regulation play an important role in the provision of universal access to electricity services in the Philippines. The Electric Power Industry Restructuring Act provides both electricity access policy and a regulatory framework. The Department of Energy plays an important role in developing innovative approaches involving various parties to accelerate the provision of energy services particularly in remote and unviable areas. On the other hand, the Energy Regulatory Commission ensures universal access of customers to electricity services at affordable rates through rate regulation, subsidy determination and service obligation.

The Energy Regulatory Commission was established by the Electric Power Industry Restructuring Act, which also abolished the existing Energy Regulatory Board. The Commission is an independent, quasi-judicial regulatory body. It is composed of a Chairman and four members. Broadly, it is responsible for promoting competition, encouraging market development, ensuring customer choice and penalising abuse of market power in the electric power industry. Its main role in the government's expanded electrification programme includes rate design, licensing and determination of the missionary electrification charge component of the universal charge. The initial budget of the Commission, set at PHP 150 million, was based on the existing budget of (the defunct) Energy Regulatory Board.

The Energy Regulatory Commission was based on the abolished Energy Regulatory Board. Though there were initial changes in leadership, the Commission retained the expertise and experience of the Board's technical staff. With the changes in the electricity supply industry, the Electric Power Industry Restructuring Act specified areas that required further strengthening. These are: evaluation of technical performance and monitoring of compliance with service and performance standards, performance-based rate setting reform, environmental standards and other areas that will enable the Commission to adequately perform its duties and functions.

New challenges

Access to electricity services and public-private partnerships

The Electric Power Industry Restructuring Act provides the legal framework for ensuring universal access to electricity services. The Energy Regulatory Commission elaborates specific rules that balance consumer protection and provision of incentives to energy access providers. The Department of Energy designs new approaches to accelerate provision of universal access through greater private-sector participation. At this stage, there is an indication that the private sector is responding to the mechanisms. It must be noted, however, that the projects being developed by private investors are in regions/provinces with the promise of attractive financial returns. The provision of electricity services in remote and unviable areas as well as services for every household (not only villages) including the poorest of the poor will remain a challenge for the government. The government must constantly seek new types of public-private partnerships, and various partnership models can be designed with the private sector for the country's unserved villages and households.

Investment incentives are necessary to stimulate private investments in remote and unviable areas. The government must also consider sources other than the ratepayers to finance these incentives since ratepayers are already burdened by high electricity tariff rates.

Other factors affecting electricity prices

The government is committed to reducing electricity prices and is currently addressing inefficiency in the electricity market. Other factors, such as global energy price trends and currency devaluation, could also potentially erode the gains in improving market efficiency.

The Philippines is poorly endowed with conventional energy resources and is highly dependent on imported primary energy. Increasing energy independence (thereby alleviating the impact of high global energy prices) requires a new energy security policy framework, for example to promote the development of indigenous energy resources and improved energy efficiency. Though specific access frameworks are vital, this issue must be also viewed in a broader national energy policy framework. Current global price trends must not be seen to hamper efforts to increase access to energy services in the remote areas and to the poorest of the poor.

Imported energy sources will remain a vital element in the country's energy security. The negative impact of high international energy prices may be exacerbated by currency devaluation since imported energy is paid for in foreign currency while energy services are paid for in local currency. The recent devaluation of the peso is an indication of the government's failure to provide a stable macroeconomic and political environment. While such questions are beyond the scope of this chapter, it must be mentioned that national economic and political governance issues have dire consequences for energy access efforts.

Renewable energies

Access to reliable and affordable electricity services can be further enhanced through utilisation of renewable energies and via distributed generation.

Renewable energy technologies can provide a cost-effective way to widen energy access in developing countries either in the form of mini-grids or individual home systems. Most of these countries, however, lack the policy, institutional and financial support for their development. In the case of the Philippines, the government supports the development of renewable energies for energy security reasons. While the Philippines has a policy framework to promote the development of renewable energies, it lacks a comprehensive regulatory framework to stimulate private investments.

Reliability is another necessary attribute of energy services. Distributed generation technologies provide a cost-effective option for improving grid-connected electricity. Distributed generation involves electricity-generating plants utilising either renewable energy or conventional fuels and integrated into distribution networks. The main characteristics differentiating distributed generation from centralised power supply relate to location, capacity and grid connection. Distributed generators are located near the point at which power is consumed. Distributed generation technologies are small in scale or can be produced economically in a range of sizes. Traditional electricity suppliers are connected to the high-voltage grid while distributed generators are connected to the grid at the distribution level.

The complexity of the structure and operation of liberalised and competitive electricity markets makes it costly for small-scale distributed generators, particularly small and intermittent producers, to deal with market competition, to undertake bilateral contracts with consumers, to meet electricity dispatch requirements (balancing requirements) and to procure back-up power. Many countries that embark on liberalisation, including the Philippines, have lacked trading arrangements and market rules that provide correct signals and appropriate incentives to facilitate the growth of distributed generation. Moreover, the integration of distributed generation in distribution networks presents both costs and benefits for the network; these need to be properly valued in order to facilitate the growth of distributed generation. The current regulatory frameworks often fail to recognise, allocate and evaluate most of these costs and benefits.

References

Department of Energy (2005), Sixth Status Report on EPIRA Implementation, Manila, Philippines.

Department of Energy (2004), Fifth Status Report on EPIRA Implementation, Manila, Philippines.

Department of Energy (2004), Update on EPIRA Implementation, Manila, Philippines.

Department of Energy (2005), Philippine Energy Plan – 2005 Update, Manila, Philippines.

Department of Energy (2003), Renewable Energy Policy Framework, Manila, Philippines.

Department of Energy, Department Circular No. 2004-05-005: "Streamlining and Rationalizing the Grant of Subsidies in the Electrification of Missionary Areas Using Solar Photovoltaic Systems", Manila, Philippines.

Department of Energy, Department Circular No. 2004-06-007: "Promoting Investment Management Contracts as One Measure in Effecting Greater Private Sector Participation in the Management and Operation of Rural Electric Cooperatives Pursuant to Section 37 of Republic Act No. 9136 and Its Implementing Rules and Regulations", Manila, Philippines.

Energy Regulatory Commission (2004), Guidelines to Implement Articles 7, 8, 14 and 28 of the Magna Carta for Residential Electricity Consumers, Manila, Philippines.

Energy Regulatory Commission (2004), A Resolution Prescribing the Timeline for the Implementation of Retail Competition and Open Access, Manila, Philippines.

Energy Regulatory Commission, Unbundling of Rates and Removal of Cross-Subsidies, Manila, Philippines.

Energy Regulatory Commission, ERC Case Nos. 2001-646 and 2001-900, Manila Electric Company (MERALCO), Manila, Philippines.

Holopainen, Lasse (2004), The Philippine Wholesale Electricity Spot Market, Investment Forum Presentation, 3 December, Mandarin Oriental Hotel, Philippines.

Republic of the Philippines, Republic Act No. 9136: An Act Ordaining Reforms in the Electric Power Industry, Amending for the Purpose Certain Laws and for Other Purposes, Manila, Philippines. 2001.

Republic of the Philippines (2002), Rules and Regulations to Implement Republic Act No. 9136, Entitled Electric Power Industry Reform Act of 2001, Manila, Philippines.

UNDP/World Bank/Energy Sector Management Assistance Program (2002), Rural Electrification and Development in the Philippines: Measuring the Economic and Social Benefits, Washington, DC.

OECD PUBLICATIONS, 2, rue André-Pascal, 75775 PARIS CEDEX 16
PRINTED IN FRANCE
(22 2006 08 1 P) No. 55339 2006